CNS stylebook

ON RELIGION — THIRD EDITION

REFERENCE
GUIDE
&
USAGE
MANUAL

Catholic News Service

Table of Contents

Introduction iv
Foreword vi
A 1
B 21
C 30
D 66
E... 72
F 86
G 92
H 95
I.. 103
J 114
K 121
L... 124
M 140
N 153
O 163
P... 172
Q 189
R 192
S... 203
T... 220
U 226
V 230
W 234
XYZ.. 237
Appendix A: Special Style Considerations 239
Appendix B: Photo Guidelines... 242
Appendix C: Endnotes... 244
Appendix D: Religious Orders, Men.. 247
Appendix E: Religious Orders, Women 250
Appendix F: U.S. Conference of Catholic Bishops..................... 258
Appendix G: Vatican Agencies... 261
Appendix H: Use of the Annuario 263
Appendix I: Vatican II Documents... 267
Appendix J: Annual Church Observances.................................... 269
Appendix K: Copyright and Trademark Law 270
Order Form 273

Introduction

It's been only five years since the publication of Catholic News Service's *Stylebook on Religion 2000,* but it is safe to say that nearly every entry in this third edition has been changed in some way. The most noticeable change -- and the one we hope will be most helpful to readers in this Internet age -- is the addition of Web addresses for most Catholic organizations, other denominations and many faith-based groups.

This edition, published 15 years after the original *CNS Stylebook,* also includes more than 100 new entries and reflects a thorough review of each previous entry in light of changes in church policy and practices, the headquarters of church organizations or the style used by The Associated Press. In some cases, the experience of the last five years has led to the realization that certain stylebook entries needed clarification or better examples, so we've done that, too.

As with each of the previous editions, this *CNS Stylebook on Religion - - Third Edition* is based on the belief that consistency is the hallmark of good writing, and accuracy its foundation. The art and craft of writing require communication that is both factual and based on commonly understood and accepted standards. Ultimately, our purpose is to help readers understand what we write.

The *CNS Stylebook on Religion* is designed specifically for the writers and editors of Catholic News Service, its clients, journalists working in the general press and other professionals who need guidelines for the correct use of words, a pattern of clear, disciplined and consistent writing and a reference guide with a religious perspective, primarily Catholic.

In the specialized area of religious news reporting, the *CNS Stylebook on Religion* draws upon Catholic News Service's 85 years of experience in the field and its presence at the focal point of a network that stretches throughout the United States and Canada and to 40 other countries.

The *CNS Stylebook on Religion* is the only resource of its kind, combining usage and reference material on religion in a single work.

This reference work contains more than 1,100 entries, many defining terms that are unique to the area of religion or that have distinct meaning in a religious context. There are also more than 200 organizations listed, with Web address and the location of their headquarters, for quick and easy reference.

The goal here is to provide guidance for style in news writing. For usage in other writing -- academic papers, formal church documents, letters addressed to church officials, etc. -- other sources may need to be consulted.

For material not covered in this book, there are other sources to which the user of the *CNS Stylebook on Religion* can refer. The Membership Photo Directory of the U.S. Conference of Catholic Bishops is the first reference for the spelling of names of U.S. bishops. For other Catholic Church officials throughout the world, the Annuario Pontificio, published by the Libreria Editrice Vaticana in Vatican City, is the first reference. See **Appendix H: Use of the Annuario** for guidance on how to use the Annuario. For guidance on other foreign names, see the entries on **Asian names**, **names** and **Spanish and Portuguese names.**

At CNS, this stylebook is the first reference for geographic names and for style, spelling and usage. *The Associated Press Stylebook and Briefing on Media Law* is the second reference for style, spelling and usage. Webster's New World College Dictionary, Fourth Edition, is the second reference for geographic names and third reference for spelling, style and usage. National Geographic Atlas of the World is the third reference for geographic names.

Other sources consulted regularly at CNS are: *The Official Catholic Directory*, also known as the Kenedy, for statistics on U.S. dioceses and the spelling of the names of U.S. priests; *Yearbook of American and Canadian Churches,* for statistics on other Christian bodies; *Our Sunday Visitor's Catholic Almanac*, for church statistics worldwide and for historical data; and the current year's *Catholic Press Directory*, for the names of U.S. and Canadian newspapers, magazines and newsletters.

The forms noted within this stylebook take precedence over those indicated in other stylebooks, dictionaries or gazetteers.

Foreword

I had the great fortune in high school to have landed for three consecutive years in the English Literature classroom of Paul Wooten. A slight but elegant man, he had an easy demeanor and an encyclopedic mind full of anecdotes and wonderful minutiae. He was a splendid teacher.

Wooten loved literature and poetry, and he taught it like he loved it. He even set aside a reading day each week. He also set aside a grammar day. He taught that like a drill sergeant. He armed his 30 boys with two books: Hodges' "Harbrace College Handbook" and Strunk and White's small but mighty "The Elements of Style." Both still sit on my desk today.

"Gentlemen," Wooten would warn as we moaned under the ever-oppressive sentence diagramming exercises, "You must learn to write well, and that means correct grammar, spelling and usage. It will be a mercy for your readers." Amen to that.

Catholic News Service's third edition of the Stylebook on Religion aims to be a mercy for readers and for the writers who serve up a daily fare of words for them.

In this edition of the Stylebook on Religion, users will find unchanged previous entries about the church's ages-old terms but many more terms updated from the last edition. Peppering this edition are Web addresses for hundreds of organizations, no doubt a handy reference for reporters and researchers.

Also in this edition, CNS adds a section on copyright and trademark law that we hope will assist all writers as they toil in the ever more complex field of intellectual property rights, whether they are creating their own work or determining how to use the work of others.

Finally, CNS thanks the people whose work made this third edition the gem it is: Nancy Frazier O'Brien for her work as supervising editor and Mark Lombard who chaired the stylebook committee; committee members Jim Lackey, Julie Asher and Nancy Hartnagel, from whose copy desk few errors ever escape; Mary Esslinger and Jerry Filteau, who arm-wrestled over dozens of entries while they copy-edited; intern Zachary Dunham, who double-checked each Web address; Barb Fraze, John Thavis, Cindy Wooden and Carol Glatz, who suggested or contributed new or revised entries; Catholic editors across the world who did the same; Nancy Wiechec and Emily Thompson for their art direction and design; Joe Larson for formatting the book and for supervising printing and distribution; and Katherine Grincewich for our new section on copyright and trademark law.

We hope that editors and writers — and anyone who communicates about religion — will find the CNS Stylebook on Religion an exceptional assistance in bringing clarity and accuracy to aspects of their writing or speaking about religion today and in the future.

Anthony J. Spence
Director and Editor in Chief
Catholic News Service

A

Abba Always capitalize when used as a proper name for God.

abbey, abbess, abbot Some monastic orders of men or women establish relatively autonomous communities. The monastery of such a community is called an *abbey.* Its head, if a woman, is an *abbess;* if a man, an *abbot.*

Capitalize and spell out *abbot* when used as a formal title before a name: *Abbot John Smith, Abbot Smith* or *Abbot John* (depending on his preference), *the abbot.*

If *abbess* is used as a formal title before a name, capitalize and spell out: *Abbess Marie Smith, Abbess Marie* (or, if she prefers, *Abbess Smith*), *the abbess.* Often, however, an abbess uses *mother* or *sister* as the title before her name. Use *mother* unless it is known that the individual prefers *sister* or *abbess: Mother Marie Smith, abbess of St. Clare Abbey; Mother Marie* (or, if she prefers, *Mother Smith); the abbess.* See **religious titles.**

Ordinarily an abbot or abbess takes office upon consenting to the election. In a territorial abbey the one chosen is *abbot-elect* until confirmed by the Vatican. See **territorial abbeys.**

Avoid using *abbacy,* an abstract term for the office or jurisdiction of an abbot or the estate or territory governed by the abbey. If it means the estate or territory, *abbey* is correct. For the office: *He was elected abbot.* not: *He was elected to the abbacy.*

abbreviations The following style rules are of special note for religious news writing:

Titles before names: Abbreviate *Msgr.* and *Rev.* Do not abbreviate *Abbot, Archbishop, Bishop, Brother, Cardinal, Deacon, Father, Mother, Patriarch, Pope, Sister* or other religious titles used before names. See **religious titles.**

Books of the Bible: Abbreviate only in endnotes and parenthetical references in texts, not in regular news uses. See **Appendix C: Endnotes.** For a list of Scripture abbreviations, see **Bible.**

Academic degrees: Ordinarily they are spelled out, but occasionally, as in a list of people and their degrees, the abbreviated form of the degree may follow the name. For names and abbreviations of the more common academic degrees conferred under church auspices, see **ecclesiastical degrees.**

To avoid alphabet soup in news writing, do not use abbreviations or acronyms for the organizations named in this book unless they are listed as acceptable. Exceptions may be made only on rare occasions. A statement that an abbreviation is acceptable on second reference does not mean that the abbreviation ought to be used. Often other forms of second reference, such as *the conference, the association, the committee, the coalition, the union,* etc., are equally acceptable or preferred.

See **acronym** and individual entries throughout this book.

aborigine, aboriginal Lowercase in all uses. These are not proper names of any race or tribe. They apply equally to the original inhabitants of any land.

abortion Official Catholic teaching condemns the intentional killing of the unborn at any time from conception on, defining conception as taking place when "the ovum is fertilized." Church teaching therefore makes a sharp moral distinction between *contraceptives,* which prevent conception, and *abortifacients,* which destroy the fertilized egg, often by preventing implantation.

Although intrauterine devices and so-called "morning-after" pills often are referred to as *contraceptives* in general usage, in official Catholic teaching they are regarded as *abortifacients* if they destroy a fertilized egg. If the distinction in church teaching is relevant to a story, it should be made clear to the reader.

In news stories, do not use the term "pro-choice" except in quotes or in titles. Use "pro-life" rather than "anti-abortion" to describe the Catholic position on life issues. But in identifying organizations or groups of people, it is best to identify the specific issues which the organization supports or opposes: *an organization that opposes abortion and euthanasia* rather than simply *a pro-life organization.*

Avoid the term "abortion rights" and instead refer to those who support or oppose keeping abortion legal. In discussing laws or legislative proposals, avoid terms like "liberal abortion laws" or "tough anti-abortion laws" in favor of more descriptive language about the specific law or proposal or terms like "laws allowing abortion" or "laws regulating abortions." Do not use "terminating pregnancy" to describe abortion.

See **artificial contraception; birth control; contraceptive sterilization; intrauterine device; natural family planning; partial-birth abortion;** and **RU-486.**

absolution In the sacrament of penance, *absolution* is the sacramental act by the priest freeing penitents of their sins. If a person is in immediate danger of death or unable to communicate, absolution may be given without confession.

General absolution, by which several penitents are absolved of their sins at the same time, is included in one of the three forms of the sacrament of penance, but its use is restricted to certain extraordinary situations. It can be given without individual confession in cases where a group of people is in danger of death or would otherwise not have access to confession and Communion for a long period of time — understood in the United States to mean for at least 30 days.

See **confession; penance;** and **sacraments.**

abstinence, days of The Catholic penitential practice of *abstinence* from meat (or another food) on certain days should not be confused with the practice of *fasting.*

The general law of the Latin Church calls for Catholics from the age of 14 to observe Ash Wednesday and all Fridays of the year, unless they are solemn feasts, as days of abstinence, in accord with provisions of the local bishops' conference.

Many bishops' conferences, however, including that in the United States, have enacted changes in the general legislation. The U.S. bishops of the Latin rite decided in 1966 that Catholics 14 and older must abstain from meat on Ash Wednesday, Good Friday and the Fridays of Lent. On other Fridays, they said, Catholics could either abstain from meat or choose another form of penance or self-denial.

In the Eastern Catholic churches, abstinence from meat is required of all Catholics, regardless of age, on all Fridays. While it is called a penitential practice, this is understood more in terms of predisposing a person to prayer, rather than as penance for one's sins.

See **fasting** and **penitential days**.

academic chairs Capitalize only proper nouns in the names of academic chairs: *John S. McDonnell Jr. endowed chair of ethics, Dr. David Lauler chair in Catholic health care ethics.* In general, use the full name of the chair sparingly.

academic degrees See **abbreviations** and **ecclesiastical degrees**.

acolyte See **altar server**.

acronym An *acronym* is an abbreviation that can be pronounced as a word. For example: *AIDS* for *acquired immune deficiency syndrome* or *FADICA* for *Foundations and Donors Interested in Catholic Activities.* A few acronyms, such as *radar, sonar, laser* and *scuba,* have entered the language as lowercase words. Most, however, require all capitals. The rules for abbreviations apply. See **abbreviations** and individual entries throughout this book.

Note that *Network* and *Renew* are not acronyms. See those entries.

"Acta Apostolicae Sedis" Latin for *Acts of the Apostolic See,* the official periodical, established in 1909, in which legislation issued by the Holy See is published. It includes writings and addresses by the pope in addition to decrees or other legislative documents issued by him and by departments of the Holy See. It is published in Latin, but texts issued in another language are usually printed in that language. In endnotes it is usually ab-breviated *AAS.*

It is not the same as *"L'Attivita della Santa Sede,"* an annual publication written primarily in Italian.

The "Acta" is rarely a source of news and rarely needs to be referenced in news copy. If it must be cited, give its full name, in quotations, and explain that it is the official periodical through which Vatican laws and decisions are published. On second reference, *the "Acta"* is acceptable. For use in endnotes, see **Appendix C: Endnotes.**

act of contrition Lowercase. Any prayer expressing sorrow for sins is an act of contrition and there is no unique prayer formula for which that is the proper name. Neither the prayer of the penitent in the sacrament of penance nor the prayer used in the first form of the penitential rite at Mass is labeled an *act of contrition* in Catholic liturgical texts.

ad hoc Latin for "for this," it means temporary or established for a special purpose. It has become part of the English language and should not be surrounded by quotation marks. Capitalize when used as part of a formal organizational name: *the Ad Hoc Committee on Catholic Charismatic Renewal.* Lowercase in other uses and do not hyphenate when used as a compound modifier: *That's an ad hoc solution, not a long-range answer to the problem.*

"ad limina" Heads of dioceses are required to make "ad limina" visits to the Vatican every five years to report on the status of their dioceses. Lowercase, put in quotation marks and include an explanatory note.

The full Latin phrase, which need not be used or translated in stories, is *"ad limina apostolorum"* (*to the thresholds of the apostles*). It refers to the pilgrimages to the tombs of Sts. Peter and Paul that a bishop is required to make during an "ad limina" visit.

See **Latin words and phrases.**

administrator In Catholic ecclesiastical usage, when a diocesan bishop dies, retires or is transferred, a *diocesan administrator* is named to govern the ordinary affairs of the diocese until a new bishop takes office. The Code of Canon Law and the Code of Canons of the Eastern Churches spell out the rules for selection of an administrator and the limits on his power.

When a pastor dies, retires or is transferred and is not immediately replaced, a *parish administrator,* usually a priest, is named to govern the parish's ordinary affairs. In Latin-rite dioceses without enough priests to provide residential pastors for all parishes, a parish may have its day-to-day governance given to a *parish administrator* who is not a priest, with a nonresident priest named pastor. A deacon, layperson or nonordained religious who administers such a parish is often called a *parish life coordinator.* See that entry.

See also **apostolic administration, apostolic administrator** and **pastor.**

"ad nutum Sanctae Sedis" The Latin phrase accompanying some ecclesiastical appointments, often abbreviated *"ad nutum S.S.,"* stands for *at the pleasure of the Holy See.* It means the appointment is indefinite and the Holy See is free to terminate it at any time. If that fact is needed in the story, avoid the technical phrase whenever possible, substituting *indefinitely, for an undefined period of time,* or a similar phrase.

Adveniat (www.adveniat.org) German Catholic aid program for the church in Latin America, funded by an annual Advent collection in churches.

Advent The season that opens the liturgical year of the Latin Church, it begins with the liturgical observance of the fourth Sunday before Christmas and ends on Christmas Eve when the liturgical observance of Christmas begins.

In Eastern Catholic churches, the yearly cycle of immovable feasts begins Sept. 1 and ends Aug. 31; the preparatory period for Christmas begins Nov. 14, the feast of St. Philip the Apostle.

See **liturgical year.**

Adventist See **Seventh-day Adventist Church.**

African-American (n., adj.) Hyphenate for consistency with AP style on others of dual heritage: *Irish-American, Polish-American,* etc. For proper names of organizations, follow the group's preference on whether to use *African-American* or *black: the Committee for African-American Catholics, the African-American Catholic Congregation, the National Black Catholic Congress.*

Ordinarily *black* is preferred when simple description by race is needed in a story. *Black* is always the preferred term when the group might include those from the Caribbean region.

However, *African-American* may be used to describe an individual or group in quoted matter or when the individual's or group's cultural heritage or sense of self-identity is relevant to the story. When mentioning the group in conjunction with other groups such as Hispanics and Native Americans, use *African-Americans.*

African-American Catholic Congregation (http://imaniaacc.org) Founded in 1989 by Father (later Archbishop) George A. Stallings Jr., a black priest of the Washington Archdiocese, who declared his definitive separation from Rome the following year. The archdiocese said he had excommunicated himself by his words and actions.

agnostic See **atheist, theist.**

AIDS, HIV Acceptable in all references for *acquired immune deficiency syndrome* and the *human immunodeficiency virus* that causes it.

Generally avoid the phrase *AIDS victim,* which some consider objectionable. Use phrases such as *person with AIDS, AIDS sufferers* or *those who have AIDS or HIV.*

AIDS patients should be used only in the specific context of medical care: *The hospital has a 16-bed ward devoted exclusively to AIDS patients.*

The national Centers for Disease Control and Prevention (www.cdc.gov) in Atlanta provide frequent updates on key national AIDS data. Use national rather than local figures in analyzing trends, since local figures can fluctuate considerably for a variety of reasons.

The Joint U.N. Program on HIV/AIDS, known as UNAIDS, is based in Geneva.

See **HIV.**

alb A long white tunic worn by priests and deacons, and sometimes by other ministers such as eucharistic ministers, for liturgical functions.

See **liturgical dress.**

Alhambra See **International Order of Alhambra.**

alleluia, hallelujah *Alleluia* is the preferred spelling for Catholic prayer usage, but *hallelujah* may be the preferred spelling for many other contexts: *The choir sang the alleluia before the Gospel. The congregation answered, "Alleluia." He said, "Hallelujah! I'm free!" Everyone stood for Handel's "Hallelujah Chorus."*

Alliance for Catholic Education (http://ace.nd.edu) A two-year program founded at the University of Notre Dame in 1994 to meet the needs of understaffed Catholic schools. Recent college graduates from Notre Dame, St. Mary's College and other colleges and universities nationwide take courses during the summers leading to a master's degree in education and teach during the academic year in Catholic schools, mainly in the South.

All Saints' Day, All Souls' Day See **holidays, holy days.**

altar server Since adults as well as children serve at the altar, *altar server* ordinarily should be used as the general term.

The official term for one who is designated to serve the priest at the altar in the Catholic Church is *acolyte.* Generally it should be reserved for more technical contexts where it is required.

The controversy in the Latin Church over the legality of female altar servers ended in 1994 when the Vatican ruled that existing church laws do not prohibit the practice. It said each bishop may decide on its advisability in his diocese, in consultation with the local bishops' conference. At their next meeting the U.S. Latin-rite bishops approved a resolution welcoming the ruling and most began to permit the practice. Female altar servers are not permitted in the laws of the

Eastern Catholic churches.

At times *altar girls* and *altar boys* may be used as generic terms for females or males serving at the altar, since most U.S. parishes rely primarily or solely on young people for their regular altar servers. Generally, however, it is preferable to use either of those terms only when the group referred to consists exclusively of young people of that gender.

See **minister, ministry.**

ambo See **lectern, ambo.**

amen An interjection meaning "May it be so," often used to conclude Christian prayers. *They said the amen. They answered, "Amen."*

America magazine (www.americamagazine.org) The national Catholic weekly published by Jesuits. Based in New York.

America Online An online service that provides access to the Internet and other special services for a fee. *AOL* is acceptable on second reference.

American Academy of FertilityCare Professionals (www.aafcp.org) Formerly the American Association of Natural Family Planning. Headquarters is in St. Louis.

American Baptist Association See **Baptist churches.**

American Baptist Churches in the U.S.A. See **Baptist churches.**

American Bible Society (www.americanbible.org) Founded in 1816 to distribute translations of the Bible, at low cost or free, around the world. Supported by more than 100 Protestant denominations, it has distributed more than a billion complete or partial copies of the Bible. Headquarters is in New York.

American Board of Catholic Missions Established in 1924 to strengthen the presence of the church in the United States and its territories by making grants to home-mission dioceses and mission projects, it was replaced in 1998 by the U.S. bishops' Committee on the Home Missions.

American Catholic Church Based in Hampton Bays, N.Y., this group is not affiliated with the Catholic Church.

American Catholic Church in the United States (www.accus.us) This group split with the American Catholic Church in Hampton Bays, N.Y., in 1998 and is not part of the Catholic Church. Headquarters is in Frederick, Md.

American Catholic Correctional Chaplains Association (www.catholiccorrectionalchaplains.org) Founded to "foster a Catholic approach to the problems and study of the correctional field."

American Catholic Historical Association (http://research.cua.edu/acha) Founded in 1919 to "promote the study of church history." Headquarters is in Washington.

American Catholic Philosophical Association (www.acpaweb.org) Founded in 1926 to promote philosophical scholarship and teaching in Catholic circles. Headquarters is in Charlottesville, Va.

American church, American Catholic Church. Do not use as a synonym for *U.S. church* except in direct quotations. Two independent federations of churches have taken the names *American Catholic Church* and *American Catholic Church in the United States.*

In references to the Catholic Church on one or both continents in the Western Hemisphere, acceptable forms of use are: *church (or Catholic Church) in North America, in South America, in the Americas.* Since the 1997 Synod of Bishops for America, there has been an effort in some church circles to refer to the church throughout the Western Hemisphere as the *church in America.*

See **American Catholic Church; Catholic Church;** and **U.S. church, U.S. Catholic Church.**

American Friends of the Vatican Library Headquarters is in Clawson, Mich.

American Jewish Committee (www.ajc.org) To avoid confusion with the *American Jewish Congress,* do not use the initials *AJC* for either group. The committee was founded in 1906 to fight bigotry and discrimination against Jews or any other minorities, to promote Jewish integration into American life and to interpret Jews to other Americans. Headquarters is in New York.

American Jewish Congress (www.ajcongress.org) To avoid confusion with the *American Jewish Committee,* do not use the initials *AJC* for either group. The congress was founded in 1918 to foster Jewish cultural development, to fight anti-Semitism and bigotry and to promote separation of church and state and the religious freedom and civil rights of all. Headquarters is in New York.

American Life League (www. all.org) A pro-life educational organization that claimed membership of 300,000 families in 2005. Its divisions include Rock for Life; the American Bioethics Advisory Commission; STOPP International, which stands for Stop Planned Parenthood; Crusade for the Defense of Our Catholic Church; and ALL Associates. National office is in Stafford, Va.

Americans United for Life (www.unitedforlife.org) Headquarters is in Chicago.

Americans United for Separation of Church and State (www. au.org) *Americans United* is acceptable on second reference. Headquarters is in Washington.

Amnesty International (www. amnesty.org) A London-based organization that monitors human rights violations, particularly the use of torture by government agents and imprisonment for political or religious beliefs. It seeks through public opinion and other international pressures to free prisoners of conscience. U.S. headquarters (www.amnestyusa.org) is in New York.

anchorite See **hermit.**

Ancient Order of Hibernians in America (www.aoh.com) *Hibernians* is acceptable on first reference, but give the full name later in the story.

Founded in New York in 1836, it describes itself as the largest and oldest Irish Catholic organization in the United States. Its aims are to promote Irish culture, defend the Catholic faith and seek fairness for the Catholics of Northern Ireland.

ancient Oriental churches See **Oriental Orthodox churches.**

Angelus This noontime prayer to

Mary is used most of the year in the Catholic Church but is replaced by the *"Regina Coeli"* during the Easter season. When the pope is in Rome or at his summer residence in Castel Gandolfo, Italy, he makes a public appearance and gives a brief talk each Sunday noon before leading the people in the Angelus or "Regina Coeli." Note that there are no quotes around *Angelus.*

See **"Regina Coeli."**

Anglican Communion (www. anglicancommunion.org) Collective name for the Church of England and at least 37 other autonomous national or regional churches in communion with the Archdiocese of Canterbury, chief diocese of the Church of England.

The archbishop of Canterbury holds a primacy of honor without juridical power among the member churches, similar to that held by patriarchs in the Orthodox churches. He convenes the Lambeth Conference, a meeting every 10 years of the world's Anglican bishops, which is one of the principal means of consultation on major matters concerning Anglican unity.

Anglicanism has its origins in Henry VIII's 16th-century break with Rome and establishment of an autonomous national church because of the pope's refusal to let him divorce his first wife. Briefly suppressed during the Catholic Restoration under Queen Mary (1553-1558), the national church was restored by Elizabeth I in 1558 and has been England's established church since then. Its titular head is the reigning monarch.

Because many Anglicans have traditionally considered themselves a national expression of the one universal church and have regarded their rupture with Rome as a juridical break rather than a doctrinal one, they are not properly called *Protestant.* In some contexts, however, they may be grouped with churches of the Reformation under the general heading of *Protestant.* See that entry.

None of the other national churches in the Anglican Communion is established by the state. The chief Anglican body in the United States is the *Episcopal Church.* See that entry.

Chief sources of Anglican belief and practice are Scripture, the Nicene Creed and Apostles' Creed, and the Book of Common Prayer, which includes the rites for celebration of the sacraments, official daily prayers (morning prayer, the service of noon, evening prayer and compline), other prayers, hymns and the Articles of Religion summarizing Anglican beliefs.

Successive revisions of the Book of Common Prayer in different countries have led to diversity in Anglican practice around the world. The traditional Anglican claim of unity among its autonomous churches in the essentials of faith has been tested in recent years by divisions over the ordination of women bishops, the blessing of same-sex marriages and the ordination in 2003 of an openly gay bishop in the U.S. Episcopal Church.

The Articles of Religion recognize only baptism and the Eucharist as sacraments necessary for salvation. Anglicans consider the other five sacraments of Catholic and Orthodox belief *sacramentals,* and they refer to the rites of those five sacraments as *sacramental rites.* Anglicans differ among themselves in their understanding of these rites and in the degree of emphasis they place on them.

The usual term for what Catholics call the Mass is, in the Anglican Church, the *Eucharist* or *Holy Eucharist.* It is also known as the *Sacrament of the Lord's Supper.* Anglicans vary in the ways they describe how Christ is present in the Eucharist and how it is related to his sacrificial death on the cross. See **church services.**

Baptism is administered to infants. Confirmation usually is given in the early teens. Anglicans refer to the anointing of the sick as *unction* and call the rite a *service of healing.* The rite for penance is called a *service of reconciliation.*

A considerable variety of emphasis in worship is permitted. At one time Anglican parishes and individuals were often identified as part of the *High Church, Broad Church* or *Low Church,* depending on their style of worship. A High-Church parish stressed the sacraments and more ritual in worship. A Low-Church parish emphasized preaching of the Gospel and simpler services. A Broad-Church parish included elements from both traditions. The terms have been abandoned for the most part in recent years and should be used only in quoted matter or historical references. If used, they should be explained.

The term *Anglo-Catholic* occasionally is used to describe those who formerly were called High-Church Anglicans. See **Catholic, catholic.**

Anglicans consider their deacons, priests and bishops ordained in apostolic succession. In 1999 the Anglican churches in Canada, New Zealand and the United States ordained women bishops. About half the member churches worldwide, including the Church of England, ordain women priests.

RELATIONS WITH CATHOLICS: The Catholic Church ruled in 1896 that Anglican ordinations are invalid because the continuity of apostolic succession was broken by 16th-century changes in the Anglican ordination rite. Catholic officials have stated that significant new obstacles to reunion have been introduced in recent years by the ordination of women priests and women bishops in the Anglican Communion, the ordination of an openly gay bishop in the U.S. Episcopal Church and the decision of some Anglican dioceses to bless same-sex unions or to recognize such blessings.

From the Anglican side, among chief obstacles to reunion are the extent and exercise of papal jurisdiction over the whole church and the Catholic understanding of infallible papal teaching authority. Linked with the problem of infallibility are difficulties over papal definitions of the Immaculate Conception and the Assumption as dogmas that must be believed.

The Catholic Church has an official dialogue with the Anglican Communion in the form of the Anglican-Roman Catholic International Commission, known as ARCIC or, when there is need to distinguish it from its predecessor, ARCIC II. The first commission met from 1970 to 1981 and in 1982 published "The Final Report," a collection of its agreed statements along with elucidations, historical notes and other background. The second commission was formed in 1982 to refine the agreements of the first commission and overcome remaining theoretical and practical obstacles to Anglican-Roman Catholic reunion. *ARCIC* is acceptable on second reference, as are *ARCIC I* and *ARCIC II* when distinguishing between the first and second commissions.

In 2001, Catholic and Anglican authorities formed the International Anglican-Roman Catholic Commission for Unity and Mission to prepare a joint affirmation of faith and promote Anglican-Catholic cooperation. As a result of internal issues in the Anglican Communion arising from the ordination of a gay bishop, the commission's meetings were put on hold in 2003 but were expected to resume in late 2005.

The U.S. Anglican-Roman Catholic dialogue group is known as ARC-USA. *ARC-USA* is acceptable on second reference, but *the dialogue group* or a similar phrase is preferable.

Annuario The *Annuario Pontificio* is the Vatican yearbook. *Annuario* is acceptable in all references and is always capitalized. Define it the first time it is used in a story. This book is the primary source on the spelling of any person's name contained in it. The only exception is U.S. bishops, for whom the Membership Photo Directory of the U.S. Conference of Catholic Bishops is the definitive source.

See **Appendix H: Use of the Annuario.**

annul Other forms are *annulling, annulled, annulment.*

In the practice of Catholic marriage courts, an *annulment* is a decision that the apparent marriage was null from the start. It declares that since there was no sacramental marriage, there is no marriage bond. The court document conveying such a judgment is called a *decree of nullity.*

Do not refer to an annulment as a church-granted divorce. Civil law varies from country to country, but most nations, including the United States, require a separate civil action of divorce or annulment to release the couple from the civil marriage bond.

See **divorce.**

anointing of the sick Note the single *n.* In the Catholic Church this sacrament, formerly known as *extreme unction* and formerly given only to those in danger of death, can now be administered to anyone who is seriously or chronically ill. The minister of the sacrament must be a priest. It is also known as the *sacrament of the sick* or the *sacrament of the anointing of the sick.* Other rites such as penance, absolution or Communion may at times accompany the anointing of the sick, but they are not part of that sacrament. In the Anglican Communion the rite is known as *unction.*

See **sacraments.**

anti-abortion See **abortion.**

Antichrist, anti-Christ Apocalyptic literature of the Bible predicts the coming of the *Antichrist,* the name given to the one who will be Christ's chief enemy. It is not uncommon for fundamentalist writers or preachers to attach the label to a currently living person: *He condemned his opponent as the Antichrist.*

The adjective *anti-Christ* does not refer to the person prophesied in the Bible. It may be applied to an attitude or action judged to be fundamentally opposed to Christ and his message: *Hating others is anti-Christ.*

Anti-Defamation League (www.adl.org) On second reference, *ADL* or *the league* are acceptable for this Jewish organization founded in 1913. Its purpose is to combat anti-Semitism through programs and services that counteract hatred, prejudice and bigotry. It is engaged in dialogue with Catholics and other Christian churches to promote mutual respect and understanding. Membership is open to all. Headquarters is in New York.

The ADL was founded by B'nai B'rith but is largely independent of it and no longer uses *of B'nai B'rith* in its name. See **B'nai B'rith.**

Antiochene, Antiochian In religious and theological references to

Antioch, the preferred adjectival form is *Antiochene*. Use *Antiochian* only in formal names of organizations which use that form.

Antiochian Orthodox Christian Archdiocese of North America (www.antiochian.org) With headquarters in Englewood, N.J., it is under the jurisdiction of the Syrian Orthodox patriarch of Antioch.

See **Orthodox churches**.

antipope, anti-pope An *antipope* is a pope set up against the one duly elected. Someone opposed to the pope, however, is *anti-pope* or *anti-papal*.

antiretroviral

Apocalypse The name used by some for the last book of the Bible. The New American Bible calls it *Revelation* or *the Book of Revelation*. Use *Apocalypse* only in direct quotations.

See **Bible**.

apocrypha, apocryphal In references to Scripture, these terms refer to writings that are not part of the accepted canon of sacred books, although at one time or another some have argued for their inclusion. Those seven books of the Old Testament which Catholics call deuterocanonical are considered apocryphal by Protestants. Catholics consider them part of Scripture; Protestants do not. For the list of those Old Testament books, see **deuterocanonical**. See also **Bible**.

apostasy The formal renunciation of one's religion. Canon 751 of the Code of Canon Law defines apostasy as "the total repudiation of the Christian faith," not just of Catholicism. A person who does this is an *apostate*. The old code also spoke of vowed religious who abandoned religious life as *apostates from religion*, but this language is not used in the new code.

Outside the religious context, it is sometimes used to describe the renunciation of political beliefs or allegiance. Do not use the term in this way in news stories, except in quoted material.

apostate See **apostasy**.

apostle, disciple *Apostle* generally refers to the Twelve whom Jesus gathered around him for special instruction and Matthias, who was chosen by lot to replace Judas. These were prime witnesses of the Resurrection and the chief leaders of the early Christian community. Paul, although not one of the original Twelve, from earliest times was ranked with them because of his leadership, writings and intense missionary activity. Other leaders in the early church were also called *apostles* at times.

Lowercase except in references to *the Twelve Apostles* or in singular references to St. Paul or one of the Twelve in which *the Apostle* is used in the form of a title: *St. Thomas the Apostle, St. Paul the Apostle*. But: *the apostle Paul; St. James, one of the apostles; the apostles Peter and Andrew*.

Disciple is used to describe those who hear and follow the teachings of Jesus, not only in New Testament times but in every age. Do not capitalize. *The Twelve Apostles were disciples of Jesus, but not all of Jesus' disciples were chosen as apostles*.

Apostles' Creed Note the apostrophe. A confession of Christian faith that gradually gained universal acceptance in the West but is not part of the traditions of the East. It is accepted in the Latin Church as an official creed and has similar standing in many Protestant churches, but Orthodox and Eastern Catholic churches do not use it.

See **Creed, creed; "filioque"; Nicene Creed;** and **Orthodox churches.**

Apostleship of Prayer (www.apostleshipofprayer.org) National office is in Milwaukee.

Apostleship of the Sea (www.aos-usa.org) Official U.S. Catholic agency for the religious, educational and charitable welfare of seafarers. Operates out of Migration and Refugee Services of the U.S. Conference of Catholic Bishops in Washington.

Apostolate for Family Consecration (www.familyland.org) Headquarters — also called Catholic Familyland — is in Bloomingdale, Ohio.

apostolic The term *apostolic* in general refers back to the Twelve Apostles, the period when they lived, the faith they held and preached, the original churches they founded or the mission of spreading the faith that followers of Christ still pursue.

In Catholic ecclesiastical usage *apostolic* also is used to characterize certain documents, appointments or ecclesiastical structures initiated by or directly dependent upon the pope or the Holy See.

See specific entries that follow.

apostolic administration, apostolic administrator *Apostolic administration* is a name used for some church jurisdictions established when, for particular, serious reasons, a diocesan structure has not been or cannot be established to care for Catholics in a certain geographical area. It is headed by an *apostolic administrator,* usually a bishop, who has full power but governs in the name of the pope. In 2005 apostolic administrations existed in Albania, Georgia, Estonia, China, the Comoro Islands, Kazakhstan and Serbia-Montenegro. A personal apostolic administration was established by Pope John Paul II in 2002 for the pastoral care of traditionalist Catholics in Brazil.

When the pope names a priest or bishop to administer a vacant diocese or archdiocese until a new residential bishop takes office, that administrator is called an *apostolic administrator* because he holds the post by papal appointment. The adjective *apostolic* is not applied to a priest or bishop elected by the local college of consultors as the interim administrator of a vacant see.

The administration, the administrator are acceptable on second reference.

For *diocesan administrator* and *parish administrator,* see **administrator.**

apostolic blessing In Catholic practice, a diocesan bishop three times a year and a pope at any time may give an *apostolic blessing.* The recipients may obtain a plenary indulgence if they say certain prayers for the pope's intentions and receive the sacraments of penance and Eucharist. The pope gives an apostolic blessing solemnly on several occasions during the year and gives it "urbi et orbi" (to the city and the world) at Christmas and Easter and immediately following his election to the papacy.

See **indulgence(s)** and **"urbi et orbi."**

Apostolic Camera The Roman Curia office headed by the *chamberlain of the Holy Roman Church.* See that entry.

Apostolic Catholic Church (www.apostoliccatholicchurch.com) This group, based in Tampa, Fla., is not part of the Catholic Church.

Apostolic Catholic Church in America (www.apostoliccatholic churchinamerica.org) This organization, with headquarters in Seattle, has no ties to the Catholic Church.

apostolic church As a historical term, *apostolic church* refers to the whole Christian Church in the apostolic era or to any of the ancient local churches founded by one of the apostles, such as those of Antioch, Rome and Alexandria.

In theological usage, *apostolic church* means a church faithful to the faith of the original apostles and/or linked to them through historical continuity. See **apostolic succession.**

Some denominations use the term *apostolic* in their name to express a conviction that their belief or structure represents a return to or restoration of the original practice and belief of the primitive church that they claim has been lost over the years by other churches.

apostolic constitution A form of papal document dealing with matters of faith or church life affecting the whole church or a sizable portion of it.

apostolic delegate A papal diplomat to the church in a nation that does not have formal diplomatic relations with the Holy See. Because he is not an envoy *to* the nation, he should always be referred to as the *apostolic delegate in* (not *to*) the country. His residence is called an *apostolic delegation.* Since apostolic delegates are always clergy, the religious title always takes precedence over the job title: Do not use *apostolic delegate* as a formal title before a name.

See **papal nuncio.**

apostolic exhortation A papal document, usually addressed to the whole church, concerning certain aspects of church life and faith. The Latin term *"adhortatio apostolica"* should be translated *apostolic exhortation.* In recent years the successive papal documents based on reflections and recommendations of the world Synod of Bishops have taken the form of apostolic exhortations.

See **encyclical** and **pastoral letter.**

apostolic nuncio See **papal nuncio.**

Apostolic Palace Capitalize this formal name of the Vatican building overlooking the right side of St. Peter's Square. The pope lives in the building, and from one of its windows on most Sundays he leads the Angelus.

Apostolic Penitentiary Formerly called the *Sacred Penitentiary,* this is one of the three tribunals of the Holy See. It has two offices. One is responsible for regulations governing indulgences. The other is a court which resolves cases of the *internal forum,* or conscience, and absolves individuals from sins or censures which are reserved to the Holy See.

The cardinal who heads the Apostolic Penitentiary is called the *major penitentiary* or *cardinal penitentiary.*

Priests commissioned by the Apostolic Penitentiary as confessors at the patriarchal basilicas, with the ability to absolve penitents from sins and censures reserved to the Holy See, are called *minor penitentiaries.*

See **ecclesiastical courts.**

apostolic prefecture Similar to an apostolic vicariate, it is generally the first step toward organization of a church hierarchy in a determined territory. It is ordinarily headed by an *apostolic prefect,* usually a priest. Apostolic vicariates generally indicate a more advanced state toward establishment of a diocese than do apostolic prefectures. In 2005 apostolic prefectures existed in Cambodia, Brunei, China, Falkland Islands, Ecuador, Ethiopia, Marshall Islands, Libya, Republic of Congo, Gabon, Nepal, Pakistan, Mongolia and Russia.

See **apostolic vicariate.**

Apostolic See One of several proper names used for the *Diocese of Rome* when referring to it as chief diocese of the Catholic Church. Use it only in quoted matter; otherwise, use more commonly recognized forms of reference, such as *Holy See, Vatican* or *Rome,* as appropriate for the context.

Apostolic Signature See **ecclesiastical courts.**

apostolic succession As used by Catholics, apostolic succession means both fidelity to the faith of the apostles and assurance of that fidelity through historical continuity in the laying on of hands in episcopal ordination. Through the laying on of hands, new bishops become members of the college of bishops and successors to the apostles, sharing in their authority to teach, sanctify and rule. See **Catholic Church.**

Catholics consider the bishops in some other churches, notably the Orthodox and Old Catholic churches, to be ordained in the apostolic succession validly, but imperfectly because of a lack of hierarchical communion with the college of bishops united with Rome. Anglicans claim apostolic succession, but the Catholic Church has rejected this claim on grounds that 16th-century changes in the Anglican ordination rite invalidated those and subsequent ordinations.

apostolic vicariate An ecclesiastical jurisdiction of the Latin Church, guided by an *apostolic vicar,* established in mission regions where the hierarchy (of the Latin rite) is not yet fully organized. Apostolic vicars, usually bishops, are nominated by the Congregation for the Evangelization of Peoples or by the Congregation for Eastern Churches, not by the Congregation for Bishops. Apostolic vicariates exist chiefly in Latin America, the Middle East and North Africa, but also in the Philippines, South Africa, Laos, Cambodia, Greece and the French islands of St. Pierre and Miquelon off the coast of Canada.

The equivalent jurisdiction in the Eastern Catholic churches is called an *exarchate.*

See **apostolic prefecture** and **exarchate, exarchy.**

apostolic visitor A person, usually a bishop, who is sent by the pope to investigate a particular problem in a local church or religious order may be called an *apostolic visitor* (not *visitator*). His investigation is called an *apostolic visitation.* The scope of his mandate is determined by the letter of appointment, but generally it involves investigating facts, evaluating views and reporting back to the Holy See, possibly with recommendations for a course of action. *Visitor* and *visitation* are acceptable on second reference.

Appalachian Ministries Educational Research Center (www.amerc.org) Located in Berea, Ky., this training center is operated by a nonprofit educational consortium of seminaries to give students exposure to the culture, economy and religious practices of Appalachia.

apparitions See **miracles, apparitions.**

archabbey A rank of honor given by the Holy See to some abbeys. The head of an archabbey is called an *archabbot.*
See **abbey, abbess, abbot.**

archbishop In Catholic usage, the title given automatically to bishops who govern archdioceses. It is also given as a personal rank to certain other bishops, especially certain high officials in the papal diplomatic corps and in Vatican departments. The adjectival form is *archiepiscopal.* Note the first *i.*

Capitalize only when used as a formal title before a name. Lowercase when it stands alone (but see **archbishop of Canterbury**). On first reference, also identify a residential archbishop by his see; identify others by their jobs, not by their titular sees: *Archbishop Daniel E. Pilarczyk of Cincinnati, Archbishop Pilarczyk, the archbishop, the archbishop of Cincinnati; Archbishop John P. Foley, president of the Pontifical Council for Social Communications, Archbishop Foley, the archbishop, the communications council president.*

Follow the same style for references to archbishops in the Anglican Communion and Eastern Catholic and Orthodox churches. In some Orthodox churches archbishops use the title *metropolitan.* See that entry.

Among the Eastern Catholic churches, a *major archbishop* and the church he heads have special standing in law. See **Eastern Catholic churches; major archbishop; "sui iuris";** and **synod.** See also **Anglican Communion; archdiocese; bishop; Catholic Church; coadjutor; Orthodox churches;** and **religious titles.**

archbishop-designate, bishop-designate Use these terms for a Catholic priest who has been named an archbishop or a bishop but has not yet been ordained to the episcopacy. If a bishop is named an archbishop, he automatically gets the title *archbishop* even before taking up his new post.

In stories reporting an episcopal appointment, use the appointee's religious title at the time of the appointment on first reference; use *(arch)bishop-designate* only on subsequent references. Lowercase *-designate* in all uses: *Msgr. John Smith was named auxiliary bishop of New York Jan. 5. Bishop-designate Smith said ....*

Similarly, one who has been named a cardinal is called *cardinal-designate* from the announcement until the consistory at which he becomes a cardinal. See **"in pectore."**

Do not use *bishop-elect, archbishop-elect* or *cardinal-elect* to refer to those who receive their office by papal appointment.

However, if an Eastern Catholic priest is elected bishop or archbishop by a patriarchal or major archiepiscopal synod of bishops, it is appropriate to call him *(arch)bishop-elect.*
See **-elect.**

archbishop of Canterbury Primate of the Church of England and the Anglican Communion. In religious or general contexts, lowercase *archbishop* except when it is used as a formal title immediately before the name of the individual.

The holder of the religious office is also a member of Great Britain's

House of Lords, however, making his title a rank of nobility. Capitalize *Archbishop of Canterbury* standing alone in stories referring specifically to his position in Parliament or listing him among British nobles, just as you would capitalize *Duke of Norfolk* or *Prince of Wales.*

See **Anglican Communion** and **primate, primatial see.**

Archconfraternity of Christian Mothers U.S. headquarters of the international organization is in Pittsburgh.

archdiocese In Catholic, Orthodox and Anglican usage an *archdiocese* ordinarily is the chief diocese of an ecclesiastical province. It is headed by an archbishop. In a few instances, sees with no suffragan dioceses have the rank of archdiocese.

Capitalize when it is part of a proper name, whether in an *of* construction or flip-flopped form: *the Archdiocese of Boston, the Boston Archdiocese.* Lowercase in plural uses or when it stands alone: *the Boston and Detroit archdioceses, the archdiocese.*

See **Anglican Communion; archbishop; Catholic Church; diocese;** and **Orthodox churches.**

archeparch, archeparchy Terms used at times in Orthodox and Eastern Catholic churches. An *archeparch* is an *archbishop.* An *archeparchy* is an *archdiocese.* If the technical character of a story requires use of the Eastern terms, explain their meaning. In most cases the more familiar Latin-rite terms should be substituted.

See **archdiocese; Eastern Catholic churches; eparch, eparchy; metropolitan;** and **Orthodox churches.**

archiepiscopal Note the first *i* in the spelling.

See **archbishop.**

archimandrite A title held by some celibate priests in the Orthodox and some Eastern Catholic churches. Use *Father* not *Archimandrite* as the title before the name: *Father John Smith; Father Smith; the archimandrite;* or *the priest.*

archpriest In the Latin Church, some principal churches in Italy and France are headed by archpriests. In some Eastern churches an archpriest may have territorial jurisdiction. In all cases treat the term as a job description, using Father, Msgr., Bishop, etc., as the personal title before the name: *Cardinal Francesco Marchisano, archpriest of St. Peter's Basilica.*

ARCIC See **Anglican Communion.**

ARC-USA See **Anglican Communion.**

Ark of the Covenant On second reference, the ark.

Armenian Apostolic Church One of the *Oriental Orthodox churches.* See that entry.

It is also called the *Armenian Church* and sometimes the *Gregorian Church* because its establishment as a national church dates to the conversion of the king of Armenia by St. Gregory the Illuminator around the year 300. Its primatial see is the Catholicate of Etchmiadzin in Armenia. It also has patriarchates in Jerusalem and Istanbul and the Catholicate of Cilicia, now located in Antelias, Lebanon.

As a result of political divisions in the 1930s, Oriental Orthodox Armenians in North America today are organized in two groups:

— The *Armenian Apostolic*

Church, Diocese of America, which since its establishment in the 19th century has been under the jurisdiction of the catholicos of Etchmiadzin. It is divided into a Canadian diocese and eastern and western U.S. dioceses, with its main headquarters in New York.

— The *Armenian Apostolic Church of America,* which split from the other church in 1933 and in 1957 placed itself under the jurisdiction of the catholicos of Cilicia. It is divided into a Canadian diocese and two U.S. prelacies, eastern and western.

artificial contraception Use of artificial means to prevent conception — the union of sperm and egg — in sexual intercourse. Catholic teaching, reaffirmed by Pope Paul VI in 1968 in the encyclical "Humanae Vitae" (Of Human Life), rejects artificial contraception as the obstruction of the natural, divinely willed life-giving power of the conjugal act. According to that teaching, the only morally acceptable methods of birth regulation are those which utilize the woman's natural periods of infertility.

Methods of birth control which do not prevent conception but prevent implantation of a fertilized egg are often described as contraceptive, but in Catholic teaching they are considered abortifacient, not contraceptive.

See **abortion; birth control; contraceptive sterilization; "Humanae Vitae"; intrauterine device; morning-after pill;** and **natural family planning.**

Ash Wednesday In Western Christianity, the first day of Lent, 46 days before Easter.

In Orthodox and Eastern Catholic churches Lent begins on the Monday 48 days before Easter. For the Orthodox this is not necessarily two days before the Western Ash Wednesday, since the Orthodox usually observe Easter on a different date.

See **Easter** and **Lent, Lenten.**

AsiaNews (www.asianews.it) A Rome-based missionary news agency. Note that the organization uses no space between Asia and News.

Asian names For countries not listed below, follow the general Western custom of given name followed by family name on first reference and family name only on second reference.

Note that the usage described below applies to individuals of the nationality or ethnic group named, which may not coincide with country of residence. Most Chinese living in Vietnam or Indonesia, for example, still give their name in the traditional Chinese form of family name first, followed by given name.

In many Asian countries, when a Christian name is added to a person's given and family names, the Christian name is always placed first on first reference, regardless of the sequence used in that country for the rest of the full name. On subsequent references, ignore the Christian name and follow the normal rules for second reference that apply for people of that nationality. For example: *Korean Cardinal Stephen Kim Sou-hwan, Cardinal Kim.* If an Asian priest or religious is known only by his or her Christian name, however, use that name on all references. See *Brother* and *Sister* usage in **religious titles.**

CAMBODIA: Family name first, followed by given name. On second reference, both names are always used: *Hun Sen, Chea Sim, Pol Pot.*

CHINA (includes Chinese names in Hong Kong, Macau, Malaysia, Singapore and Taiwan): Family name first, followed by given names; family name on second reference: *Alex Mok*

Wing-kee, Mok; Mao Tse-tung, Mao.

INDONESIA: Given name first, followed by family name if there is one. Many, especially Christians, follow the Western style, but many Javanese use only one given name, such as *Suharto,* or their second name is derived from their father: *Megawati Sukarnoputri* (daughter of Sukarno), *Megawati.* Family name or single name used for second reference.

KOREA: Names are generally three words (excluding Christian name), with family name first. Use family name on second reference (see Cardinal Kim on p. 17). North Korean names generally have no hyphens; South Korean names usually have the second and third names hyphenated, with a lowercase letter after the hyphen: *Kim Il Sung* (North); *Kim Young-sam* (South).

LAOS, THAILAND: Given name, followed by family name. Given name on second reference. *Suvicha Saengmanee, Suvicha.* The exception is for bishops, use family name on second reference: *Cardinal Michael Michai Kitbunchu, Cardinal Kitbunchu.*

MALAYSIA: See Chinese names above. Christians or Indians follow Western style. As Malays (Muslims) usually have one given name followed by father's name or, for some males, Mohammed, use the given name on second reference: *Anwar Ibrahim, Anwar.*

PAKISTAN: The name Masih (Urdu for "Messiah") is often added after the names of male Christians, as Mohammed is for male Muslims, especially when there is no family name. In these cases, use the single given name instead of the family name on second reference. Mian is an honorific; do not use.

VIETNAM: Family name, followed by given names. In general for second reference, use the last of three Vietnamese names or the last two of four such names: *Cardinal Jean-Baptiste Pham Minh Man, Cardinal Man.*

Assemblies of God See **Pentecostal churches.**

assisted suicide The act of providing the means by which another person can cause his or her own death in order to end pain or suffering. Do not use as a synonym for *euthanasia,* which is an act or omission that intentionally brings about another's death in order to end pain or suffering.

Use *physician-assisted suicide* only in cases where a proposal or law specifically says only doctors can provide those means.

Official Catholic teaching admits circumstances in which a patient may refuse useless or extraordinarily burdensome treatment, but it rejects any form of euthanasia or assisted suicide.

See **euthanasia.**

Associated Church Press (www.theacp.org) A professional Christian journalism association with Protestant, Catholic and Orthodox member publications. Headquarters is in Stoughton, Wis.

Association for Social Economics (www.socialeconomics.org) Formerly the Catholic Economics Association.

Association for Spiritual, Ethical and Religious Values in Counseling (www.aservic.org) Formerly the National Catholic Guidance Conference, it is now a division of the American Counseling Association.

Association of Catholic Colleges and Universities (www.accunet.org) A voluntary association of regionally accredited colleges and universities in the United States. There were 213 institutional members in the 2004-05 school year. Headquarters is in Washington.

Association of Catholic Diocesan Archivists Established in 1979 to promote professionalism in the management of diocesan archives in the United States. Headquarters is in New Orleans.

Association of Marian Helpers (http://marian.org/association) Headquarters is in Stockbridge, Mass.

Assyrian Church of the East (www.cired.org) Formerly but no longer regarded as a Nestorian church. This ancient Christian church flourished for many centuries within the Persian Empire and once extended into central Asia as far as China. For various theological and political reasons, it adopted the Christology espoused by Nestorius and broke with the church in the Roman Empire after Nestorius was condemned at the Council of Ephesus in 431. Since that time it has not been in full communion with any other church. With the invasions of Tamerlane in the 14th century, the church was almost annihilated and reduced to small communities in what is now eastern Turkey. During the chaos and massacres of World War I, most Assyrians fled south into modern Iraq, where most live today. The Assyrians celebrate seven sacraments and allow married men to be ordained to the priesthood, although the bishops must be celibate. The church has a total membership of about 400,000. The Christological differences between the Assyrian Church of the East and the Catholic Church were resolved in November 1994 when Pope John Paul II and the Assyrian patriarch signed a common Christological declaration. In light of modern scholarship, the Assyrians are no longer regarded as holding the positions condemned as heretical in 431.

This church should not be referred to as part of any grouping of churches, such as Orthodox or Oriental Orthodox, and it should no longer be referred to as Nestorian. In 2005, the patriarch, Mar Dinkha IV, lived in Morton Grove, Ill., a suburb of Chicago.

An official theological dialogue between the Catholic Church and the Assyrians has been meeting annually since 1995. There is a parallel dialogue between the Assyrians and the Chaldean Catholic Church, formed by a group of Assyrians who broke away and joined the Catholic Church in the 16th century. The goal of this dialogue is the reintegration of the two churches.

In 2001, the Vatican Congregation for the Doctrine of the Faith ruled that the ancient anaphora of Addai and Mari, used for most of the liturgical year in Assyrian celebrations of the Holy Eucharist, can be considered valid. Later that year, the Pontifical Council for Promoting Christian Unity ruled that in cases of pastoral necessity it is permissible to let Chaldean Catholics receive Communion at an Assyrian Holy Eucharist and to let Assyrians receive Communion at a Chaldean Holy Eucharist. It left it to the authorities of the two churches to decide when or how to implement such permission but said the provision could be applied only in cases of need "and is not to be equated with full eucharistic communion" between the two churches.

atheist, theist An *atheist* is one who believes there is no God.

A *theist* is one who believes in at least one divine being. Someone who believes there is only one God is a *monotheist.* Someone who believes in several gods is a *polytheist.*

An *agnostic* is neither a theist nor an atheist. An agnostic believes it is impossible to know whether or not there is a God.

Deist is not a synonym for *theist.* A deist rejects revelation or authority as a source of belief, believing in God purely on rational grounds. The deists of the 17th and 18th century generally viewed God as the original creator of the universe and its laws but rejected the concept of God's continuing involvement in creation.

at risk Hyphenate only when used as an attributive adjective: *at-risk youths.* But: *teens at risk.* Unless it is self-evident from the context, define the specific danger of which the group is considered to be at risk, e.g., starvation, teen pregnancy.

auditor A term used in the Catholic Church for an individual, usually a layperson, who is invited to attend a meeting of church officials but has no formal voice in its proceedings. Papally appointed lay auditors attend sessions of the world Synod of Bishops. A group of them attended the last session of the Second Vatican Council. Do not use as a formal title before a name.

If non-Catholic representatives are invited to such a meeting, they are called *observers* or *observer delegates,* not *auditors.*

In diocesan church courts, an official who gathers evidence and testimony for the court may be called an *auditor* or *instructor.* See **ecclesiastical courts.**

Do not use *auditor* to express the Italian *uditore* when it is used by the Vatican as a job description in curial departments and the diplomatic corps.

When applied to a member of the Roman Rota, it refers to a *judge.*

When applied to staff members in other curial departments or in Vatican embassies around the world, it should be paraphrased as *an official, an aide, a staff member, an assistant,* etc. There is no single job title in English that corresponds exactly to *uditore* in those offices.

Augsburg Confession See **Lutheran churches.**

auxiliary A bishop assigned to a Catholic diocese or archdiocese to assist its residential bishop is usually an *auxiliary bishop.* Capitalize when used as a title before a name: *Auxiliary Bishop John G. Noonan of Miami.* Lowercase in other uses: *Bishop Noonan, an auxiliary bishop of Miami.*

When an auxiliary bishop is mentioned in a story, the story should always state that he is an auxiliary and give the name of his diocese. Ordinarily this should be done by means of a formal title with the person's full name and diocese on first reference. On second reference the title should be shortened to *Bishop.*

Auxiliary refers to jurisdiction, not to sacramental ordination. Someone may be *named an auxiliary bishop,* but he is *ordained a bishop.* Between his appointment and his ordination he is a *bishop-designate,* not *auxiliary-designate* or *auxiliary bishop-designate.*

See **archbishop-designate, bishop-designate; coadjutor;** and **titular see.**

award categories Do not capitalize categories such as best picture, best foreign film or best actress in stories about presentation of such awards as the Oscars or the Emmys.

B

Bacau Use this spelling for the city in East Timor and for the name of the diocese listed in the *Annuario* as *Baucau.*

baldacchino Preferred to *baldachin* or *baldaquin* as the spelling for a canopy made of rich brocade that is carried in church processions or placed over an altar, or a permanent altar canopy on pillars, such as the bronze baldacchino over the main altar of St. Peter's Basilica in Rome.

baptism One of two sacraments (along with the Eucharist) accepted by most Christian churches. Baptism is considered one of the three sacraments of initiation (along with confirmation and the Eucharist) by Catholic and Orthodox churches. Protestant churches generally do not regard confirmation as a sacrament, but Anglican churches describe it as a *sacramental rite.*

Some Protestant churches consider baptism valid only if it is given after a person has personally professed faith in Christ. They usually refer to this as *believer baptism.* The Catholic Church and others which accept or practice *infant baptism* may object to the term *believer baptism* on grounds that it implies that baptized infants are outside the community of believers. These churches prefer the term *adult baptism* to describe the baptism of those who receive the sacrament at a later age, after personally professing the faith.

The rite of baptism varies among the churches. The sacrament can be conferred either by *immersion* in water or by the *pouring* of water in Catholic teaching and practice. Some churches accept only immersion or only pouring. Some use *aspersion (sprinkling),* in which the minister lets water trickle from his hand onto the head of the person being baptized.

See **Rite of Christian Initiation of Adults** and **sacraments.**

Baptist churches Baptists trace their origins to several early 17th-century breaks from English Congregationalism. They form the largest Protestant denomination in the United States, with more than 29 million members. They are noted for their emphasis on personal religious experience, the autonomy of each congregation, religious freedom and separation of church and state.

Scripture is the only authoritative rule of faith, and each member is free to interpret it according to his or her own conscience. Despite lack of a creedal or confessional standard, Baptists are generally agreed in recognizing Christ's divinity and humanity, the Trinity, human sinfulness and the necessity of grace for salvation. Some believe redemption was meant for all, while others believe in a form of predestination or limited redemption.

Baptists reject infant baptism because they consider personal testimony of one's faith in Christ a prerequisite for baptism. It is generally administered by immersion.

They generally reject the notion of sacraments. They term baptism and the Lord's Supper *ordinances,* carried out in obedience to the Lord's commands in Scripture. They consider the Lord's Supper a memorial meal and baptism an emblem of the believer's faith. Worship services tend to be simple, with an emphasis on preaching.

With their emphasis on the autonomy of the local congregation, they use the term *church* only for the local unit. Larger agencies of coordination and cooperation generally define themselves with terms such as *association, conference, convention, fellowship* or the plural *churches.*

In addition to more than 20 major Baptist bodies are dozens of smaller ones, some consisting of only a few congregations.

The largest body is the Southern Baptist Convention in North America (www.sbc.net), with more than 16 million members in 2005. The largest black body is the National Baptist Convention, U.S.A. (www.national baptist.com), with about 7.5 million members. A listing of main Baptist bodies and their headquarters is contained in the Yearbook of American and Canadian Churches.

The Baptist World Alliance (www.bwanet.org) is an association of 211 Baptist conventions and unions throughout the world serving about 80 million Baptists, of whom more than 32 million have been baptized. It fosters communication and consultation among its members and helps promote evangelical, educational and service work by Baptist churches. Headquarters is in Falls Church, Va.

The Baptist Joint Committee on Public Affairs (www.bjcpa.org), supported by 14 U.S. Baptist groups, monitors church-state concerns in legislation and public policy related to religious liberty and church-state separation. Headquarters is in Washington.

CLERGY: Baptist clergy are *ministers.* A minister who leads a congregation is a *pastor.* See **religious titles.**

RELATIONS WITH CATHOLICS: The Baptist World Alliance maintains an official dialogue with the Catholic Church. The U.S. Catholic Church has had bilateral consultations with the American Baptist Convention and the Southern Baptist Convention, but in 2005 such contacts continued only through the Faith and Order Commission of the National Council of Churches.

bar mitzvah, bat mitzvah See **Judaism.**

basic ecclesial communities See **small Christian communities.**

basilica A church to which special privileges are attached. Most are *minor basilicas,* but a few of special importance are called *major basilicas.* Among these, four in Rome are primary and are usually the ones referred to as the major basilicas: St. Peter's, St. John Lateran, St. Mary Major and St. Paul Outside the Walls. Another example of a major basilica is the Franciscan church in Assisi, Italy, where St. Francis of Assisi is buried. Capitalize *basilica* only when used as part of a proper name: *St. Peter's Basilica, the Basilica of St. Paul Outside the Walls.*

Many basilicas, including St. Peter's, are not cathedrals. The cathedral church of Rome, which is the pope's cathedral, is St. John Lateran.

For the full proper names of basilicas in the United States, follow the form used in the Kenedy directory: *St. Mary's Basilica* in Phoenix; *Cathedral Basilica of the Sacred Heart* in Newark, N.J.; *Basilica of the National Shrine of the Immaculate Conception* in Washington.

Context and relevance should determine whether *basilica* or another appropriate term (e.g. *church, cathedral, shrine*) is used on subsequent references to a church that has been designated a basilica.

B.C.E. See **C.E., B.C.E.**

beatification See **canonization.**

Beatitude, beatitude *His Beatitude* is a formal title of respect for a Catholic patriarch or Orthodox metropolitan. It should not be used in news stories except in quoted matter. If used, it should be capitalized along with the preceding modifier *His* or *Your: "Everyone should stand when His Beatitude enters the room,"* he said. See **religious titles.**

Capitalize the phrase *Eight Beatitudes*, but lowercase in other forms of reference: *She lives the Eight Beatitudes. "Blessed are the peacemakers" is one of the beatitudes.*

Beginning Experience (www.beginningexperience.org) A weekend program to help divorced, separated and widowed people. Designed by and for Catholics, it is open to people of all faiths. Its international ministry center is in South Bend, Ind.

Belfast Agreement See **Good Friday Agreement.**

Benediction, blessing Capitalize *Benediction* when referring to a Catholic religious service consisting of prayers and hymns, usually with the Eucharist displayed on the altar. It also is called *Benediction of the Blessed Sacrament.*

The term *blessing* is preferable to *benediction* (lowercase) when referring to other rites or acts of blessing: *the blessing at the end of Mass; the blessing of the fleet; the parish's annual blessing of animals.*

Benemerenti Medal See **papal honors.**

Bible Capitalize *Bible, Scripture* and *Scriptures* when used as terms for the sacred writings of Christianity or Judaism. Do not use quotation marks. Lowercase the adjectives *holy* and *sacred* when they are used to describe the Bible: *the holy Bible, sacred Scripture.*

Lowercase the adjective *biblical: biblical literature, a biblical figure.* Also lowercase *bible* when it refers to any other authoritative writings, religious or nonreligious: *The Koran is the bible of the Muslims. The Wall Street Journal is his bible.*

Capitalize, without quotation marks, the names of individual books of the Bible and the standard collective names for portions of it: *the Book of Genesis, St. Paul's Letter to the Romans, Old Testament, New Testament, the Pentateuch, the Synoptics, the Gospels.* Also capitalize different versions of the Bible: *King James Version, Standard Version,* etc. But in general, references to stories in the Bible should be lowercase: *the parable of the prodigal son, the story of Jonah and the whale, the parable of the good Samaritan,* etc.

Hebrew Scriptures may be a preferable term for *Old Testament* in stories dealing with Judaism or Christian-Jewish relations. In this context, *Christian Scriptures* means the *New Testament.* See **apocrypha, apocryphal** and **deuterocanonical.**

For books of the Bible, use the names and spellings of the New American Bible. Two key variant names that could cause confusion are: Apocalypse (abbrev. Apoc or Apc), which is the Book of Revelation; and Ecclesiasticus (abbrev. Ecclus), which is Sirach, NOT a variant spelling of Ecclesiastes. Substitute the New American Bible names for Apocalypse and Ecclesiasticus unless direct quotation requires their use.

Any Bible passages quoted by the

In footnotes or parenthetical citations use the abbreviations used in the New American Bible. Do not use periods. For citations listing chapters and verses by number, use these forms: *Mt 3:10, 17-18; Jn 10:12; 14:3, 10-12; 1 Pt 4:5*. See **Appendix C: Endnotes.**

The following table shows the books of the Bible in their order of appearance, with the abbreviations used in the New American Bible.

OLD TESTAMENT

Abbreviation	**Book**
Gn	Genesis
Ex	Exodus
Lv	Leviticus
Nm	Numbers
Dt	Deuteronomy
Jos	Joshua
Jgs	Judges
Ru	Ruth
1 Sm	1 Samuel
2 Sm	2 Samuel
1 Kgs	1 Kings
2 Kgs	2 Kings
1 Chr	1 Chronicles
2 Chr	2 Chronicles
Ezr	Ezra
Neh	Nehemiah
Tb	Tobit
Jdt	Judith
Est	Esther
1 Mc	1 Maccabees
2 Mc	2 Maccabees
Jb	Job
Ps(s)	Psalms
Prv	Proverbs
Eccl	Ecclesiastes
Song	Song of Songs
Wis	Wisdom
Sir	Sirach
Is	Isaiah
Jer	Jeremiah
Lam	Lamentations
Bar	Baruch
Ez	Ezekiel
Dn	Daniel
Hos	Hosea
Jl	Joel
Am	Amos
Ob	Obadiah
Jon	Jonah
Mi	Micah
Na	Nahum
Hb	Habakkuk
Zep	Zephaniah
Hg	Haggai
Zec	Zechariah
Mal	Malachi

NEW TESTAMENT

Abbreviation	**Book**
Mt	Matthew
Mk	Mark
Lk	Luke
Jn	John
Acts	Acts of the Apostles
Rom	Romans
1 Cor	1 Corinthians
2 Cor	2 Corinthians
Gal	Galatians
Eph	Ephesians
Phil	Philippians
Col	Colossians
1 Thes	1 Thessalonians
2 Thes	2 Thessalonians
1 Tm	1 Timothy
2 Tm	2 Timothy
Ti	Titus
Phlm	Philemon
Heb	Hebrews
Jas	James
1 Pt	1 Peter
2 Pt	2 Peter
1 Jn	1 John
2 Jn	2 John
3 Jn	3 John
Jude	Jude
Rv	Revelation

writer and any English-language translations of texts should use the New American Bible as their source. The most up-to-date version of the New American Bible is on the Internet at www.usccb.org/nab/bible/index.htm. For translating Bible passages into Spanish, use the latest Spanish-language Bible available until the U.S. bishops and CELAM publish their official joint Spanish-language Bible. If other versions of the Bible are used in quoted material, identify the version used, if possible.

Spell out the name if the book is mentioned in the text of a story: *He cited Genesis as his proof. He read from the Gospel of Luke.*

Capitalize *Book, Letter* and *Gospel* when they are used as part of the name of a book in the Bible: *the Book of Job, the Letter to the Ephesians, the Gospel of St. Luke.* See **Gospel(s), gospel** and **letter, epistle.**

The *Pentateuch* is not a separate book of the Bible but the proper collective name for the first five books of the Bible taken together. This collection enjoys special status among Jews as the *Torah,* or *law.*

The Gospels of Sts. Matthew, Mark and Luke, which parallel one another closely in overall narrative structure, are the *synoptic Gospels.* Lowercase *synoptic* as an adjective, but capitalize the collective noun: *the Synoptics.*

Bible Belt The term was coined in 1925 by H.L. Mencken to describe those sections of the United States where fundamentalist beliefs prevail. To Catholics, Bible Belt attitudes have been associated traditionally with anti-Catholic prejudice. In some contexts the term may be considered offensive. It should be used with care.

biblical events Like some major events of secular history, certain major events of salvation history have names that are capitalized when they are used as a unique reference to an event but lowercased when they are used in their common meaning: *the Exodus, the Passion.* But: *the Hebrew nation's exodus from Egypt under Moses; Christ's passion and death.*

Capitalize the name of a major event in the life of Jesus in references that do not use his name, but lowercase if the word is used with his name or a pronoun referring back to him: *The Last Supper, Crucifixion, Resurrection and Ascension are central to Christian belief.* But: *Jesus foretold his resurrection from the dead.*

Apply the same principle to major events in the life of his mother: *the Assumption, Mary's assumption into heaven.*

binate, trinate When a priest celebrates two Masses on the same day, he *binates.* When he celebrates three, he *trinates.* The verbs are intransitive. The noun forms are *bination* and *trination.*

The terms are part of clerical argot. They ordinarily should not be used. If used, they must be explained.

bingo Not a trademark.

birth control Do not use as a synonym for *artificial contraception. Birth control* is a general term that means any method of limiting births. It encompasses *abortion, artificial contraception, contraceptive sterilization* and *natural family planning.* See those entries.

bishop In the teaching of the Catholic and Orthodox churches and others that have an episcopal or hierarchical form of government, *bishop* is the highest order of ordained ministry, or the fullness of the ordained priesthood.

Capitalize when used as a formal title before a name. Lowercase in other uses. When *bishop* is used as a formal title before a name, it is used before the name on all references.

When it is used as a formal title and accompanied by another modifier:

— Capitalize *auxiliary* or *coadjutor*. In the Episcopal Church, also capitalize *suffragan* or *assistant*. Capitalize *presiding* when used as part of the title of the chief bishop of a denomination in a nation. All these modifiers are part of the formal title. On second reference the modifier should not be repeated as part of the formal title before a name. See **auxiliary; coadjutor;** and **Episcopal Church.**

— Lowercase other modifiers, such as *retired* or *-designate*. These are merely descriptive, not part of the formal title.

In the Catholic Church, the proper term for the chief bishop of a diocese is *diocesan bishop* or *residential bishop*, not *ordinary*. See **ordinary** and **residential bishop.**

See **archbishop; archbishop-designate, bishop-designate; eparch, eparchy; religious titles**; and entries for individual denominations.

bishop-designate, bishops-designate See **archbishop-designate, bishop-designate.**

bishops' conferences Unless it is used as part of the formal name of a national episcopal conference in an English-language form printed in the *Annuario*, do not capitalize the words *bishops' conference*. Some examples: *the U.S. Conference of Catholic Bishops, the Canadian Conference of Catholic Bishops, the Southern African Catholic Bishops' Conference,* but *the U.S. bishops' conference, the French bishops' conference, the Polish bishops' conference.*

black See **African-American.**

Black Muslims See **Muslim(s).**

Blessed See **canonization.**

Blessed Sacrament Capitalize, but use only in quoted matter or certain phrases such as *Benediction of the Blessed Sacrament, devotion to the Blessed Sacrament, exposition of the Blessed Sacrament*. Otherwise use *Eucharist* or *Communion* as appropriate.

See **Benediction, blessing** and **Eucharist, eucharistic.**

Blessed Virgin See **Mary.**

blessing See **Benediction, blessing.**

Blue Army of Our Lady of Fatima (www.bluearmy.com) U.S. branch of the World Apostolate of Fatima, an international organization that promotes the 1917 message of Our Lady of Fatima to abandon sin and build peace through prayer, especially the rosary. Blue Army is acceptable on second reference. Headquarters and shrine are in Washington, N.J.

Blue Mass See **Red Mass.**

B'nai B'rith (http://bnaibrith.org) Acceptable in all references to affiliates in the United States or elsewhere of *B'nai B'rith International*, a fraternal organization of Jewish men. Founded in 1843, it has affiliates in more than 50 countries and emphasizes community service, social action and public affairs. The full name is needed on first reference only if the story concerns a formal statement, action or policy by the leadership of the full international body. *B'nai B'rith* is Hebrew for *Sons of the Covenant.* Headquarters is in Washington.

See **Anti-Defamation League.**

body of Christ Lowercase *body* in all references: *The church is the body of Christ. The Eucharist is the body and blood of Christ.*

Book of the Gospels A ceremonial liturgical book composed of the four Gospels. In Orthodox and Eastern Catholic tradition it is arranged as full Gospels in the traditional sequence of authors. For its revived use in the Latin Church it is usually arranged in the order of Gospel readings for the Sundays and major feasts of the liturgical cycle. The 2000 General Instruction of the Roman Missal said only the Book of the Gospels, not the Lectionary, is to be carried in the opening procession at Mass. When it is used, it is placed on the altar at the start of Mass and taken to the ambo for the proclamation of the Gospel. It is also used in the rites of ordination of deacons and bishops.

book reviews See **Appendix A: Special Style Considerations.**

Boy Scouts The coordinating agency of Catholic involvement is the *National Catholic Committee on Scouting.* See that entry. For *Catholic awards,* see that entry.

Boys Town (www.girlsandboys town.org) Two words, no apostrophe, for the Nebraska town for delinquent boys established in 1922 by Father Edward J. Flanagan. Acceptable in datelines. The form: *BOYS TOWN, Neb. (CNS)* —. While the dateline has not changed, since 2000 the institutional name has been changed to *Girls and Boys Town.* See that entry and **datelines.**

Brahma, Brahman *Brahma* is the supreme being in Hinduism.

A *Brahman* is a member of the priestly Hindu caste, the highest level in the caste system. The term also is capitalized when used to refer to a breed of cattle.

See **Hindu, Hinduism.**

Bread for the World (www. bread.org) A nonprofit, nondenominational Christian citizens' movement that advocates policy changes to ease hunger in the United States and abroad. Headquarters is in Washington.

Brest, Union of The 1596 reunion of a segment of the Ruthenian Orthodox Church with the Catholic Church, it resulted in the establishment of what today are the Ukrainian, Ruthenian and Belarusian Catholic churches. See **Eastern Catholic churches** and **uniate churches.**

Brooklyn Although it is a part of New York City, because of the division of the city into two Catholic dioceses, *Brooklyn* is acceptable in datelines and text of stories concerning the Catholic Diocese of Brooklyn or institutions or activities related to the diocese. The form: *BROOKLYN, N.Y. (CNS)* —. See **datelines.**

brother A man who has taken vows in a religious order and is not ordained or preparing for the priesthood is a *brother.* If a man is ordained he is identified as a priest and the title before his name is *Father.* If he is a student for the priesthood, no title should be used, but the religious order to which he belongs should be identified.

Generally identify by religious community in first reference: *Franciscan Brother John Smith, Christian Brother Joseph Jones.* On second reference, use the first name if the person is known that way: *Brother John, Brother Joseph.* Otherwise, use the last name on second reference: *Brother Smith, Brother Jones.* Do not use the abbreviation *Bro.* See **religious titles.**

Do not capitalize *brother* or *brothers* when standing alone: *The priests and brothers protested in front of the South African Embassy in Washington.*

Originally priests in religious orders were also called brothers, and the term *lay brother* was used to refer to members who were not ordained. The distinction is still used in some technical writing, but in general writing *brother* implies *unordained,* making *lay brother* redundant.

See **order, congregation, society; religious;** and **Appendix D: Religious Orders, Men.**

Buddha, Buddhism Buddhism began as a reformist movement in Hinduism. Its basic teachings were developed by Siddhartha Gautama (whose name also appears as Gautama Siddhartha), an Indian prince who lived about 563-483 B.C., and who in meditation reached enlightenment about pain and the way to overcome it. His disciples called him the Buddha, or Enlightened One.

In 2005 an estimated 373 million people, mostly Asians, were Buddhists. They have significant numbers in India, China and Korea and form a majority of the population in Japan, Thailand, Burma, Cambodia, Laos and Tibet. In 2005 an estimated 2.9 million Buddhists lived in the United States and more than 300,000 in Canada.

BELIEFS: The central doctrine of Buddhism is the belief that correct understanding and the elimination of desires, gradually achieved in successive incarnations through meditation and asceticism, will enable the soul to reach nirvana, a state of complete enlightenment and peace. Only nirvana frees one from the cycle of death and rebirth. One's karma, or fate, determines that all of one's actions, no matter how small, will affect one's next life after rebirth.

The chief guidelines for reaching nirvana are:

— The Four Noble Truths: All existence entails suffering; it is caused by desire; it may be overcome by conquering desire; and the means to achieve that is the Eightfold Path.

— The Eightfold Path: Right knowledge of the Four Noble Truths; right resolve to curb malice; right speech; right behavior; right occupation; right effort to free oneself from evil and retain the good; right control of the senses and thought; and attainment of inner peace and joy through meditation.

ORGANIZATION: Buddhist organization varies widely from culture to culture. In broad terms, the sangha, or ideal Buddhist community, is a religious order made up of monks, nuns and the laity. Monks are not to be separated by rank or privilege but play the primary role in preserving and spreading the religion. Monks and nuns practice the full path of asceticism and meditation, while lay followers are called on to avoid vices and practice the virtues leading to salvation. See **religious titles.**

In Buddhism four major groups emerged over time, each with different emphases in doctrine and practice. These main groups are Hinayana or Theravada, Mahayana, Mantrayana and Zen.

DIALOGUE: The U.S. Catholic Church held its first national consultation with Buddhists in 1989. The Monastic Interreligious Dialogue has included Buddhist monks since 1981. The Vatican in recent years began sending greetings to Buddhist leaders to mark Vesakh, a celebration of the Buddha's life.

Unofficial Web sites devoted to information on Buddhism include www.buddhanet.net and http://buddhism.about.com.

Bureau of Catholic Indian Missions Headquarters is in Washington.

bylines See **Appendix A: Special Style Considerations.**

Byzantine rite One of the five main ritual groups into which Eastern Catholics are divided.
See **Eastern Catholic churches.**

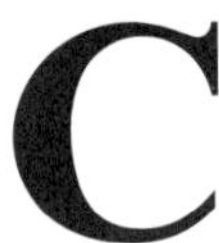

CAFOD See **Catholic Agency for Overseas Development.**

Calix Society (www.calixsociety. org) An association of Catholic recovering alcoholics, it is affiliated with Alcoholics Anonymous. The word *calix* is Latin for *chalice.* Headquarters is in St. Paul, Minn.

Call to Action (www.cta-usa.org) An independent national organization based in Chicago, its aims are to promote Catholic social teaching and action, greater lay participation in church decisions and certain changes in church teaching and practice, including the ordination of women and married men to the priesthood. It traces its roots to a national conference in Detroit in 1976 that was convened under the sponsorship of the U.S. Catholic bishops but proposed some controversial changes that were not accepted into church practice. Headquarters is in Chicago.

Calvary, cavalry The place Jesus was crucified was *Calvary.*

Certain combat troops, formerly mounted but now often in motorized armored vehicles, are described as *cavalry.*

camerlengo See **chamberlain of the Holy Roman Church.**

Campaign for Human Development See **Catholic Campaign for Human Development.**

Camp Fire Girls For *Catholic awards,* see that entry.

Cana conference, pre-Cana conference Often used as terms for church-sponsored marriage preparation courses. *Cana* is capitalized because it refers to the biblical town where Jesus attended a wedding feast.

Candlemas, Candlemas Day The liturgical feast for Feb. 2 is the Presentation of the Lord, but it is also known as Candlemas because the liturgy of the day includes a special rite before Mass of the blessing of candles for sacred uses.

canon For its use in references to the Code of Canon Law and Code of Canons of the Eastern Churches, see **canon law.** For usage as a religious title, see **religious titles.** Canon can also refer to the books of the Bible officially accepted by the church as divinely inspired (*the canon of the Bible)*, the complete works of an author *(the Alexandrian canon)* or the part of the Mass between the preface and Communion, centering on the consecration of the bread and wine (*the Roman Canon)*.

canonization The Catholic Church's process leading to canonization involves three major steps. First is the declaration of a person's heroic virtues, after which the church gives him or her the title *Venerable.* Second is beatification, after which he or she is called *Blessed.* The third step is canonization, or declaration of sainthood.

Do not use the title *Venerable* in any reference, except where it is unavoidable in direct quotes.

In a beatification story, the first reference to the person should indicate he or she was beatified but should use the title or name under which the person was best known during his or her lifetime. Do not refer to a person as "the venerable" or "the blessed." *The pope beatified Sister Alphonsa Muttathupadathu of the Immaculate Conception. Sister Alphonsa....*

For canonization stories, the first reference to the new saint should include the title "St." However, in subsequent references, use the name by which the person is or was best known. *St. Elizabeth Ann Seton, Mother Seton; St. Francesco Antonio Fasini, Father Fasini; St. Pius X, Pope Pius.*

At various steps in the canonization process, evidence of alleged miracles is presented to church authorities. In general, two miracles need to be accepted by the church as having occurred through the intercession of the prospective saint. When referring to these, say: "a miracle was attributed to the intercession of the new saint" or a similar phrase. See **miracles, apparitions.**

canon law When referring to the codified body of general laws governing the Latin rite of the Catholic Church, capitalize *Code of Canon Law, Canon 110,* etc.; lowercase *canon law* and *the code.*

When referring to a particular paragraph of a canon that is divided into numbered paragraphs, use the forms: *the first paragraph of Canon 116; Canon 116, Paragraph 1;* or (in endnotes) *Canon 116.1.* For plural references: *Canon 116, Paragraphs 1 and 3; Canon 116.1 and .3.*

A few canons have subsections within a paragraph. If the paragraph is unnumbered, use the forms: *the second subsection of Canon 119; Canon 119, Subsection 2;* or (in endnotes) *Canon 119.2.* If the paragraph is numbered:

Canon 112, Paragraph 1, Subsection 3 or (in endnotes) *Canon 112.1.3.* Note capitalization and figures when *paragraph* or *subsection* is followed by the numeral, and lowercase if preceded by spelled-out ordinal number.

For quotations in English from the code, use the Canon Law Society of America's 1999 *Code of Canon Law, Latin-English Edition.* The only official version of the code is the one in Latin, but ordinarily there is no need in news stories to state the source of translation.

In printed texts of the code, the numbers of numbered paragraphs are preceded by a *paragraph* symbol. Subsection numbers are followed by a small *o* in superscript. While the footnote forms are identical for reference to a numbered paragraph and to a subsection in an unnumbered paragraph, there can be no confusion in practice, since either form can have only one reference in the canon cited.

The code's name in Latin is "Codex Iuris Canonicis," and it is sometimes referred to by its Latin initials, "C.I.C.," or by the shortened form, the "codex." If such references are used in quoted matter, explain their meaning. Outside quoted matter always use English forms of reference.

Eastern Catholic churches are governed in common by the *Code of Canons of the Eastern Churches.* This code, promulgated in 1990, is designed to respect the proper traditions and laws of each church within its own territory. It establishes more universal legislation for those churches outside their home territories, however.

Since the Eastern code's system of numbering and dividing canons is the same as the Latin code's, the same style guidelines apply for references to specific canons.

The Eastern code's name in Latin is "Codex Canonum Ecclesiarium Orientalium" and it is sometimes referred to by its Latin initials, "C.C.E.O." If such references are used in quoted matter, explain their meaning. Use English forms of reference outside quoted matter.

Canon Law Society of America (www.clsa.org) An organization of canon lawyers. Headquarters is in Alexandria, Va.

Canterbury See **archbishop of Canterbury** and **Anglican Communion.**

cantor In Catholic usage, one who intones hymns, psalms or antiphons at liturgical services. For Jewish usage, see **Judaism.**

cardinal Capitalize only when it is part of a formal name, such as *College of Cardinals,* or a personal title immediately preceding a name: *Cardinal William H. Keeler, Cardinal Keeler.*

For consistency with all other personal titles, on first reference place *Cardinal* before the given name, not after: *Cardinal Roger M. Mahony,* NOT *Roger Cardinal Mahony.*

Do not, however, change the proper names of institutions, organizations or awards named after cardinals: *Catholic Theological Union's Joseph Cardinal Bernardin Center for Theology and Ministry.*

See **Catholic Church; conclave, consistory; "in pectore"; patriarch;** and **titular church.**

cardinal-designate, cardinals-designate See **archbishop-designate, bishop-designate.**

Cardinal Mindszenty Foundation (www.mindszenty.org) Founded in 1958 "to combat communism with knowledge and facts," it is named after Hungarian Cardinal Jozsef (note spelling) Mindszenty, imprisoned from 1949 to 1956. Headquarters is in St. Louis.

Caritas ... Name used by bishops of many nations for their national coordinating agencies for Catholic charities and social services, usually with the name of the country following. For example: *Caritas Chile, Caritas India.* On second reference the country name may be dropped but *Caritas* remains capitalized. When the name is used, explain that it is a national Catholic charities organization. The comparable national organization in the United States is called *Catholic Charities USA.*

See that entry and **Caritas Internationalis.**

Caritas Internationalis (www.caritas.org) A confederation of 162 Catholic relief, development and social services organizations working in more than 200 countries around the world. U.S. members are Catholic Relief Services, Catholic Charities USA and Catholic Campaign for Human Development. *Caritas* is acceptable on second reference. Headquarters is in Vatican City.

Castel Gandolfo A small town south of Rome where the pope has a summer villa. The dateline should read: *CASTEL GANDOLFO, Italy (CNS) —.*

See **datelines.**

catechetics The field of religious education in which the doctrinal and moral principles of faith are taught. The adjective is *catechetical.*

The teacher is a *catechist,* more commonly called a *religious educator* or *CCD teacher* in most U.S. applications. In many other parts of the world, however, particularly in Latin America, Africa and Asia, *catechist* is the preferred term. In areas with few priests, catechists often hold a prominent or even primary role in the leadership of local Catholic communities.

A single book that explains the basic teachings of a faith systematically is a *catechism.* Some catechisms are written for children of different ages, some for adults. The papally approved official compendium of Catholic teaching is the *Catechism of the Catholic Church.* See that entry.

The process of teaching the faith is called *catechesis.* The verb form is *to catechize.* These two terms generally should be explained when used. Outside quoted matter or technical contexts requiring their use, synonymous descriptive phrases such as *religious education* or *to teach the faith* are preferred.

See **catechumen; Confraternity of Christian Doctrine;** and **Rite of Christian Initiation of Adults.**

Catechism of the Catholic Church No *The* in the formal title. On second reference, use *the catechism.*

catechumen An unbaptized person being formed in Christian faith and life in preparation for entry into the church. The period of preparation is called the *catechumenate.* For already baptized Christians who are preparing for entry into full communion with the Catholic Church, the correct term is *candidate,* not *catechumen.*

See **Rite of Christian Initiation of Adults.**

cathedra The bishop's chair in a cathedral.

Catholic, catholic In lowercase, *catholic* means *universal: Her tastes in art and literature are catholic.*

Note that in the creedal statement, "I believe in one, holy, catholic and apostolic church," *catholic* is used in this nondenominational sense.

Whenever it is used in a denominational sense, *Catholic* is capitalized. If it is not otherwise qualified, *Catholic* means *Roman Catholic.* When referring to other individuals or denominations which are not united with Rome but describe themselves as *Catholic* — such as the *Polish National Catholic Church, Old Catholic, Anglo-Catholics* — other modifiers or information must be supplied to make it clear to the reader that *Roman Catholic* is not meant.

In most contexts, *Catholic* is preferable to *Roman Catholic* in all references to the *Roman Catholic Church* or its members. *Roman Catholic* should be used, however, whenever it is needed to distinguish between Roman Catholics and others who describe themselves as Catholic.

See **Catholic Church.**

Catholic Academy for Communication Arts Professionals (www. catholicacademy.org) New name since 2002 for Unda-USA. U.S. affiliate of Signis. Headquarters is in Dayton, Ohio. See **Signis.**

Catholic Advertising Network Operates through Catholic Press Association in Ronkonkoma, N.Y.

Catholic Agency for Overseas Development (www.cafod.org.uk) A British Catholic aid agency. CAFOD or the agency are acceptable on second reference.

Catholic Aid Association (www. catholicaid.com) Fraternal life insurance society. Headquarters is in St. Paul, Minn.

Catholic Alumni Clubs International (www.caci.org) Founded in 1957 for single Catholics with professional education.

Catholic Association of Teachers of Homiletics (www.cathomiletics.org)

Catholic awards For honors conferred by the pope, see **papal honors.** See also **Christophers.**

Capitalize *award, medal,* etc., only when used as part of the full formal name: *the Laetare Medal, the medal, the John Courtney Murray Award, the award.*

Some Catholic awards given in the United States are:

— The *Gabriel Awards,* given by the Catholic Academy for Communications Arts Professionals for contributions to value-centered broadcasting. Some specific awards have their own formal names, such as *Gabriel Personal Achievement Award.* Acceptable on second reference for any of the awards: *a Gabriel, the Gabriel, the Gabriels.*

— The *John Courtney Murray Award,* named after a leading U.S. Jesuit theologian of the 20th century and given by the Catholic Theological Society of America for contributions in theology.

— The *Laetare Medal,* given annually by the University of Notre Dame to an outstanding Catholic. It receives its name from Laetare Sunday, the fourth Sunday of Lent, because the recipient traditionally is announced on that day.

— The *Role of Law* award, given by the Canon Law Society of America for contributions in church law.

—The *St. Francis de Sales Award,* given by the Catholic Press Association for contributions to Catholic journalism.

— The *U.S. Catholic Award,* given by Chicago-based U.S. Catholic magazine for contributions to the cause of women in the church.

For girls in Girl Scouts, Camp Fire Girls, Junior Catholic Daughters of the Americas and Junior Daughters of Isabella, the chief Catholic religious awards are: *Family of God* medal (ages 7-9), *I Live My Faith* medal (ages 9-11) and *Marian Medal* (ages 12-15). They are coordinated by the National Federation for Catholic Youth Ministry. The Girl Scouts also award the *Spirit Alive medal* (ages 15-17), *St. Elizabeth Ann Seton medal* (adult) and *St. Anne medal* (adult).

In the Boy Scouts of America, the Catholic religious awards for Cub Scouts are the *Light of Christ* emblem and the *Parvuli Dei,* Latin for *God's little ones.* For Boy Scouts in the Latin Church it is the *Ad Altare Dei,* Latin for *to God's altar;* in the Eastern Catholic churches it is the *Light Is Life* emblem.

Catholic Biblical Association of America (http://cba.cua.edu) A professional association of Scripture scholars and teachers founded in 1936. *Catholic Biblical Association* is acceptable on all references. Headquarters is in Washington.

Catholic Book Publishers Association (www.cbpa.org) Headquarters is in Rockford, Ill.

Catholic Campaign for Human Development (www.usccb.org/cchd) The U.S. Catholic bishops' domestic anti-poverty program. The word *Catholic* was added to its name in 1998. Started in 1970, it is funded through an annual collection in Catholic parishes. One-fourth of the money collected in each diocese is administered by the diocese for local projects; three-fourths goes to the national office in Washington, which uses it to fund educational programs and self-help projects around the country. *CCHD* is acceptable on second reference, but *the campaign* or *the program* is preferred.

Catholic Campus Ministry Association (www.ccmanet.org) Headquarters is in Cincinnati.

Catholic Central Union of America Founded in 1855 to promote "the development and vigor of Christian principles in personal, social, cultural, economic and civic life," it is one of the oldest U.S. Catholic lay organizations. *Catholic Central Union* is acceptable on second reference. Headquarters (the "central bureau") is in St. Louis.

Catholic Charities USA (www. catholiccharitiesusa.org) Formerly the National Conference of Catholic Charities. Founded in 1910 to advance the charitable and social-service activities of the Catholic community, it includes diocesan and other Catholic social-service agencies and individuals in its membership. Headquarters is in Alexandria, Va.

Catholic Church The worldwide body of followers of Christ united with their local bishops in full union with the pope. Members consider the pope, as bishop of Rome, the chief vicar of Christ on earth and sole successor of the apostle Peter. They believe the pope, as head of the college of bishops, holds ultimate doctrinal and jurisdictional authority over the whole church in virtue of Christ's promise, "Whatever you bind on earth shall be bound in heaven; and whatever you loose on earth shall be loosed in heaven."

In Catholic belief, each bishop through membership in the college of bishops shares in the teaching, preaching, sanctifying and governing mission entrusted by Christ to the original Twelve Apostles. The bishops trace their authority back to the apostles through an unbroken line of laying on of hands.

The shared authority — often called *collegiality* — of the bishops is particularly manifest when a pope summons an ecumenical council, a meeting of all bishops to address current pastoral, doctrinal or disciplinary issues in the church. Council actions must be approved by the pope, however, before they can take effect. See **collegiality** and **Vatican councils.**

Papal infallibility — the Catholic teaching that the pope can speak without error in formal teaching on matters of faith or morals — is considered by many non-Catholic Christians to be one of the chief obstacles to unity with the Catholic Church. Use of the power requires that the pope formally declare and define a teaching as a matter which must be believed. This is rarely used and was last invoked by Pope Pius XII in 1950, when he declared that Mary was assumed bodily into heaven at the end of her life on earth.

During his pontificate Pope John Paul II and his doctrinal officials gave increasing attention to what the Second Vatican Council called the infallibility of the world's bishops in communion with the pope when, "in their authoritative teaching concerning matters of faith and morals, they are in agreement that a particular teaching is to be held definitively and absolutely." The pope pronounced the teaching that only men can be ordained priests to be such a teaching and revised church laws to provide penalties for persistent dissent against such teachings. Top officials of the

Congregation for the Doctrine of the Faith described several other church teachings as being among those which cannot be revised and must be held definitively by Catholics.

Papal primacy — the Catholic teaching that the pope can exercise direct authority over the church anywhere in the world — is also an obstacle to reunion for most non-Catholic Christians. Many non-Catholic ecumenists would be willing to accept a primacy of honor, such as that held within the Anglican Communion by the archbishop of Canterbury or among the Orthodox churches by the patriarch of Constantinople, but not the worldwide jurisdictional authority accorded to the pope by Catholics. See **primacy.**

The *Roman Curia* is the official collective name for the Catholic Church's central administrative and judicial departments and their officials, who are appointed by the pope. The term refers only to the agencies of the Holy See, not to the diplomatic corps, the Synod of Bishops, pontifical educational institutions, the agencies of Vatican City State or the Palatine Administration. The *Curia* is acceptable as a shortened form in all references. The adjective is *curial.* Apart from stories specifically discussing the Vatican's institutional structures, however, the terms are usually unnecessary. A *curial official* is a *Vatican official,* offices of the *Curia* are *Vatican* offices or departments of the *Holy See,* etc. See **Appendix G: Vatican Agencies.**

The *College of Cardinals* is a group of men chosen by the pope as his chief advisers. Most are heads of major dioceses around the world or of the major departments of the Vatican. Cardinals are generally appointed to be members of at least one Vatican agency, and occasionally all cardinals may be convened to discuss major issues of church administration. At age 80 they retain membership in the college and the title of cardinal, but they lose an active role. The maximum number of active cardinals, which can be changed by the pope, was raised to 120 by Pope Paul VI in 1973. When Pope John Paul II named cardinals in 1998, he allowed the number of voting cardinals to exceed 120 but reaffirmed that the normal maximum would continue to be 120. When the papacy is vacant, the cardinals under age 80 gather in Rome for a closed meeting, called a *conclave,* at which a new pope is elected by majority vote. Cardinals are given honorary title to churches in Rome. Cardinals named *"in pectore"* are not part of the college until their names are made public and they are installed: Do not include them in figures for current membership in the college. See **cardinal; conclave; consistory; "in pectore";** and **titular church.**

In the Latin rite used by most Catholics, there are no national "churches" in the sense that applies in other denominations. For the Catholic Church that exists in a particular country or region but does not have its own distinctive rite, phrases such as *the French church* or *the Catholic Church in France* are acceptable; outside quoted matter, generally avoid phrases such as *the French Catholic Church,* where the conjunction of capitalized words suggests that a proper title is being given. See **American church, American Catholic Church; Catholic, catholic;** and **U.S. church, U.S. Catholic Church.**

Bishops within most nations are organized into a national conference. While primary authority rests with each bishop within his own diocese, the conference has legal responsibility for some nationwide church policies and programs, such as norms for seminaries, religious education and liturgical practice. A conference may also serve as a forum for discussion and decisions by the bishops regarding a range of pastoral concerns or matters of government relations and public policy, even though it has no binding authority as a conference in such areas. The U.S. Conference of Catholic Bishops, based in Washington, is the national organization of Catholic bishops in the United States. See **bishops' conferences** and **Appendix F: U.S. Conference of Catholic Bishops.**

In the Eastern Catholic churches, formed mainly by Catholics who live in Eastern Europe or the Middle East or who trace their origins to those regions, there are national churches. They and the archbishops who head them have considerable autonomy in ritual and discipline, but they acknowledge the authority of the pope. Some Eastern churches are headed by patriarchs. See **Eastern Catholic churches.**

The chief local divisions of the Catholic Church are archdioceses and dioceses. They are headed, respectively, by archbishops and bishops, who are responsible for church life within their territory. An archdiocese is essentially the same as a diocese in its internal government, but the archbishop is chief bishop of an ecclesiastical province. The province consists of the archdiocese, or metropolitan see, and the dioceses, or suffragan sees, linked to it. The bishops of the province are to gather at least once every three years to propose a list of priests considered good candidates to be named bishops. The metropolitan court is ordinarily the first court of appeals for cases tried in diocesan courts within a province. See **ecclesiastical courts** and **see.**

In Eastern Catholic churches, the church jurisdictions are called eparchies (singular: eparchy) and archeparchies (singular: archeparchy) and the bishops who head them are eparchs or archeparchs. Except in stories specifically about the establishment of a new eparchy, use the more familiar Latin-rite terms: *Archbishop Stefan Soroka of the Ukrainian Archdiocese of Philadelphia.*

All diocesan bishops are required to visit Rome once every five years to report on the state of their dioceses. See **"ad limina."**

MEMBERSHIP: In 2005 the Vatican estimated there were 1.08 billion Catholics in the world, making up 17.3 percent of the world's population. In the United States, Catholics form the largest single body of Christians, with nearly 68 million members, about 23 percent of the U.S. population.

BELIEFS: The essential elements of Catholic belief are contained in the Bible and in the church's tradition, the body of prayer, practice and teaching developed over the centuries that Catholics believe is both guided by Scripture and its authentic interpreter.

Both the official teaching authority of the church, vested in the pope and the bishops, and the content of that teaching are referred to as the *magisterium.* See that entry.

The Mass is the central act of worship. Christ is believed to be present in the Eucharist, which is consecrated during Mass. The Mass and other official acts of public worship, including the celebration of the other sacraments, together form the church's liturgy. See **liturgy, devotions** and **Mass.**

Catholics celebrate seven sacraments: baptism, confirmation and Eucharist (the three sacraments of initiation), penance (also called the sacrament of reconciliation), matrimony, holy orders and the anointing of the sick. See **sacraments** and individual entries.

See **religious titles.**

Catholic Church Extension Society (www.catholic-extension.org) Although *Catholic Church Extension Society* remains the formal name for this U.S. Catholic home mission organization founded in 1905 to extend the work of the Catholic Church in rural or isolated areas of the United States, *Catholic Extension* is acceptable on any reference. Headquarters is in Chicago.

Catholic Coalition on Preaching (www.preachingcoalition.org)

Catholic Committee of Appalachia Headquarters is in Wittensville, Ky.

Catholic Common Ground Initiative (www.nplc.org/common ground.htm) Begun by Cardinal Joseph L. Bernardin of Chicago shortly before his death in 1996, this initiative is coordinated by the National Pastoral Life Center in New York.

Catholic Communication Campaign (www.usccb.org/ccc) The U.S. church's program to assist media-related efforts reflecting Christian values. Supported by an annual national collection, the campaign funds U.S. projects in broadcasting, the Catholic press, education and training, technology and public policy, and religious communications in developing nations. Half of the funds collected in the diocese during the campaign remain in the diocese for local projects. Headquarters, called the *Office for the Catholic Communication Campaign,* is in Washington.

Catholic Daughters of the Americas (www.catholicdaughters. org) Headquarters is in New York.

Catholic Engaged Encounter (www.engagedencounter.org)

Catholic Extension See Catholic Church Extension Society.

Catholic Familyland See Apostolate for Family Consecration.

Catholic Foreign Mission Society of America (Maryknoll) See **Maryknoll** and **order, congregation, society.**

Catholic Golden Age (www. catholicgoldenage.org) For Catholics 50 years old or older. Headquarters is in Olyphant, Pa.

Catholic Health Association (www.chausa.org) *CHA* is acceptable on second reference. Headquarters is in St. Louis, but the president and CEO is based in Washington.

Catholic International Federation for Sports and Physical Education (www.ficep.org) Headquarters is in Paris.

Catholic Knights of America (www.ckoa.com) Fraternal insurance society. Headquarters is in St. Louis.

Catholic Kolping Society of America (www.kolping.org) Devoted to the spread of Catholic social teaching.

Catholic League for Religious and Civil Rights (www.catholic league.org) *The league* is acceptable on second reference. Headquarters is in New York.

Catholic Legal Immigration Network (www.cliniclegal.org) Acceptable on all references for *Catholic Legal Immigration Network Inc.* A nonprofit legal-services corporation, also known as *CLINIC,* founded by the U.S. Catholic bishops in 1988 to serve as a national support and resource center for dioceses in providing immigration services to their indigent and low-income clients. *CLINIC* is acceptable on second reference, but it should be introduced by an explanatory phrase such as: *the network, also known as CLINIC.* It is based in Washington.

Catholic Library Association (www.cathla.org) Headquarters is in Pittsfield, Mass.

Catholic Marketing Network (www.catholicmarketing.com) Headquarters is in Irving, Texas.

Catholic Medical Association (www.cathmed.org) Formerly the National Federation of Catholic Physicians' Guilds. Headquarters is in Needham, Mass.

Catholic Medical Mission Board (www.cmmb.org) Founded in 1928, it sends medical supplies and medical and paramedical volunteers to poor missionary countries. Headquarters is in New York.

Catholic Medical Students Association (www.cathmsa.org) Headquarters is in Oak Park, Ill.

Catholic Movement for Intellectual and Cultural Affairs (www.pax-romana.org) U.S. affiliate of *Pax Romana.* See that entry.

Catholic Near East Welfare Association (www.cnewa.org) Founded in 1926 by Pope Pius XI, its mission is fourfold: to provide humanitarian support to the people of the Middle East, northeast Africa, India and Eastern Europe, regardless of creed; to support the endeavors of Eastern Catholic churches everywhere; to promote the union of Catholic and Orthodox churches; and to educate North Americans about the churches and people it serves.

In 1949, Pope Pius XII founded the Pontifical Mission for Palestine as an emergency relief agency, uniting all Catholic agencies working on behalf of Palestinian refugees, and placed the agency under the direction of the Catholic Near East Welfare Association, whose secretary-general serves as its president.

In the Middle East, the agency is known as the Pontifical Mission, but in the United States and Canada the work of the mission should be identified with Catholic Near East Welfare Association.

The association's magazine is called *One.*

Except in quoted material, do not use *CNEWA;* use *the association* or *the agency* instead.

The association's main office is in New York, but in 2005 it also had offices in: Addis Ababa, Ethiopia; Amman, Jordan; Asmara, Eritrea; Beirut, Lebanon; Ernakulam, India; Jerusalem; Ottawa; and Rome.

Catholic Network of Volunteer Service (www.cnvs.org) Formerly *International Liaison,* it coordinates the placement of Catholic lay missionaries worldwide and in the United States. Headquarters is in Takoma Park, Md.

Catholic News Service (www.catholicnews.com) The oldest and largest editorially independent Catholic news agency in the world, it was formed by the U.S. bishops in 1920 as the *National Catholic Welfare Conference News Service,* with the logo *NCWC.* It changed its name to *Na-*

tional Catholic News Service, with the logo *NC,* when the National Catholic Welfare Conference became the U.S. Catholic Conference in 1967. In 1989 it dropped *National* from its name to reflect more accurately its international character.

When mentioning *Catholic News Service* in the body of a story, use the full name on first reference. *CNS* is acceptable on second reference.

In datelines:

WASHINGTON (CNS) —.

Catholic Online (www.catholic. org) Headquarters is in Bakersfield, Calif.

Catholic Order of Foresters (www.catholicforester.com) Fraternal insurance society. Headquarters is in Naperville, Ill.

Catholic Press Association (www.catholicpress.org) *CPA* is acceptable on second reference. An association of U.S. and Canadian Catholic newspapers, magazines, newsletters and general publishers. The annual *Catholic Press Directory* is the primary source for the names of Catholic newspapers, magazines and newsletters named in it. Headquarters is in Ronkonkoma, N.Y.

Catholic Relief Services (www. catholicrelief.org) The overseas aid agency of U.S. Catholics and a member of Caritas Internationalis. See that entry. *CRS* is acceptable on second reference. Headquarters is in Baltimore.

Catholic Theological Society of America (www.jcu.edu/ctsa) Headquarters is at John Carroll University in Cleveland.

Catholic Truth Society (www. cts-online.org.uk) An organization founded in England in 1869 to disseminate information about the Catholic Church and defend it against attacks, the society has branches in several English-speaking countries.

Catholic University of America, The (www.cua.edu) Note that *The* is part of the title. *Catholic University* is acceptable on second reference. Founded in 1887 by the U.S. bishops as their national university, it is supported in part by an annual national collection. It can give ecclesiastical degrees in three fields — canon law, philosophy and theology — and is the only university in the United States with a school of canon law. It is located in Washington.

Catholic War Veterans (www. cwv.org) Headquarters is in Alexandria, Va.

Catholic Worker Movement (www.catholicworker.org) *Catholic Worker* is acceptable on all references. Founded by Dorothy Day and Peter Maurin in 1933, this loosely structured lay social-reform movement is devoted to nonviolence, simplicity of life and service to the poor. Catholic Worker communities in many U.S. cities run soup kitchens for the hungry and hospitality houses for the homeless. The movement publishes a newspaper in New York called *Catholic Worker* seven times a year.

Catholic Workman (www. catholicworkman.org) Fraternal and insurance society. Headquarters is in New Prague, Minn.

Catholic Youth Foundation USA (www.cyfusa.org) Formerly the National Foundation for Catholic Youth, it is affiliated with the National Federation for Catholic Youth Ministry in Washington.

Catholic Youth Organization

CYO is acceptable on second reference, but only in historical references or references to diocesan offices or parish groups that still use this as their proper name. The former National CYO Federation is now the National Federation for Catholic Youth Ministry and most U.S. dioceses and parishes have adopted different names for their youth groups.

Catholics Against Capital Punishment

(www.cacp.org) Headquarters is in Bethesda, Md.

Catholics for a Free Choice

(www.catholicsforchoice.org) This organization, based in Washington, supports expanded access to abortion and contraception for women in the United States and abroad and has led an effort to end the Vatican's status as a permanent observer at the United Nations. It was denounced in 1993 by the U.S. bishops' 50-member Administrative Committee, which said the group "merits no recognition or support as a Catholic organization" and is funded mostly by non-Catholic sources.

Catholics Speak Out

(www.quixote.org/cso) Formed in 1986 as a project of the Quixote Center in Hyattsville, Md., to oppose alleged injustices in the church.

Catholics United for the Faith

(www.cuf.org) A Catholic lay movement founded in 1968 to promote orthodoxy in Catholic teaching and practice. Headquarters is in Steubenville, Ohio.

CCD See **Confraternity of Christian Doctrine.**

C.C.E.O. See **canon law.**

C.E., B.C.E. The Jewish equivalents, respectively, of *A.D.* and *B.C.*

C.E. stands for the *common era* that Judaism and Christianity share. *B.C.E.* means *before the common era.* The terms were adopted by Jews to deal with the Gregorian calendar without accepting the Christian perspective of viewing Christ's birth as the central event of history.

Use with dates only in quoted matter or in stories dealing with Judaism or Jewish-Christian relations in which the term has significance. When used, it must be explained. The forms should be *287 C.E.* and *287 B.C.E.,* since the full phrase would read, *in the year 287 of* (or *before) the common era.*

See **Jewish calendar.**

CELAM Acceptable on second reference to the *Latin American bishops' council* (not *conference).* See that entry.

celebrant Use *celebrant* only for the priest or minister who leads a religious rite, especially the one who presides at the Eucharist: *Father Smith was the celebrant but Father Jones gave the homily.*

In Catholic usage, if two or more priests celebrate Mass together they are called *concelebrants,* not *co-celebrants.* The concelebrant who leads the group usually is called the *chief celebrant* or *principal celebrant.*

See **Mass** and **president, presiding.**

Use *celebrator,* not *celebrant,* for a participant in a nonreligious celebration: *Thirty New Year's Eve celebrators were arrested.*

celibacy, chastity *Celibacy* refers to a decision to live chastely in the unmarried state. At ordination, a diocesan priest or unmarried deacon in the Latin Church makes a *promise of celibacy,* not a *vow.*

Chastity in its general sense does not mean abstinence from sexual activity as such, but moral sexual conduct.

Marital chastity means faithfulness to one's spouse and moral conduct in marital relations.

The religious *vow of chastity,* taken by brothers, sisters and priests in religious orders, is a solemn promise to God to live the virtue of chastity by not marrying and by abstaining from sexual activity. See **order, congregation, society** and **vow, promise**.

cenobite A technical word for any member of a monastic community that has a communal form of life: the opposite of a *hermit.* In the Latin Church nearly all men and women in monastic religious orders are cenobites; few are hermits. See **hermit.**

Avoid the word if possible; explain it if it is used. Male cenobites can be called *men religious, monks, priests* (if ordained) or *brothers* (if not ordained). Female cenobites can be called *women religious, nuns* or *sisters.*

censer, censor, censure A *censer,* also called a *thurible,* is an ornamented container in which incense is burned, especially at religious rites. The one who carries it is a *censer-bearer* or *thurifer.*

For clarity's sake use *cense,* not *incense,* as the verb form for the ritual act of perfuming with incense: *He incensed the people* could be construed to mean *He got the people angry.*

A *censor* is an official empowered to prohibit or permit publication of a work or to order changes before publication. In Catholic ecclesiastical usage, a censor — often referred to by the full Latin phrase, *"censor li-brorum"* — is a theologian deputized by a bishop or religious superior to judge the fidelity to church teaching of a written work. See **imprimatur, "nihil obstat."** When used as a verb, *censor* means to prohibit publication, restrict use or require changes in content before publication.

A *censure* is a penalty; *to censure* is to express strong disapproval or to condemn. In Catholic ecclesiastical usage, *censures* constitute one class of penalties that can be imposed for violating certain church laws.

Center for Applied Research in the Apostolate (http://cara.georgetown.edu) *CARA* is acceptable on second reference for this independent Catholic research agency. It is located at Georgetown University in Washington.

Center for Media Literacy (www.medialit.org) Formerly called the Center for Media and Values. It is located in Santa Monica, Calif.

Center of Concern (www.coc.org) An independent Catholic think tank on international social issues founded in 1971 by the Jesuits. It is located in Washington.

Central Association of the Miraculous Medal (www.cammonline.org) Headquarters is in Philadelphia.

Central Conference of American Rabbis See **Judaism.**

chair of Peter A symbol of episcopal, and especially papal, teaching authority, it stems from the early Christian practice of bishops preaching while seated in their official chair facing the people. The expression *"ex cathedra,"* used to describe solemn papal definitions regarded as infallible by Catholics, means *"from the chair."* The actual "chair of St. Peter" behind the main altar in St. Peter's Basilica could not have belonged to St. Peter, as a pious tradition held. The oak, iron and ivory in the chair were from several centuries after St. Peter's death. Lowercase *chair* except in references to the *feast of the Chair of Peter,* the Feb. 22 liturgical feast that dates back to the fourth century.

chalice The goblet used at Mass to hold the consecrated wine. It may also be called a *cup.* For the vessel used to hold Communion wafers, see **ciborium.**

chamberlain of the Holy Roman Church *Chamberlain* is acceptable on second reference to the cardinal who is assigned to take charge of the goods and temporal affairs of the Holy See between the death of one pope and the election of the next. Until the Curia reform of 1967, he had those duties during a papal reign as well. The office the chamberlain heads is called the *Apostolic Camera.*

Chamberlain is preferable to *camerlengo,* an Italian term taken over into English. If *camerlengo* is used its meaning should be explained, but it should be lowercased and without quotation marks.

chancellor In Catholic ecclesiastical usage, the *chancellor* of a diocese is the chief archivist of its official records. He or she is also automatically a notary and secretary of the diocesan curia, or central administration, and may have a variety of other duties as well. Do not use as a title before the name in this sense.

chapter In Catholic ecclesiastical usage, an elected or appointed body of officials with authority or responsibilities assigned to it by law.

In each religious order a *general chapter* is the highest authority. It determines general legislation for the order and elects the order's general superior. Its membership is determined by the order's constitution, following norms established by canon law.

A *provincial chapter* of an order elects the superior of the province and legislates for the province.

Some dioceses have a *chapter of canons,* composed of diocesan priests appointed by the bishop, with responsibilities governed by local church laws. If the chapter is assigned to cathedral responsibilities it is called a *cathedral chapter.* Cathedral chapters exist in many European dioceses but are not common in the United States.

charism, charisma Use *charism* to refer to a gift that Christians believe is given by God to an individual for the benefit of the Christian community. While *charism* often is used to refer to extraordinary manifestations such as speaking in tongues or healing, in Catholic teaching it also refers to other gifts of ministry and service. *The Second Vatican Council said that through their ordination bishops receive the charisms of teaching, sanctifying and ruling.*

Use *charisma* to refer to a personal quality in some individuals which draws the attention, admiration or allegiance of others. *A candidate needs more than intelligence, experience and hard work. She needs charisma.*

charismatic renewal See **charismatics.**

charismatics Also called *neo-Pentecostals* in some non-Catholic circles, charismatics emphasize the living presence of the Holy Spirit in the church. The charismatic movement grew rapidly in the 1960s and '70s as a spiritual-revival movement within Catholic and mainline Protestant churches.

Unlike the Pentecostals of the early 20th century, who formed new denominations, charismatics have generally remained within their original denominations. See **Pentecostal churches.**

Charismatic groups may be formed along denominational or ecumenical lines. They are generally characterized by a close sense of community and mutual spiritual support and by openness to spontaneity and emotional expressiveness in worship and community prayer. They are open to the manifestation of special gifts of the Spirit, or *charisms,* such as the speaking in tongues and spiritual healing cited by St. Paul in his First Letter to the Corinthians, but the presence of such extraordinary gifts is not considered an essential part of a charismatic community.

Within the Catholic Church, overall support and coordination of the charismatic movement is provided by such organizations as the Rome-based *International Catholic Charismatic Renewal Services,* which has a papally appointed episcopal moderator, and the U.S.-based *National Service Committee of the Catholic Charismatic Renewal.* See those entries. Bishops' conferences have appointed national episcopal moderators in a number of countries, and many dioceses have diocesan moderators who oversee the activities of local groups.

"Charter for the Protection of Children and Young People" The document adopted by the U.S. bishops at their Dallas meeting in June 2002 and revised and extended five years in 2005. Among other things, it required all U.S. dioceses and Eastern-rite eparchies to put in place policies and procedures regarding allegations of sexual abuse of children by clergy or church personnel, mandated external audits and reports to assess compliance, and established a bishops' Office of Child and Youth Protection and a National Review Board to assist implementation. *The charter* is acceptable on second reference. To implement the charter legislatively, the bishops adopted *"Essential Norms."* See that entry and **National Review Board**.

chastity See **celibacy, chastity.**

chasuble The outer vestment of a priest celebrating Mass. Liturgical norms guide the color to be used for the various liturgical seasons, feast days and other observances. The similar vestment sometimes worn by deacons is a *dalmatic.*

See that entry and **liturgical dress.**

Chicano, Chicanos Although not always derogatory, *Chicano* should be avoided as a routine description for U.S. citizens or residents of Mexican descent. *Mexican-Americans* is preferred. *Hispanic, Spanish-speaking* or similar terms should be used when referring to a group that may include people of Caribbean or Central or South American descent as well as those of Mexican descent. See **Hispanic** and **Latino, Latinos.**

Chicano has been adopted by some social activists of Mexican descent and may be used when activists use it to describe themselves. When applied to a woman or exclusively female group, the feminine forms are used: *Chicana, Chicanas.*

Chief Administrators of Catholic Education (www.ncea.org/

departments/cace) Headquarters is at the National Catholic Educational Association in Washington.

Chinese Catholic Patriotic Association Formed by the Chinese government in 1957, eight years after the communist takeover of China, it does not accept ties to the Vatican. Although it has ordained many bishops "elected" without papal approval, the Chinese church has kept alive the line of apostolic succession with ordinations by validly ordained bishops, and Hong Kong church leaders have said at least two-third of the government-approved bishops have reconciled secretly with the Vatican.

An underground church in China, estimated to number in the millions, professes loyalty to the pope, and at the parish level there is some mingling of the two churches.

Use the full name of the association on first reference, but *patriotic association* is acceptable on second reference.

Chinese names See **Asian names.**

chorbishop In the Maronite, Chaldean and Syrian Catholic churches, some priests who are close assistants to the bishop may be ordained as chorbishops. They have the power to confer minor orders, including subdiaconate, but not diaconate or priesthood. Thus, a chorbishop is neither simply a priest nor a bishop. A Maronite bishop's protosyncellus, or vicar general, receives the title of chorbishop by virtue of his office even if he has not been ordained a chorbishop. Taken from the Greek *chora,* which means *country,* the term referred in early centuries of Christianity to a priest or bishop who was given charge over a rural area of a diocese. See **protosyncellus.**

Use *Chorbishop* before the name on all references: *Chorbishop John D. Faris, Chorbishop Faris.*

See **religious titles.**

chorepiscopus, "chorepiskopos" The Latin and Greek forms, respectively, for *chorbishop.* No quotation marks around the Latin, since it has been taken over into English, but it is not a widely known term. Use *chorbishop.* See that entry.

chrismation See **confirmation.**

chrism Mass The annual Mass concelebrated by a bishop and the priests of his diocese at which the bishop blesses oils for sacramental use throughout the diocese for the coming year. It is to be celebrated Holy Thursday morning or, if that presents a pastoral difficulty, on an earlier day near Easter. It is distinct from the *Mass of the Lord's Supper* celebrated in parishes on Holy Thursday.

See **holy oils** and **Mass.**

Christ Catholic Church (www.cccint.org) Founded in 1968 and based in Niagara Falls, Ontario, this group is not affiliated with the Roman Catholic Church.

Christ Child

Christian Appalachian Project (www.christianity.com/cap) Founded in 1964 by Father Ralph Beiting as an interdenominational organization to help the Appalachian people help themselves. Headquarters is in Lancaster, Ky.

Christian Brothers Investment Service (www.cbisonline.com) It is located in New York.

Christian Church (Disciples of Christ) (www.disciples.org) The parenthetical phrase is part of the formal name of this denomination. Born on the American frontier in the early 1800s as a movement to unify Christians, in 2005 it had nearly 800,000 members in the United States and Canada. Its national offices are in Indianapolis.

It was formed by the merger in 1832 of two parallel but separate unity movements: Alexander Campbell's Disciples and Barton W. Stone's Christians.

The full name should be used on first reference, but *the Disciples* is acceptable on second reference. The local congregation, however, usually is called a *Christian Church* or a *Church of Christ.*

Do not confuse member churches of the *Christian Church (Disciples of Christ)* with the churches of the *Churches of Christ* or those of the *Christian Churches and Churches of Christ.* See **Churches of Christ.**

The local congregation of Disciples elects its elders and deacons, owns its own property and has full control over its budget and program. It conducts an ordination ceremony for new permanent officers.

BELIEFS: Intentionally noncreedal, the church considers the New Testament, as interpreted by each individual, the sole norm of faith and discipleship. It administers baptism by immersion to those who have made an adult profession of faith in Christ, but most congregations accept as transfers those who have been baptized by other forms in other denominations. The Lord's Supper, also called Communion, is celebrated weekly and is the center of the Disciples' prayer and worship life. Christians of all denominations are admitted to Communion.

The church accepts baptism and the Lord's Supper as sacraments. See **dominical sacraments.**

Although congregations are basically autonomous, they are united in voluntary regional and general associations. A General Assembly, which meets every two years and has voting representation directly from each congregation, oversees national programs and policies.

Thoroughly ecumenical in orientation, the Disciples were among the founders of the National Council of Churches and the World Council of Churches, and they are members of *Churches Uniting in Christ.* See that entry.

CLERGY: Preaching elders, who form the clergy, are *ministers.* A minister who leads a congregation is a *pastor.* See **religious titles.**

RELATIONS WITH CATHOLICS: The Disciples of Christ maintain an official dialogue with the Catholic Church. It began in 1967 as a U.S. dialogue and later expanded to an international dialogue.

Christian Churches Together in the USA (www.christianchurchesto gether.org) This national ecumenical forum delayed its originally planned 2005 launching to give more churches time to become founding members. It is the first national ecumenical organization of Christian churches in the United States to include as a full member the Catholic Church. The U.S. Conference of Catholic Bishops voted to become a member in November 2004.

The organization is intended as a forum of participation through which Christian churches can pray and witness together, and grow in mutual understanding. Business is to be conducted chiefly through its annual General Assembly and, between assemblies, through a steering committee composed of three representatives from each of the five major church families. These are the Catholic, Orthodox, historical Protestant, historical racial and ethnic, and evangelical and Pentecostal

The organizational plan of Christian Churches Together says that it welcomes as members "churches, Christian communities and national Christian organizations that: believe in the Lord Jesus Christ as God and savior according to the Scriptures; worship and serve the one God, Father, Son and Holy Spirit; and seek ways to work together in order to present a more credible Christian witness in and to the world."

The organization can take positions or issue statements as a body only if all its members agree; a single no vote can block a statement, but members also have an option to "stand aside," neither supporting a statement nor blocking it.

The size of a church's delegation to the General Assembly is determined by the number of members the church has: Each church may send one representative for each 5 million members or fraction thereof. In addition, up to 20 percent of the assembly may be composed of representatives of national Christian organizations. The USCCB has sole authority to determine which national Catholic organizations can be admitted.

The shortened version of the name, *Christian Churches Together,* is acceptable on second reference but do not use the abbreviation *CCT.*

Christian Family Movement
(www.cfm.org) National office is in Evansville, Ind.

Christian Foundation for Children and Aging (www.cfcausa.org)
Promotes sponsorship of children and the elderly at Catholic missions around the world. Headquarters is in Kansas City, Kan.

Christianity The largest of the world's religious faiths, with an estimated 2 billion adherents in 2005. Catholics form the largest segment, with an estimated membership of nearly 1.1 billion.

Of other major Christian faith groups, the Orthodox are estimated to number about 219 million, Anglicans about 80 million and Protestant traditions collectively about 376 million. Various other groups within the Christian tradition, such as the Oriental Orthodox and Old Catholic churches, or those derived from Christian belief, have an estimated 225 million adherents. The quality of membership estimates varies because denominations use different methods of counting membership and because no current census figures are available in some denominations.

Most Christians consider essential elements of Christian faith to include belief in the three divine persons in God, discipleship in Christ, belief that he is the Son of God and savior of the world, and belief in the Bible as divinely revealed and a primary guide for judging the authenticity of Christian truths.

Many believe that Christ's death is the ultimate fulfillment of God's covenant with Abraham and the other Old Testament patriarchs that was solidified in the Mosaic covenant. The Catechism of the Catholic Church calls Christ's death "the sacrifice of the New Covenant, which restores man to communion with God."

Some denominations that reject what other Christians consider essential or that rely on claimed revelations subsequent to the Bible often are classified as Christian in general groupings of world religions because they profess varying degrees of belief in Christ and the Bible and derive historically from the Christian faith tradition. Among these are Unitarians and Jehovah's Witnesses, who reject Trinitarian belief, and the Latter-day Saints, Seventh-day Adventists and members of the Unification Church, who claim beliefs based on post-biblical divine revelations. Many Christians, however, consider such groups new religions outside the Christian tradition.

See individual entries for the main Christian denominations and non-Christian religions.

Christian Life Communities (www.clc-usa.org) Formerly known as *Sodalities of Our Lady.* National office is in St. Louis. World headquarters is in Rome.

Christian Science Church See **Church of Christ, Scientist.**

Christ-like

Christmas, Christmas Day The feast of the Nativity of Christ, a holy day of obligation celebrated Dec. 25. As a U.S. federal holiday, it is observed on Friday when it falls on Saturday, on Monday when it falls on Sunday.

The Armenian Catholic Church and Armenian Orthodox Church celebrate Epiphany, Jan. 6, as the chief observance of Christ's manifestation on earth. This is sometimes called the *Armenian Christmas.*

Currently there is a 13-day difference between the Gregorian and Julian calendars. When the Orthodox churches that continue to use the Julian calendar celebrate Christmas, it is Jan. 7 on the Gregorian calendar.

During the 20th century most Orthodox churches started observing immovable feasts such as Christmas according to the Gregorian calendar. The Orthodox churches of Jerusalem, Russia and Serbia and the Greek Orthodox monasteries of Mount Athos retained use of the Julian calendar.

Never use the abbreviation *Xmas.*

Christmas Eve Dec. 24.

Christmas season In general usage, *Christmas season* has come to refer primarily to Christmas itself and the period of shopping, caroling and other preparations leading up to it. In Catholic liturgical usage, the season begins with Christmas and ends with the feast of the Baptism of the Lord, the Sunday after Epiphany.

See **liturgical year.**

Christology (n.), **Christological** (adj.)

Christophers (www.christo phers.org) Do not use *The* before the name. Also called the *Christopher Movement.* Founded in 1945, it has no formal organization or meetings for general membership. Through radio and television programs and the publication *Christopher News Notes,* it tries to stimulate individual initiative to promote Christian values in society.

The organization sponsors the *Christopher Awards,* annual awards for artistic excellence affirming human values in the fields of books for adults, books for children, films and television specials. Headquarters is in New York.

church Do not capitalize unless it is used as part of the formal name of a building, a congregation or a denomination. *Holy Redeemer Church, the United Methodist Church.*

Lowercase in plural uses when two formal names are combined: *Trinity Lutheran and Holy Redeemer churches, the Catholic and Methodist churches, Orthodox churches.*

Lowercase *church* when it is used in an institutional or general theological sense: *Father Smith said the church will not ordain women. The church is the people of God.*

In references to local Catholic entities, generally use *church* for the building, *parish* for the organization and its people: *The roof of St. Odilia Church was destroyed by a tornado. Members of St. Odilia Parish raised the money for a new roof in two days.* It is also correct, however, to use *church* as a synonym for *parish* in such contexts: *the members of St. Odilia Church.*

Use a possessive form (for example: *St. Mary's Church)* in a full name only if it is officially in the formal name. For names of Catholic churches in the United States, consult the Kenedy directory.

See **parish** and **saint.**

Churches of Christ (http://church-of-christ.org) Formed in 1906 in a split from the *Christian Church (Disciples of Christ),* this loose cooperative fellowship has more than 15,000 independent congregations with a total U.S. membership of more than 2 million. Closely allied in spirit and origins is a fellowship called *Christian Churches and Churches of Christ,* with more than 5,500 independent congregations whose combined membership is more than 1 million.

Churches of Christ congregations broke away from the Disciples primarily over the Disciples' missionary societies, which the Churches of Christ regarded as denominational activity. They also opposed use of instrumental music in worship and use of the title *Reverend* as unscriptural.

The fellowship of *Christian Churches and Churches of Christ* consists chiefly of congregations which broke with the Disciples later over what they regarded as denominationalism, especially around 1968 when the Disciples reorganized their national structures.

Strictly congregationalist in structure, each local church in either fellowship is autonomous. The churches consider themselves strictly nondenominational and regard all denominational forms of church government as an infringement on the authority belonging to Christ alone.

They teach that baptism is necessary for salvation and practice adult baptism by immersion. They celebrate the Lord's Supper only as a memorial of Christ's passion and death, usually using unleavened bread and grape juice for Communion.

Because of their anti-denominational thrust, they are not active in interdenominational dialogues.

Since the church opposes use of the title *Reverend*, do not use religious titles for Churches of Christ clergy.

See **Christian Church (Disciples of Christ).**

Churches Uniting in Christ (www.cuicinfo.org) Formed in 2002 as a covenantal relationship of nine U.S. Christian churches, Churches Uniting in Christ is an outgrowth of and successor to the *Consultation on Church Union.* See that entry.

Each member church retains its own identity and decision-making structures, but has pledged to draw closer in sacred things, including regular sharing of the Lord's Supper and common mission, especially a mission to combat racism together. Each church also committed itself to undertake an intensive theological dialogue aimed at providing a foundation for the mutual recognition and reconciliation of ordained ministry among all member churches by 2007.

According to figures in the 2005 Yearbook of American and Canadian Churches, combined inclusive membership of the member churches is about 18 million. They are the African Methodist Episcopal Church, African Methodist Episcopal Zion Church, Christian Church (Disciples of Christ), Christian Methodist Episcopal Church, Episcopal Church, International Council of Community Churches, Presbyterian Church (U.S.A.), United Church of Christ and United Methodist Church.

In 2005, the Evangelical Lutheran Church in America was a participant as a "partner in mission and dialogue" and other communions were exploring various possibilities of relating to the consultation.

Do not use the acronym *CUIC* (pronounced *quick*) except in quoted material.

churchgoer

Church in Wales Note the *in*. An autonomous church of the Anglican Communion.

See **Anglican Communion.**

Church of Christ, Scientist (www.tfccs.com) The terms *Christian Science* and *Church of Christ, Scientist* are acceptable as references to this denomination formed by Mary Baker Eddy in 1879. Her study of the Bible and experiences of spiritual healing led Eddy to form the church "to reinstate primitive Christianity and its lost element of healing."

BELIEFS: Christian Science is based on the spiritual interpretation of God's word in the Bible explained in Eddy's 1875 textbook, *Science and Health With Key to the Scriptures*. It describes fundamental reality as spiritual and God as "the divine Principle of all that really exists." According to Christian Science, this spiritual creation is wholly good and God does not create death, disease or sin. These are not real, therefore, but result from the failure of the human mind to understand and obey God. Prayer-based physical cure and moral reformation, reached through an understanding of God and the individual's unbroken relationship with him, stand as proof of this spiritual view of creation.

The original church in Boston is the mother church and international headquarters of Christian Science. Each branch church is governed by its own democratically chosen board. The first branch church established in a community is known as First Church of Christ, Scientist. If another is formed in the same community, it is called Second Church of Christ, Scientist. In 2005, the church had about 2,000 branch churches and a presence in 139 countries. Church policy forbids publication of membership figures.

The church has no clergy. Each congregation elects *readers* to lead Sunday worship, which is built around lesson-sermons consisting of citations from the Bible and the Christian Science textbook. Christian Science *practitioners* carry on healing work and spiritual guidance as a full-time vocation. *Lecturers* are appointed by the international directors to give public lectures on Christian Science. All these offices are open to men and women. None are used as formal titles before a name. See **religious titles.**

Each church maintains a Christian Science Reading Room as a bookstore and community center open to the public for spiritual inquiry.

Christian Scientists are involved in ecumenical and interfaith activities in their communities but Christian Science is not involved in formal dialogue with the Catholic Church.

Church of Christ Uniting Name used briefly for the union of churches that is now *Churches Uniting in Christ.* See that entry.

Church of England (www.cofe. anglican.org) See **Anglican Communion.**

Church of Ireland (www.ireland. anglican.org) See **Anglican Communion.**

Church of Jesus Christ of Latter-day Saints (www.lds.org) Note the hyphen and lowercase *d.* Include the full proper name in any story describing the institution or its activities. A media style guide distributed by the church describes use of the terms *Mormon Church* or *Mormons* as "incorrect and confusing," and says the preferred terms on second reference are *the church* or *the Latter-day Saints.* However it may not always be possible in news stories to avoid use of the terms *Mormon Church* or *Mormons.*

It is not a Protestant church: Its teachings are drawn from the writings of founder Joseph Smith Jr., who claimed he received them from the angel Moroni in the 1820s in upstate New York. His followers split into factions after his death in 1844. The Mormons, the largest group, went West under the leadership of Brigham Young and founded Salt Lake City, which remains their headquarters. See **Protestant.**

Latter-day Saints form a majority of the population of Utah and have a membership of about 12 million worldwide, including more than 5.5 million in the United States.

Smith's three books of revelations — *The Book of Mormon, The Doctrine and Covenants* and *The Pearl of Great Price* — plus the Bible (King James Version) form the Mormon scriptures. Mormons also accept ongoing revelation through the president of the church.

Smith's earlier writings were more Christian in tenor, but his later writing introduced beliefs in spiritual pre-existence before birth, a finite and developing God, an understanding of the Trinity as tritheism, belief that good men may become gods, polygamy and a view of the United States as holding a special providential position in the world, with its Constitution divinely inspired. Polygamy was renounced as effective church teaching in 1890, although a small, excommunicated splinter sect continues to advocate and practice it.

Nearly every male over the age of 11 holds some rank of lay priesthood, starting with deacon and moving up through teacher, priest, elder, member of the First Quorum of Seventy or high priest. Only those 18 or older may hold the ranks of elder and above. Lowercase these ranks in all uses. Do not use them as formal titles before a name. See **religious titles.**

Women may not be priests or general authorities.

Latter-day Saints are not active in ecumenism.

NOTE: Only the Church of Jesus Christ of Latter-day Saints uses a hyphen and lowercase *d* in its formal name. Among the splinter groups formed after Smith's death, the largest is the Community of Christ, formerly known as the Reorganized Church of Jesus Christ of Latter Day Saints, with about 250,000 members worldwide. Its headquarters is in Independence, Mo. See **Community of Christ.**

Church of Scotland See **Presbyterian churches.**

church services Capitalize the formal names of church services or liturgical celebrations: *Mass, Benediction, Stations* (or *Way) of the Cross, Liturgy of the Hours,* etc. Lowercase descriptive substitutes or added modifiers: *solemn Benediction, funeral Mass, daily prayer of priests.*

Lowercase the names of the sacraments, except Eucharist. See **rite of ... and sacraments.**

For the Latin-rite Mass and its parts, or comparable services in other rites and denominations, see **Mass.**

In other services or liturgical rites, lowercase descriptive names of actions that form part of the rite. For example: *anointing of the forehead, pouring of the water, baptismal rite, exchange of vows, nuptial blessing, confession, absolution, blessing of the casket,* and, within the Liturgy of the Hours, *morning prayer, readings, daytime prayer, evening prayer* and *night prayer.*

Note: Terminology for church services varies among denominations and among different rites within the Catholic Church, and in recent years many denominations have changed terms. Check with denominational officials for current official usage.

See **liturgical books; liturgy, devotions; Liturgy of the Hours;** and **prayers.**

ciborium The plural is *ciboria.* A cup with a cover, used to distribute Communion or to store remaining wafers in the tabernacle. The ciborium may be stemmed or unstemmed. If a very shallow, unstemmed vessel is used, it may be preferable to call it a *Communion plate.*

The cup that holds the wine is called a *chalice.* See that entry.

CIDSE See **International Cooperation for Development and Solidarity.**

cincture The cord which serves as a belt over the priest's alb.
See **liturgical dress.**

Citizens for Educational Freedom (www.educational-freedom. org) A nonsectarian group promoting public aid to those in private schools through tuition tax credits and vouchers. Headquarters is in St. Louis.

clergy Ordinarily used as a collective term for a group of *priests, ministers* or *rabbis: a clergy conference, the clergy of the diocese, the city's clergy.* Do not use *clergymen* to refer to a group that can or does include women.

In some technical uses in the Catholic Church, *clergy* comprises all those ordained: bishops, priests and deacons. If the term is used in this sense, the story should make it clear that the term refers to others as well as priests. Use caution in referring to a *clergy shortage* when you mean a *shortage of priests,* or to *priests* distributing Communion when the group also includes *deacons.* See **hierarchy.**

clerical titles See **religious titles.**

CLINIC See **Catholic Legal Immigration Network.**

cloning Although *cloning* is most frequently used to describe the reproduction of the genetic twin of another organism, scientists use three terms to describe different processes for duplicating biological material. *Recombinant DNA technology* or *DNA cloning* refers to the transfer of a DNA fragment to create artificial DNA, a common practice in molecular biology labs. *Reproductive cloning* is a technology used to generate an organism that has the same nuclear DNA as another currently or previously existing organism. *Therapeutic cloning*, or *embryonic cloning*, is the production of human embryos to harvest stem cells, or cells that can replicate and differentiate into specialized cells, for use in research.

CNS See **Catholic News Service.**

coadjutor A *coadjutor bishop* sometimes receives special faculties with his appointment. He automatically becomes head of the diocese upon the death or retirement of its bishop.

Unlike auxiliary bishops, coadjutors receive the title *archbishop* if they are assigned to an archdiocese.

On first reference, the proper title takes the form: *Coadjutor Archbishop Joseph Serge Miot of Port-au-Prince, Haiti; Coadjutor Bishop Salvatore R. Matano of Burlington, Vt.* On second reference: *Archbishop Miot, the archbishop; Bishop Matano, the bishop.* Second references to the coadjutor or the coadjutor (arch)bishop should be avoided unless the person's role as coadjutor is immediately relevant to that part of the story.

See **archbishop-designate, bishop-designate** for guidelines on appointment stories.

Code of Canon Law, Code of Canons of the Eastern Churches See **canon law.**

college of bishops A collective term for the world's Catholic bishops.

See **Catholic Church** and **collegiality.**

College of Cardinals See **Catholic Church.**

college of consultors A diocesan body of six to 12 priests chosen by the bishop from among the members of the diocesan council of priests. Canon law requires the bishop to consult with his college of consultors before making certain decisions. When a diocese becomes vacant, the college of consultors is to elect a diocesan administrator within eight days unless the Holy See provides otherwise.

collegiality In Catholic usage, collegiality in the strict sense refers to the shared responsibility and authority that the college of bishops headed by the pope has for the teaching, sanctification and governance of the church.

By analogy the term has been applied also to shared authority or a consultative or collaborative style among smaller groups of bishops and on other levels of church governance: *The U.S. bishops worked collegially on their peace pastoral. Bishops are often asked to show collegiality with their priests in establishing diocesan policies. The parish council praised the pastor for his collegial style.*

Theologians and church authorities sometimes refer to collegiality in its strict sense as *effective collegiality,* and in the analogous sense as *affective collegiality.* In most cases the technical terms should be avoided in favor of paraphrases such as: *full collegiality, collegiality in the strict sense* for *effective collegiality;* or: *a collegial style, a collegial approach, a style of collegiality* for *affective collegiality.*

Colosseum The ancient stadium in Rome. The generic word is *coliseum.*

COMECE See **Commission of the Bishops' Conferences of the European Community.**

Coming Home Network (www. chnetwork.org) An organization founded in 1993 by a group of former Protestant clergy and their spouses who joined the Catholic Church. Offers newsletters, retreats and other resources to help others who want to become Catholic. Headquarters is in Zanesville, Ohio.

Commission of the Bishops' Conferences of the European Community (www.comece.org) The commission, with headquarters in Brussels, Belgium, is made up of representatives of Catholic bishops' conferences of the European Union. Include the phrase *known by the acronym COMECE,* but avoid multiple uses of the acronym; instead, use phrases such as *the commission.*

Commission on Religion in Appalachia (www.geocities.com/appal cora) Formed in 1965 by 17 denominations, the commission in 2005 included two dozen partner denominations and community groups. It works to empower the people of Appalachia to demand their rights to an education, economic opportunities, adequate health care and safety, and equal opportunity in work. Headquarters is in Charleston, W.Va.

committee While committees of Congress may be capitalized in both full form and shorter, flip-flopped form (for example: *Senate Committee on Budget, Budget Committee),* the committees of religious bodies and other organizations do not enjoy the same national familiarity.

Apart from Congress, capitalize only the full, formal name of any committee. Lowercase shortened or flip-flopped versions of the formal name. In the U.S. Conference of Catholic Bishops, for example: *the Committee*

on Canonical Affairs, the canonical affairs committee; the Committee on Women in Society and in the Church, the committee on women.

For committees of the U.S. bishops, see **Appendix F: U.S. Conference of Catholic Bishops.**

Communion and Liberation (www.clonline.org) A lay ecclesial movement founded in Italy in 1954, it is aimed at educating its members in Christian maturity and collaborating in the church's mission in contemporary life. It took its present name in 1969, and it was present in some 70 countries in 2005. Female members of *Memores Domini,* an organization of men and women from Communion and Liberation who have made promises of poverty, chastity and obedience, cared for Pope Benedict XVI's apartment, as of 2005. International headquarters is in Milan, Italy.

Communion, communion Capitalize all references to the sacrament, but not adjectives modifying it or nouns it modifies: *first Communion, holy Communion, a Communion service, the Communion cup.* See **Eucharist, eucharistic** and **sacraments.**

Capitalize as part of the proper name, *the Anglican Communion.* The Anglican churches are the only ones who use *communion* as a proper term in this way.

Capitalize *Holy Communion* as the proper name of the eucharistic worship service of the Lutheran churches and some other Protestant churches that use this term for the whole service at which Communion is given. *"A Catholic may participate in a Lutheran Holy Communion service but may not receive Communion during it,"* the bishop said.

Anglicans used to refer to their main worship service as *Holy Com-*

munion. The usage still occurs, although many Anglicans now call the service *the Eucharist.*

Lowercase *communion* for all uses outside the church service, the sacrament or proper names: *the communion of Anglican churches, the communion of saints, the Catholic principle of communion with Rome, churches in communion with one another, the communion of spouses in marriage.*

The theological idea of the church as *communion* — as a fellowship or community grounded in and expressive of the divine communal life of the Trinity — started to receive particular emphasis in the 1990s in intra-Catholic and ecumenical discussions as an important and fruitful way of understanding the nature of the church and of advancing the unity of the churches. In reporting on these discussions, use the English term *communion* whenever possible instead of the Latin *"communio"* or the Greek *"koinonia"* often employed by some participants. When *"communio"* or *"koinonia"* is used, it should be placed in quotation marks and its meaning explained.

See **Anglican Communion; church services;** and **intercommunion.**

communion of saints Lowercase. The Christian belief affirmed in the Apostles' Creed does not refer only to the saints in heaven. From ancient times it has referred to the entire body of Christ, his followers living and dead. This is expressed in fuller form in Pope Paul VI's "Credo of the People of God," quoted in the Catechism of the Catholic Church: "We believe in the communion of all the faithful of Christ, those who are pilgrims on earth, the dead who are being purified and the blessed in heaven, all together forming one church."

From this stems a belief in the *intercession of the saints in heaven* on behalf of those still on earth, held by Catholics, Orthodox and some other Christians, but not by all.

Community of Christ (www.cofchrist.org) Formerly known as the Reorganized Church of Jesus Christ of Latter Day Saints, it is the largest of several groups that split from the Church of Jesus Christ of Latter-day Saints in conflicts over succession after the death of founder Joseph Smith Jr. This denomination was formed in 1860 by Smith's son Joseph Smith III. It claims to be the authentic continuation of the original church and shares basic Mormon beliefs, but it has also developed its own distinctive beliefs and practices. In 1984 it voted to accept women priests. Do not use *Mormon* to describe this church or its members. It has a U.S. membership of about 250,000, with headquarters in Independence, Mo.

See **Church of Jesus Christ of Latter-day Saints.**

Community of Sant'Egidio (www.santegidio.org) *Sant'Egidio Community* also is acceptable on first reference. This Catholic group runs soup kitchens and other social-service programs in Rome and has been involved in mediating political disputes in Africa and Eastern Europe. *Sant'Egidio* or *Sant'Egidio Community* is acceptable on second reference. There is no space between *Sant'* and *Egidio.*

Compendium of the Catechism of the Catholic Church

Compendium of the Social Doctrine of the Church

composition titles See Appendix A: Special Style Considerations.

concelebrant Not *co-celebrant.* See **celebrant.**

conclave In Catholic ecclesiastical usage a *conclave* is a closed meeting of the College of Cardinals, ordinarily held at the Vatican, to elect a new pope. Lowercase. Do not confuse it with a *consistory.*

See that entry and **Catholic Church.**

concordance An alphabetical index of words in the Bible cross-referenced to their location. Because these are reference works, do not place titles in quotation marks: *The NIV Complete Concordance is a concordance to the New International Version Bible.*

concordat A public treaty between the Holy See and a secular state, its purpose is to conserve and promote the interests of religion and especially to safeguard the spiritual rights of Catholics in a country.

Capitalize in specific references: *the Concordat of Worms, the Concordat of Fontainebleau.* But lowercase *the Vatican-Italy concordat, the concordat with Spain.*

Conference for Pastoral Planning and Council Development (www.cppcd.org) Formed in the early 1990s from the merger of the National Pastoral Planning Conference and the Parish and Diocesan Council Network.

Conference of International Catholic Organizations (www.oic-ico.org) An umbrella group, with 35 member organizations, founded in 1927 to foster collaboration and agreement among international Catholic organizations and to promote international understanding. Headquarters is in Fribourg, Switzerland.

Conference of Major Superiors of Men (www.cmsm.org) Acceptable in all references for the *Conference of Major Religious Superiors of Men's Institutes of the United States Inc.,* a membership organization of the heads of male religious orders or provinces in the United States. *CMSM* is acceptable on second reference. Headquarters is in Silver Spring, Md.

confess In general usage the word ordinarily implies guilt or fault and must be used with care. In religious usage it may have two distinct meanings: admission of faults or profession of belief. See **confession.**

confession Lowercase. Confession is only part of the sacrament of penance or reconciliation, not another term for the sacrament. Phrases such as *going to confession,* however, imply reception of the sacrament. See **absolution; penance;** and **sacraments.**

The *confessor* is the priest who hears the confession. The one who confesses is a *penitent.*

Confession of faith is a term commonly used by Lutherans and others to express what Catholics usually call a *profession of faith.* Lutheran churches and some others are called *confessional churches* because they view as their primary identifying characteristic their adherence to a particular *confession* or statement of beliefs. Lowercase except in the proper name of a particular statement of belief: *the Augsburg Confession.*

confirmation One of the three sacraments of initiation, along with baptism and Eucharist, in the belief of Catholics, Orthodox and some other churches. Rejection of confirmation as a sacrament by Martin Luther was an element of the Protestant Reformation.

Most Protestant churches do not consider confirmation a sacrament, but some have a nonsacramental ceremony called confirmation, often marking the end of childhood religious education and entry into adult membership in the church. Anglicans, who generally receive confirmation in their teens, refer to the rite as a *sacramental rite*. See **Anglican Communion.**

Recently some Protestant churches have begun to introduce a confirmationlike chrism ceremony into baptismal rites, but they do not consider it a separate sacrament or call it confirmation.

Confirmation usually is administered to infants along with baptism in the Orthodox churches and some Eastern Catholic churches. Many churches of the East call confirmation *anointing* or *chrismation.*

Among Latin-rite Catholics in many countries and most areas of the United States, confirmation usually is administered during the teen years to those baptized in infancy. Thinking and practice regarding the time of reception are in flux.

For belief and practice in individual denominations, consult authorities of the denomination in question.

See **Rite of Christian Initiation of Adults** and **sacraments.**

Confraternity of Catholic Clergy (www.catholic-clergy.org) Based in Chicago.

Confraternity of Christian Doctrine The abbreviation *CCD* as a popular synonym in the United States for Catholic parish-based *religious education* is acceptable on all references in quoted matter, but explain within the text of the story what it means. Although *CCD* is still widely recognized as a synonym for religious education of children from kindergarten through high school, when used in this sense it is generally an anachronism. At the diocesan level, most former *CCD* offices are now called offices of *religious education* or of *Christian formation.* A few still use *CCD* as part of their name, usually in the form: *department of religious education-CCD.* At the national level, the religious education component of the confraternity has been taken over by the U.S. Conference of Catholic Bishops' Department of Education.

The *Confraternity of Christian Doctrine* continues to exist as a separately incorporated entity directed by the USCCB Administrative Committee, which is the confraternity's board of trustees. It licenses religious and spiritual literature, especially the Lectionary for Mass and the New American Bible. Use the full name on first reference to this national body. Use *the confraternity,* not the acronym, on second reference. It is located in Washington.

See **catechetics.**

congregation Those gathered for a religious service are called a *congregation. Worshipers, participants, the assembly, the gathering* or *those present* are among acceptable alternatives.

A *congregation* is not an *audience,* a term which suggests that the people are merely spectators, not participants in the event.

Congregation also is a term used for some Vatican departments: *the Congregation for Catholic Education.* Capitalize only proper names. See **Appendix G: Vatican Agencies.**

For *religious congregations,* see **order, congregation, society.**

congregational Lowercase when referring generically to the form of church polity or governance in which authority is democratic, vested in the congregation. The other two chief forms of church polity are *episcopal,* in which bishops hold authority, and *presbyterian,* in which designated elders hold authority.

Churches that call themselves *Congregational* (capitalized) form only one branch among churches that have a congregational form of government. See **Congregational churches.**

Congregational churches The term *Congregational* still is used by some churches as part of a formal name. Their members are called *Congregationalists.* The Puritans who settled in Massachusetts in 1620 were among the first Congregationalists, and in the 19th century Congregationalism flourished across the country despite substantial losses in the early part of that century to the Unitarian movement. See **Unitarian Universalist Association.**

The Congregational Christian Churches was the main national group that called itself Congregational in the 20th century. It dropped the term in 1961, four years after it merged with the Evangelical and Reformed Church to form the *United Church of Christ.* See that entry.

In 1955 a small group of churches that resisted the then-developing merger formed the National Association of Congregational Christian Churches. Churches in the association have more than 65,000 members. The association conducts business through an annual meeting and through its national headquarters in Oak Creek, Wis. It is not incorporated and has no legal authority over member congregations.

Congregationalists hold that Christ is their savior and the only head of the church and that the Bible is a sufficient rule of faith and practice. They consider Christian character, rather than adherence to a particular creed or set of doctrines, as the chief measure of church membership.

Each local church is autonomous in worship, ministry and teaching, but regional associations of Congregational churches promote cooperation and oversee licensing and ordination of ministers.

The clergy are *ministers.* A minister who heads a congregation is a *pastor.* See **religious titles.**

consecrate, consecration The priest *consecrates* the bread and wine at Mass. Catholics believe that at the *consecration* these elements become Christ's body and blood.

Those who take religious vows of poverty, chastity and obedience live a *consecrated life.* In the Catholic Church the *consecrated life* is lived not only by members of religious institutes but also by members of secular institutes. See **institute.**

Consecrate used to be the preferred term for a number of other liturgical actions for which different terminology is more commonly employed today. In these cases do not use *consecrate* or its variants except in quoted matter:

— New bishops are *ordained,* not *consecrated.* The bishop formerly called the *consecrator* is called the *ordaining bishop.* Former *co-consecrators* usually are described now by phrases such as *other ordaining bishops.* See **ordain, ordination.**

— New churches and altars are *dedicated* or *blessed,* depending upon the ceremony used, but not *consecrated.* The ceremony is a rite of *dedication* or *blessing.*

— Sacred vessels such as the chalice and paten are *blessed.*

Within the ordination ceremony for a deacon, priest or bishop, however, there is a *prayer of consecration.* When a religious professes vows, there is a prayer at the conclusion of the rite that is called an *act of solemn blessing or consecration.*

conservative In popular references to a religious denomination or individuals or groups within a religious body or family, this term often is used to signal contempt for sincerely held religious convictions. In general, do not apply it to an individual or group except in quoted matter or when someone uses it as a self-description.

Capitalize only when it is part of a formal name adopted by a group, for example, *Conservative Jews.* See **Judaism.**

Conservative can have many different meanings, among them: one who insists on strict adherence to historical doctrinal formulations of his religion, one who insists on a strict moral code, one who objects to proposed changes in the structure or discipline of his religious body, or one who links personal religious beliefs to a conservative political philosophy. In place of using the *conservative* label, it is usually preferable to say what specific views or practices an individual or group supports or opposes.

See **liberal.**

Conservative Judaism See **Judaism.**

consistory A formal meeting of the College of Cardinals convened and presided over by the pope. Lowercase in all uses.

The 1983 Code of Canon Law says an *ordinary consistory* is called to conduct "serious" but frequently occurring business of the church "or to carry out certain very solemn acts." For such a meeting the pope may convene all cardinals or only those who are then in Rome. Usually only those living in or visiting Rome are asked to attend a consistory to approve causes for beatification and canonization. Cardinals from around the world are usually convened when an ordinary consistory is called to create new cardinals.

Only an ordinary consistory involving solemn ceremonies can be *public,* or open to those who are not cardinals.

An *extraordinary consistory* of all cardinals is called for "special needs of the church or the conducting of more serious affairs." Only cardinals are allowed to attend.

A meeting of cardinals to elect a pope is not a consistory but a *conclave.* See that entry.

Consortium Perfectae Caritatis An organization of U.S. Catholic sisters founded in 1971 to promote religious renewal with a stress on faithfulness to church norms, it was disbanded as part of the 1992 agreement under which the Vatican formed *the Council of Major Superiors of Women Religious.* See that entry.

consul, consulate See **council, counsel.**

Consultation on Church Union A U.S. Christian unity movement, 1962-2002. At the consultation's 1999 plenary assembly, delegates from the nine member churches unanimously adopted a foundational agreement for a new relationship of covenanted communion. Following confirmation of that decision by each of the churches, they formalized the change in 2002 by dissolving the consultation and entering into their new relationship as *Churches Uniting in Christ.* See that entry.

The consultation developed rapidly in the '60s, consolidated in the '70s, and in 1984 developed a theological basis for partnership and eventual full communion called *The COCU Consensus.* A December 1988 document, *Churches in Covenant Communion,* expanded on the consensus statement and proposed a plan for the nine member churches to enter into covenant communion during the next decade, each church retaining its own distinctive governance, structures and traditions. At the 1999 plenary, delegates found the only remaining obstacle to full mutual recognition of ministries was an inability to reconcile the corporate oversight by ruling elders of the Presbyterian Church (U.S.A.) with the insistence in the Episcopal Church of oversight by individual bishops ordained in unbroken historic apostolic succession. The 1999 plenary also approved *A Call to Christian Commitment and Action to Combat Racism,* calling racism "the most church-dividing issue in the United States."

The preferred form for second reference is *the consultation.* Avoid *COCU* except in quoted matter or proper names that employ the acronym, such as *The COCU Consensus.*

contraceptive sterilization When a person undergoes a sterilization procedure to avoid having children rather than to correct an adverse medical condition, it is called *voluntary* or *contraceptive sterilization.* The Catholic Church considers contraceptive sterilization immoral.

See **birth control.**

convert (n., v.) This entry concerns only the use of *convert* and *conversion* to describe a change in religious adherence. When used in this sense, except in quoted matter, *convert* and *conversion* should be used only when a change of fundamental religious belief or affiliation is involved, not for a movement from one branch or denomination of Christianity, Buddhism, Islam, Judaism, etc., to another within the same basic faith group. Thus: *He was a Buddhist before he converted to Catholicism at the age of 25.* But: *Raised a Lutheran, she became Catholic in 1995.*

corporal A linen cloth spread on the altar at the beginning of Mass by the priest, on which the eucharistic elements rest.

corporal, spiritual works of mercy The corporal works of mercy are: feeding the hungry, giving drink to the thirsty, clothing the naked, visiting the imprisoned, sheltering the homeless, visiting the sick and burying the dead.

The spiritual works of mercy are: counseling the doubtful, instructing the ignorant, admonishing sinners, comforting the afflicted, forgiving offenses, bearing wrongs patiently and praying for the living and the dead.

CORPUS See **National Association for an Inclusive Priesthood**.

Corpus Christi Latin for *the body of Christ.* The Catholic feast formerly known by that name is now called the *feast of the Body and Blood of Christ.* Continue to use *Corpus Christi,* however, for traditional devotions, especially processions, connected with the observance: *a Corpus Christi procession,* NOT: *a Body and Blood of Christ procession.*

See **holidays, holy days.**

Cor Unum Acceptable on second reference for Pontifical Council Cor Unum, Latin for "one heart." It was founded by Pope Paul VI in 1971 to allow each pope to distribute funds for disaster relief and development projects. The money comes from contributions to the pontiff by dioceses, religious institutes, parishes, Catholic schools and individuals worldwide. Cor Unum also oversees the work of two charitable agencies founded by Pope John Paul II — the John Paul II Foundation for the Sahel region of northern Africa, for projects working against drought and desertification, and the "Populorum Progressio" Foundation to aid indigenous peoples and peasant farmers in Latin America and the Caribbean.

council (n.), **counsel** (n. and v.) Do not confuse with *consul.*

In Catholic ecclesiastical usage, *council* usually refers to a body which has only consultative or advisory power: *diocesan pastoral council, parish council, priests' council.* Those on such councils are ordinarily called *members* rather than *councilors.* See **pastoral council** and **priests' council.**

Councils of religious orders are also consultative, but their members are usually called *councilors.*

Reserve *councilman, councilwoman* for members of a civil legislative body such as a city council.

Councils of bishops — *ecumenical councils,* national *plenary councils, provincial councils* and *councils of hierarchs* — have deliberative power, subject to approval by the Holy See.

For such ecclesiastical councils, see specific stylebook entries or consult the Code of Canon Law, Code of Canons of the Eastern Churches or other references.

Used as a verb, *counsel* means *advise* or *recommend.* The noun *counsel* means *advice* or *recommendation.* Apply it to a person or group of persons only when referring to *lawyers giving legal advice or representing a client in court.* Many organizations, for example, use *general counsel* as the term both for their office of legal advice and for the head of that office.

Use *counselor* for other individuals who give advice. In ecclesiastical usage, a *pastoral counselor* is a person trained to give pastoral assistance to people facing various difficulties.

In diplomatic language, a *counselor* — NOT *councillor, councilor, counsellor* or *consul* — is a legal adviser at an embassy. *Counselor* is the proper translation of *consigliere* as used by the Vatican to describe certain embassy staff posts.

In diplomatic language a *consul* is the head of a *consulate,* the office or residence in a foreign city which handles the commercial affairs and personal needs of citizens of the appointing country. It is not an *embassy.* The Vatican does not have any consuls or consulates.

Council for American Private Education (www.capenet.org) Headquarters is in Germantown, Md.

Council of European Bishops' Conferences (www.ccee.ch) Formed in 1995 for bishops from Eastern and Western Europe. Do not use the acronym CCEE. Headquarters is in Sankt Gallen, Switzerland. Do not confuse with the *Commission of the Bishops' Conferences of the European Community.* See that entry.

council of hierarchs In Eastern Catholic churches, a legislative body of a metropolitan church "sui iuris." Lowercase except when used as part of a formal name. The council, composed of all ordained bishops of the archdiocese and dioceses that form the metropolitan church, is headed by the metropolitan archbishop. In the United States, only the Ruthenian or American Byzantine Catholic Church, headed by the Byzantine Archeparchy of Pittsburgh, is a metropolitan church "sui iuris."

See **Eastern Catholic churches** and **"sui iuris."**

Council of Major Superiors of Women Religious (www.cmswr. org) Acceptable in all references for the *Council of Major Superiors of Women Religious in the United States of America.* Formed in 1992 at the request of some superiors of women religious, the council is the second canonically recognized organization of its type in the United States. The other is the *Leadership Conference of Women Religious.* See that entry.

CMSWR is acceptable on second reference, but *the council* is preferred. Headquarters is in Washington.

Counter-Reformation The 16th-century Catholic response to the *Reformation.* See that entry.

Couple to Couple League (www.ccli.org) A group founded in 1971 to teach and promote natural family planning. Headquarters is in Cincinnati.

Courage (http://couragerc.net) A group founded in 1990 by Father John Harvey, an Oblate of St. Francis de Sales, to support homosexual Catholics who want to live in accordance with church teaching. A related movement for parents and other family members and friends of people with same-sex attractions is called *Encourage.* See **homosexuality.** Headquar-

ters for both Courage and Encourage are in New York.

court-case names Capitalize, but do not use quotation marks around, the names of court cases and rulings: *Roe v. Wade, Bob Jones University v. United States.*

On second reference, it is acceptable to use only part of the case name unless confusion would result: *In Roe the Supreme Court said .... In the Bob Jones University case ....* Usually the first name cited in a case is the name used alone on second reference, but not always. For example, *Felton v. Aguilar* often is called *Aguilar* on second reference.

The first part of a civil-case name is the name of the plaintiff or principal plaintiff; the last part is the name of the defendant or principal defendant. In a criminal case, the first part is the name of the government jurisdiction conducting the prosecution. In an appeal, the first part of the case name refers to the appellant, or the one who brings the appeal, and the second to the appellee, or respondent. If a person is a party, only his or her last name need be used; if an organization is a party, its full name is given.

If there are two or more plaintiffs or defendants, the courts may refer to the others as *et al.* In news writing the Latin abbreviation should be replaced with its English equivalent, *and others.* The *and others* may be dropped on second reference and often may be dropped on first reference, depending on the context in which it appears.

courtesy titles Do not use the courtesy titles *Mr., Mrs., Miss* or *Ms.* on first or subsequent references except in direct quotations. For the courtesy titles of those in ministry or religious life, see **religious titles.**

Use *Dr.* as a courtesy title only on

first reference to medical doctors.

In stories in which a husband and wife or two other people with the same last name are mentioned, use either the first names only or the first and last names on second reference, depending on what fits the story best.

In stories involving children up to about 15 years of age, use the first name on second reference.

Covenant, Old and New See **Christianity** and **Judaism.**

creationism See **evolution.**

Creed, creed Capitalize when used as part of the proper name of specific formulations of Christian faith but lowercase when standing alone or in other uses: *Apostles' Creed, Nicene Creed,* but*: They said the creed. Self-interest is his only creed.*

Credal and *creedal* are both acceptable forms of the adjective.

See **Apostles' Creed; "filioque"; Nicene Creed;** and **Orthodox churches.**

cremation In the teaching and practice of the Catholic Church, interment of the body in a cemetery or mausoleum is the preferred practice to symbolize most fully Christian respect for the body. In response to materialist and anti-Catholic elements in 19th-century European cremation movements, the church forbade Catholics to direct that their bodies be cremated. That ban was partially lifted in 1963, and the Catechism of the Catholic Church says, "The church permits cremation, provided that it does not demonstrate a denial of faith in the resurrection of the body."

The laws and liturgical norms of the Eastern Catholic churches make no mention of cremation. The general liturgical law of the Latin Church makes provision for committal of cremated remains but not for their presence at a funeral Mass. In some countries, however, including the United States and Canada, Latin-rite bishops have sought and received permission from Rome to permit funeral Masses with cremated remains present. In those countries it is up to each diocesan bishop to determine whether that practice will be permitted in his diocese.

In stories about funeral, burial and cremation practices, use of the term *cremains* as a shortened form of reference to *cremated remains* is acceptable, but its meaning should be explained on first reference. In an obituary, however, some readers may regard that 20th-century coinage as a flippant or irreverent form of reference to the remains of the person who died. In obituaries, use *ashes, remains* or the full form, *cremated remains.* See **obituaries.**

crosier Preferred to *crozier* as the spelling for the staff that is one of a bishop's symbols of office. It may also be called a *pastoral staff.* When capitalized, *Crosier* is the name of a religious order.

See **liturgical dress.**

cross, crucifix Lowercase. An object is a *crucifix* only if it depicts Christ on a cross. If it does not have the figure of Christ, it is a *cross.* A crucifix also may be called a cross, but a plain cross may not be called a crucifix.

If a proper name is used to describe a style or kind of cross, capitalize only the proper name: *Maltese cross, Greek cross, Latin cross.* Do not capitalize other style names: *patriarchal cross, jeweled cross.*

If *cross* is part of the proper name of an award or badge, it is capitalized: *Distinguished Service Cross.*

Crossroads (www.crossroad swalk.org) Founded in 1994 as a response to Pope John Paul II's call for young people to take an active role in the pro-life movement, Crossroads sponsors an annual pro-life walk across the United States. Its national office is in Columbia, Md.

crown The cap, modeled after the Byzantine imperial crown and worn as liturgical dress by most Orthodox and Catholic bishops of the Byzantine-rite churches and certain high-ranking priests of those churches. It may also be called a *miter*, but it is more commonly called a *crown* or *episcopal crown*.

See **kamelaukion; liturgical dress;** and **miter.**

Crusades, Crusaders Capitalize references to the medieval Christian wars for control of the Holy Land and soldiers who fought them. Lowercase all other uses unless they form part of the proper name of an organization or movement: *her crusade against taxes* but *Campus Crusade for Christ.*

cult In its neutral or generic use, *cult* denotes any *act or system of veneration or worship.* In current popular usage, however, it nearly always carries a derogatory connotation of *aberrational religious practice* or *excessive devotion to an individual religious leader and his or her beliefs.* In this derogatory sense it is often used to refer to new religious movements or sects that use manipulative techniques to attract followers or to make them psychologically dependent on the sect and its leaders.

Description of a new religious movement or sect as a *cult* implies a negative editorial judgment. Do not use the term without attribution to a source.

See **religious movements** and **sect.**

curate See **religious titles.**

Curia When capitalized, this is a shortened form, acceptable in all references, for the *Roman Curia,* the church's central administrative offices. The term must be explained when used. See **Catholic Church.**

Capitalize *curia* when used as part of the formal name of a diocesan central office, but lowercase in other uses: *The Los Angeles archdiocesan Office of the Moderator of the Curia; Msgr. Royale M. Vadakin, archdiocesan moderator of the curia.*

Lowercase *curial* (adj.) in all uses: *a top curial official.*

Cursillo movement (www.natl -cursillo.org) The movement, which began in Spain in 1949 as a Christian renewal effort, has become popular in the United States. It seeks to promote individual and organized apostolic action. Cursillo means "little course." Individuals are initiated into the movement through a three-day weekend focused on prayer, study and Christian action. Participants are called *Cursillistas.* The National Cursillo Center is located in Dallas.

"custos" of the Holy Land The Franciscan minister provincial in the Middle East, appointed by the Vatican to coordinate the reception of pilgrims to the Christian sites of the Holy Land and sustain the Christian presence there. The office he heads is the *Franciscan Custody of the Holy Land.* Use *"custos,"* not *custodian* in news stories, but define the term if used.

Unlike other ministers provincial of the Franciscan order, the "custos" is not elected but named by the Holy See. Although not a bishop, he is a member of the Assembly of Catholic Ordinaries of the Holy Land, the local bishops' conference.

Cycle A, Cycle B, Cycle C See liturgical year.

CYO See **Catholic Youth Organization.**

D

dais, podium, rostrum All refer to a raised platform or stage used for public speaking. Speakers stand *on* them, not *in* or *behind* them.

The terms are not used to refer to the place in a Catholic church from which one reads the Scriptures or preaches a homily.

See **lectern, ambo; pulpit;** and **roster, rostrum.**

dalai lama *Lamaism* is the name given to Tibetan Buddhism, which is a mixture of Mahayana Buddhism, Hinduism and the indigenous Bon religion. Monks of Lamaism are called *lamas.* Since the 16th century the chief monk has been given the title *dalai lama,* and from the early 17th century until 1959 he was temporal as well as spiritual ruler of Tibet. Lowercase in plural or general references, but capitalize when referring to a particular dalai lama, since the title is used as his name. See **Buddha, Buddhism** and **Hindu, Hinduism.**

The 14th Dalai Lama, Tenzin Gyatso, was born in 1935 and became Dalai Lama in 1940. He fled to India in 1959 following an unsuccessful Tibetan uprising against Chinese communist rule. He has lived in exile since.

dalmatic The outer vestment sometimes worn by a deacon at Mass, similar to the *chasuble* worn by the priest.

See that entry and **liturgical dress.**

Dames of Malta See **Knights of Malta.**

Damien-Dutton Society for Leprosy Aid (www.damienleprosy society.org) Headquarters is in Bellmore, N.Y.

datelines The CNS list of cities that stand alone in datelines may vary from those chosen by our main secondary style and reference source, The Associated Press. The current CNS lists follow:

U.S. CITIES

No state with the following:

ATLANTA	MILWAUKEE
BALTIMORE	MINNEAPOLIS
BOSTON	NEW ORLEANS
CHICAGO	NEW YORK
CINCINNATI	OKLAHOMA CITY
CLEVELAND	PHILADELPHIA
DALLAS	PHOENIX
DENVER	PITTSBURGH
DETROIT	ST. LOUIS
HONOLULU	SALT LAKE CITY
HOUSTON	SAN ANTONIO
INDIANAPOLIS	SAN DIEGO
LAS VEGAS	SAN FRANCISCO
LOS ANGELES	SEATTLE
MIAMI	WASHINGTON

FOREIGN CITIES

No country with the following:

BEIJING	MONTREAL
BERLIN	MOSCOW
DJIBOUTI	NEW DELHI
GENEVA	OTTAWA
GIBRALTAR	PANAMA CITY
GUATEMALA CITY	PARIS
HAVANA	QUEBEC CITY
HONG KONG	ROME
JERUSALEM	SAN MARINO
KUWAIT CITY	SAN SALVADOR
LONDON	SINGAPORE
LUXEMBOURG	TOKYO
MACAU	TORONTO
MEXICO CITY	VATICAN CITY
MONACO	

Note these special cases:

— Because of their particular linkage with Catholic institutions, the following datelines are acceptable: *BOYS TOWN, Neb.*; *BROOKLYN, N.Y.*; *MARYKNOLL, N.Y.*; and *NOTRE DAME, Ind.*

— Because of its wide recognition and unique international status, *UNITED NATIONS* stands alone in datelines.

— The town in which the pope's summer residence is located is two words. The form in datelines: *CASTEL GANDOLFO, Italy.*

For the correct dateline for the Catholic University of Louvain in Belgium, see **Louvain, Catholic University of.**

dateline selection Use datelines on every story. A story without a byline may carry whatever dateline is appropriate, usually the site of the news event. A story with a byline must carry a dateline corresponding with the writer's location, either at the time of writing or at the time of gathering information for the story. A correspondent writing from the capital or a major city of a foreign country may use the capital or the major city as a dateline on an event that occurred elsewhere. It is appropriate in such circumstances to use a byline.

Daughters of Isabella (www.daughtersofisabella.org) Founded in 1897, originally as a ladies' auxiliary of a local council of the Knights of Columbus, but no longer formally linked with the men's group. Headquarters is in New Haven, Conn.

deacon, diaconate Note the *i* in *diaconate*. In the Catholic Church, diaconate is the first of three ranks in ordained ministry. From about the fifth century until the Second Vatican Council it was used in the Latin Church almost exclusively to describe the final stage in preparation for ordination to the priesthood. The council decreed that the diaconate also could be restored as a permanent and separate rank in the Latin Church and that married men may be ordained to this rank. Pope Paul VI restored the permanent diaconate in 1967.

Deacons studying for the priesthood are *transitional deacons.* Those not planning to be ordained priests are called *permanent deacons.* Since not all permanent deacons are married, *married deacons* is not a synonym for *permanent deacons.*

It is not necessary to identify a deacon by his marital, permanent or transitional status unless it is relevant to the story and not already clear from the context. When status is relevant, often identification by other concrete information — such as naming the wife of a married deacon or stating a transitional deacon's place of seminary studies or a permanent deacon's place or length of service — will indicate his status to the reader without using terms such as *transitional* or *permanent.* For example, for a transitional deacon: *Deacon John Jones, a fourth-year theology student at St. Mary's Seminary; Deacon Jones, who is to be ordained a priest next May.* Or, for a permanent deacon: *Deacon Sam Smith, who has assisted at St. Rita Parish for 15 years; Deacon Smith, a chaplain at Mercy Hospital since 1998.*

Capitalize when used as a formal title before a name: *Deacon John Jones, Deacon Jones.* Lowercase in other uses.

See **religious titles.**

Dead Sea Scrolls

dean In Catholic ecclesiastical usage *dean* is not used as a formal title before a name. When parishes of Catholic dioceses are organized geographically into *deaneries,* the priest responsible for each deanery is the *dean,* but treat this as a job description: *Father John Smith, dean of Deanery 11; Father Smith.* See **deanery.**

At the Vatican, the chief judge of the Roman Rota, called the *decano* in Italian, in English is called the *dean: Msgr. Antoni Stankiewicz, dean of the Roman Rota; Msgr. Stankiewicz.*

In Anglican ecclesiastical usage a priest who is rector of a cathedral is called a *dean.* Do not use this as a formal title before the name: *the Rev. John Smith, dean of Grace Cathedral; Rev. Smith.*

See **religious titles.**

deanery One form of division of a diocese into smaller groupings of parishes. Usually deaneries are formally named simply by a number or by a geographic designation. Capitalize *deanery* only when it is used as part of a formal name: *Deanery 7, Grand County Deanery, Southeast Deanery.* Lowercase in all other uses.

See **dean.**

decision-maker, decision-making

defrock (v.), **defrocked** (adj.) Restrict use of these terms to cases in which a priest faces removal or has been removed from clerical office against his will — by a criminal trial or imposed administrative act — since defrocking has a negative connotation of deprivation of office. A neutral term that refers equally to involuntary and voluntary return of a cleric to the lay state is *laicization.* See that entry.

Do not use unfrock, which can also mean simply to undress. See **suspended priests.**

deist See **atheist, theist.**

denomination Religious usage to denote an individual Christian church body, especially when approached from the underlying view that all such bodies are part of the one indivisible church of Christ despite their diverse doctrinal, organizational and liturgical forms (*denominational* differences). This religious use of the term is of 18th-century English and American Protestant origin, and it is not widely used today outside North America.

Denomination and its other forms (for example: *denominational, interdenominational, nondenominational*) may be used loosely in plural references that include Catholic or Orthodox churches along with Protestant churches. But the Catholic and Orthodox churches should not be called *denominations* except when grouped with Protestant bodies.

The terms should never be used in references that include Jewish or other non-Christian bodies.

See **ecumenical, interreligious; interdenominational, interfaith;** and **nondenominational.**

-designate See **archbishop-designate, bishop-designate.**

deuterocanonical Term used to describe seven Old Testament books considered part of the canon of Scriptures by the Catholic Church but considered apocryphal by Protestant churches. The seven are *Tobit, Judith, Wisdom, Sirach, Baruch* and *1 and 2 Maccabees.*

See **apocrypha, apocryphal** and **Bible.**

devil Lowercase *devil* but capitalize proper names applied to the devil such as *Satan* and *Lucifer.* See **Satan.**

devotions See **liturgy, devotions.**

diaspora Capitalize only in reference to the dispersion of the Jews outside their homeland. Historically, this dates from the Babylonian exile in the sixth century B.C., but it continues in use today in reference to Jews living outside Israel: *The United States has the largest community of Jews in Diaspora.* Lowercase all other references to the dispersion of a group with common beliefs or background: *the African diaspora, the Ukrainian community in diaspora.*

dicastery A major Vatican department. Despite its use by the Holy See, this meaning of the word is not given in standard English dictionaries. Avoid the term when possible and explain it when it must be used, as in direct quotes or in references to one of the Vatican's *interdicasterial commissions.* Each dicastery has its own proper name that does not use the term *dicastery.* For example: *Secretariat of State, Congregation for Bishops, Pontifical Council for the Laity.*
See **interdicasterial.**

Dignity (www.dignityusa.org) An unofficial support organization for gay, lesbian, bisexual and transgender Catholics. Headquarters is in Washington.
See **homosexuality.**

Diocesan Fiscal Management Conference (www.dfmconf.org) Headquarters is in Waterville, Ohio.

diocese The standard term in the Catholic, Orthodox and Anglican churches for an ordinary territorial division of the church headed by a bishop. The chief diocese of a group of dioceses usually is called an *archdiocese.* See that entry, **archbishop** and **bishop.**

In Catholic usage worldwide, a diocese ordinarily takes its name from the *see city,* the community where the bishop resides and his cathedral is located. See **see.** In Europe and the Middle East this is generally true of Anglican and Orthodox dioceses as well. In the United States most Anglican and Orthodox dioceses are named according to the geographic region they encompass: *the Episcopal Diocese of West Missouri.*

Some Orthodox and Eastern Catholic churches may call a diocese an *eparchy.* Use *diocese* unless the technical character of the story requires use of *eparchy.* See **eparch, eparchy.**

Capitalize only as part of a proper name: *the Diocese of New Ulm, Minn., the New Ulm Diocese, the diocese.* For a diocese that includes a state in its formal name, drop the phrase naming the state and use the state abbreviation instead: *the Diocese of Springfield, Ill.,* not *the Diocese of Springfield in Illinois.* If a state or country name must be inserted within a formal name, place it in parentheses: *the New Ulm (Minn.) Diocese.* It is preferable to avoid such constructions when possible.

See **Catholic Church; Eastern Catholic churches; Episcopal Church;** and **Orthodox churches.**

disciple See **apostle, disciple.**

Disciples of Christ See **Christian Church (Disciples of Christ).**

dispensation In Catholic ecclesiastical usage, an exemption from a church law. One is dispensed *from* a law or obligation, or dispensed *to* do something ordinarily not permitted. *He needed a dispensation to be married in a non-Catholic church. Be-*

cause of her health she was dispensed from fasting.

dispensationalism A form of Christian biblical fundamentalism that views history as a succession of divinely ordained periods culminating in the second coming.

Divine Liturgy The proper name used by many Eastern Catholics for the eucharistic liturgy.
See **Mass.**

Divine Mercy Sunday Pope John Paul II inaugurated this annual feast honoring devotion to Christ's tender mercy for all humanity on the Second Sunday of Easter in 2000, when he canonized St. Faustina Kowalska, the Polish nun and visionary of Jesus as the divine mercy.

divorce If a person is divorced, it should be mentioned in a story only if it is directly relevant. The same rules of relevancy should be applied to women as to men.
Do not use *divorcee* for a *divorced woman.*
Even if a person's divorce or divorced status is relevant, it does not belong in the lead unless it is a central element of the story. Place the information in the body of the story.
In the Catholic Church civil divorce does not entail exclusion from the sacraments. A person is excluded from the sacraments if he or she remarries outside the church while still bound by a valid previous marriage. See **annul.**

Diwali A Hindu feast commemorating the victory of light over darkness.

doctor For one who has a medical doctorate, use *Dr.* as a formal title before the full name on first reference only: *Dr. C. Everett Koop, Koop; Dr. Joyce Brothers, Brothers.*
Except in quoted matter, do not use *Dr.* as a formal title before the name of those with doctorates in fields other than medicine. If the person's academic credentials are relevant to the story, describe them as part of the story narrative: *John Smith, a philosophy professor; Smith, who has doctorates in philosophy and European history.*
For clergy and religious who have academic doctorates the religious title takes precedence. Do not use *Dr.* as part of or in place of the formal religious title before such names, even if the person is widely known that way, except in quoted matter.
WRONG: *the Rev. Dr. Joan Brown Campbell, Dr. Campbell; the Rev. Dr. Martin Luther King Jr., Dr. King.*
RIGHT: *the Rev. Joan Brown Campbell, Rev. Campbell; the Rev. Martin Luther King Jr., Rev. King.*
WRONG: *Dr. George Carey, archbishop of Canterbury; Dr. Carey.*
RIGHT: *Archbishop George Carey of Canterbury, Archbishop Carey.*
See **religious titles** and **reverend.**

doctor of the church Lowercase singular and collective references to this select group of saints whose writings have had a particularly notable influence on Catholic theology or spirituality. Do not use as a formal title before a name. *In 1997 St. Therese of Lisieux was proclaimed a doctor of the church. She was the 33rd person and the third woman to be listed among the doctors of the church.* Do not confuse with *Fathers of the Church.* See that entry.

documents Capitalize, without quotation marks, universally used names of historic and public documents such as *treaties, laws, decrees, charters, constitutions* and *court decisions.* For example: *Magna Carta, U.S. Constitution, Treaty of Versailles, Declaration of Independence, Bill of Rights, Augsburg Confession, Gettysburg Address, Civil Rights Act of 1964.*

Lowercase standard descriptive names of documents that are common to many organizations, even if a particular organization capitalizes such names in its internal communications: *the union's constitution and bylaws; the parish's mission statement; the association's charter.*

Lowercase descriptive names that are not used as proper titles. For example: *the U.S. bishops' pastoral letter on the economy, the Vatican norms for general absolution, the organization's statement on racism.*

Use quotation marks and capitals for proper names of documents that serve as unique titles: *the bishops' economic pastoral,* "Economic Justice for All: Catholic Social Teaching and the U.S. Economy."

For the documents of the Second Vatican Council, see **Appendix I: Vatican II Documents.**

For papal documents, use capitals and quotation marks for official titles in Latin or another non-English language; use capitals and quotation marks for a standard title in English, either as it appears in an English version issued by the Holy See or as established by common practice in the United States. Capitalize and enclose in quotation marks only the title itself, not terms such as *encyclical, apostolic constitution* or *apostolic exhortation* that describe the nature of the document. See **encyclical.**

dominical sacraments Baptism and the Lord's Supper (the Eucharist). So named because of the clear scriptural evidence that they were mandated by *the Lord ("Dominus"* in Latin), these are generally the only two recognized as sacraments by Protestant denominations.

Dormition of Mary, feast of the The name usually used in the Eastern Catholic and Orthodox churches for the Aug. 15 feast celebrated in the Latin Church as the *feast of the Assumption,* commemorating the bodily assumption of Mary into heaven.

Druzism A sect founded in Egypt in 1017 in a break from Ismaili Islam. Most *Druze* live in scattered communities in Israel, Syria and Lebanon. There are also immigrant Druze communities in the United States, Canada, Europe and Latin America. They have their own scriptures, written in the 11th century. Unlike Muslims, they do not practice fasting, pilgrimage to holy places or praying in mosques. They believe in human reincarnation and regard the 11th-century Fatimid Caliph al-Hakim as an incarnation of God. Druzism is a closed religion that does not seek converts or try to propagate its teachings outside its own community.

due process This general term for the protection of rights in judicial proceedings has been adopted in Catholic ecclesiastical usage to refer as well to a set of procedures or guidelines, adopted by a diocese, eparchy or other Catholic institution, to resolve disputes equitably without recourse to church or civil courts. Due process guidelines vary, but they generally include forms of conciliation, mediation or arbitration.

earth In most uses *earth* is a common noun. It is capitalized as a proper noun only when it is used as the proper name of our planet in conjunction with the proper name of another astronomical body — not including the sun and moon, which also are used ordinarily as common nouns.

Note that theological statements such as *when Christ was on earth, during our life on earth* or *the church on earth* are not meant to distinguish the planet Earth from Mars or the moon. They mean the world of time, space and history, as distinct from eternity, heaven or life after death.

Not capitalized: *Where on earth were you? The space shuttle returned to earth after two weeks in orbit. The earth rotates around the sun. Christ came to earth to redeem the world.*

Capitalized: *Venus and Earth are nearly the same size. Every 75 years Halley's comet approaches Earth.*

Easter The chief feast in the liturgical calendars of all Christian churches, it commemorates Christ's resurrection from the dead. The feast always falls on Sunday: *Easter Sunday* is redundant.

The date of Easter is calculated by lunar cycles — it is the first Sunday after the first full moon of spring — because Christ's death and resurrection were linked to the Passover, a feast calculated according to the Jewish lunar calendar.

In the Catholic Church and Protestant churches Easter falls between March 22 and April 25 inclusive. All of the Orthodox churches — including those which have adopted the Gregorian calendar for other purposes — continued to use the older Julian calendar to calculate the date for Easter, which the Orthodox ordinarily call *Pascha.* As a result, their Easter or Pascha sometimes coincides with that of the West, but it is often one, four or five weeks later.

At a 1997 meeting in Aleppo, Syria, an ecumenical group of scholars issued a proposal, called the Aleppo Statement, under which all churches would use the same method of calculation and celebrate Easter/Pascha on a common date. Members of the North American Orthodox-Catholic Theological Consultation endorsed the Aleppo Statement at a meeting in Washington in 1998. As of 2005, however, it had not been adopted and remained only a recommendation.

Use *Pascha* as an alternative name for Easter only when it is relevant, as in contexts discussing differences in Western and Orthodox observance, and explain the term when it is used.

The Catholic liturgical observance of Easter begins with the Easter Vigil service, which is celebrated Saturday night. See **liturgical time.**

For preparatory periods preceding Easter, see **Easter triduum; Easter Vigil, vigil of Easter; Holy Week;** and **Lent, Lenten.**

Easter duty A popular term for the obligation of Catholics in the Latin Church to receive Communion at least once a year, during the Easter season. The governing law is Canon 920 of the Code of Canon Law. The season for this purpose includes Holy Week as well as the period from Easter to Pentecost. For U.S. Catholics, however, the period for fulfilling the Easter duty begins with the first Sunday of Lent and ends with Trinity Sunday, a week after Pentecost.

Church law for the Eastern Catholic churches encourages frequent reception of Communion but does not impose an annual obligation as a matter of law.

Eastern Catholic churches The term is used for Catholic churches with origins in Eastern Europe, Asia or Africa that have their own distinctive liturgical and legal systems and are identified by the national or ethnic character of their region of origin.

Each Eastern church is considered fully equal in dignity to the Latin tradition within the Catholic Church, although members of the Latin Church dominate numerically. Eastern Catholics enjoy the same dignity, rights and obligations as members of the Latin Church.

General law for all the Eastern Catholic churches is spelled out in the Code of Canons of the Eastern Churches, promulgated in 1990. See **canon law.**

According to the code, the Eastern Catholic churches, each with its own particular law, fall into four categories: those headed by patriarchs (Chaldean, Armenian, Coptic, Syrian, Maronite and Melkite churches); those headed by major archbishops (Ukrainian, Syro-Malabar and Syro-Malankara churches); those headed by metropolitans (Ethiopian, Romanian and American Ruthenian churches); and other churches "sui iuris" (Bulgarian, Greek, Hungarian, Italo-Albanian and Slovak churches, as well as a diocese covering all of the former Yugoslavia). See **"sui iuris."** The Belarusian, Albanian, Georgian and Russian Eastern Catholic churches have no hierarchy.

These 22 churches trace their roots to five ritual families or groups. They are:

—Alexandrian: Coptic and Ethiopian churches.

—Antiochene: Syro-Malankara, Syrian and Maronite.

—Armenian: Armenian church.

—Byzantine: Albanian, Belarusian, Bulgarian, Georgian, Greek, Hungarian, Italo-Albanian, Melkite, Romanian, Russian, American Ruthenian, Slovak, Ukrainian and Yugoslavian churches.

— Chaldean: Chaldean and Syro-Malabar churches.

In the United States, the following Eastern Catholic churches had their own church jurisdictions in 2005:

— Armenian Catholics: Eparchy of Our Lady of Nareg, based in New York.

— Chaldean Catholics: Eparchy of St. Thomas in Southfield, Mich.

— Maronite Catholics: Eparchy of St. Maron in Brooklyn, N.Y., and Eparchy of Our Lady of Lebanon in Los Angeles, based in St. Louis.

— Melkite Catholics: Eparchy of Newton in Newton, Mass.

— Romanian Catholics: Eparchy of St. George in Canton, Ohio.

— Ruthenian Catholics (often referred to as American Byzantine): Archeparchy of Pittsburgh, with eparchies of Passaic, N.J.; Parma, Ohio; and Van Nuys, Calif.

— Syrian Catholics: Eparchy of Our Lady of Deliverance in Newark, N.J.

— Ukrainian Catholics: Archeparchy of Philadelphia and eparchies of St. Nicholas in Chicago and Stamford, Conn., and St. Josaphat in Parma, Ohio.

In the United States there are also a small number of parishes of the Coptic, Syro-Malabar, Syro-Malankara and Ethiopian Catholic churches. Since they have no hierarchy of their own in this country, they fall under the jurisdiction of the local Latin bishops.

As a group the members of these churches are *Eastern Catholics* and the churches are *Eastern Catholic churches.* In general, avoid using the word *rite* unless it is needed to avoid confusion between nationality or geographic location and ritual membership. Avoid the terms *uniate* and *uniate churches* when referring to Eastern Catholic churches. Many members of those churches consider those terms derogatory. Also avoid using the term *Roman* when speaking of Eastern Catholics. Although they are in union with Rome, it is not the patriarchal see of their church or the center of their liturgical, cultural and canonical tradition, as it is with Catholics of the Latin Church.

LITURGY: The eucharistic worship service is called the *Divine Liturgy,* not the Mass, in most Eastern churches. Maronites call it the *Divine Service of the Holy Mysteries.* Communion ordinarily is given under both forms, and ordinarily leavened bread is used.

The Eastern churches often admit married men to the priesthood in their regions of origin but do not permit marriage after ordination. Outside their regions of origin, Eastern Catholic churches may not admit married men to ordained ministry without a dispensation from the Holy See.

Like the Orthodox, most Eastern Catholic churches administer the three sacraments of initiation together in infancy, and the priest is the ordinary minister of all three. They use *anointing* or *chrismation* as the term for the sacrament called *confirmation* in the Latin tradition. Practice governing the sacraments of initiation may vary from church to church or from one country to another within a church, however. Some Eastern Catholic communities in the United States, for example, have adopted the Latin tradition of giving first Communion after the child reaches the use of reason, generally about age 7.

ORGANIZATION: New bishops are ordinarily elected by a synod of the bishops of the church, subject to papal confirmation. Eastern Catholics worldwide number between 16 million and 17 million, according to Vatican figures.

The Vatican agency which has responsibility for these Catholics is the Congregation for Eastern Churches. Many of the churches are headed by patriarchs. Others may be headed by a major archbishop or archbishop. Some smaller ones may be headed by a bishop or apostolic administrator. In general, the names of jurisdictions and titles of clergy in the Eastern churches should be adapted to the Latin equivalent unless the technical nature of the story requires use of the Eastern terms. Some examples: *archeparchy* (archdiocese), *eparchy or exarchy* (diocese), *archeparch* (archbishop), *eparch or exarch* (bishop).

See **archimandrite; Catholic Church; chorbishop;** and **religious titles.**

Eastern Orthodox churches
See **Orthodox churches.**

Eastern rite (n.), **Eastern-rite** (adj.) In general, avoid these terms in describing Eastern Catholic churches, unless needed to distinguish between the Catholic Church of the Latin rite and those of the Eastern rites.

For the individual Eastern Catholic churches the term *rite* may be needed in some contexts to clarify the difference between geographical or national references and references to the kind of ecclesiastical affiliation one has. Use *Romanian-rite Catholics* or *Romanian-rite Catholic Church,* for example, when the reader might understand *Romanian Catholics* to mean *Catholics who live in or come from Romania*, regardless of ritual affiliation, or *Romanian Catholic Church* to mean *the Catholic Church (Latin-rite and Romanian-rite) in Romania.*

Eastern-rite churches See **Eastern Catholic churches**.

Easter season, Easter time In Catholic practice, the period that begins with Easter and ends with Pentecost. It is also called *Eastertide* or *Paschaltide.*

Easter triduum The three-day period of liturgical observance, sometimes called the *sacred triduum,* which begins with the Mass of the Lord's Supper on Holy Thursday evening and ends with evening prayer on Easter. The term should be explained when used. On second reference *the triduum* is acceptable. *Triduum* is lowercase because it simply means a three-day period.

Easter Vigil, vigil of Easter *Easter Vigil* refers to the Catholic religious service, held between sundown Holy Saturday and dawn Easter morning, which is the high point of the church's liturgical year. It is capitalized because it is the proper name of a specific religious ceremony.

The *vigil of Easter* is an alternative way of describing the day before Easter. Use the preferred form *Holy Saturday* except in quoted matter.

See **Holy Week.**

Easter Week The period from Easter through the following Sunday. Eastern Catholics call it *Bright Week.*

"Ecclesia Dei" The 1988 papal document setting out terms for the reconciliation of Lefebvrites (followers of the late Archbishop Marcel Lefebvre) with Rome. Its title means "the church of God." It includes permission for returning priests and religious to retain their spiritual and liturgical traditions, including use of the Tridentine Mass, provided they accept the teachings of the Second Vatican Council and the validity of the new order of the Mass. It also encourages bishops to make greater use of the 1984 Vatican permission for limited use of the Tridentine Mass as revised in 1962.

The papal commission overseeing reconciliation is the *Pontifical Commission "Ecclesia Dei."*

See **Lefebvre, Archbishop Marcel** and **Tridentine Mass.**

ecclesial, ecclesiastical, ecclesiological Meanings of these three terms overlap. Choice of the proper word depends on the connotation one is seeking to convey.

Ecclesial means having to do with the church in general or the life of the church. For example: *Religious life is ecclesial* means that men and women religious are part of the life of the church; their work and witness are in the church and for it.

Ecclesiastical should be restricted to contexts referring to official structures or legal or organizational aspects of the church. For example: *Religious life is ecclesiastical* means that it is a structured reality of the church, that it is governed by church laws and norms, etc. Often *church* can replace *ecclesiastical* as a modifier: An *ecclesiastical* law, post, jurisdiction, etc., is a *church* law, post, jurisdiction, etc.

Ecclesiological means having to do with the theology of the church and its structures and practice: *The rise of bishops' conferences is one of the most important ecclesiological developments since the Second Vatican Council, the theologian said.* If the term must be used, it should be explained.

ecclesiastical courts Courts in the Catholic Church are called *tribunals* in technical writing, but *courts* is usually preferable in news writing. The Code of Canon Law spells out their structure, procedures and jurisdiction. Most of their cases involve requests for marriage annulments. The church's main court system consists of:

— *Diocesan or archdiocesan courts*: First courts of trial for most cases.

— *Metropolitan, interdiocesan or regional courts*: They are appellate courts. In the United States the metropolitan court, located in an archdiocese, is usually the appellate court for all cases tried in dioceses within the province of that archdiocese. For cases first tried in an archdiocesan court, the metropolitan court of another archdiocese is designated as the appellate court.

Note that *metropolitan* refers to an appeals court, *archdiocesan* to a court of first trial. Although the two courts in a particular archdiocese may share facilities and personnel, they are distinct in name and function.

Since 1983, regional or interdiocesan courts have been established in some parts of the United States as appellate courts for marriage cases only. Canada has a system of regional appellate courts nationwide.

— *Tribunal of the Roman Rota*: When an appeals court disagrees with the decision of a primary court, the case may go to the church's central appellate court, the Roman Rota. It is also the primary court of trial for certain cases reserved to the Holy See by law or decree. Theoretically either party in any court case may appeal to the Rota at any stage in the case, but this possibility is rarely invoked in practice. *Rota* is acceptable on second reference. The chief judge is called the *dean of the Rota.* In most contexts it is preferable to use *judge,* not *auditor,* to refer to the Rota's judges.

— *Supreme Court of the Apostolic Signature*: The church's supreme court, it deals primarily with questions of the procedures and jurisdiction of the other courts, although at times it handles substantive case decisions. *Apostolic Signature* is acceptable on second reference. Do not use the Latin, *Signatura,* or the Italian, *Segnatura,* in English-language references to the court.

— *Apostolic Penitentiary*: A special court. See **Apostolic Penitentiary.**

PERSONNEL: Lowercase all titles of ecclesiastical court officials, treating the terms as job descriptions rather than formal titles. The main officials of diocesan, metropolitan and regional courts are *judges, defenders of the bond, promoters of justice, advocates* and *auditors.*

An auditor, also called an *instructor* in some dioceses, gathers evidence and testimony for the court. Advocates argue on behalf of the parties they represent. A promoter of justice, the equivalent of a prosecuting attorney in civil law, is assigned in all penal cases and in contentious cases involving the public good as determined by law or the bishop. The defender of the bond, assigned in all cases involving nullity of ordination or nullity or dissolution of marriage, presents evidence in favor of the sacramental bond.

The primary judge of every diocesan court is the bishop, but in practice he delegates that task to a judge called the *"officialis"* in Latin. Some U.S. courts have begun to use the English terms *chief judge* or *judicial vicar* for the "officialis." If a diocese still uses "officialis" in its listing, use *chief judge*. A *"vice officialis"* is an *assistant chief judge*. Some courts refer to him as *vice judicial vicar.*

OTHER TERMS: The person who brings a case to court is the *petitioner.* The other party is the *respondent.* Sometimes, particularly in penal cases, they are called, respectively, the *plaintiff* and the *defendant.*

The court of first trial is referred to in church law as the *court of first instance.* The court of first (second, third) appeal is a *court of second (third, fourth) instance.* In news writing, the ecclesiastical terms should be avoided in favor of language parallel to that used for civil courts: *diocesan court, lower court, court of appeals, appellate court, central appeals court,* etc.

ecclesiastical degrees Degrees conferred, in accord with norms established by the Holy See, by pontifically chartered Catholic institutions or faculties of higher learning.

Use words, not abbreviations, to describe ecclesiastical degrees in a story: *Sister Smith received a doctorate in canon law. Jones has a licentiate in sacred theology from the Gregorian University in Rome.*

Some of the common ecclesiastical degrees are *S.T.B., S.T.L.* and *S.T.D.* (bachelor's, licentiate and doctorate in sacred theology), *J.C.B., J.C.L.* and *J.C.D.* (bachelor's, licentiate and doctorate in canon law), *S.L.L.* and *S.L.D.* (licentiate and doctorate in sacred liturgy), and *S.S.D.* (doctorate in sacred Scripture). Formerly these were commonly called *pontifical* degrees, but now *ecclesiastical* is preferred.

Most degrees offered by Catholic colleges, universities and seminaries in the United States, including degrees in theology and related sciences, are *civil degrees* because they are based on the granting institution's civil charter, accreditation and degree requirements, not on pontifical charter and requirements. Except when discussing what kind of degrees a school can confer, the distinction between civil and ecclesiastical degrees ordinarily is not relevant to a story; it is enough to name accurately the degree a person has earned.

Ecclesiasticus A name formerly used for the *Book of Sirach.* Do not use.

See **Bible.**

ecumenical, interreligious In Christian religious usage, the first meaning of *ecumenical* is *universal, of or concerning the church as a whole.* It is used in this sense in phrases such as *ecumenical council* (a council of the whole church) and *ecumenical patriarch* (the patriarch of Constantinople, recognized as first among equals by the whole body of Orthodox churches).

The second meaning, derived from the first but more common in use, is *furthering or intending to further the unity or unification of Christian churches.*

The term refers only to the unity or fellowship of *Christians.* Use it only for organizations, movements, actions, etc., guided by the goals of improving relations among the Christian churches and restoring Christian unity.

Use *interreligious* to describe religious relations that involve non-Christians.

Both *ecumenical* and *interreligious* ordinarily approach the question of relations between religious groups from the standpoint of their purpose — fostering mutual respect, understanding, fellowship, unity, etc. If only organizational participation or support by different groups is intended, the terms *interfaith* and *interdenominational* may be more appropriate.

See **interdenominational, interfaith.**

ecumenical council See **Vatican councils.**

ecumenical patriarch See **Orthodox churches.**

ecumenism Do not use *ecumenicism* or *ecumenicalism.*

editor's notes See **Appendix A: Special Style Considerations.**

elder In some Christian denominations *elders* hold offices of ministry or governance.

See **Church of Jesus Christ of Latter-day Saints; Presbyterian churches;** and **religious titles.**

-elect Hyphenate and lowercase when attached to a title or office between the time a person is elected to a position and the assumption of the position: *President-elect Doe, the president-elect; Abbot-elect Smith, the abbot-elect.*

Use *-designate,* not *-elect,* to describe intended officeholders who have received that office through appointment by a superior or a governing board, not by a vote of peers or constituents. In Catholic practice, superiors of religious orders or congregations usually are selected by an electoral process, so the use of *-elect* is appropriate in most cases; but pastors, bishops, archbishops and cardinals usually receive office by appointment and should be called *-designate* between the time of appointment and entry into office. See **archbishop-designate, bishop-designate.**

An exception: When a bishop or patriarch of an Eastern Catholic church is elected by the bishops of that church, even if Rome's prior assent to nominees or subsequent confirmation is required, that person is properly called a *bishop-elect* or *patriarch-elect.*

e-mail addresses When using an e-mail address in a story, advisory or editor's note, capitalize the initial letters of the person's name, e.g., *JLackey@catholicnews.com, NOBrien@catholicnews.com.* But: *cns@catholicnews.com.*

emarginate, emarginated Both are adjectives that mean *having a notched or truncated edge.* When they are used in social-justice or liberation-theology contexts to refer to the poor or powerless (those *placed on the fringes* of society), the usage is erroneous.

For correct usage, see **marginalize.**

emeritus, retired Although the Vatican has begun to call retired residential bishops *bishop emeritus* (for example: *Archbishop Emeritus John R. Quinn of San Francisco),* the usage is not yet widespread in practice. Nor does the Vatican use it for all bishops — only for former heads of dioceses and Vatican agencies. For consistency, use *retired,* always lowercase, for all Catholic bishops who have retired. For example: *Bishop Patrick V. Ahern, retired auxiliary of New York; retired Archbishop Patrick F. Flores of San Antonio; Cardinal Anthony J. Bevilacqua, retired archbishop of Philadelphia.*

In other contexts, when *emeritus* is appended to a person's title to indicate his retention of the title after retirement, capitalize it only when it is used as part of a formal title before the name. Lowercase it in all other uses.

Eminence A formal title of respect for a cardinal, it should not be used in news stories except in quoted matter. If used, it should be capitalized along with the preceding modifier *His* or *Your: "I will do it if His Eminence wishes,"* he said.

See **Excellence, Excellency** and **Holiness.**

Encourage (http://couragerc.net/Encourage.html) An organization for family members and friends of people with same-sex attractions.

See **Courage** and **homosexuality.**

encuentro Spanish for *encounter*, encuentros have been held at diocesan and national levels to celebrate the multiculturalism of the U.S. church. The last national encuentro was in Los Angeles in 2000.

encyclical A papal document addressed to the whole church. Capitalize the titles of encyclicals and place within quotation marks. Use either the English or Latin title, whichever the encyclical is more generally known by: *"Humanae Vitae,"* but *"Faith and Reason."* When using Latin titles, translate them or describe the content of the document within the text of the story. When a Latin title is the primary form of reference, use capitals and quotation marks for an English form of reference only if the English is a direct translation of the Latin; otherwise treat the English as a descriptive paraphrase, lowercase and without quotation marks. For a chronological list and description of all encyclicals since 1740, consult the Catholic Almanac. See **apostolic exhortation** and **pastoral letter.**

Here is a list of the modern social encyclicals, which appear with some frequency in the news, with the more common form of reference given first, along with year of issuance and author:

— "Rerum Novarum" (on capital and labor), 1891, Pope Leo XIII. Considered the starting point of modern social teaching by the popes.

— "Quadragesimo Anno" (on reconstructing the social order), 1931, Pope Pius XI. The second major social encyclical, it marked the 40th anniversary of "Rerum Novarum."

— "Mater et Magistra" ("Mother and Teacher," on Christianity and social progress), 1961, Pope John XXIII.

— "Peace on Earth" ("Pacem in Terris"), 1963, Pope John XXIII.

— "Populorum Progressio" ("The Progress of Peoples"), 1967, Pope Paul VI.

— "On Human Work" ("Laborem Exercens"), 1981, Pope John Paul II.

— "On Social Concerns" ("Sollicitudo Rei Socialis"), 1987, Pope John Paul II.

— "Centesimus Annus" ("The Hundredth Year"), 1991, Pope John Paul II.

— "Evangelium Vitae" ("The Gospel of Life"), 1995, Pope John Paul II.

See **"Humanae Vitae."**

endnotes See **Appendix C: Endnotes.**

English Language Liturgical Consultation An association formed in 1985 by English-speaking ecumenical liturgical organizations to improve cooperation in liturgical projects across denominational and national boundaries. It is a successor to the International Consultation on English Texts, which existed from 1969 to 1975 and promoted the development and use of commonly acceptable liturgy texts.

It meets biennally in conjunction with the congress of the *Societas Liturgica.* See that entry. Coordinated through the offices of the *International Commission on English in the Liturgy* in Washington. See that entry.

enrollment See **incardination.**

Enthronement of the Sacred Heart in the Home (www.sscc.org/enthronement.html) Headquarters is in Fairhaven, Mass.

eparch, eparchy An *eparch* is a *bishop.* An *eparchy* is a *diocese.* Use the more familiar Latin-rite words unless the technical character of a story, such as the founding of a new eparchy, requires use of these Eastern Catholic and Orthodox terms.
See **Eastern Catholic churches.**

episcopal, Episcopal Lowercase *episcopal* when it is used to refer to a bishop or group of bishops or to the form of church governance in which ordained bishops have authority: *episcopal vicar, episcopal conference, episcopal ordination. The Catholic, Orthodox, Anglican, Lutheran and Methodist churches have an episcopal form of government.*

Capitalize *Episcopal* in references to the Episcopal Church. Do not use *Episcopalian* as an adjective or *Episcopal* as a noun: *Three Episcopalians were present. The chairman is an Episcopal priest.*
See **Episcopal Church.**

Episcopal Church (www.episco palchurch.org) In news writing this is the preferred form in almost all contexts to refer to the U.S. member of the Anglican Communion formerly known as the *Protestant Episcopal Church in the U.S.A.* In 1967 U.S. Episcopalians formally adopted *Episcopal Church* as an official alternate name, and now they rarely use the longer form.

For general Episcopal beliefs, practices, governance and relations with the Catholic Church, see **Anglican Communion.**

In 2005 the Episcopal Church said it had between 2 million and 3 million members, mostly in the United States. It also has dioceses in Central and South America and elsewhere overseas.

National policies are determined by the *General Convention,* which meets every three years. It is a bicameral legislature, comprised of a House of Bishops and a House of Deputies. The House of Deputies is formed by equal numbers of clergy and laity. A 38-member *Executive Council,* elected by the convention, carries out decisions of the convention and oversees the church's national programs and activities.

The head of the church nationally is the *presiding bishop,* who is also called the primate. The primate is elected by the House of Bishops and confirmed by the House of Deputies, and holds office for nine years or until shortly after the election of a successor at the General Convention nearest the primate's 70th birthday if that occurs before nine years. National offices of the church are at the Episcopal Church Center in New York.

Although Episcopal dioceses are grouped into eight regional U.S. provinces and one Latin American province, there are no Episcopal archdioceses or archbishops in the United

States. A provincial synod, with two houses following the model of the General Convention, coordinates regional activities.

A bishop heads each diocese. He or she may have a coadjutor, suffragan or assistant bishop as well. A coadjutor has right of succession. The clergy of the diocese and lay representatives from each parish form a diocesan convention, which adopts a budget, elects its bishop or bishops, and elects delegates to the General Convention and provincial synod.

The congregation has the right to select its own rector, with the consent of the bishop. The rector and elected lay members form a *vestry,* the governing body of the parish or local church.

Do not capitalize terms such as *vestry, diocesan convention* or *provincial synod* unless they are used as part of the formal names of particular bodies.

The Episcopal Church ordained its first women priests in 1974, its first woman bishop in 1989 and its first openly gay bishop in 2003.

The Episcopal Church entered full communion with the Evangelical Lutheran Church in America in 1999.

The Episcopal Church is a member of *Churches Uniting in Christ.* See that entry.

epistle See **Bible** and **letter, epistle.**

Equestrian Order of the Holy Sepulcher of Jerusalem See **Knights of the Holy Sepulcher.**

eremite See **hermit.**

eschatology (n.), **eschatological** (adj.) If possible, avoid using these technical terms. If used, they must be explained. *Eschatology* is the Christian theological study of death and what follows: resurrection, divine judgment, immortality, heaven, hell, etc. An *eschatological* perspective or orientation refers to a view in which one's life with God after death is considered of primary importance.

Eskimo, Eskimos Derived from an Ojibwa word meaning "eaters of raw flesh," the word is considered derogatory by many of the Native American people it is used to describe. The preferred term is *Inuit.*

See **Inuit.**

"Essential Norms" Vatican-approved laws adopted by the U.S. bishops in 2002 to implement legislatively their *"Charter for the Protection of Children and Young People."* See that entry. The texts of the charter and norms are available on the Web at www.usccb.org/ocyp. Requirements of the norms include written policies on sexual abuse and child protection in every diocese, an assistance coordinator for abuse victims, a diocesan review board and various mandated procedures for dealing with abuse allegations and with the accused priest or deacon.

Eternal Word Television Network (www.ewtn.com) *EWTN* is acceptable on second reference. In some media material, such as program listings, *EWTN* is acceptable on all references. Headquarters is in Irondale, Ala.

"Ethical and Religious Directives for Catholic Health Care Services" The directives guide Catholic health care facilities in addressing a wide range of ethical questions, such as abortion, euthanasia, care for the poor, medical research, treatment of rape victims, surrogate motherhood, in vitro fertilization, prenatal testing, nutrition and hydration for the terminally ill and organ donation. Most recently revised by the bishops in 2000, they also offer guidance to bishops on the circumstances under which mergers or consolidations of health facilities in their dioceses should be approved.

Eucharist, eucharistic Capitalize *Eucharist*. Lowercase *eucharistic* except as part of a formal title: *the International Eucharistic Congress.*

See **Communion.**

eucharistic adoration See **Forty Hours devotion** and **perpetual adoration**.

eucharistic minister See **extraordinary minister of holy Communion.**

eucharistic sharing Preferable to the more inclusive term *intercommunion* when referring to the participation in the Eucharist of one ecclesial community by a member of another community.

In some churches various forms of intercommunion with certain other churches, including eucharistic sharing, are permitted. When referring to a practice that violates a church's rules, make it clear that you are talking about a form of *unauthorized intercommunion* or *unauthorized eucharistic sharing.*

See **Communion, communion** and **intercommunion.**

European Union The organization's ruling document is the *European constitution* or *European Union constitution.*

euthanasia An act or omission that intentionally brings about death in order to end pain or suffering.

Official Catholic teaching admits circumstances in which a patient may refuse treatment considered useless or extraordinarily burdensome, but it rejects any form of euthanasia — that is, any act or omission designed to cause death in order to eliminate suffering. Avoid using *mercy killing* as a synonym for euthanasia.

Do not use as a synonym for *assisted suicide,* in which someone provides the means by which another person can cause his or her own death. Use *physician-assisted suicide* only in cases where a proposal or law specifically says only doctors can provide those means.

Church teaching describes assisted suicide as illicit in all cases. See **assisted suicide.**

evangelical (n., adj.) Lowercase except when used as part of a formal name: evangelical Christians, evangelicals. But: *the Evangelical Methodist Church.*

Historically, *evangelical* was used as an adjective meaning Gospel-related or describing dedication to preaching the Gospel. It comes from the Greek word for good news, *"evangelion."*

Today it also is used as a noun. In this use it refers to Christians who emphasize the need for a definite, adult commitment or conversion to faith in Christ and the duty of all believers to persuade others to a decision accepting Christ. Evangelicals tend to focus on Reformation principles of faith alone, Scripture alone and grace alone, de-emphasizing sacraments, ecclesiastical structure and adherence to particular doctrinal formulations. They make up the entire membership of some denominations and are numerous in other denominations.

An international Catholic-evangelical theological consultation is sponsored by the Pontifical Council for Promoting Christian Unity and the Theological Commission of the World Evangelical Fellowship.

See **evangelist, Evangelist, evangelizer; National Association of Evangelicals; World Evangelical Alliance; Reformation;** and entries for individual denominations.

Evangelical Friends International-North American Region See **Quakers.**

Evangelical Lutheran Church in America See **Lutheran churches.**

evangelist, Evangelist, evangelizer Reserve *evangelist* for a preacher or revivalist who seeks conversions by preaching to groups, usually without regard for any denominational affiliation audience members may have. One who does so by television is a *televangelist.* Do not use either term as a formal title before a name. See **televangelist, televangelism.**

When capitalized, *Evangelist* refers to a writer of one of the four Gospels: *Luke the Evangelist.*

An *evangelizer* is anyone who tries to draw others to the Gospel by word and witness: *In Catholic teaching all baptized people are called to be evangelizers.*

See **evangelize, evangelization.**

evangelize, evangelization These verb and noun forms for *preaching the Gospel* or *spreading the Gospel* have entered U.S. Catholic vocabulary only in recent years. Because they may still be unfamiliar to some readers, make an effort to accompany the first or second reference with an explanatory phrase: *He said the role of all Christians in evangelization, or spreading the Gospel, is often underestimated.*

Do not use *proselytize,* which is usually used with negative connotations of sectarianism or hard-sell evangelism, as a synonym for *evangelize.* See **proselytize.**

Eve, eve Capitalize when it is used immediately after the name of a holiday or feast day as a proper name for the day before: *New Year's Eve, Christmas Eve, St. Agnes' Eve.*

Lowercase in all other uses: *the eve of victory, the eve of Christmas.*

evolution In biological terms, the belief that higher forms of plant and animal life, including humans, developed from lower forms. Charles Darwin originated the theory of evolution by natural selection in the 19th century, but some U.S. states banned the teaching of evolution in public school classrooms until the early 20th century.

Contrasting theories include *creationism,* also called *creation science,* a belief that the Bible, interpreted literally, gives an accurate scientific description of the origins of the universe and of life on earth, and *intelligent design,* the belief that natural law and chance alone are not adequate to explain all natural phenomena.

Creationists generally reject scientific theories of evolution and of the origins of the universe as contradicting divine revelation.

The Catholic Church teaches that God is creator of all things and, in the words of the Catechism of the Catholic Church, "upholds and sustains them in being, enables them to act and brings them to their final end." While it rejects certain evolutionary hypotheses as contradicting fundamental doctrines, it does not view the Bible as scientific literature. Ordinary Catholic teaching and theology have long been comfortable with the basic idea of evolution as a way in which God carries out his creative activity.

In 2004, a document of the International Theological Commission said evolutionary explanations of biological development were acceptable as long as they did not exclude God as a transcendent cause or exclude the universe as a setting for "a radically personal drama" involving God and man.

A new controversy erupted the following year, however, when Austrian Cardinal Christoph Schonborn wrote in The New York Times that an "unplanned process of random variation and natural selection," both important parts of evolutionary thinking, are incompatible with Catholic belief that there is a divine purpose and design to nature.

EWTN See **Eternal Word Television Network.**

exarch The person, ordinarily a bishop, who heads an exarchate. Use *bishop* rather than *exarch* whenever possible: *Bishop Georges Kahhale Zouhairaty of the Melkite Catholic Exarchate of Venezuela.*

With the elevation of the Armenian Catholic Exarchate of the U.S.A. and Canada to an eparchy in 2005, there were no exarchates in the United States or Canada.

See **Eastern Catholic churches** and **exarchate, exarchy.**

exarchate, exarchy A form of church jurisdiction sometimes established for Eastern Catholics or Orthodox Christians living outside their native land. Either *exarchate* or *exarchy* is acceptable. In 2005 no Eastern Catholic jurisdiction in the United States or Canada used *exarchate* in its name. Lowercase except in formal titles: *Melkite Catholic Exarchate of Venezuela; the Melkite exarchate.*

An exarchate is similar to an apostolic vicariate in the Latin Church: It is established in an area where there are enough Catholics of that rite to form a stable hierarchical structure and self-government, but where the church is not sufficiently established to create a diocese. It can be described as *a church jurisdiction similar to a diocese.*

See **apostolic vicariate** and **Eastern Catholic churches.**

excardination See **incardination.**

Excellence, Excellency A formal title of respect for bishops and archbishops, it should not be used in news stories except in quoted matter. If used, it should be capitalized, along with the preceding modifier *His* or *Your: "We are completely at Your Excellency's disposal," he told the bishop.*

See **Eminence** and **Holiness.**

exclusive language See **inclusive language.**

excommunication An extreme form of church penalty, reserved for especially serious offenses committed by church members. It is one of three ecclesiastical censures. The other two are interdict and suspension. These punishments are known as "medicinal penalties," since they are intended to heal the harm caused by the offense and at the same time lead the offender to a return to good standing within the church. Excommunication and interdict can be incurred by any believer, but suspension is reserved to clerics.

The penalty exists in two forms: *"ferendae sententiae,"* meaning that it is imposed following a formal judicial or administrative process, and *"latae sententiae,"* meaning that it is incurred automatically at the time of the offense. Certain especially grievous acts, such as procuring a completed abortion, heresy, schism, apostasy, a confessor violating the seal of confession, or a sacrilegious use of the Eucharist, automatically bring about excommunication. Refer to someone under excommunication as *the excommunicated person,* not *the excommunicant.*

A person who has been excommunicated remains a member of the church subject to its legislation, unless the person has left the church by means of a formal act. According to the 1983 Code of Canon Law, those who are excommunicated are banned from all ministerial participation in ceremonies of public worship and may not celebrate the sacraments or sacramentals, receive the sacraments, or exercise any ecclesiastical offices, ministries or functions. Also, an excommunicated person cannot act as a sponsor in baptism or confirmation. See **interdict** and **suspended priests**.

exegesis Critical analysis and interpretation of the Bible. The adjective is *exegetical.* The practitioner is an *exegete.* Avoid using these terms when possible. In place of *Exegetes are divided on the exegesis of that passage,* write: *Bible scholars are divided on how to interpret that passage.*

exorcism A religious rite used to rid a person or place of an evil spirit. The Catholic Church cautions that the rite should be used sparingly and only after an investigation has ruled out psychological or other causes as an explanation of the phenomena attributed to the evil spirit.

The verb form is *exorcise.*

Extension (Society) See **Catholic Church Extension Society**.

extraordinary minister of holy Communion The term preferred by the Vatican over *eucharistic minister* for laypeople who distribute Communion at Mass or a Communion service or who bring the Eucharist to those unable to attend Mass.

The Vatican document "Redemptionis Sacramentum" ("The Sacrament of Redemption"), issued in 2004 by the Congregation for Divine Worship and the Sacraments, said only bishops, priests or deacons are true ministers of the Eucharist and laypeople deputized to assist in distributing Communion must be called "extraordinary ministers of holy Communion." It rejected substituting "special" for "extraordinary" or "Eucharist" for "holy Communion."

Use *eucharistic ministers* if the group includes only clergy or the distinction between lay and ordained ministers is not relevant.

The 2004 document said at any given Mass all available priests or deacons should step up to distribute Communion before any laypeople are called on to do so.

See **minister, ministry**.

extreme unction Former name for the Catholic sacrament of anointing of the sick. Do not use.

See **anointing of the sick** and **sacraments**.

faculty The legal term in Catholic usage for authorization, given by the law itself or by a church superior, to perform certain official church acts. In most contexts more commonly recognized terms such as *authorization* or *power* are preferred.

Faculty ordinarily is not used for powers that come automatically with ordination itself or with appointment to a particular ecclesiastical office. For example, by virtue of his office a pastor has the power to assist at marriages in his parish. When that authority is delegated to another priest or deacon, or to a layperson where this is permitted, the person to whom the authority is delegated is said to have received the *faculty* to assist at marriages. Other acts involving conferral of faculties are *hearing confessions* and *preaching*.

When a priest has one or more faculties suspended or withdrawn, it does not mean he has been suspended from all priestly ministry. Report which specific faculties were suspended: *Bishop Jones has ordered Father Smith not to preach or hear confessions.* For suspension from all priestly ministry, see **suspended priests.**

FADICA (www.fadica.org) *Foundations and Donors Interested in Catholic Activities,* an international organization with about 46 foundation and individual members.

FADICA is acceptable on first reference, but the full name of the organization should be given in the body of the story. Headquarters is in Washington.

Faith & Reason Institute (www.frinstitute.org) Acceptable on all references for the *Faith & Reason Institute for the Study of Religion and Culture.* Note the ampersand. It is located in Washington.

Family Federation for World Peace and Unification (www.familyfed.org) New name for the Unification Church, founded by the Rev. Sun Myung Moon in South Korea in 1954. The Unification Church is like Islam and the Church of Jesus Christ of Latter-day Saints in that it considers Christ a prophet but bases its beliefs on new divine revelations given to its founder. Do not describe it as *Protestant.* See that entry.

Its authority structures and recruitment techniques have led many Christian theologians to consider it a cult. It has been criticized also for creating a variety of social-action and international-affairs organizations that are allegedly secretive about their relationship with the Unification Church.

Rev. Moon, who was born in Korea Jan. 6, 1920, claims to have had private revelations from Christ, Moses and Buddha. The first was a vision in 1936 in which he says Christ commissioned him to carry out Christ's unfinished task of saving the world from Satan and Satan's representatives in the world, communists. He began preaching his beliefs in 1946 and was excommunicated from the Presbyterian Church two years later.

While building his church in South Korea in the 1950s and '60s, Rev. Moon also built an international manufacturing and trading empire. In the early 1970s he embarked on a massive international missionary effort and in 1971 moved from South

Korea to New York. In the 1990s he moved to Uruguay. Church membership worldwide is estimated at between 1 million and 3 million. U.S. followers are estimated at between 30,000 and 50,000. Related organizations include the Women's Federation for World Peace and the Summit Council for World Peace.

International headquarters is in Seoul, South Korea, and U.S. headquarters is in Washington.

Members were derisively referred to as *"Moonies"* in the 1970s. If the term is used, it should be placed in quotes and identified as a nickname widely used at that time.

BELIEFS: The chief source of Unification Church doctrine is Rev. Moon's 1952 book, "Divine Principle." It says Jesus was a prophet sent by God to be the Messiah, but he was not God and failed in his messianic mission when he was crucified before he was able to restore divine rule on earth through procreative marriage. Christ's followers formed a provisional second Israel, but Rev. Moon is said to be forming a third Israel, the fullness of divine rule based on restoration of the family, which will unite divided Christians and believers of other faiths in a single world religion.

The theology in "Divine Principle" is strongly influenced by yin-yang motifs in which reality is understood in terms of complementary passive, feminine principles and active, masculine principles. Unification Church members are expected to follow a strict code of sexual morality, with Rev. Moon and his ministers deciding who will be married and when. Sometimes massive weddings are celebrated at which several thousand arranged marriages are solemnized in a single ceremony. Followers often refer to Rev. Moon and his wife, Hak Ja Han, as Father and Mother.

CLERGY TITLES: Use *the Rev.* on first and *Rev.* on subsequent references.

Family of the Americas (www.familyplanning.net) A pro-life organization that promotes natural family planning worldwide. It is based in Dunkirk, Md.

Family Rosary (www.familyrosary.org) An organization founded in 1942 by Holy Cross Father Patrick J. Peyton to promote praying of the rosary. It has offices in Albany, N.Y., and North Easton, Mass.

Family Theater Productions (www.familytheater.org) The television, movie and video arm of *Family Rosary*. See that entry. Headquarters is in Hollywood, Calif.

fasting In Catholic practice in the Latin Church, *fasting* can mean not taking nourishment at all during a particular time or limiting one's food consumption during a given day to one main meal and two smaller meals, with no solid foods in between. This should not be confused with the penitential practice of *abstinence,* which refers to avoiding particular kinds of food, especially meat. Note, however, that fast days are also days of abstinence; days of abstinence are not necessarily fast days.

The laws of fasting and days of fasting in Eastern Catholic churches differ from those in the Latin Church. Catholics of the Eastern churches observe fast days by refraining from meat, dairy products and eggs. This is required of Catholics of all ages on the first day of Lent (two days before the start of Lent in the Latin Church) and on Good Friday. Consult authorities of individual churches to determine if they have other fast days.

Church law for the Latin Church requires Catholics ordinarily to fast from all food and drink except water or medicine for at least one hour before receiving Communion. Eastern churches generally follow the same rule, but it is up to each church to determine its laws of Communion fast. Consult authorities of individual churches to determine what their laws say.

Church law for the Latin Church establishes Ash Wednesday and Good Friday as penitential days of fast. Those aged 18 through 59 ordinarily are obliged to observe these fast days by not eating between meals and by having no more than one main meal and two smaller meals. Consult authorities of other churches for information on their laws and practices.

In coverage of *protest fasts,* state the extent of the fast. For example: *a water-only fast, a bread-and-water fast, a fast from all solid foods, a 24-hour liquids-only fast.*

See **abstinence, days of** and **penitential days.**

Father Use *Father* (not *the Rev.)* as the formal title before the name of Catholic and Orthodox priests in all references, unless they have a religious title that takes precedence, such as *Msgr.* Never abbreviate Father. Use *the Rev.* for Anglican or Episcopal priests to avoid problems with second reference to female priests.

Do not use *Father* alone or *the father* to refer to a priest.

WRONG: *He said Father told him so. The father has a new parish.*

RIGHT: *He said Father Smith told him so. The priest has a new parish.*

See **religious titles.**

Fathers of the Church Collective name given to those ancient Christian writers whose theological discourses and writings, taken collectively, are considered a foundation for orthodox Christian doctrine. Some are also called *doctors of the church,* but that title is accorded to some later theologian-saints as well. See **doctor of the church.**

Because the term may be unfamiliar to some readers, it is generally preferable to avoid *Fathers of the Church* and substitute alternative phrases such as *early Christian theologians, ancient Christian writers,* etc.

When used, capitalize. Like *Crusaders,* it is a proper name given to a historical group of people, even though scholars may debate whether or not certain individuals ought to be included in the group.

feast of Do not capitalize the word *feast* in *feast of the Immaculate Conception, feast of St. Francis of Assisi,* etc.

In news writing, *feast* is an appropriate generic term to describe any day set aside to honor the Lord or Mary or events in their lives or to celebrate the memory of a saint or saints. In the general calendar of the Latin Church, liturgical observances are ranked in a complex order of precedence in which the four main rankings are, in descending order, *solemnity, feast, obligatory memorial* and *optional memorial.* Unless the technical rank of precedence is relevant to the story, however, use *feast of* or other nontechnical terms in all uses.

The rules of precedence and a list of rankings in the General Roman Calendar are contained in the introductory material of the *Sacramentary.* See that entry.

Federation of Diocesan Liturgical Commissions (www.fdlc.org) Headquarters is in Washington.

Federation of Vietnamese Catholics in the United States (http://liendoanconggiao.com) Web site is in Vietnamese but includes several contacts by e-mail. Headquarters is in Riverdale, Ga.

fellow A *fellow* can be male or female. The word has no sexist connotations when used as an adjective *(fellow worker, fellow citizen)* or as a noun in standard usage *(a companion, a partner, one of a corresponding pair, a holder of an academic fellowship, a member of a learned society, etc.).*

In certain colloquial uses, however, some people find the word offensive because it suggests male clubbishness or condescension toward women: *Treat her just like one of the fellows.* Unless needed in quoted matter, avoid such colloquial uses.

See **sexism, sexist language.**

Fellowship of Catholic Scholars (www.catholicscholars.org) An interdisciplinary organization of Catholics founded in 1977 to defend and promote the Catholic faith. An academic doctoral degree or its equivalent is needed for full membership. Doctoral students can hold associate membership. Headquarters is in Notre Dame, Ind.

Fellowship of Catholic University Students (www.focusonline.org) A national outreach to college campuses, both to secular and Catholic schools, it was represented on 25 campuses in early 2005. Avoid the acronym FOCUS except in quoted material. Headquarters is in Greeley, Colo.

Fellowship of Reconciliation (www.forusa.org) An interfaith pacifist organization. Headquarters is in Nyack, N.Y.

"filioque" The phrase, meaning *"and the Son,"* that was added to the Nicene Creed in the West in centuries following the original conciliar formulation. The churches of the East objected to what they considered an unwarranted change in the conciliar profession of faith, and the "filioque" controversy was among the factors that contributed to a hardening of positions following the Great Schism of 1054.

The original text of the creed says the Holy Spirit "proceeds from the Father." With the addition it says the Holy Spirit "proceeds from the Father and the Son."

See **Nicene Creed** and **Orthodox churches.**

First Catholic Slovak Ladies Association (www.fcsla.com) Headquarters is in Beachwood, Ohio.

First Catholic Slovak Union (Jednota) (www.fcsu.com) Headquarters is in Independence, Ohio.

first Communion Lowercase *first.* See **Communion, communion.**

first confession Lowercase. *First penance* and *first reconciliation* have become the preferred terms in pastoral practice in many areas, but *first confession* is still widely used. All three terms are acceptable in news writing.

First Friday, First Saturday Capitalize *first* in the name of the devotion, but not in references to the day on which it occurs: *Some Catholics observe First Fridays out of devotion to the Sacred Heart of Jesus. They attend Mass and receive Communion on the first Fridays of nine consecutive months. The First Saturday devotions, in honor of the Immaculate Heart of*

Mary, consist of confession, Communion and recitation of five decades of the rosary on the first Saturdays of five consecutive months.

First Nations See **Indians.**

501(c)(3) Describes a nonprofit organization that is exempt from taxation under Section 501(c)(3) of the Internal Revenue Service code.

Focolare, Focolare movement (www.rc.net/focolare) Started in Trent, Italy, by Chiara Lubich in 1943, this Catholic lay movement claims more than 87,000 members and about 2 million "friends and adherents" in over 180 nations. It is also known as the *Work of Mary.* Its aim is world unity through the living witness of Christian love and holiness in the family and small community.

A female member is a *Focolarina* (pl. *Focolarine);* a male member is a *Focolarino* (pl. *Focolarini);* the plural for a mixed group is *Focolarini.* Whenever possible, however, use *members of Focolare, a Focolare member* or similar alternatives. Some members live in community in homes called *Focolare centers.* Larger centers or towns of Focolare members established in various parts of the world usually bear the name *Mariapolis.* In 1986 the first such larger center in North America was established in Hyde Park, N.Y., with the name *Mariapolis Luminosa.*

Movement members include single men or women who take vows of poverty, chastity and obedience but are not members of any religious order; married persons and families; diocesan priests; members of various religious orders who join the movement while remaining with their order; apostolic volunteers, whose branch is called the *New Humanity Movement;* and young people, who belong to the youth branch called *Gen,* which is short for *New Genesis.* Members of the youth movement are called *the Gen.* U.S. headquarters is in Hyde Park.

Food for the Poor (www.food forthepoor.org) A Christian relief and development agency, based in Deerfield Beach, Fla.

footnotes See **Appendix C: Endnotes.**

foreign names See **names** and **Appendix A: Special Style Considerations.**

Forty Hours devotion A eucharistic devotion consisting of continuous adoration of the Blessed Sacrament, solemnly exposed, by shifts of people for 40 hours. The length of the devotion comes from the calculation that Jesus was in the tomb for 40 hours before he rose from the dead.

See **liturgy, devotions** and **perpetual adoration.**

Foundations and Donors Interested in Catholic Activities See **FADICA.**

Franciscan Custody of the Holy Land See **"custos" of the Holy Land.**

fraternal organizations See individual entries in this book for Catholic and some other religious organizations.

In general, capitalize the proper names of such organizations. For example: *Knights of Columbus, Catholic Daughters of the Americas.* Also capitalize words denoting membership: *the Knights, a Knight, a Daughter.* These words are not being used in their common noun sense.

Capitalize the formal titles of officeholders when used before a name: *Supreme Knight Carl Anderson.* Do not, however, capitalize those titles that serve as clear functional descriptions of office, such as *chairman, president, vice president, secretary* or *treasurer,* unless the individual holds the position as a full-time post.

free-market (adj.)

Freemasonry See **Masons.**

Free the Fathers (www.ftf.org) Founded in 1983 to work for the release of clergy imprisoned in China, it is based in Chattanooga, Tenn.

free-trade (adj.) But North American Free Trade Agreement.

friars Members of any of several mendicant orders, especially the Augustinians, Carmelites, Dominicans and Franciscans. Do not use interchangeably with the word *monks.* Do not use as a title before a name. *Father* (for those ordained) and *Brother* (for the nonordained) take precedence as religious titles: *Among the Franciscan friars at the game were Father John Smith and Brother Patrick Murphy.* Do not capitalize *friar* except when it is used as part of a proper name: *Some Franciscan friars are members of the Order of Friars Minor. The Franciscan Friars of the Atonement is an order dedicated to Christian unity.*

friend of the court A person or organization which is not a party to a court case but speaks to the court as a bystander affected by or interested in the case. The plural is *friends of the court.* Hyphenate when used as a compound modifier: *a friend-of-the-court brief.* Avoid the Latin, *amicus curiae* (pl. *amici curiae).*

Friends United Meeting See **Quakers.**

fundamentalism The term originally identified two independent but allied strains of Protestant thought:

— As an early 20th-century reaction against liberals who were thought to be reducing Christianity to modern sociological or psychological ideas, fundamentalism sought to protect what its adherents considered the 12 "fundamentals" of the faith — such as the doctrine of human sinfulness, the need for grace and God's word and the sufficiency of Jesus Christ for salvation — from modern rationalism and naturalism.

— As a movement defending the literal interpretation, inerrancy and infallibility of Scripture, biblical fundamentalism opposed modern forms of biblical criticism and scientific theories of evolution seen as contrary to the Bible. See **evolution.**

When used as a neutral term without further qualification, *fundamentalist* generally refers to one who emphasizes a strict, literal interpretation of the Bible. If used in a broader sense it almost always carries pejorative connotations.

In general, do not describe any particular group as *fundamentalist* unless the group applies the word to itself. When a source uses the term to describe a religious attitude, movement or segment of Christianity, report what the source means by the word.

funeral liturgy, rites, services See **Mass** and **obituaries.**

G

G-7, G-8 See **Group of Seven, Group of Eight.**

G-24 See **Group of 24.**

Garden of Eden

gay See **homosexuality.**

Gehenna Also capitalize *Hades,* but lowercase *hell.*

Gen See **Focolare, Focolare movement.**

gender-neutral language See **inclusive language.**

general absolution See **absolution.**

gene therapy Research or procedures aimed at correcting faulty genes responsible for disease development.

genome All the DNA in an organism, including its genes. The *Human Genome Project,* completed in 2003, was a 13-year project, coordinated by the U.S. Department of Energy and the National Institutes of Health, which identified all the approximately 20,000-25,000 genes in human DNA and determined the sequence of the 3 billion chemical pairs that make up human DNA. See **gene therapy** and **genomics.**

genomics The study of genes and their function.

gentile Originally it meant *foreigner.* Hence its various meanings: among Jews, any person not a Jew, often specifically a Christian; among Latter-day Saints, any person not a Latter-day Saint. The former usage among Christians to mean anyone neither Jewish nor Christian — that is, a pagan or heathen — has largely disappeared.

Gethsemane, Garden of Gethsemane

Girls and Boys Town (www.girl sandboystown.org) The name since 2000 of the institution founded in 1922 as Boys Town by Father Edward J. Flanagan. The original Girls and Boys Town is located in Boys Town, Neb.

In 2005 there were 15 other Girls and Boys Town campuses around the country. The organization also operates Boys Town Research Hospital in Omaha, Neb.

Girl Scouts For *Catholic awards,* see that entry.

gnosticism The term early Christians used to describe various sects that arose in the second century which exalted arcane knowledge, mixing Christian belief with pagan speculation and theories. "Gnosis" is the Greek word for knowledge.

Repudiated as heretics, gnostics claimed that salvation could be obtained only through the knowledge and acceptance of certain divinely revealed mysteries which they alone possessed. Until the 20th century most of what was known about gnosticism came from the anti-gnostic writings of Christian theologians of the second and third centuries. That has changed since 1945, when an ancient library of about 50 gnostic works in Coptic, including the so-called Gospel of Thomas, was discovered in a cemetery near the modern Egyptian village of Nag Hammadi.

God, god(s) Capitalize *God* or words that mean *God* in reference to the divine being of all monotheistic religions. Capitalize all nouns used as names for this being: *God the Father, God the Son, Holy Ghost, Holy Spirit, Our Lord, Yahweh, Elohim, Jehovah, Allah,* etc. Lowercase personal pronouns: *he, him, thee, thou.* See **Jesus** for guidelines on lowercasing secondary names used descriptively rather than as names.

Lowercase *god, goddess* and their plural forms when referring to the deities of polytheistic religions and cultural mythologies, but capitalize their proper names: *the sun god; a goddess of fertility; Gaea, the earth goddess and mother of the Titans; the war god Thor, son of Odin.*

Lowercase *god* in metaphorical references: *Power is his god.*

Also lowercase in solid compounds such as *godchild, goddamned, godlike, godliness.* Capitalize in hyphenated compounds only when reference is clearly to the God of the Bible: *God-fearing, God-given.*

-goer No hyphen: *Massgoer, festivalgoer, churchgoer, moviegoer, theatergoer.*

Good Friday The day Christians commemorate the crucifixion of Jesus, the Friday before Easter. It is not part of Lent.

See **Easter triduum; Holy Week;** and **Lent, Lenten.**

Good Friday Agreement Sometimes called the *Belfast Agreement,* it was signed in Belfast, Northern Ireland, on April 10, 1998, by representatives of the British and Irish governments. It was approved by the voters of Northern Ireland and the Irish Republic in separate referendums in May 1998.

The agreement set up a power-sharing government in Northern Ireland and established the 108-member Northern Ireland Assembly, a North-South Ministerial Conference and a British-Irish Council. By late 2005, its full implementation was viewed more hopefully after the Irish Republican Army formally ended its campaign and destroyed its weapons.

good news Lowercase, even when referring to the Gospel.

Gospel(s), gospel Capitalize as a noun or an adjective when it refers to any or all of the first four books of the New Testament, the message they contain or an excerpt from them proclaimed in a religious service: *the synoptic Gospels, this Sunday's Gospel, preaching the Gospel, the Gospel message, the Gospel mandate to love your enemies, the Gospel story of the loaves and fishes.*

Lowercase in derived uses: *He is a gospel singer. That's the gospel truth. He preaches the church's social gospel.*

See **Bible** and **letter, epistle.**

Grail, The (www.grail-us.org) An international movement of women that works in educational, religious, cultural and social areas for the full development of all people. U.S. headquarters is in Loveland, Ohio.

Graymoor Ecumenical and Interreligious Institute (www.geii.org) It is located in New York.

Greek Catholics, Greek Catholic Church In some places, especially in Europe, it is not uncommon for people to use *Greek Catholic* as a way of referring collectively, not to inhabitants of Greece who are Catholic, but to the Eastern Catholic churches whose patrimony is the Byzantine tradition or to members of those churches. While this usage is legitimate, it can be confusing to those unfamiliar with it. Except in quoted matter, use *Byzantine* when referring to all churches of that family or the name of the individual church or churches referred to — Ukrainian, Ruthenian, Romanian, etc. When *Greek Catholic* is used in quotations, explain to the reader what is meant. For example, *He said, "It was wrong not to invite a single Greek (Byzantine) Catholic."*
See **Eastern Catholic churches.**

Greek Orthodox Archdiocese of America See **Orthodox churches.**

Greek Orthodox Church See **Orthodox churches.**

Gregorian chant Also called *plainsong* or *plainchant.* From the ninth century to the middle of the 20th century, this was the mainstay of liturgical music in the Latin Church, in part because of its rhythmic affinity to the Latin language. Its use in everyday worship has nearly disappeared with the introduction of modern languages into the liturgy following the Second Vatican Council. Gregorian chant is sung unharmonized. Originally it was sung without instrumental accompaniment.

Gregorian University See **Pontifical Gregorian University.**

Group of Seven, Group of Eight *G-7* or *G-8* is acceptable on second reference. On first reference or very high in a story explain what the group is. Originally it was composed of seven wealthy industrialized nations — the United States, United Kingdom, Germany, France, Japan, Italy and Canada — whose political leaders and finance ministers meet to develop policy agreements on global economic issues. Russia was added in 1997, but it has not participated in every meeting since then. When Russia participates it is the *G-8*; when it does not, it is the *G-7.*

Group of 24 *G-24* is acceptable on second reference. On first reference explain what the group is. It was formed in 1972 to represent the interests of developing countries in negotiations on international monetary affairs. Members are: Algeria, Argentina, Brazil, Colombia, Democratic Republic of Congo, Egypt, Ethiopia, Gabon, Ghana, Guatemala, India, Iran, Ivory Coast, Lebanon, Mexico, Nigeria, Pakistan, Peru, Philippines, South Africa, Sri Lanka, Syria, Trinidad and Tobago, and Venezuela.

Guard of Honor of the Immaculate Heart of Mary Headquarters is in New York.

Hades Also capitalize *Gehenna,* but lowercase *hell.*

Hail Mary, Hail Marys

hallelujah See **alleluia, hallelujah.**

hanged, hung Use *hanged* as the past tense of *hang* only when referring to an individual suspended by the neck from a rope until dead.

Hung is the correct past tense for all other uses. Note that Christ was *hung* on a cross: The soldiers did not suspend him by the neck from a rope.

Hansen's disease See **leper, leprosy.**

Hanukkah Preferred spelling for the eight-day Jewish Feast of Lights, commemorating the rededication of the Temple by Judas Maccabaeus in 165 B.C. Other variants include *Chanukah* and *Hanukka.*

The feast occurs in December or late November. On the eve of each successive day of the feast, one more candle on the nine-candle Hanukkah menorah is lighted, so that on the eve of the eighth day all nine — the kindling candle plus the eight used to mark the days — are lighted.

Most non-Jewish calendars list only the first day of the feast as Hanukkah.

Hasidic Jews See **Judaism.**

he, him, his Lowercase personal pronouns referring to God.
See **God, god(s).**

health care No hyphen, even in compound modifiers.

heaven

heavenly bodies See **earth.**

Heavily Indebted Poor Countries Initiative. *HIPC Initiative* is acceptable on second reference for this debt reduction plan developed by the World Bank and International Monetary Fund in 1996 to help heavily indebted poor countries reduce their foreign debt if they meet certain conditions. Revisions made in 1999 provided for faster, deeper and broader relief and linked external debt relief to internal poverty reduction and social development in eligible countries. The revised program is called the *Enhanced HIPC Initiative.* Apart from references to the initiative, do not use *HIPC* (or *HIPCs*) as shorthand for *heavily indebted poor country* (or *countries*) except in quoted matter. As of mid-2005, 27 of 38 potentially eligible countries had received debt reductions under the initiative.

Hebrew See **Jewish, Hebrew, Judaic.**

Hebrew Scriptures See **Bible.**

hell Lowercase, but capitalize *Gehenna* and *Hades.*

her Except in quoted matter, use *it,* not *her,* to refer to the Catholic Church.

here Do not use as a form of reference to the location of the story because it forces readers to refer back to the dateline. If you must refer to the location within a story, repeat the name of the community.

heresy Defined by the Code of Canon Law as "the obstinate denial or obstinate doubt after the reception of baptism of some truth which is to be believed by divine and Catholic faith." A person who is guilty of heresy is a *heretic*. Care must be taken in using the terms, however, because opinions may vary about whether denial of a particular belief constitutes *heresy*.

hermeneutics A technical term best avoided when possible. In Scripture scholarship it means the study of different methods of analyzing and interpreting the Bible.

hermit The adjective is *hermitic* or *hermitical*. Preferred to *eremite, eremitic* or *anchorite, anchoritic* in references to those who live a life of religious consecration in solitude.

Hermitic life was a standard form of religious consecration in the early centuries of Christianity. In the West it has been largely obscured by the communal forms of monasticism, apart from minor hermitic revivals in the 11th and 13th-14th centuries. Canon 603 of the 1983 Code of Canon Law, responding to some renewed interest in hermitic life, said anyone taking religious vows as a hermit should be under the direction of the local bishop. See **cenobite.**

Do not confuse *hermitic* with *hermetic,* which refers to alchemy, magic or airtight seals.

hierarchy Lowercase. In Catholic practice the term is used most commonly to refer collectively to the bishops of the world or of a particular region. In technical uses, however, it may refer to all those who are ordained: deacons and priests as well as bishops.

In Eastern Catholic churches bishops are sometimes referred to as *hierarchs*. The term may also apply to ordained religious superiors or diocesan administrators who are not bishops, but in most news contexts the more familiar term *bishops* can be used. See **council of hierarchs.**

Hindu, Hinduism The chief religion in India and the religious basis of its caste system, Hinduism is notable among the non-Christian religions for its mysticism and spiritual emphasis. Hindus worldwide may number more than 760 million. Among world religions only Christianity and Islam have more adherents. In North America there are an estimated 1.1 million Hindus.

Of the major world religions Hinduism is the oldest and may date back to prehistoric times. Its essence is spiritual self-discovery. One of its central teachings is reincarnation: The soul is immortal and enters a new body when the old one dies. It may be reincarnated in human or animal form. An individual's karma, or fate in the next life, is determined by every action and thought in this life. The caste, or social status into which a person is born, is the result of actions in the previous incarnation.

Reincarnation continues until a soul attains perfection through meditation and renunciation. This endpoint of the cycle, called "moksha," or liberation, is a state of complete enlightenment and peace in which the soul is united with the one absolute being, the Brahman. Yoga is one of the main schools of philosophy and spiritual discipline developed in Hinduism to achieve spiritual perfection.

The Brahman, which is impersonal, is manifested in three main forms: Brahma, the god of creation; Vishnu, the god of preservation; and Siva, the god of destruction. One of Vishnu's most important incarnations is Krishna, chief hero of Hinduism. The mother goddess, Devi, has several personifications, among them Uma, a benevolent force, and Durga or Kali, a destructive force. While Hindu philosophers emphasize the higher deities and some approach monotheism, in popular religious practice there are innumerable other deities and saints who receive prayers and offerings. In Hindu belief animals also have souls and may be worshiped as gods.

Chief writings of Hinduism are the Vedas, the Puranas or Epics, the Ramayana, the Mahabharata, the Bhagavad-Gita and the Manu Smriti.

The Vedas are collections of poetry and prose that deal with ritual, theology and philosophy. They include hymns called mantras; the Brahmanas, which deal mainly with religious ritual; the Aranyakas, which focus on meditation and asceticism; and the Upanishads, philosophical and mystical teachings.

Hindu religious and social law, including the Indian caste system, is based on the Manu Smriti.

Religious practice in Hinduism varies widely. Among the thousands of sects, some have almost no structure while others are highly organized. There is no single creed or doctrine that can be cited as defining Hinduism.

Ritual leaders in both temples and homes are often from the Brahman, or priestly, caste. Holy men who are spiritual teachers often are called gurus. Because of the diversity of practice, however, there is no single classification of religious leaders and their roles.

In the 1990s, the Vatican began sending greetings to Hindu leaders to mark Diwali, the Hindu feast commemorating the victory of light over darkness.

See **Brahma, Brahman.**

HIPC Initiative See **Heavily Indebted Poor Countries Initiative.**

His ... When used as part of a formal title of respect *(His Holiness, His Majesty, His Excellency,* etc.), *His* should be capitalized, but such deferential titles are out of place in news writing except in quoted material. See separate entries in this book under the main word for formal titles sometimes applied to members of the clergy.

Hispanic Use *Hispanic* as a noun or adjective when referring to U.S. residents who trace their origins, especially their cultural origins, to Spain or to any country of Latin America. The preferred term in the Western United States, however, is *Latino.* Use this and similar terms — *Latina, Latinos, Latinas* — only in reference to groups that are exclusively Western. However, in popular usage *Hispanic* and *Latino* are becoming synonymous. In common usage, the term *Hispanic* traces its roots to the U.S. Census Bureau, which began using this term as a catch-all phrase for all Spanish-speaking immigrants and their descendants. In some documents, the U.S. bishops' Secretariat for Hispanic Affairs has begun using the term *Hispanic/Latino,* but retains *Hispanic* in its formal name.

Spanish-speaking is not strictly synonymous with *Hispanic,* since not all Hispanics in the United States speak Spanish or have it as their first language. Some speak only English. Portuguese is the native language of those from Brazil.

See **Chicano, Chicanos** and **Latino, Latinos.**

HIV Acceptable on all references, but it must be explained as *human immunodeficiency virus* or *the virus that causes AIDS.* Avoid the redundant *HIV virus.*

See **AIDS, HIV.**

holidays, holy days Capitalize the names of designated days of celebration or remembrance. Also capitalize the word *day* or *eve* if used as part of the name. Some examples: *New Year's Eve, New Year's Day, April Fools' Day, Mother's Day, May Day, Ash Wednesday, Easter, St. Patrick's Day, Hanukkah.*

Do not capitalize *eve* in *eve of* phrases: *Christmas Eve,* but: *the eve of Christmas.*

Do not capitalize *feast* when it precedes the name of a day of Christian religious observance: It is not part of the proper name. It may be capitalized, however, in other contexts if it is an integral part of the name, such as the *Feast of Lots* and *Feast of Lights* in Judaism. These holidays are never known simply as *Lots* or *Lights.* See **feast of; Jewish holy days;** and individual entries listed there.

The *holy days of obligation* in Latin-rite Catholic usage are feasts on which Catholics are obliged to assist at Mass. In the United States these are: Mary Mother of God, Jan. 1; Ascension (of the Lord), 40 days after Easter; Assumption (of the Blessed Virgin Mary), Aug. 15; All Saints' Day, Nov. 1; Immaculate Conception (of the Blessed Virgin Mary), Dec. 8; and Christmas (the Nativity of Jesus), Dec. 25.

In addition to these, there are four other holy days of obligation prescribed in the general law of the Latin Church which are observed differently in the United States. Two of these — St. Joseph, March 19, and Sts. Peter and Paul, June 29 — are observed by U.S. Catholics on the same days but without the obligation to assist at Mass. For Epiphany, Jan. 6 in the general church calendar, the observance and obligation are transferred to the first Sunday after Jan. 1. For the Body and Blood of Christ, the second Thursday after Pentecost in the general calendar, the observance and the Mass obligation are transferred to the following Sunday.

In other countries and different U.S. dioceses, other variations on the holy days of obligation may occur.

In church law, Sundays of the year and the holy days of obligation together are described as the *days of precept.*

Holy days of obligation common to the Eastern Catholic churches, beyond Sundays, are the feasts of: Epiphany, Jan. 6; Ascension, 40 days after Easter; Holy Apostles Peter and Paul, June 29; the Dormition of Holy Mary Mother of God, Aug. 15; and Christmas (the Nativity), Dec. 25. As in the Latin Church, an Eastern church can, with Vatican approval, suppress a holy day of obligation or transfer its observance to Sunday. Some Eastern churches celebrate Jan. 6 as the feast of the Theophany, which refers to the baptism of Jesus, not to the visit of the Magi.

The *federal legal holidays* in the United States are: New Year's Day, Martin Luther King Jr. Day, Washington's Birthday, Memorial Day, Independence Day, Labor Day, Columbus Day, Veterans Day (no apostrophe), Thanksgiving and Christmas. The extent to which the federal holiday calendar is observed by states or by private employers varies. The holiday observance for Washington's Birthday often is called *Presidents Day* (no apostrophe), but that is not the official federal designation.

Holiness A formal term of respect for a pope or an Orthodox patriarch, it should not be used in news stories except in quoted matter. If used, it should be capitalized along with the preceding modifier *His* or *Your: "I gave the message to His Holiness personally," she said.* The parallel term of respect for the ecumenical patriarch of Constantinople is *His All Holiness.*

See **Beatitude, beatitude**; **Eminence;** and **Excellence, Excellency.**

holism, holistic Not *wholism, wholistic.*

Holocaust The killing of 6 million Jews before and during World War II in the Nazi attempt to exterminate the race. The Hebrew word for it, *Shoah,* should be capitalized and explained if used. A recently begun religious observance recalling the Shoah is called *Yom Hashoah.* See **Shoah** and **Yom Hashoah.**

Lowercase *holocaust* when used in the common meanings of a *burnt offering* or a *great loss of life, especially by fire.*

Holy, holy When this adjective of reverence is inextricably or almost always linked with a noun to form a proper name, the adjective is capitalized along with the noun; if the adjective is dispensable, it is treated as merely descriptive and lowercased.

For example, *Eucharist, Communion, Bible, Scripture(s)* and *Mass* can stand alone as proper names. If they are modified by *holy,* it is merely descriptive and is not capitalized. Similarly, common nouns such as *baptism, orders, matrimony, church* and *martyrs* have the same meaning when modified by *holy.* It is merely descriptive and does not give the resulting phrase the character of a proper name: Neither the adjective nor the noun is capitalized.

When *holy* is placed before some common nouns, however — such as *land, father, see, sepulcher* and *door* — the resulting phrase is a proper name for a unique entity: *Holy Land, Holy Father,* etc.

For the most common uses, see individual entries in this stylebook. The same general principles apply to *sacred.* See **sacred, Sacred.**

SPECIAL CASES: Although *Spirit* and *Trinity* can stand alone as proper names, *Holy Spirit* and *Holy Trinity* also are accepted as integral proper names by almost universal usage. For capitalization of *holy* when used before *Communion* as the name of a church service, see **holy Communion** and **Mass.**

Holy Childhood Association (www.worldmissions-catholicchurch.org/hca) Acceptable on all references to the *Pontifical Association of the Holy Childhood.* Founded in 1843 to promote missionary awareness among Catholic children and to support missionary work with children, it is one of the four *pontifical missionary societies* governed by the Vatican Congregation for the Evangelization of Peoples. U.S. headquarters is in New York.

See **pontifical missionary societies.**

holy Communion Capitalize *holy* only when the term is used, as in the Lutheran churches, to refer to a full church service. For the sacrament, *Communion* is also acceptable on all references.

See **church services** and **sacraments,** but especially the note at the end of **Mass.**

holy days See **holidays, holy days.**

Holy Door A large bronze door, to the right of the main entrance to St.

Peter's Basilica, which is sealed with bricks except during a holy year. The pope ceremonially removes the brick seal to start a holy year and reseals the door at the end of the year. Capitalize.

See **holy year.**

Holy Family

Holy Father Like other honorific titles, this title of respect for the pope should not be used except in quoted matter or in special contexts for the sake of a particular literary effect. When it is used, it should be capitalized.

Use *the pope* or *the pontiff,* or name the individual: *Pope John XXIII.*

See **pontiff** and **pope.**

Holy Ghost See **Holy Spirit.**

Holy Hour A devotional exercise made up of meditation, vocal prayer and singing, with exposition of the Blessed Sacrament. It draws its inspiration from Christ's words to the apostles at Gethsemane: "Can you not watch one hour with me?" Although it can take place at any hour, Thursday or Friday evening is the preferred time, because of the link to Christ's passion.

Holy Land A religious term for the region east of the Mediterranean that is sacred in varying degrees to Judaism, Christianity and Islam. Always capitalize. Broadly speaking it means biblical Palestine, which corresponds roughly to the modern state of Israel and the Palestinian and occupied territories. In popular Christian usage it refers primarily to the area encompassing sites associated with the life of Jesus.

Do not use in datelines. Do not use in text except in quoted matter or in contexts in which the area's religious or biblical importance is of primary concern: *On a pilgrimage to the Holy Land, they visited Jerusalem, Nazareth and Bethlehem.* Many popular Holy Land sites are in Israel. Notable exceptions are Bethlehem and Jericho, both in the Palestinian Territories.

See **Israel** and **Jerusalem.**

Holy Name Society, National Association of the (www.holy namesociety.info) Founded to make reparation for misuse of Jesus' name, it seeks to deepen the spiritual life of its members by organizing retreats, Holy Hours and other spiritual and devotional exercises at the parish and diocesan level. In 2005, the national communications office was in Baltimore and its newsletter was published in Buffalo, N.Y.

holy oils The collective term for the oils used in baptism, confirmation (or chrismation), ordination of priests or bishops and the anointing of the sick. In the Latin Church, these are blessed by the bishop at the *chrism Mass*, ordinarily celebrated on the morning of Holy Thursday.

See **chrism Mass.**

holy orders Also called *orders* or *the sacrament of orders.* Often the word *holy* must be added to avoid confusion with other meanings of *order.*

In the Catholic and Orthodox traditions there are three orders, each part of the one sacrament: deacon, priest or presbyter and bishop. In those traditions, only a bishop can confer any order. Protestant churches generally do not consider ordination a sacrament as Catholics do, but many have ordained ministries. See entries for individual denominations.

In the Catholic Church ordination is a prerequisite for many forms of liturgical or sacramental leadership, governance and authoritative teaching. All those ordained are technically members of the clergy and of the hierarchy. But *clergy* often is used in a popular sense to refer only to priests or to priests and bishops, and *hierarchy* is often used as a synonym for bishops.

See **Catholic Church; clergy; deacon, diaconate; hierarchy;** and **sacraments.**

Holy See Always capitalize. This term of reverence for the Diocese of Rome, as the chief diocese of Catholic Christendom, is used to refer to the pope and his Curia — congregations, tribunals and offices — in their role of authority over and service to the Catholic Church around the world.

In most news contexts *the Vatican* is a preferable synonym. The more precise term *Holy See* may be needed, however, if the context requires a clear distinction between the central offices serving the whole church and those of the local government of Vatican City State — as in stories about the finances of the Holy See.

Another synonym, *Apostolic See,* should be avoided except in quoted matter.

See **Catholic Church; Rome, Diocese of; Vatican City State;** and **Appendix G: Vatican Agencies.**

Holy Spirit Now preferred over *Holy Ghost* in most usage. *Holy Ghost* may be used in quoted matter or as part of the proper name of an organization or institution. When used alone, *Spirit* should be capitalized when it refers to the Holy Spirit.

Holy Spirit Association for the Unification of World Christianity See **Family Federation for World Peace and Unification.**

Holy Trinity Capitalize when used, but *the Trinity* is sufficient outside quotes or proper names in which *Holy* is used, such as *Holy Trinity Church.*

Holy Week The week before Easter, beginning with Palm Sunday, also called Passion Sunday. Always capitalize. The other days: Monday, Tuesday and Wednesday of Holy Week, Holy Thursday or Maundy Thursday, Good Friday and Holy Saturday, also called the vigil of Easter.

In the Eastern Catholic and Orthodox churches, Holy Week is not part of Lent. In the Latin Church, Lent ends at the start of the Mass of the Lord's Supper on Holy Thursday evening, when the Easter triduum starts.

See **Lent, Lenten.**

holy year *Holy* or *jubilee years* are called by the pope — ordinarily every 25 years (1900, 1925, 1950, 1975). In 1933 and 1983 popes called extraordinary holy years to mark the 1,900th and 1,950th anniversaries of Christ's death and resurrection. Lowercase indefinite or plural references, but capitalize all references to a specific holy year: *Workers of the world should be united for peace, said Pope John Paul II in a Holy Year celebration for workers.*

For Holy Year 2000, also capitalize *Great Jubilee of the Year 2000,* a formal designation, but lowercase other forms of reference, such as *the jubilee year, the year of jubilee.*

Traditionally a holy year begins with the pope opening the Holy Door of St. Peter's Basilica on Christmas Eve and ends with the sealing of the door one year later. See **Holy Door.**

home schooling, home school, home-schooler, home-schooled

homosexuality Many Christian churches in recent years have faced divisive struggles over issues relating to homosexual orientation and activity, especially whether to recognize homosexual unions, whether to bless such unions and whether to admit to church ministry individuals who are homosexually active.

The Catechism of the Catholic Church summarizes key points of Catholic teaching on the subject. It calls homosexual acts "intrinsically disordered" but says men and women who have deep-seated homosexual tendencies "must be accepted with respect, compassion and sensitivity. Every sign of unjust discrimination in their regard should be avoided." Church leaders have supported some forms of legislation to protect homosexuals against violence and unjust discrimination, but they have opposed efforts to legalize marriage for homosexuals and some forms of legislation that they regard as eroding traditional family status and sanctioning homosexual behavior.

Gay and *lesbian* are acceptable as adjectives or nouns in references to male or female homosexuals, respectively, but should be used sparingly, since some object to use of the words as synonyms for *homosexual*.

Among the unofficial support groups of homosexual Catholics are Courage, which supports church teaching on abstinence from homosexual activity, and Dignity, which since 1989 has held the position "that we can express our sexuality physically in a unitive manner that is loving, life-giving and life-affirming."

See **Courage; Dignity; Encourage;** and **Rainbow Sash.**

"Humanae Vitae" This 1968 encyclical by Pope Paul VI is on married love and procreation. It reaffirmed church teaching that artificial contraception is morally wrong. In English its title means *of human life.* Use the Latin title, but within the story explain the content of the encyclical.

Avoid calling it an encyclical "on artificial contraception," which implies that the whole encyclical was on that topic.

Avoid saying that the encyclical or the church "bans" artificial contraception. This suggests a disciplinary or legislative prohibition rather than a moral teaching. Refer to the first paragraph of this entry for model language.

See **artificial contraception; birth control;** and **natural family planning.**

Human Genome Project See **genome.**

Hungarian Catholic League of America Headquarters is in Providence, R.I.

hymns When writing about Scripture texts or standard prayers set to music without reference to a specific melodic version, capitalize but do not place in quotation marks unless such marks are needed for a particular foreign-language title. *The choir sang the Our Father and the Agnus Dei.*

See **Mass** and **prayers** for guidelines on capitalization and foreign-language prayer titles.

When writing about a hymn originally written as a song or about a specific musical composition of a prayer, place the title in quotation marks: *They sang "Silent Night" and Gounod's "Ave Maria."*

I

ICEL See **International Commission on English in the Liturgy.**

ICET Do not use. See **International Consultation on English Texts.**

illicit See **valid, licit.**

imam Any Muslim is an *imam* when he leads prayer in a mosque. Every mosque has at least one designated imam, but if no regular imam is present any suitable male can be the imam. Some who hold stable positions as prayer leaders or as community religious leaders use *imam* as a title. Capitalize only when it is used as the formal title before a name.
See **Islam** and **religious titles.**

Immaculate Conception A Catholic dogma concerning Mary and the name of a feast in her honor celebrated Dec. 8. It refers to the Catholic belief that Mary, by special divine favor in anticipation of her role in salvation, was without sin from the moment she was conceived.

Do not confuse this, as many do, with the *virgin birth,* which refers to the Christian belief that even after conceiving and bearing Jesus, Mary remained a virgin. See **virgin birth.**

The declaration of the Immaculate Conception as a defined dogma of faith by Pope Pius IX in 1854 is seen as an obstacle to Christian unity by many Protestants and Orthodox.

imprimatur, "nihil obstat" No quotes around *imprimatur,* a Latin word that has become part of standard English, but explain its meaning.

In Catholic usage the *imprima-* *tur,* which means "let it be printed," is official permission by the competent church authority to publish a book which touches on matters of Catholic faith or moral teaching. The main church laws governing the imprimatur are found in Canons 822-832 of the 1983 Code of Canon Law.

In U.S. practice, the imprimatur is usually given by the bishop of the place where the book is published. Some authors, particularly diocesan priests, deacons and men religious, seek the imprimatur from their own bishop or religious superior. Liturgical books and Scripture translations require approval by a bishops' conference or the Holy See.

The *"nihil obstat,"* Latin for "nothing stands in the way," is a judgment by an official church censor that a book does not contain errors in faith or moral teaching. Censors are theologians appointed by diocesan bishops, religious superiors or other competent church authorities to review new books. See **censer, censor, censure.**

Other terms of permission to publish once commonly used for Catholic books: *"Imprimi potest" (it can be printed)* and *"cum permissu superioris" (with the superior's permission).*

incardination Legal term in the Latin Church for the attachment of a deacon or priest to his diocese, religious institute or society, personal prelature or (in some cases) secular institute. Church law forbids "unattached or transient clerics." A cleric who transfers from one jurisdiction to another must be simultaneously *incardinated in* the one he transfers to and *excardinated from* the one he leaves.

A diocesan priest who joins a secular institute remains incardinated in his diocese unless he receives a special Vatican grant for incardination into the institute.

In the Eastern Catholic churches, *enrollment* is the term used for a cleric's attachment to his eparchy, monastery, religious order, etc.

Incarnation Literally "enfleshment," this refers to the Christian belief that Jesus was both fully human and fully divine. Christmas is sometimes called the feast of the Incarnation. Capitalize only when there is no reference to Jesus Christ in the sentence: *He spoke about the Incarnation* but *Christians believe in Jesus' incarnation and resurrection.*

incense Use as a verb only in the sense of *arouse anger.*

See **censer, censor, censure.**

inclusive language Also called *gender-neutral language.* It denotes word usage which does not ascribe maleness or femaleness to mixed groups, inanimate objects or individuals whose gender is unknown or undefined. It refers especially to avoidance of the tendency in most cultures to use male terms when referring to mixed groups or undefined individuals. For example: *Everyone is the master of his own fate. I love all mankind. God created man. We are all brothers.*

In English-speaking church circles, debates over inclusive language have focused particularly on terminology used in worship, Scripture translations and official statements by church authorities. At issue are the use of male terms for God and the use of female terms for the church as well as the use of male terms for mixed groups or undefined individuals.

This entry addresses three issues:

news-writing style, translations from other languages and news coverage of debates about gender in language.

WRITING STYLE: Whenever possible, avoid using gender-related terms to refer to mixed groups of people or to individuals whose gender is unknown or undefined. At the same time, do so as unobtrusively as possible. Do not use awkward, stilted or grammatically incorrect constructions to avoid the use of a gender-related word.

Often gender-neutral phrasing is easy. Sometimes creative reconstruction of a whole sentence or paragraph is needed to avoid an undesirable gender-related term or phrase.

It is grammatically correct to say *man, men, mankind* to refer to all members of the human race, but it is better to use gender-neutral words such as *the human race, people, all people.* In some contexts *persons* or *humankind* may be acceptable, but usually in a news context these would appear stilted or awkward and should be avoided. Do not manufacture words such as *firepeople* or *waitperson.* See **layman, laywoman, layperson** and **-person, -people**.

The pronoun *it* is always correct in English when referring to an inanimate object or a group or organization made up of people. Do not use *she* for a hurricane, ship, church, nation, etc., except in quoted matter.

In news writing the phrase *he or she* is rarely acceptable outside quoted matter if the simple and grammatically correct *he* conveys the meaning. Never use awkward forms with slashes, hyphens or parentheses, such as: *(s)he, s-he, his/her, him/her, he(she),* etc. Do not use a plural pronoun when the referent is singular. Do not replace the relative pronoun with an indefinite pronoun such as *one, one's* or *oneself.*

WRONG: *Every leader is responsible to their constituents.*

RIGHT: *Every leader is responsible to his constituents.*

BUT BETTER: *All leaders are responsible to their constituents.*

WRONG: *Each person must account for one's actions.*

RIGHT: *Each person must account for his actions.*

BUT BETTER: *People have to account for their actions.*

If a speaker regularly uses bad grammar to avoid masculine pronouns, in many cases it may be better to paraphrase than to correct the grammar within quotations.

TRANSLATIONS: In general, follow the same rules for translation as for news writing: Gender-neutral terms are preferable to gender-related terms if they accurately convey the meaning of the original and do not result in awkward, stilted or ungrammatical English.

Do not impose on a translation a gender neutrality which was not in the original. If the pope says, *"carissimi fratelli,"* it means *dear brothers,* not *dear brothers and sisters.* If he says *"uomini,"* it can be translated as *people* unless it appears in a context that clearly refers only to *men.*

COVERING NEWS ABOUT GENDER AND LANGUAGE: The opposite of *gender-neutral* is *gender-specific* or *gender-related,* not *sexist.* The terms *sexist* and *nonsexist* imply value judgments and should not be used without attribution to the person expressing those views. If *inclusive* is used, its opposite is *exclusive.*

See **sexism, sexist language.**

Index of Forbidden Books First published in 1559 and periodically revised and updated, the index was an official list of books drawn up by the Vatican which were considered dangerous to faith or morals and could not be read by Catholics without special permission. Its last revision was published in 1948. In 1966 the Vatican's doctrinal congregation decided to discontinue the index.

Because it is a reference work, *Index of Forbidden Books* stands without quotation marks. On second reference *the index* is acceptable. The English form is preferred to the Latin, *Index Librorum Prohibitorum.*

Indians *American Indian* is preferred over *Native American* for native peoples in the United States. In Canada, among preferred forms of reference are *native peoples* and *First Nations. Native American* is acceptable in quotes and in names of organizations. Lowercase *native* in all other uses.

Customs, rituals, dress, crafts, art forms and languages may vary greatly from tribe to tribe and region to region. Whenever possible, be specific: *a Hopi dance, a Sioux word, a Mohawk carving.*

In writing news about American Indians, avoid disparaging or offensive words such as *brave, redskin, squaw, wampum* or *warpath.*

indulgence(s) Canon 992 of the Catholic Church's Code of Canon Law says, "An indulgence is a remission before God of the temporal punishment for sin, the guilt of which is already forgiven." It adds that this is done "under certain and definite conditions with the help of the church which ... dispenses and applies authoritatively the treasury of the satisfactions of Christ and the saints."

If all punishment is remitted, the indulgence is described as *plenary.* If only part is remitted, it is called *partial.*

In the complex history of indulgences, the granting of them in return for contributions to church projects in the late Middle Ages was one of the abuses that helped spark the Reformation. The Catholic teaching on indulgences remains a source of division between Catholic and non-Catholic churches.

indult In church law it is an exemption from a general requirement granted by a church authority, such as the pope or a bishop, to the Catholics of a particular place or group. In most news contexts if the term is used it must be explained. Usually it is preferable to substitute a more familiar phrase such as *church permission, Vatican permission, permission from the bishop.*

infallibility See **Catholic Church.**

Inner Light See **Quakers.**

"in pectore" The appropriate English idiom to translate this Latin phrase is *in the heart, in his heart* or *secretly.* A translation should be given if either the Latin phrase or its Italian equivalent, "in petto," is used.

When a pope announces that he has named a cardinal "in pectore," the person secretly named is not a cardinal in fact. He does not become a cardinal until he is named publicly and installed. If he or the pope should die before he is named publicly, he never becomes a cardinal. Until he is installed he has no standing in the College of Cardinals and cannot participate in its activities. The only effect of having been named a cardinal "in pectore" is that if he is actually installed in the College of Cardinals he gains seniority retroactively to the time he was named "in pectore."

Because his status is that of a secret *cardinal-designate,* not an actual cardinal, he should not be counted when the number of cardinals is given. When the existence of a secretly named cardinal is relevant to a story, his status is that of an addendum or footnote to the actual list, not an integral part of the College of Cardinals.

See **cardinal** and **Catholic Church.**

institute The Code of Canon Law defines a *religious institute* as "a society in which members, according to proper law, pronounce public vows ... and live a life in common as brothers or sisters." Apart from technical uses, religious institutes are more commonly referred to as *religious orders* or *congregations.* General church law governing such institutes is contained in Canons 607-709 of the code. See **order, congregation, society; religious;** and **secular institutes.**

Institute is also the comprehensive term in the Eastern Catholic churches for monasteries, religious orders and congregations, societies of common life and secular institutes. Canons 410-572 of the Code of Canons of the Eastern Churches govern such institutes. In the Eastern traditions monastic life has special prominence among the forms of consecrated life.

Institute for Continuing Theological Education (www.pnac.org/general/institute.htm) Established in 1970, it is sponsored by the Pontifical North American College in Rome. Twice a year it offers a three-month program of theological updating in Rome for U.S. priests.

Institute for the Works of Religion Use this form, not variations, when there is need to give the proper name for the Vatican bank. In most cases *Vatican bank* (lowercase *b)* is sufficient. Avoid the initials *IOR* except in quoted matter. If used, *IOR* must be explained as the initials of the bank's name in Italian.

See **Vatican bank** and **Appendix G: Vatican Agencies.**

Institute of Hispanic Liturgy (http://liturgia.cua.edu) Use this name rather than the Spanish *Instituto de Liturgia Hispana.* It is located in Washington.

Institute on Religion and Democracy (www.ird-renew.org) An ecumenical alliance of U.S. Christians working to reform their churches' social witness in line with the institute's dual commitment to historic Christian teachings and to democracy. It is located in Washington.

Institute on Religious Life (www.religiouslife.com) Founded in 1974 to promote religious vocations and adherence to church teaching on religious life. It is located in Chicago.

"instrumentum laboris" A Latin term used by the Holy See to identify a *working paper* or *working document,* usually a document sent out beforehand to provide a common basis for discussion at an international meeting. Ordinarily the Latin term is best avoided in news writing in favor of descriptive English phrases.

See **"lineamenta"** and **schema.**

intelligent design See **evolution.**

intercommunion In accord with Webster's New World use this form, not *inter-Communion,* for the agreement or practice of two ecclesial communions by which each admits members of the other communion to its sacraments. Mutual participation in the Eucharist *(Communion)* is usu-

ally the most significant element of the broader mutual sharing *(intercommunion)* of faith and life to which the word refers.

The Methodist Church practices what it calls *open communion,* welcoming to its sacraments Christians of any denomination.

The Catholic Church does not practice intercommunion in a general way. On an individual basis, if certain conditions are met it may permit a Catholic to receive a sacrament in another ecclesial community or a non-Catholic to receive certain sacraments in the Catholic Church. This practice is more accurately described as *admission to the sacraments,* since it does not refer to a general reciprocal arrangement for all members of the two ecclesial communities.

Much news about *intercommunion* in the Catholic Church concerns the practice of unauthorized *eucharistic sharing* by individual Catholics at non-Catholic services or non-Catholics at Catholic services. In those cases *intercommunion* is a correct but loose term, and the more precise phrase *eucharistic sharing* is preferred. When reporting on a practice that is unauthorized, make that fact clear in the story.

See **Communion, communion** and **eucharistic sharing.**

interdenominational, interfaith *Interdenominational* is a term used mostly by American Protestants. It means *having the support or participation of more than one denomination.* It is used properly only to refer to the involvement of various Christian Protestant denominations, although at times it is used more loosely to include Catholic or Orthodox churches as well. It should never be used to refer to a group that includes non-Christians.

Interfaith means *having the sup-*

port or participation of more than one faith group. It may be used with reference to groups composed only of Christians or to groups composed of Christians and non-Christians.

Both *interdenominational* and *interfaith* refer to an organization or activity from the standpoint of the religious affiliation of its participants or supporters. If you wish to refer to an organization or activity in terms of a religious purpose of fellowship, understanding, etc., the more appropriate term may be *ecumenical* or *interreligious.* See **denomination** and **ecumenical, interreligious.**

interdicasterial *Dicastery* is a Vatican term for the congregations and other major departments of the Roman Curia. Following the 1988 Curia reforms, several *permanent interdicasterial commissions* have been formed to provide a means for better communication and cooperation among those departments on matters where their areas of competency overlap. A 1997 Vatican instruction on distinctions between lay and priestly ministry was issued by an ad hoc interdicasterial commission composed of leaders of six Vatican congregations and two pontifical councils.

Standard English dictionaries do not define *dicastery* in the way it is used by the Vatican and do not have an entry for *interdicasterial.* When *interdicasterial* must be used, explain that it means *interdepartmental.* Often it is more helpful to the reader to use other descriptive phrases instead, such *as a Vatican commission composed of the heads of six Vatican agencies.*

The permanent interdicasterial commissions and their members are listed at the end of the section on congregations in the Annuario.

See **dicastery** and **Appendix G: Vatican Agencies.**

interdict An extreme form of church penalty, reserved for especially serious offenses committed by church members. It is one of three ecclesiastical censures. The other two are excommunication and suspension. These punishments are known as "medicinal penalties," since they are intended to heal the harm caused by the offense and at the same time lead the offender to a return to good standing within the church. Excommunication and interdict can be incurred by any believer, but suspension is reserved to clerics.

The penalty exists in two forms: *"ferendae sententiae,"* meaning that it is imposed following a formal judicial or administrative process, and *"latae sententiae,"* meaning that it is incurred automatically at the time of the offense. Some violations of church law that can bring about an interdict are provoking disobedience of ecclesiastical superiors, publicly inciting opposition to church authority, promoting or taking office in a forbidden society, or celebrating or receiving a sacrament through simony. Refer to someone under interdict as *the interdicted person.*

An interdict entails the same liturgical restrictions as excommunication. Also, an interdicted person cannot act as a sponsor in baptism or confirmation. However, the interdict does not affect any governmental functions of governance or personal prerogatives in the church, such as privileges, eligibility for various offices or the receiving of income. The 1983 Code of Canon Law reaffirmed personal interdicts but did not retain local interdicts, that is, censures of groups of believers who live in a certain territory. See **excommunication** and **suspended priests**.

Interfaith Alliance (www.inter faithalliance.org) Do not capitalize

The in the name. Headquarters is in Washington.

International Anglican-Roman Catholic Commission for Unity and Mission See **Anglican Communion.**

International Catholic Charismatic Renewal Services (www.iccrs.org) Located in Rome.

International Catholic Child Bureau (www.bice.org) Headquarters is in Brussels, Belgium, with other offices in Geneva and Paris.

International Catholic Committee of Nurses and Medico-Social Assistants Headquarters is in Brussels, Belgium.

International Catholic Conference of Scouting (www.cics.org) Headquarters is in Rome.

International Catholic Deaf Association (www.icda-usa.org) U.S. headquarters is in Landover Hills, Md.

International Catholic Federation of Youth Organizations (www.fimcap.org) Headquarters is in Antwerp, Belgium.

International Catholic-Jewish Liaison Committee Established in December 1970 as the official link between the Pontifical Commission for Religious Relations With the Jews and the International Jewish Committee on Interreligious Consultations, it held its first meeting in Paris in 1971 and its 18th in Buenos Aires, Argentina, in 2004. Its goal is to explore questions "concerning our mutual relationship" and those "of common concern."

International Catholic Migration Commission (www.icmc.net) Headquarters is in Geneva.

International Catholic Movement for Intellectual and Cultural Affairs See **Pax Romana.**

International Catholic Organization for Cinema and Audiovisual See **Signis.**

international Catholic organizations See **Conference of International Catholic Organizations.**

International Catholic Rural Association (www.icra-agrimissio.org) Headquarters is in Rome.

International Catholic Stewardship Council (www.catholicstewardship.org) Headquarters is in Washington.

International Catholic Union of the Press (www.ucip.ch) *UCIP,* after the initials in French, is acceptable on second reference. There are seven branches: International Federation of Dailies; International Federation of Periodicals; International Federation of Catholic Journalists; International Federation of Catholic News Agencies; International Catholic Federation of Teachers and Researchers in the Science and Techniques of Information; International Federation of Church Press Associations; and International Federation of Book Publishers. Headquarters is in Geneva.

International Commission on English in the Liturgy *ICEL* is acceptable on second reference. It was established in 1963 as a joint commission of Catholic bishops' conferences in 26 participating countries where English is spoken. Its purposes are to provide good English translations of official liturgical texts by pooling scholarly resources and to promote the use of common texts in all English-speaking countries. Each bishops' conference is free to adopt or reject any text ICEL proposes.

Do not use *committee* in place of *commission.* ICEL used to refer to itself for some purposes as the International Committee on English in the Liturgy, but it has abandoned that alternative usage as unnecessary and confusing. Headquarters is in Washington.

International Consultation on English Texts Existed from 1969 to 1975. A similar group formed in 1985 is called the *English Language Liturgical Consultation.* See that entry.

International Cooperation for Development and Solidarity (www.cidse.org) A network of 15 Catholic development agencies in Europe and North America. Include the phrase *known by the acronym CIDSE,* but do not use the acronym on subsequent references, except in quoted material. Headquarters is in Brussels, Belgium.

International Council of Catholic Men-Unum Omnes (www.unum-omnes.com) Headquarters is in Rome.

International Federation of Catholic Medical Associations (www.fiamc.org) Headquarters is in Rome.

International Federation of Catholic Universities (www.fiuc.org) Headquarters is in Paris.

International Federation of Rural Adult Catholic Movements Headquarters is in Assesse, Belgium.

International Jewish Committee on Interreligious Consultations Formed by representatives of the American Jewish Committee, the Anti-Defamation League, B'nai B'rith International, the Central Conference of American Rabbis, the Israel Jewish Council for Interreligious Relations, the Rabbinical Assembly, the Rabbinical Council of America, the Union of American Hebrew Congregations, the Union of Orthodox Jewish Congregations of America and the World Jewish Congress, it serves as the Jewish side of the *International Catholic-Jewish Liaison Committee.* See that entry.

International Liaison Now known as *Catholic Network of Volunteer Service.* See that entry.

International Military Apostolate Headquarters is in Bonn, Germany.

International Movement of Apostolate in the Independent Social Milieux (www.miamsi.com) Headquarters is in Rome.

International Movement of Apostolate of Children Headquarters is in Le Plessis Robinson, France.

International Movement of Catholic Agricultural and Rural Youth (www.mijarc.net) Headquarters is in Brussels, Belgium.

International Movement of Catholic Students (www.imcs-miec.org) A branch of Pax Romana. See that entry. Headquarters is in Paris.

International Order of Alhambra (www.orderalhambra.org) Fraternal order of Catholic men dedicated to assisting people with mental disabilities. It also works to preserve and commemorate Catholic historical places, events and persons of international or regional importance. Headquarters is in Baltimore.

International Task Force on Euthanasia and Assisted Suicide (www.internationaltaskforce.org) Formerly called the International Anti-Euthanasia Task Force. Headquarters is in Steubenville, Ohio.

International Union of Superiors General (www.uisg.org) Catholic organization of the heads of women's religious orders. The parallel men's group is the *Union of Superiors General.* Headquarters is in Rome.

International Young Christian Workers (www.jociycw.net) Headquarters is in Brussels, Belgium.

Internet Capitalize in all uses for this global computer network that preceded and includes the World Wide Web. When reporting on the online presence of an organization that does not have *www* as part of its Internet address, refer to the address as an *Internet* site, not a *Web* site. When giving such an address in the body of a story or at the end, use the initial seven characters — *http://* — to make clear to readers that it is an Internet address. For example: *http://ace.nd.edu,* not *ace.nd.edu.*
See **online** and **World Wide Web.**

internuncio. A papal envoy with the rank of minister rather than ambassador.
See **apostolic delegate** and **papal nuncio.**

Inter-Regional Meeting of Bishops of Southern Africa Includes bishops from Angola, Lesotho, Mozambique, Sao Tome and Principe, and Zimbabwe.
Do not confuse with the *Southern African Catholic Bishops' Conference.* See that entry.

interregnum The term still used for the period between the death of one pope and the election of the next, although *reign* generally is no longer appropriate to describe a pontificate.
See **reign (papal).**

interreligious See **ecumenical, interreligious** and **interdenominational, interfaith.**

intifada Arabic for shaking or awakening, the word is used to describe two Palestinian uprisings against Israeli military rule — the first from 1987 until the 1993 peace agreement between the Palestine Liberation Organization and Israel, and the second beginning in 2000. Do not capitalize or use quotation marks. If the meaning is not clear from the context, add an appositive phrase: *the intifada, or Palestinian uprising.*

intrauterine device *IUD* is acceptable on second reference. The IUD is called a contraceptive in secular definitions, but Catholic moral teaching refers to it as an abortifacient because it prevents, not conception, but the implantation of the fertilized egg.
See **abortion** and **artificial contraception.**

Inuit (n., adj.) Webster's New World says this is "now the preferred term in Canada" for Eskimos. Many Inuits consider *Eskimo* derogatory. Use *Inuit* but explain in the story that this is the name by which Eskimos prefer to be known. See **Eskimo, Eskimos.**
The Inuit are not Indians. Phrases

such as *Indians* and *Inuit, Native Americans* or, especially in Canada, *native peoples* should be used if the Inuit are meant to be included in a reference.

The plural form may be *Inuit,* especially in references to the people collectively (as in the preceding paragraph), or *Inuits,* especially in references to members speaking or acting as individuals (as in the first paragraph of this entry).

See **First Nations** and **Indians.**

invalid See **valid, licit.**

Irish American Unity Conference (www.iauc.org) Begun in 1983 in Chicago, the conference describes itself as "a nationwide and wholly American organization created to bring about the withdrawal of British troops and the peaceful reunification of Ireland." Headquarters is in Washington.

Islam Followers are called *Muslims.* Both *Islamic* and *Muslim* are acceptable adjectives, but *Muslim* is used chiefly to refer to the people themselves, while *Islamic* generally is used in reference to the religious beliefs, customs and laws of Islam.

The sacred book of Islam is the *Quran.* Do not use *Koran,* a spelling once popular but now largely out of use. See **Quran.**

Daily Islamic prayers may be said anywhere, but Muslims are expected to gather at a mosque for public worship at noon on Friday, their weekly holy day. Arabic is the official language of the Quran and of Islamic prayers, but Islam stretches far beyond the Arab world. The largest Muslim community in the world is in Indonesia. Islam is the predominant religion throughout North Africa and the Middle East and in many parts of southern Asia. In 2005 there were an estimated 1.25 billion Muslims, making Islam second only to Christianity among the world's religions. About 5.2 million of them lived in the United States and Canada.

Islam is the youngest of the world's three major monotheistic religions. Like followers of the other two — Judaism and Christianity — its followers believe that there is but one God, called Allah by Muslims, who is all-powerful, just and merciful. In order to become a Muslim legally, it is sufficient to declare before a witness the basic testimony of faith, "There is no God but God and Mohammed is his messenger." See **Mohammed.**

The Quran includes many of the stories — or variations of them — also found in the sacred writings of Jews and Christians. Muslims regard Abraham, Moses and Jesus as early prophets of their faith.

Islam sets five duties for its adherents:

— Belief in God and Mohammed as his prophet.

— Prayer, especially the five daily prayers that are said facing Mecca.

— Almsgiving, also called the "purifying tax" or *zakat.*

— A total fast from dawn to dusk throughout the month of Ramadan, the ninth month of the Muslim year. Since the Islamic calendar is lunar, in each solar year Ramadan takes place about 10 days earlier than it did the previous solar year.

— If possible, a *hajj,* or pilgrimage to Mecca, during one's lifetime.

Mecca, in modern-day Saudi Arabia, is Islam's holiest city. It is the site of Islam's holiest shrine, the Kaaba, a cube-shaped black rock that is the destination of pilgrimages to Mecca.

Medina, home of the Mosque of Mohammed, where Mohammed was buried, is the second-holiest city.

Jerusalem, Islam's third-holiest city, is the site of al-Aqsa Mosque, the sanctuary for the nearby Dome of the Rock where Islamic tradition says that Mohammed ascended into heaven in a vision.

BRANCHES: Islam's largest branches are the *Sunni* and the *Shiite.*

About 90 percent of all Muslims are *Sunnis.* The Saudis, who sometimes are called Wahhabi Muslims, are a subgroup of the Sunnis.

Shiites form a majority only in Iran, but they form a substantial minority in Iraq, Lebanon and Bahrain. Significant Muslim offshoots of the Shiites include:

— *Ismaili:* East African, Indian and Pakistani Muslims whose hereditary spiritual leader is the Aga Khan.

— *Alawite:* A small group, chiefly in Syria and Lebanon.

Druzism originated as a breakaway sect in Ismaili Islam but the *Druze* are not considered Muslim. See **Druzism**.

ISLAMIC LAW: In Islamic tradition all Muslims should, if possible, live under an Islamic government that promotes Muslim belief and practice. While Turkey maintains an officially secular government, other predominantly Islamic nations incorporate Islamic law, called the *Shariah,* in varying degrees into their form of government.

CATHOLIC-MUSLIM RELATIONS: The Vatican has a Commission for Religious Relations With the Muslims under its Pontifical Council for Interreligious Dialogue and the council co-sponsors several ongoing dialogues with Muslim leaders and Islamic institutions. The president of the council delivers an annual message to Muslims at the close of Ramadan. The Holy See has diplomatic relations with most Islamic countries.

In the United States several regional dialogues were initiated in the 1990s under the joint sponsorship of the bishops' conference and national Muslim organizations, and there are a number of ongoing local Catholic-Muslim dialogues.

See **imam; Muslim(s); Ramadan;** and **Shariah.**

Israel Originally used for the Jewish people of biblical times, now it is used most often to refer to the modern Jewish state. The biblical people were *Israelites.* Citizens of the modern state are *Israelis.* About five-sixths of Israelis are Jewish. Most of the Israeli minority consists of Arabs. The official languages are *Hebrew* and *Arabic.*

Jerusalem stands alone in datelines.

The Vatican and Israel established full diplomatic relations in 1994, six months after the Dec. 30, 1993, signing of the "Fundamental Agreement Between the Holy See and the State of Israel."

See **Holy Land; Jerusalem; Jew; Jewish, Hebrew, Judaic;** and **Judaism.**

italics The CNS Stylebook on Religion gives guidelines for the transmission of news and features under the ASCII (American Standard Code for Information Interchange) standard, which does not provide for the use of different typefaces or underlining. It therefore calls for the use of quotation marks to set off many words or phrases that would be set off with italics in typesetting or underlined in typescript: foreign words, titles of books and other major compositions, words used as words, etc.

General rules for the use of italics are given in the "Italicization" chapter at the beginning of Webster's Third New International Dictionary.

IUD See **intrauterine device.**

J

Januarius, St. Note the spellings *liquefy* and *liquefaction.*

St. Januarius, patron saint of Naples, Italy, is believed to have been martyred during the persecution of Christians in 305 by the Roman Emperor Diocletian. A vial of his blood, kept in the Naples cathedral, is said to liquefy three times a year — on the Saturday before the first Sunday in May, the feast of the transfer of the saint's relics to Naples; Sept. 19, his feast day; and Dec. 16, the local feast commemorating the averting of a threatened eruption of Mount Vesuvius in 1631 through the intervention of St. Januarius.

The Vatican does not officially recognize the liquefaction as a miracle.

Jehovah's Witnesses (www.watchtower.org) A millennialist religious body founded in 1872 by Charles Taze Russell. Because it rejects the divinity of Christ and the doctrine of the Trinity, it should not be called a Protestant church. See **Protestant.**

The Witnesses are also known corporately as the *Watch Tower Society.* Their leader is the person elected as director by the corporate officers of the *Watch Tower Bible and Tract Society of Pennsylvania,* the *Watchtower Bible and Tract Society of New York Inc.,* and the *International Bible Students Association,* which is located in England. The three corporations publish Witness literature and coordinate Witness activities.

Witnesses call their congregations *companies* and their churches *kingdom halls.* They have more than 1.1 million U.S. members and a worldwide membership of 6.5 million in 232 countries, although more than twice that many participate in the annual Memorial of Christ's death.

Jehovah's Witnesses refer to God as Jehovah to stress their belief in the true God revealed in the Bible. They reject Trinitarian theology as a pagan invention and think of Jesus Christ as Jehovah's highest creature and agent. Sinful people can be reconciled to Jehovah through Jesus, and he will come again after the Battle of Armageddon to establish the kingdom of God, a theocracy on earth in which the just will reign forever. All people will be re-created and given a second chance at salvation during the millennium, but those who reject it by wickedness will be annihilated. Millions who obey Jehovah may live in immortal bliss on earth, but only Jesus and the 144,000 specially chosen by Jehovah will reign as spiritual creatures in heaven. See **millennium, millenary.**

Witnesses rely heavily on the apocalyptic literature of Scripture, especially the Book of Daniel and the Book of Revelation, as guides for interpreting world affairs as signs of the coming of that kingdom.

All those who join Jehovah's Witnesses are baptized by immersion, making them ordained ministers and citizens of the theocracy. All are expected to devote time to announcing God's kingdom to others and to have no loyalty toward earthly reigns of government, business or organized religion, which are considered tools of Satan. While they uphold a strict moral code, they have faced bans, persecution and hostility in many countries because they refuse, as a violation of God's law, to salute a flag, perform military service or participate in politics. They also have come into conflict with the law for refusing blood transfusions because of a biblical injunction to abstain from blood.

They do not have sacraments. Baptism is considered a sign of their dedication to the service of Jehovah. The only feast they observe is a communion service once a year on Nisan 14 — the day before the start of Passover in the Jewish calendar. Only those who believe they are among the 144,000 elect are allowed to receive the bread and wine at this memorial service.

Their rejection of all other organized religion has kept them outside the ecumenical movement.

Witnesses consider themselves a company of ministers, but they generally disavow ministerial titles. Most members are *kingdom publishers,* part-time workers who generally devote at least 10 hours a month to distributing literature and five hours a week to kingdom hall meetings. Some of these devote vacation time to evangelizing and are called *auxiliary pioneers. Pioneers* (also called *general pioneers)* support themselves with secular jobs but devote 100 hours or more a month to Witness activities. S*pecial pioneers* or *missionaries,* who work full time evangelizing, are supported by the society. Those who work full time at the world headquarters in Brooklyn, N.Y., are not considered special pioneers. None of these terms is used as a formal title before a name. See **religious titles.**

Jerusalem A holy city to Jews, Muslims and Christians. Its religious importance to people of many countries is a source of pressures to give the city a special international status. The Vatican supports such a status.

In 1980 Israel declared a united Jerusalem as its capital. Most nations refused to recognize the unification, and many protested it by refusing to move their embassies from the recognized capital, Tel Aviv.

Several divisions of the city are distinct realities described by proper nouns:

— *East Jerusalem:* The portion under Jordanian rule from the 1949 partition until 1967, when Israel occupied the West Bank (Jordanian land west of the Jordan River) and annexed East Jerusalem. All of the Old City is in East Jerusalem.

— *West Jerusalem:* The portion of the city that has been part of Israel since the state was created with the 1949 partition of Palestine.

— *Old City:* The part of Jerusalem bounded by the ancient city walls. It occupies less than a square mile and forms a small part of the modern city.

— *Jewish Quarter, Christian Quarter, Armenian Quarter and Muslim Quarter:* The four major sectors into which the Old City is traditionally divided. Within the Christian Quarter are the Church of the Holy Sepulcher and the headquarters of the Latin, Melkite Catholic, Greek Orthodox and Coptic patriarchates.

Other prominent features of Jerusalem include:

— In the Old City: the *Via Dolorosa,* believed to mark the route Jesus followed to his crucifixion; *Temple Mount,* which Orthodox Jews consider too sacred to walk on; the *Western Wall,* or the chief standing remnant of the retaining wall that surrounded the Temple of Solomon; the *Dome of the Rock,* the site in Islamic tradition where Mohammed ascended into heaven in a vision; and *al-Aqsa Mosque.*

— In Jerusalem but outside the Old City: the *Garden of Gethsemane,*

Mount of Olives, Mount Zion, Church of the Dormition, Holocaust Memorial and *Hebrew University.*

Jesuit Conference (www.jesuit. org) It is located in Washington.

Jesuit Refugee Service (www. jesref.org) An international Catholic organization founded in 1980 to "accompany, serve and defend the rights of refugees and forcibly displaced people." JRS is acceptable on second reference, but do not use in headlines.

Jesuit Volunteer Corps (www. jesuitvolunteers.org) International headquarters is in Washington.

Jesus *Jesus Christ, the Christ, Christ, Son of God, God the Son, the Messiah, One, Good Shepherd, Christ Child* and a variety of other titles, depending on context, may be used in news stories referring to the person Christians consider the lord and savior of the world. See **God, god(s).**

For nouns or phrases other than those given above in italics (for example: *redeemer, savior, lord, son of man, the word):* Treat the words as descriptive (lowercase) if one of the primary names of Jesus appears within the sentence; treat them as proper nouns if they appear alone: *She believes that the redeemer is Christ, the Son of God. Jesus is our lord and savior.* But: *Christmas marks the birth of the Redeemer. He said the Son of Man was born in Bethlehem.* For consistency, if a sentence has a pronoun referring back to Jesus in the previous sentence, do not capitalize secondary titles in the second sentence: *They believe in Jesus. He is their savior.*

Personal pronouns referring to him are lowercase.

For events in the life of Jesus, see **biblical events.**

Jesus Christ of Latter-day Saints, Church of See **Church of Jesus Christ of Latter-day Saints.**

Jew The general term for any adherent of Judaism or descendant of the ancient Hebrews, male or female. Do not use *Jewess.*

See **Jewish, Hebrew, Judaic** and **Judaism.**

Jewish calendar The day is from sundown to sundown, not from midnight to midnight. The months and the years are based on lunar cycles. The Jewish new year, Rosh Hashana, usually occurs in September on the Gregorian calendar but sometimes in October.

Years are calculated from the time of creation as projected from the Scriptures. The Jewish year 5766, for example, began Oct. 4, 2005 — actually sundown Oct. 3 — and ends Sept. 22, 2006. Add 3,760 years to the Christian calendar from Jan. 1 to Rosh Hashana, or 3,759 from Rosh Hashana to Dec. 31, to determine what year it is on the Jewish calendar.

See **C.E., B.C.E.** and **Jewish holy days.**

Jewish congregations See **Judaism.**

Jewish, Hebrew, Judaic The three adjectives are used in different ways.

Jewish is the general term referring to the people descended from Abraham or the religious and cultural heritage associated with them: *the Jewish state, the Jewish religion, a Jewish celebration, the Jewish calendar, a Jewish gathering, the New York Jewish vote,* etc.

Hebrew today refers primarily to the language used in modern Israel and in Jewish prayers and sacred writings:

"Shoah" is the Hebrew word for "holocaust." Christians usually call the Hebrew Scriptures the Old Testament.

Hebrew also can be used as a noun or adjective to refer to the Jewish people of biblical times. Depending on time and context they were also known in biblical times by various other names, including *Israel, Israelites, Judeans* and *Jews.*

Judaic should be used only in reference to the religious beliefs or theological traditions of the Jewish religion: *the Judaic concept of God, the relationship of justice and peace in Judaic thought.*

See **Israel** and **Judaism.**

Jewish holy days The main holy days in Judaism are *Hanukkah, Passover, Purim, Rosh Hashana, Shavuot, Sukkot* and *Yom Kippur.* See those entries.

Of these, *Rosh Hashana* and *Yom Kippur* are the high holy days.

Use *Passover,* not *Pesach,* as the ordinary term for the Passover observance.

In recent times many Jews have begun to observe *Yom Hashoah,* the Day of the Holocaust, shortly after Passover. See **Yom Hashoah.**

The *Seder* is not a separate holy day but a meal-and-prayer observance at the start of *Passover.* See **Seder.**

Observance of each feast begins on the eve of the feast and ends at sundown on the day of the feast. See **Jewish calendar** and **liturgical time.**

John Carroll Society (www. johncarrollsociety.org) A Catholic lay association in the Archdiocese of Washington that sponsors a Red Mass on the Sunday before the opening of the Supreme Court's October term. It is traditionally attended by members of the high court, Cabinet officers and members of the local judiciary.

John Paul I, Pope The pope who preceded Pope John Paul II in 1978 served for 34 days, not 33.

Jubilee USA Network (www. jubileeusa.org) The U.S. branch of a London-based international movement called Jubilee Research (www. jubilee2000uk.org), following up on the Jubilee 2000 efforts to relieve heavily indebted poor countries of their external debt by the end of 2000. U.S. headquarters is in Washington.

jubilee, year of See **holy year.**

Judaeo-Christian See **Judeo-Christian.**

Judaic See **Jewish, Hebrew, Judaic.**

Judaism In general, each local synagogue or temple of Judaism is autonomous. In some European countries, however, there is a chief rabbi who may represent the nation's Jewish community and adjudicate some questions of religious law.

In Israel the Sephardic and Ashkenazi chief rabbis form a rabbinical court that decides on certain questions. The Sephardim trace their lineage to Spain or Portugal before their expulsion in the 1490s. The Ashkenazim are those whose ancestors settled in eastern and northern Europe. The distinction is based on cultural and linguistic differences, not faith or theology.

In 2005 there were nearly 15 million Jews worldwide, about 6.4 million of them in the United States and Canada.

Originating with Abraham and Sarah in the second millennium before the common era and solidified in the Mosaic Covenant, Judaism was at that time unique in its exclusive worship of one God as creator and ruler of the universe. It is the oldest of the monotheistic religions, and the monotheistic faiths of both Christianity and Islam are rooted in it.

Central to Jewish belief is the covenant with which the one personal, loving God chose Abraham and his descendants as his special possession for all time, calling them to worship him alone and obey his will.

The revelation of God's will is found especially in the *Torah,* the first five books of the Bible, but also in his revelation through the prophets and the life of his people. See **Bible.**

The *Talmud,* a written compilation of rabbinic thought, occupies a special place as a guide to understanding and interpreting religious faith and practice.

There are three main branches of Judaism today. In the United States each branch has North American rabbinical and lay synagogal organizations, all based in New York, which foster cooperation and communication.

— *Orthodox* Jews follow strictly the biblical dietary laws, Sabbath observance, ritual forms and traditional holy days. They uphold the perennial authority of the Talmud. They prayerfully await the coming of the promised Messiah, who is to inaugurate an age of justice and peace. Within the spectrum of Orthodox Judaism, among the strictest are the *Haredi* and *Hasidic* Jews.

The chief North American organizations are the Orthodox Union (www. ou.org) and the Rabbinical Council of America (www.rabbis.org). In 2005, they said they had 1,000 synagogues in North America.

— *Reform* Jews emphasize the ethical aspects of Judaism and view the traditional and biblical dietary laws and ritual forms as ancient customs that must be adapted to modern life. Separation of men and women in the synagogue is not required, men need not wear the prayer shawl or yarmulke, work is permitted on the Sabbath and daily public worship is not required. They expect the coming of a messianic age but not necessarily a personal Messiah. This branch sometimes is referred to as *Reformed,* but the correct term is *Reform.* Reform Judaism originated in Germany at the start of the 19th century and was introduced in the United States in 1841.

The chief North American organizations are the Union for Reform Judaism (formerly Union of American Hebrew Congregations) and the Central Conference of American Rabbis (both at http://rj.org). In 2005, they said they had 1.5 million members in more than 900 congregations.

— *Conservative* Jews agree with the Reform movement's general position of modernization and adaptation but reject what they consider too radical an abandonment of religious customs and traditions. They observe the Sabbath and dietary laws but permit modification where necessary. The Conservative movement began in Germany in the middle of the 19th century as a reaction to the Reform movement and became a significant force in U.S. Judaism near the end of that century.

The chief North American organizations are the United Synagogue of Conservative Judaism (www.uscj.org) and the Rabbinical Assembly (www. rabbinicalassembly.org). In 2005, they said they had 1.5 million members in 760 congregations.

Many U.S. Jews do not indicate a preference for a particular branch of Judaism.

The *National Council of Synagogues,* also based in New York, serves as a spokesman for and coordinates policies of the North American rabbinical and lay synagogal organizations of the Reform and Conservative branches of Judaism. The four organizations constitute the council.

Other significant national organizations of U.S. Jews include the *American Jewish Committee, American Jewish Congress, B'nai B'rith* and the *Anti-Defamation League.* See those entries.

In all branches when a boy reaches 13, the age of religious responsibility, he becomes a *bar mitzvah,* which means *son of the commandment. Bar mitzvah* also refers to the ceremony marking this passage to adulthood. Conservative and Reform congregations have an analogous ceremony for a 12-year-old girl to become a *bat mitzvah (daughter of the commandment).*

WORSHIP: Ten mitzvahed Jews constitute a *minyan,* the minimum needed to form a synagogue or hold communal prayer services. There are three Sabbath services in the synagogue: Friday evening, Saturday morning and Saturday evening. Of equal or greater importance is the family prayer service, initiated by the mother, welcoming the Sabbath at the Friday evening meal in Jewish homes.

In Orthodox Judaism only men may be counted in a minyan or hold the posts of rabbi, cantor or president of the congregation. Reform Judaism has long admitted women to all those positions, and in recent years Conservative Judaism also has done so.

The *president of the congregation* and the *cantor* are the chief leaders of worship in the synagogue. Any mitzvahed Jew may be elected president of the congregation or lead a synagogue service.

Rabbis are primarily the scholars, teachers and interpreters of religious law in Judaism, not the leaders of worship. They may lead worship, however, and they usually conduct wedding ceremonies. *Jewish rabbi* is redundant: Do not use it.

CATHOLIC-JEWISH RELATIONS: The Second Vatican Council's 1965 Declaration on the Relationship of the Church to Non-Christian Religions, "Nostra Aetate," marked a dramatic shift in official Catholic attitudes toward Judaism. That document and subsequent official guidelines and statements have sharply condemned all forms of anti-Semitism and affirmed the continuing validity of God's covenant with the Jews. The Catholic Church has urged greater mutual understanding through dialogue and has instituted changes in Catholic education, liturgy, preaching, biblical scholarship and other fields to improve Catholic appreciation of Christianity's debt to Judaism.

At the international level official dialogue is coordinated by the *International Catholic-Jewish Liaison Committee.* See that entry.

In the United States the *National Workshop on Christian-Jewish Relations,* begun in 1973 by the Catholic-Jewish relations office (then a secretariat) of the bishops' Committee on Ecumenical and Interreligious Affairs, usually draws about 1,000 participants. The office maintains ongoing relations with a number of national Jewish organizations.

After the Synagogue Council of America was disbanded in 1998, the U.S. bishops' committee began holding two twice-yearly consultations on topics of mutual concern — one with the National Council of Synagogues, for Reform and Conservative Jews, and the other with the Orthodox Union and Rabbinical Council of America.

Local dialogues are active in a number of U.S. cities.

See **Jewish calendar; Jewish, Hebrew, Judaic; Jewish holy days; religious titles;** and **Zionism.**

Judeo-Christian Not *Judaeo-Christian*. However, the word can be offensive to some Jews because often it is used in ways that subsume Jewish thought into Christian tradition without reflecting the distinctiveness of the Jewish tradition. It should be avoided outside of quotes. A phrase such as *Jewish and Christian traditions* would be preferable.

Junior Catholic Daughters of the Americas, Junior Daughters of Isabella For *Catholic awards* for both youth groups, see that entry.

K

kamelaukion The brimless cylindrical black hat worn by some Orthodox and Eastern Catholic bishops, monks and, in some Orthodox circles, other celibate clergy. It may be worn with or without a black veil attached. It can serve as part of liturgical garb or simply as part of formal clerical wear. The plural is *kamelaukions*. If the term is used, explain it. In most cases a simple descriptive reference is better: *black hat, black hat and veil, brimless black hat*, etc.

There are several variant spellings of *kamelaukion*. Use this form, the only one listed in Webster's Third New International Dictionary.

See **crown; liturgical dress;** and **miter.**

Kenedy directory Its true name is *The Official Catholic Directory*. Either form is acceptable on all references, but the nature of the directory should be explained in the story. On second reference, *the directory* is acceptable. It is published annually by P.J. Kenedy & Sons, based in Wilmette, Ill.

kingdom of God

knight In Catholic ecclesiastical usage, *knight* may refer to:

— A member of a fraternal society. For example: *Knights of Columbus, Knights of Peter Claver.* In stories about such organizations, *the Knights* is acceptable on second reference. A member is called a *Knight*. See **fraternal organizations.**

— A member of the *Knights of Malta.* See that entry.

— A recipient of a papal honor of knighthood. For example: *Knights of St. Gregory, Knights of the Golden Spur.* Capitalize *knight* only when it is part of the equestrian order's full name. Some recipients are given higher honorary rank, such as *commander.* Do not use *commander, knight* or *sir* immediately before the person's name as a title: *The pope named John Jones a Knight of St. Sylvester. Jones became a knight with the rank of commander Dec. 21.* Follow the same style rules for *Knights of the Holy Sepulcher,* which operates under the protection of the Holy See.

Knight is lowercased when standing alone in these cases because the pope, like the sovereign of England, is exercising a traditional right of honoring persons by enrolling them in equestrian orders.

See individual entries and **papal honors.**

Knights Hospitaller See **Knights of Malta.**

Knights of Columbus (www. kofc.org) A Catholic fraternal organization founded in the United States in 1882. On second reference *the Knights* is acceptable.

Most of its 1.6 million members are in the United States, but it has councils in Canada, Mexico, Philippines, Dominican Republic, Puerto Rico, Panama, the Bahamas, the Virgin Islands, Guatemala, Guam, Saipan and Poland.

A supreme council governs the Knights. It consists of the international officers and representatives from the state councils in the United States, provincial councils in Canada and national councils in other countries.

Beneath each state, provincial or national council are parish-based local councils within their territory. Lowercase *council* except when it is followed by the council number: *supreme council; Illinois council; Council 9726 in Red Oak, Iowa.*

A member is a *Knight: John Jones, a fourth-degree Knight from New York.* Capitalize the formal titles of supreme, state or local council officials only if used immediately before the name and if *Knight* is part of the title: *Supreme Knight Carl Anderson; Deputy Supreme Knight Ellis D. Flinn; state council Grand Knight James Johnson; Deputy Grand Knight John Jamison.* But: *supreme treasurer William J. Van Tassel; state council warden Sam Smith; local secretary Steven Smythe.*

The Knights have no ladies' auxiliary. They sponsor a youth organization, the *Columbia Squires.* Headquarters is in New Haven, Conn.

See **fraternal organizations.**

Knights of Malta (www.orderof malta.org) Acceptable on all references for the *Sovereign Military Order of the Hospital of St. John of Jerusalem, of Rhodes and of Malta.* Also known as the *Knights Hospitaller* and as the *Knights and Dames of Malta,* this Catholic organization is the oldest order of chivalry in existence. On second reference *Knights* is acceptable.

Founded in the 11th century as a religious confraternity, it became an international military order in the 12th century. It reached a peak of military and political power in the 14th to 16th centuries, when its navy and island strongholds in the Mediterranean stopped repeated Ottoman advances toward southern Europe. Its power declined in the 17th and 18th centuries, and it ceased to be a significant political force soon after it lost Malta to Napoleon I in 1798.

Today, as a combined religious order and chivalric order with about 11,000 members, it engages in extensive hospital work, emergency medical assistance and relief work for refugees and the needy. It retains international recognition as a sovereign state and has diplomatic relations with 63 countries. A number of its members are leading figures in political, business or professional life. It began admitting women to its leadership ranks in 1998.

The Knights are ruled by a grand master, who is elected for life from among the order's top class, the *knights of justice.* Only men of noble lineage who take vows of poverty, chastity and obedience can be knights of justice. A second class, *knights of obedience,* is also restricted to those of noble lineage. A third class, open to women and men without noble lineage, includes several grades of knights and dames.

Capitalize *Knight of Malta, Dame of Malta* and *Knight* and *Dame* used without modifiers when referring to individuals as members of the organization. See **fraternal organizations.**

Do not, however, capitalize the names of the different classes and grades of the Knights of Malta when given in full: *Smith is a member of the knights of justice of the Knights of Malta. Peters is a knight of magistral grace. Jones is a dame of honor and devotion.* Such phrases are clearly those used by the organization. Unlike *knight* standing alone, they need no capitals to signal a departure from ordinary meaning.

Knights of Peter Claver (www. knightsofpeterclaver.org) No *St.* in the name of this fraternal society of black Catholics founded in 1909. On second reference *Knights* is acceptable. A ladies auxiliary founded in 1922 is known as *Ladies of Peter Claver.* On second reference *Ladies* is acceptable. The two often meet or act jointly as the *Knights and Ladies of Peter Claver.* Their combined membership is 35,000.

Capitalize the title of each organization's top officer when used immediately before the name: *Supreme Knight Arthur C. McFarland, Supreme Lady Mary L. Briers.* Capitalize *Knight* and *Lady* when used to identify a person as a member of the group. Headquarters is in New Orleans.

See **fraternal organizations.**

Knights of St. Gregory Acceptable on all references to *Knights of St. Gregory the Great,* a pontifical order of chivalry bestowed by the pope on individuals for their service to the church.

For usage, see **knight.** See also **papal honors.**

Knights of St. Sylvester Acceptable on all references for *Knights of St. Sylvester the Pope,* a pontifical order of chivalry bestowed by the pope on individuals for their service to the church.

For usage, see **knight.** See also **papal honors.**

Knights of the Holy Sepulcher (Not *Sepulchre)* Acceptable on all references for the order of chivalry also known as the *Equestrian Order of the Holy Sepulcher of Jerusalem* or the *Knights of the Holy Sepulcher of Jerusalem.* The order is under the patronage of the Holy See. It is governed by a papally appointed cardinal, who is grand master, and the Latin-rite patriarch of Jerusalem, who is grand prior.

Because of its similarity to the honorific pontifical orders of chivalry, lowercase the title *knight* except when it is used as part of the proper name: *Knight of the Holy Sepulcher.*

For usage, see **knight.** See also **papal honors.**

Knights of the Immaculata See **Militia of the Immaculata.**

Koran See **Quran.**

kosher A description of food fixed in accord with strict dietary and ceremonial laws of Judaism. Lowercase.

See **Judaism.**

Ku Klux Klan On second reference *the Klan* or *KKK* is acceptable for any of the organizations known collectively as the *Klan in America,* even though some of them do not use the full name *Ku Klux Klan.* Members are called *Klansmen.*

While white supremacy has always been the central tenet of the KKK, significant strains of anti-Semitism and anti-Catholicism remain a part of Klan ideology.

Leaders of the Klan organizations form an *Imperial Board,* which meets occasionally to coordinate activities.

Titles of leaders vary from group to group but usually are drawn from mythological and chivalric literature. Capitalize titles such as *imperial wizard* and *grand dragon* when used as formal titles before a name.

In a March 1987 statement on the Klan and other racist organizations, the Administrative Board of what is now the U.S. Conference of Catholic Bishops said: "We state unequivocally that Catholics who join the Ku Klux Klan, or any organizations that actively promote racism, act in violation of Catholic teaching. These organizations are a scandalous contradiction to all that we hold sacred and teach in the name of Jesus Christ."

L

Ladies of Charity of the United States Headquarters is in St. Louis.

Ladies of Peter Claver See **Knights of Peter Claver.**

Laetare Medal See **Catholic awards.**

laicization The process in the Catholic Church by which a priest is returned to the lay state, sometimes as a penalty for a serious crime or scandal, but usually at his request. Do not say *reduced to the lay state,* which suggests a negative view of laypeople.

A laicized priest is barred from priestly ministry. Usually he is also dispensed from the promise of celibacy and all other priestly obligations. If he is a member of a religious order he also is dispensed from his religious vows. The letter of laicization usually contains restrictions against holding certain jobs or leadership functions in the church, but the former priest remains a Catholic in good standing.

Since 1989 the Vatican Congregation for Divine Worship and the Sacraments has handled voluntary requests for laicization, which must ordinarily be sought on grounds that the ordination was invalid for some reason, and for dispensation from clerical duties. Since 2001 the Vatican Congregation for the Doctrine of the Faith has had jurisdiction over penalties, including laicization, for clergy who have committed certain grave church crimes, including violation of the seal of confession and sexual abuse of minors. The pope personally had to approve every laicization for any reason until 2003, when the doctrinal congregation received authority to laicize for certain serious crimes and to do so without a trial in certain "grave and clear cases." Published cases since then indicate, however, that Pope John Paul II continued to approve each case personally until his death.

A *laicized priest* also may be referred to as a *former priest* or *resigned priest.* Use *inactive priest* only for those who have left active ministry without being laicized. Do not use the title *Father* for a man who has been laicized or who has left active ministry.

See **defrock, defrocked** and **suspended priests.**

LAMP (www.lampministries.org) A Catholic lay missionary association that focuses on evangelization among the urban poor. Its full name is Lay Apostolic Ministries with the Poor. Headquarters is in Bronx, N.Y.

L'Arche (www.larche.org) An ecumenical and interreligious movement founded in 1964 to provide group homes and spiritual support for developmentally disabled people. L'Arche, which in English is "the Ark," had more than 120 communities in 30 countries in 2005. Its formal title is the International Federation of L'Arche Communities.

Do not use the word *the* before its name, since it is already part of the name.

last rites Not a sacrament, but the collective term for those sacramental rites and prayers that may be used in whole or in part in pastoral care for the dying. Sacramental rites may include *penance, anointing of the sick* and *Communion,* which is called *viaticum* when it is given to someone approaching death. See **anointing of the sick; Communion, communion;** and **penance.**

Do not confuse *last rites* with the funeral and committal rites following death. See **obituaries.** Also, do not call the anointing of the sick a *last rite* except when it is given to someone near death. Once used only for those in danger of death, it is used more broadly now for those whose health is debilitated by sickness or old age.

Last Supper But lowercase when modified by a possessive referring to Jesus: *Before his last supper with the Apostles, Jesus washed their feet.* In such cases, a variation on the phrase — *his final meal* or *his last meal* — may be preferable.

See **biblical events.**

Lateran Pacts The treaty, financial agreement and concordat signed between the Holy See and Italy on Feb. 11, 1929. Under the treaty, the Vatican recognized the Italian state and Italy recognized the pope's absolute independence and sovereignty over Vatican City. Under the financial agreement, Italy agreed to compensate the Holy See for the loss of the Papal States by paying 750 million lire in cash and 1 billion lire in interest-bearing bonds. The concordat regulated the status of religion and the church in Italy; a revised concordat was signed in 1984.

Latin American bishops' council (www.celam.org) Do not call it a *conference. CELAM,* the acronym for the council's Spanish name, *Consejo Episcopal Latinoamericano,* is acceptable on second reference. Found-ed in 1955, it is an administrative and coordinating agency of 22 national bishops' conferences of Latin America. Member conferences elect their representatives on the council. Headquarters is in Bogota, Colombia.

Latin Church A synonym for the Roman Catholic Church, which is comprised of all Catholics of the Latin rite. Use only in technical contexts in which it is needed to distinguish it from the Eastern Catholic churches. In some cases *Latin rite* (or the adjective *Latin-rite)* may be preferable as a means of making that distinction. Care must be taken, however, to ensure that no confusion would result regarding the Latin language.

Avoid using *Roman Church* (without Catholic) as a synonym for *Latin* Church, since this could be understood to mean only the church of the diocese or city of Rome.

See **Catholic Church; Eastern Catholic churches;** and **Roman Catholic Church.**

Latin Liturgy Association (www.latinliturgy.com) Founded in 1975 to promote the use of Latin language and music in approved rites of the Catholic Church.

Latin Mass Not a synonym for *Tridentine Mass.* See that entry.

Latino, Latinos The term preferred for most Hispanics in the Western United States. When referring to a woman or to a group composed solely of women, the singular is *Latina,* the plural is *Latinas.* In general, use *Hispanics* when referring to a group from various parts of the country. However, in popular usage *Hispanic* and *Latino* are becoming synonymous. In common usage, the term *Hispanic* traces its roots to the U.S. Census

Bureau, which began using this term as a catch-all phrase for all Spanish-speaking immigrants and their descendants. The U.S. bishops' Secretariat for Hispanic Affairs has begun using *Hispanic/Latino* in some of its documents, but retains its name with *Hispanic* only.

See **Chicano, Chicanos** and **Hispanic**.

Latin rite (n.), **Latin-rite** (adj.) See **Catholic Church** and **Latin Church.**

Latin words and phrases Some Latin words and phrases in ecclesiastical usage which occur frequently in the news are listed separately in this book.

If a Latin word or phrase is listed in Webster's New World in regular boldface type, indicating that it has become a part of the English language, do not surround it with quotation marks. If it is not listed in Webster's or is listed there in italics, place it within quotation marks.

See **encyclical; hymns; Mass; prayers;** and **Appendix I: Vatican II Documents** for use of Latin in those contexts.

The following is a list of some abbreviations, words, phrases and sayings that occasionally occur in Catholic contexts, with English translations and, where needed, a description of the context in which they are likely to occur. In this list a word is capitalized only if it is always capitalized or if it begins a complete sentence. Words given in parentheses are optional insertions in or additions to the phrase. In many Latin sayings, for example, the verb *is ("est")* is usually dropped.

— "adhortatio apostolica." See **apostolic exhortation.**

— "ad limina." See that entry.

— "ad multos annos": *many years* (or: *long life)*. Often used as a toast marking a birthday or jubilee.

— "ad nutum Sanctae Sedis." See that entry.

— "alter Christus": *another Christ.* Said of a priest to describe the character he receives at ordination.

— A.M.D.G.: *for God's greater glory* (initials for "ad maiorem Dei gloriam"). Motto of St. Ignatius of Loyola, founder of the Jesuits.

— "Annuit coeptis": *He (God) has favored our undertakings.* Inscription above the eye representing divine providence on the reverse of the Great Seal of the United States.

— "Benedicamus Domino": *Let us bless the Lord.*

— "Christifidelis": *a Christian.* The plural, "Christifideles," is usually translated *the faithful.*

— C.I.C. and C.C.E.O. See **canon law.**

— "communicatio in sacris": *intercommunion.* Literally: communication in sacred things. See **intercommunion.**

— "communio": *communion.* See **Communion, communion.**

— "cum et sub Petro": *with and under Peter.* That is, in unity with and under the leadership of the pope.

— "cura animarum": *the (pastoral) care of souls.*

— "Deo gratias": *Thanks be to God.*

— "Ecce sacerdos magnus (qui in diebus suis placuit Deo)": *Behold the great priest (who in his time was pleasing to God).* The beginning of a hymn often used as the entrance song at a rite led by a bishop. Capitalize first three words when used as the title of the hymn.

— "ecclesia docens, ecclesia discens": *the teaching church, the learning church.* Usually said with reference to bishops and laity, respectively.

Either half of the phrase may be used separately.

— "ecclesia reformata, ecclesia (semper) reformanda": *a reformed church, a church (always) in need of reform.* A popular phrase during the Second Vatican Council.

— "Extra ecclesiam nulla salus": *Outside the church there is no salvation.* An axiom, first stated by Origen in the third century, to express the Catholic doctrine that the church is necessary for salvation. It does not mean that formal membership in the Catholic Church, sacramental baptism, or even a profession of belief in Christ is needed for salvation.

— "fides quaerens intellectum": *faith seeking understanding.* A description of the nature of theology.

— "Habemus papam": *We have a pope.* The opening words of the announcement of a new pope.

— IHS. A compressed version of Jesus' name in Greek, consisting of the first three letters; the middle letter is not a capital "h" but a capital *eta, a long "e."* The letters are: *iota, eta, sigma.* Several Latin meanings, based on interpreting the middle letter as an "h," have been attached to the symbol. These include: "Iesus, hominum salvator" : *Jesus, savior of the people;* "In hoc signo (vinces)": *In this sign you will conquer;* and "In hac (cruce) salus": *In this (cross) is salvation.*

— imprimatur. See **imprimatur, "nihil obstat."**

— "In necessariis unitas, in dubiis libertas, in omnibus caritas": *In essentials unity, in doubtful matters freedom, in all things charity.*

— "in persona Christi (capitis)": *in the person of Christ (the head).* Said of the priest's sacramental role, especially in celebrating the Eucharist; with *"capitis"* added it emphasizes the male character of the person so acting.

— "I.N.R.I." Initials for the Latin inscription on the cross recorded in the Gospels: "Iesus Nazarenus, Rex Iudaeorum": *Jesus the Nazarene, King of the Jews.*

— "instrumentum laboris." See that entry.

— "Laudetur Jesus Christus": *Praised be Jesus Christ.*

— "Lex orandi, lex credendi": *One's prayers express one's beliefs.* Literally: *The law of praying is the law of believing.* The verb "est" *(is)* usually is omitted but sometimes is placed after "orandi" or after "credendi." No comma if the verb is used.

— "lineamenta." See that entry.

— "mirabile dictu." Literally *wonderful to say.* An interjection often punctuated with an exclamation mark. When used sincerely, this is an expression of surprise or wonder, but often it is used sarcastically or sardonically in the way one might say: *The poll showed that most Americans — what a surprise — want peace.* An effective translation of the Latin idiom depends on the context. Similar exclamations, less often used, are: "mirabile visu" *(a wonder to behold)* and "mirabile auditu" *(wonderful to hear).*

— "motu proprio." See that entry.

— "novus ordo (Missae)": *new order (of the Mass).* Not a proper term for the 1969 order of the Mass, it is often used by opponents of the 1969 order as a pejorative epithet.

— "novus ordo seclorum": *a new order of the ages.* Inscription below the pyramid on the reverse of the Great Seal of the United States. "Seclorum" is a rare variant spelling of "saeculorum."

— "Ora et labora": *Pray and work.* The motto of St. Benedict and the Benedictine order.

— "Pax vobiscum": *Peace be with you.* If said to an individual, the singular is used: "Pax tecum."

— "per omnia saecula saeculorum (Amen)": *world without end (Amen).* The standard ending of many Latin prayers, it also may be translated: *forever and ever.*

— "placet": See that entry.

— "Quo vadis (Domine)?": *Where are you going (Lord)?*

— "Requiescat in pace": *May he (she) rest in peace.* The plural is: "Requiescant in pace."

— "Roma eterna (est), ecclesia sempiterna": *Rome is forever, the church forever and ever.*

— "Roma locuta (est), causa finita (est)": *Rome has spoken, the case is closed.*

— "sensus fidei": *sense of the faith.* Or: *understanding of the faith.*

— "sensus fidelium": *the sense of the faithful.* Or: *the (common) understanding of the faithful.*

— "sola fides": *faith alone.* Also "sola Scriptura": *Scripture alone.* Theological slogans of the Reformation, expressing beliefs that faith alone is necessary for salvation and that Scripture is the only sure source of God's revealed truth.

— "sui iuris": *of its own right.* See that entry.

— "urbi et orbi": *to the city and the world.* See that entry and **apostolic blessing.**

— "ut unum sint": *that they may be one.* Often translated more freely: *that all may be one.* From Jesus' prayer in Gethsemane, often cited as the Gospel mandate for Christian unity.

Latter Day Saints, Latter-day Saints See **Church of Jesus Christ of Latter-day Saints.**

lauds A term sometimes used for morning prayer in the *Liturgy of the Hours.* See that entry.

lay ecclesial ministers Lay Catholics who are engaged full time or part time in public positions of ministry and community leadership in the church such as parish life coordinators or parish directors of music, liturgy, catechetics or youth ministry. Such ministry is described as *ecclesial* because it involves substantial collaboration with the pastoral ministry of the ordained as part of parish or diocesan staff or a pastoral leadership team, acting in the name of the church and often as a church-authorized leader or director of some area of ministry. The number of people receiving salaries as full- or part-time lay ecclesial ministers in U.S. parishes was estimated at more than 30,000 in 2005, and some 2,000 more were engaged in such ministries at least 20 hours a week on an unpaid basis. See **parish life coordinator.**

Do not use *lay ecclesial minister* as a title or job description for an individual; instead, use that person's specific job description: *director of religious education, parish music director, youth ministry director,* etc.

Also see the **minister, ministry** entry.

lay ecclesial movements Also called *Catholic lay associations* or *lay movements,* these organizations may also include priests and deacons but are made up predominantly of laypeople. In late 2004, the Vatican published a directory listing 123 international lay associations, movements and communities approved by the church.

layman, laywoman, layperson, laypeople When a gender-neutral term is sought, *layperson* is the preferred singular form but *laypeople* is generally the preferred plural.

Note: Although these words ordinarily should be written with no hyphen or space, this does not prevent the use of *lay* as a separate adjective when it modifies two or more nouns or when it is used in a parallel construction with another adjective modifying the same noun: *lay men and women, ordained and lay men, lay and religious women.*

In general language, laypeople are ordinary people — those outside a particular group, especially a group defined by professional expertise: *To the layperson, legal language may be confusing.*

In Catholic ecclesiastical usage, *layperson* may mean:

— Any member of the church who is not among the ordained clergy. This is the technical meaning in canon law. In this sense, religious sisters and brothers are laypeople.

— Any church member who is neither ordained nor a member of a religious order. When the Second Vatican Council spoke of the laity, it used the term in this more common meaning.

See **inclusive language.**

lay ministries See **altar server; extraordinary minister of holy Communion; lector;** and **minister, ministry.**

Lay Mission-Helpers Association (www.laymissionhelpers.org) Headquarters is in Los Angeles.

Leadership Conference of Women Religious (www.lcwr.org) *LCWR* is acceptable on second reference for this membership body of major superiors of sisters' orders in the United States. Since 1992 a second such body, the *Council of Major Superiors of Women Religious,* has also existed. See that entry. Headquarters is in Silver Spring, Md.

lectern, ambo A *lectern* is the reading desk or stand, in a church or elsewhere, on which a speaker places books or notes. The speaker stands *at* or *behind* it, not *on* it.

An *ambo* is the place in a Catholic church from which, according to liturgical norms, the Scriptures are read and the homily may be preached. It may consist only of a lectern, or it may consist of a raised platform and the lectern on it. Apart from technical uses, *lectern* is ordinarily preferred in references to the place from which the reader reads or the homilist preaches.

The norms also allow the delivery of the homily from the area of the presidential chair, however.

In most Latin-rite churches a *pulpit,* properly speaking, no longer exists or no longer is used.

See **dais, podium, rostrum** and **pulpit.**

Lectionary One of two books used for Mass, it contains the Scripture readings for each day. The other, the *Sacramentary,* contains the prayers used at Mass. As of 2005, there were indications that for several years the Vatican has wanted the name *Roman Missal* to replace *Sacramentary* as new national editions of that book are published.

In practice, usually the Lectionary is divided into at least two volumes, but ordinarily any individual volume or the entire set can be referred to, without distinction, as *the Lectionary.* In multivolume format usually the first volume contains the readings of Sundays, feasts of the Lord and certain other major feasts, set in a three-year cycle of readings. Additional volumes contain the readings for weekdays and all the lesser feasts of saints and Masses for various other occasions. The readings for weekdays and saints' feasts are set in a two-year cycle.

See **liturgical books; liturgical year; Mass; Roman Missal;** and **Sacramentary.**

lector In Catholic ecclesiastical usage, a person assigned to read any of the Scripture readings except those from the Gospels during a Mass or other public worship service. Only a priest or deacon may proclaim the Gospel at Mass.

Lector is correct in all contexts, but *reader* is generally preferred except in more technical references to the lay ministry of *lector.* Do not use as a formal title before a name.

Do not use *lector* as a verb, and do not use *lectoring* as a description of the ministry. The verb is *to read;* the job of the reader is *reading.*

Canon 230 of the Code of Canon Law states that only qualified "men" may be "installed on a stable basis in the ministries of lector and acolyte." It adds, however, that "laypersons can fulfill the function of lector during liturgical actions by temporary deputation."

See **minister, ministry.**

lecturer Always treat it as an occupational description, not as a formal title before a name.

See **Church of Christ, Scientist.**

Lefebvre, Archbishop Marcel The French traditionalist, founder of the Society of St. Pius X, who was excommunicated in 1988 when he illegally ordained four bishops to continue the movement after him. The Mass he and his followers celebrate is the Tridentine Mass, which was superseded by the revised order of the Mass after the Second Vatican Council. Do not say the Tridentine Mass was *banned* or *outlawed,* since limited use continues to be authorized.

The Tridentine Mass is celebrated only in Latin, but Latin is the original language of the new order of the Mass as well — and is used at times to celebrate according to the new rite — so it is incorrect to use Latin Mass as a term intended to distinguish the older rite from the newer one.

Archbishop Lefebvre, who died in 1991, rejected the liturgical reforms and concepts of religious freedom and ecumenism as formulated by Vatican II.

The Pontifical Commission "Ecclesia Dei," established in 1988 to reconcile Lefebvrites who did not wish to break with Rome, takes its name from the Latin title of the papal document spelling out the terms for reconciliation.

See **"Ecclesia Dei"; Society of St. Pius X;** and **Tridentine Mass.**

legate An individual appointed by the pope as his personal representative at a religious event such as a eucharistic congress often is given the title, for that event, of papal *legate.* Do not use as a formal title before the individual's name.

Legatus (www.legatus.org) An organization of Catholic business leaders formed in 1987 by Domino's Pizza founder Thomas S. Monaghan. Headquarters is in Naples, Fla.

Legion of Mary (www.legionof mary.org) U.S. headquarters is in St. Louis.

Lent (n.), **Lenten** (adj.) In the Latin Church, the period in the liturgical year from Ash Wednesday through Holy Thursday, three days before Easter. Since the 1969 reform of the Roman calendar, it comprises 44 days, including the Sundays, which are part of the penitential period.

Before 1969 Lent was described

in the Latin Church as a 40-day period of penance before Easter. This calculation was reached by excluding the six Sundays during the period, which were not considered penitential days, and counting Good Friday and Holy Saturday, which were formerly treated as part of Lent.

In Eastern Christianity, both Catholic and Orthodox, Lent often is called *Great Lent* or *the Great Fast*. In Eastern traditions it begins two days earlier than in the West, on Monday, and ends liturgically the Friday before Palm Sunday. Palm Sunday and its vigil mark a transition to Passion Week, a period that is liturgically distinctive and more penitential. Eastern Catholic traditions sometimes refer to three lesser penitential periods as minor fasts. These are the periods before the Nativity (Dec. 25), the feast of Sts. Peter and Paul (June 29), and the feast of the Dormition of Mary (Aug. 15).

For the method of computing when Easter occurs, see **Easter.**

See **abstinence, days of; Ash Wednesday; Easter triduum; fasting; Holy Week; liturgical year;** and **penitential days.**

leper, leprosy The preferred term today is *Hansen's disease,* after the 19th-century Norwegian physician who discovered its cause, although in many contexts it may be necessary to explain on first or second reference that this is leprosy.

When possible, avoid use of the word *leper,* a term offensive to those with Hansen's disease because of the long history of social rejection and stigma associated with the illness before a cure was found. In some countries, however, *leper* and *leprosy* are the only terms used. Note also that it is anachronistic to use *Hansen's disease* in references to biblical stories or events: *Jesus cured a man with leprosy,* not: *Jesus cured a man with Hansen's disease.*

lesbian See **homosexuality.**

letter, epistle Unless confusion could result, use *letter* rather than *epistle: St. Paul's letters to the Corinthians, the letters of the apostles in the Bible.* But *in the epistles and Gospels* (where a departure from the usual phrase could confuse readers).

As a general rule, the letters of St. Paul should be called *letters;* those by Sts. James, Peter, John and Jude may be called *epistles* for the sake of recognition, if it is not immediately clear from the context that the reference is to a book of the Bible.

For formal titles of specific letters, use the form given in the New American Bible, but lowercase the initial *the* or skip it if the author's name is inserted before the title: *the Letter of Jude, the First Letter of John, the Second Letter of Peter, the Letter to the Romans* or *St. Paul's Letter to the Romans* (but not: *the Letter of St. Paul to the Romans* — the words *of St. Paul* are not part of the title).

Lowercase all uses of *epistle* and any uses of *letter* outside formal titles: *the first letter of St. Paul to the Corinthians, St. John's second epistle, the first epistle of St. Peter, St. Paul's letters to the Ephesians and the Philippians.*

See **Bible** and **Gospel(s), gospel.**

Leuven Now the preferred spelling for the city in the Flemish part of Belgium. It used to be known more commonly by its French name, *Louvain.* Use *Leuven* in datelines and text: *LEUVEN, Belgium (CNS) —.*

See **Louvain, Catholic University of.**

liberal In popular references to a religious denomination or individuals or groups within a religious body or family, this term often is used to signal contempt for sincerely held religious convictions. In general, do not apply it to an individual or group except in quoted matter or when it is used by someone as a self-description.

Liberal can have many different meanings, among them: one who accepts or prefers new formulations of some traditional doctrines, one who emphasizes context and the complexity of life in interpreting moral norms, one who seeks changes in current church structures and discipline, or one who links personal religious beliefs to a liberal political philosophy. It is generally better to state what views or practices an individual or group supports or opposes than to use the *liberal* label.

See **conservative.**

Liberal Catholic Church (www.liberalcatholic.org) Founded in 1916, it has world headquarters in San Diego and an American province based in New York. It is not part of the Roman Catholic Church.

liberation theology Also called *a theology of liberation,* it is a theology that finds in Scripture the principles and inspiration for working to free people from unjust social patterns and structures. It originated in Latin America in the 1960s and '70s and still is identified chiefly as a Latin American phenomenon, but liberation theologies have been developed in Africa and Asia and among African-Americans, Hispanics and women in the United States.

Vatican documents in 1984 and 1986 praised liberation theology for drawing attention to the "essential truth" that "the Gospel of Jesus Christ is a message of freedom and a force for liberation"; but they warned against dangers such as a tendency to ignore personal conversion and freedom from sin as the most fundamental liberation, and tendencies to employ Marxist social analysis, theories of class struggle or other ideological concepts that are incompatible with Christian teaching.

The Vatican documents neither condemned liberation theology nor endorsed it, but rather supported some aspects of the movement and criticized others.

licit See **valid, licit.**

Life Teen (www.lifeteen.org) Founded in an Arizona parish, this international Catholic ministry included 950 programs in 20 countries in 2005. Its stated goal is to serve the church and lead all teens closer to Christ by providing resources and training that encourage vibrant eucharistic celebrations and opportunities for teens to grow in their faith. Its headquarters is in Mesa, Ariz.

limbo A theological postulate, developed by medieval theologians, of a state after death of natural happiness, but without the beatific vision that is perfect communion with God, for those innocent of personal sin who died without baptism.

When the Catechism of the Catholic Church discusses heaven, purgatory and hell, it makes no mention of limbo as another possible destination of the soul. It states that "at the very moment of death" the soul of each person undergoes "a particular judgment that refers his life to Christ: either entrance into the blessedness of heaven — through a purification or immediately — or immediate and everlasting damnation."

"lineamenta" A Latin term used by the Holy See for a preliminary document outlining topics to be treated at a meeting. Generally the word is best avoided in news writing in favor of English terms such as *outline* or *background paper.* Although the Latin word is plural in form, it may take singular verbs and pronouns if it is used to refer to the document as a whole: *"The 'lineamenta' is not the final word, but it is a good basis to start the discussion," he said.*

See **"instrumentum laboris"** and **schema.**

liquefy, liquefaction Not *liquify* or *liquification.*

See **Januarius, St.**

Lithuanian Catholic Religious Aid Headquarters is in Maspeth, N.Y.

Little Flower, Society of the (www.littleflower.org) Headquarters is in Darien, Ill.

liturgical books Capitalize but do not enclose in quotation marks the proper names of official liturgical books containing the rites, prayers and readings used by a denomination for its public worship.

Liturgical books in the Latin Church include: the *Roman Missal, Lectionary for Mass, Sacramentary, Roman Pontifical, Roman Ritual, Liturgy of the Hours, Book of Blessings, Rite of Ordination of Bishops, Presbyters and Deacons* (formerly *Ordination of Deacons, Priests and Bishops*), *Holy Communion and Worship of the Eucharist Outside Mass, Rite of Baptism of Children, Order of Celebrating Marriage* (formerly *Rite of Marriage), Rite for the Dedication of a Church or Altar, Rite of Confirmation, Rite of Christian Initiation of Adults, Pastoral Care of the Sick: Rites of Anointing and Viaticum* (formerly *Rite of Anointing), Rite of Penance, Order of Religious Profession* and *Order of Christian Funerals* (formerly *Rite of Funerals).* See **rite of ....**

In the Anglican Communion, the chief liturgical book is the *Book of Common Prayer.*

For the proper names of official liturgical books of the Eastern Catholic or other churches, consult with officials of the church in question.

liturgical calendar The official calendar of seasonal and other feasts observed by a particular church or rite.

In the Latin Church the general or universal liturgical calendar, formerly known as the ordo, is often called the *Roman calendar.* Individual religious orders, nations or dioceses may have certain feasts or remembrances on their calendar that are not part of the universal calendar.

See **liturgical year** and **ordo, "ordo."**

Liturgical Conference (www. liturgicalconference.org) Formed in 1940 as a Catholic organization, in 1979 it merged with the Lutheran Society for Worship, Music and the Arts. It is devoted to ecumenical and liturgical renewal within the churches. Headquarters is in Evanston, Ill.

liturgical dress Lowercase all items of liturgical dress, including *alb, chasuble, cincture* and *stole.*

See **alb; chasuble; cincture; crosier; crown; dalmatic; kamelaukion; miter; pallium;** and **stole.**

liturgical time In Jewish religious practice, when the sun sets on one day the next day begins. Eastern Catholic and Orthodox churches generally maintain this practice by beginning the liturgical observance of each day on its eve with evening prayer.

In Latin-rite Catholicism, the practice is maintained chiefly in the observance of Sundays, holy days and other major feasts, when first vespers of the feast is said on the eve of the feast. This liturgical reckoning of time underlies the practice of observing Sundays and other holy days of obligation with Masses celebrated on the eve of the feast.

Unless there is a particular reason to refer to the eve of a feast, story references should treat the feast as beginning on the day it is listed on the calendar.

See **liturgical calendar; liturgical year;** and **Sunday, weekend.**

liturgical year In the Latin Church and in other Western churches it begins with Advent, the fourth Sunday before Christmas, and ends the following year on the Saturday before Advent.

The temporal cycle of the calendar is built around weeks of the year in relation to Sundays and other key feasts of the Lord and the church — Christmas, Easter, Ascension, Pentecost. Because of the changing time of Easter, which is calculated according to the lunar calendar, and the yearly shift of the dates of Sundays, nearly all the observances of the temporal cycle are on different dates each year.

The Orthodox and Eastern Catholic churches have a one-year cycle of liturgical readings. Since the Second Vatican Council, however, the Latin Church and many Protestant churches have adopted a three-year cycle for the liturgical readings for Sundays, feasts of the Lord and other major feasts. When referring to readings of a particular cycle or year, the forms are *Cycle A, Cycle B, Cycle C* or *Year A, Year B, Year C.* Cycle C is used in years evenly divisible by three, such as 2007. Since the liturgical year and the calendar year do not coincide, these calculations refer to the calendar year in which the bulk of the cycle occurs. Thus Cycle C begins with Advent in 2006.

The fixed or sanctoral cycle consists mainly of feasts of Mary and the saints that are observed on the same date each year. In the Latin Church, the liturgical readings for weekdays and most feasts of the sanctoral cycle follow a two-year cycle, referred to as *Year I* and *Year II.* Year I readings are used in odd-numbered years, Year II in even-numbered years.

In the majority of Orthodox and Eastern Catholic churches, Sept. 1 marks the beginning of the liturgical year of fixed feasts. The feast of St. Philip the Apostle, Nov. 14, marks the beginning of the preparatory period for Christmas, comparable to Advent in the West. The cycle of movable feasts has Easter as its focus. It begins with three weeks plus a day (four Sundays) of pre-Lent and continues with six weeks of Lent, Passion Week, Easter, the Easter season, Ascension, Pentecost and then Sundays of ordinary time, which are counted sequentially until the start of the next pre-Lent.

liturgy, devotions *Liturgy* is the collective name for the official rites and acts of public worship in the Catholic Church. It also may be used in its popular meaning as a synonym for the Mass. Lowercase in those uses, but capitalize *Divine Liturgy* as the proper name for the Mass in Eastern Catholic churches.

The main liturgical rites of Roman Catholicism are contained in four books: the *Roman Missal, Roman Pontifical, Roman Ritual* and *Liturgy of the Hours.* Although these are called *books,* since the postconciliar liturgical reforms each usually is broken down into several separate publications with different names. For example, books based on the Roman Missal are the Sacramentary and the Lectionary. See **liturgical books.**

The missal contains rites for the Mass; the pontifical has rites celebrated by a bishop; the ritual has blessings, consecrations and sacraments other than the Eucharist and holy orders; and the Liturgy of the Hours has the official daily prayer of the church. Acts of eucharistic worship outside Mass, such as Benediction of the Blessed Sacrament or the administering of Communion to the sick, are also liturgical and are contained in the ritual. See **Forty Hours devotion** and **perpetual adoration.**

Devotions is the general term for all private prayer and all public but nonliturgical acts of prayer or devotion. Devotional acts include such things as the rosary and other Marian devotions, novenas and the Way of the Cross. Some of the main approved devotions in the church are collected in a book called the "Enchiridion Indulgentiarum." The English translation is called the "Handbook of Indulgences." See **Stations of the Cross.**

Capitalize *Liturgy of the Word* and *Liturgy of the Eucharist,* the proper names of the two main parts of the Mass, and *Liturgy of the Hours.*

See **Liturgy of the Hours** and **Mass.**

Liturgy of the Hours The preferred term in the Latin Church for the official liturgical prayers sanctifying the parts of each day. Generally avoid the older terms, *Roman Breviary* or *Divine Office,* except in historical references or quotations, and then explain that it means the Liturgy of the Hours. In popular usage a prayer book containing the Liturgy of the Hours in convenient arrangement for daily prayer may be called a *breviary,* but the name should not be applied to the prayers inside: *He read from his breviary. He prayed the Liturgy of the Hours. They recited morning prayer together.*

General church law in the Latin Church requires ordained ministers — bishops, priests and deacons — to pray the Liturgy of the Hours daily. Some religious orders and lay institutes require their members to observe this prayer. Church norms encourage all Catholics to make it, especially the primary hours of morning and evening prayer, part of their prayer life. The norms also strongly encourage communal celebration of the Liturgy of the Hours whenever possible.

As reformed after the Second Vatican Council, the Liturgy of the Hours consists of *morning prayer, daytime prayer* (also called *midmorning, midday* or *midafternoon prayer,* depending on the time of its celebration), *evening prayer, night prayer* and the *office of readings.* The office of readings is suitable for use at any time of day or night. Treat the terms for the parts of the Liturgy of the Hours as descriptive terms, lowercased.

The terms *lauds* (for morning prayer) and *vespers* (for evening prayer) may still be used for community services described that way by their organizers: *The new bishop presented his credentials to the priests of the diocese at a vespers service in the cathedral.* In the Anglican Communion the evening prayer often is called *evensong.*

Other terms from the earlier structure of the Liturgy of the Hours — *matins, prime, terce, sext, none, compline* — are generally no longer applicable, except in some religious community contexts.

The *Angelus* and *"Regina Coeli,"* prayers often used to mark noontime and evening, are not part of the Liturgy of the Hours. See those entries.

In the Orthodox and Eastern Catholic churches, the terminology, rules and forms of celebration of the Liturgy of the Hours may vary. Parish celebration of morning and evening prayer holds a stronger place in many Eastern traditions than in the West. Secular clergy generally are encouraged but not required by law to pray the Liturgy of the Hours daily. In monastic communities it is usually a required and central part of daily life. For specific practices consult authorities of the church in question.

living will Do not capitalize or put in quotations. Because legislative proposals on living wills vary widely, give details of the proposal in question.

Londonderry, Derry The town in Northern Ireland is *Londonderry.* It is the see city of the *Diocese of Derry.* Catholics in Northern Ireland also call the town *Derry.* Use *Londonderry* in datelines, but *Bishop Seamus Hegarty of Derry.*

Lord See **Jesus** and **Our Lady, Our Lord.**

Loreto, Loretto *Loreto* is the proper spelling for the town in Italy to which Mary's house allegedly flew. Religious orders and parishes often use the alternate spelling, *Loretto.* Follow the usage of the individual order or parish.

L'Osservatore Romano The Vatican daily newspaper. Avoid use of the word *official* in describing it. Always capitalize and do not put in quotes. On second reference, *L'Osservatore* is acceptable: *L'Osservatore's editorial.*

Do not duplicate the article (*the L'Osservatore*), but it is usually bet-
ter to restructure the sentence than to drop the article from the proper name *(the text in L'Osservatore,* not *the Osservatore text).*

Louvain This is the French name for the city of *Leuven, Belgium.* Use *Leuven* in datelines.

See **Leuven** and **Louvain, Catholic University of.**

Louvain, Catholic University of Acceptable in historical references to the university founded in 1425 in Leuven, Belgium. It was split into two universities, however, following student riots in 1967.

The *Catholic University of Leuven* is the proper name of the Flemish-language institution, which remained at the original site.

The *Catholic University of Louvain* is the proper name of the French-language institution. It also is called the *Catholic University of Louvain-la-Neuve.* It occupies a new university city called *Louvain-la-Neuve* which was built a few miles south of Leuven, near the town of Ottignies. The new campus formally opened in 1972. Each university has its own schools, faculties and degrees, although they cooperate and allow cross-enrollment in courses.

Stories concerning only the Flemish institution should identify it as the *Catholic University of Leuven* and should be datelined *LEUVEN, Belgium (CNS)* —. If background is necessary, the body of the story should explain that the university and city used to be known more commonly by their French name, Louvain.

Stories concerning only the French institution should identify it as the *Catholic University of Louvain* and should be datelined *LOUVAIN-LA-NEUVE, Belgium (CNS)* —. If background is necessary, the body of the story should explain that this is one of two modern universities formed in the 1960s when the original Catholic University of Louvain was split into separate French- and Flemish-language institutions.

In 2005 the U.S. national seminary in Belgium was still called the *American College of the Catholic University of Louvain.* In stories about that institution, whose students may enroll in either university, the traditional university name may be used. If more detail is needed, the two universities may be referred to jointly as *the Catholic universities of Leuven and Louvain.* The seminary is located in Leuven.

Lucifer Lowercase *devil* but capitalize proper names applied to the devil such as *Satan* and *Lucifer.*

See **Satan.**

Lutheran churches Named after Augustinian monk Martin Luther, whose 95 Theses criticizing elements of Catholic belief and practice marked the start of the Reformation in 1517. It was only after publication of the Augsburg Confession in 1530, however, that any Lutheran churches, properly speaking, could be said to exist.

The Lutheran churches are called *confessional* churches because Lutheran identity is defined primarily by adherence to the body of beliefs declared in the *Augsburg Confession* and other 16th-century confessions and documents that, along with the ancient Apostles' Creed, Nicene Creed and Athanasian Creed, were collected in 1580 in the *Book of Concord.* The Book of Concord is the basic collection of doctrinal writings expressing what Lutherans believe is taught in Scripture. Aside from Scripture itself, it is the primary authority for Lutheran belief and teachings.

Polity, or form of governance, traditionally has been a low priority among Lutherans. Some Lutheran churches, including the largest U.S. body, have bishops. The local congregation usually is governed by a council, consisting of the clergy and elected laypeople, which may be headed by the pastor or another council member. Ministers are ordained, but ordination is not considered a sacrament.

National church bodies are made up of congregations and governed by conventions. Congregations are grouped into territorial districts or synods whose functions vary. The term *synod* also is used in the names of some national bodies.

The Lutheran World Federation, founded in 1947, is a global communion of Lutheran churches with headquarters in Geneva. In 2005 it said it had 138 member churches, 11 congregations and one council in 77 countries, representing 66 million of the world's 69.5 million Lutherans. Its highest decision-making body is a world assembly which meets every six or seven years. Between assemblies the federation is governed by a 49-member council, which meets annually, and its executive committee.

The mosaic of Lutheran churches in the United States today is a product of numerous ethnic migrations (especially German and Scandinavian), internal divisions over theology and, especially in the past century, efforts at intraconfessional ecumenism that resulted in eucharistic sharing and acceptance of one another's ministers and often the merger of previously separate bodies.

The American Lutheran Church, the Lutheran Church in America and the Association of Evangelical Lutheran Churches in America merged in 1988 to form the *Evangelical Lutheran Church in America* (www.elca.

org). In 2005, it said it had just under 5 million members. It is headed by a presiding bishop, called the *bishop of the church,* and divided into 65 synods, each headed by a bishop. Headquarters is in Chicago. It is a member of the World Council of Churches and National Council of Churches. It ordains women and is considered theologically liberal within the Lutheran tradition because it does not adhere to strict literal interpretation of Scripture. ELCA is acceptable on second reference.

In Canada the 1988 U.S. merger was anticipated in 1986 when the American Lutheran Church, which had become an autonomous Canadian body in 1967, merged with the three Canadian synods of the Lutheran Church in America to form the *Evangelical Lutheran Church in Canada.* The parallel U.S. and Canadian bodies have a formal working relationship that includes provisions for exchange of pastors and eucharistic sharing.

In 1997, the ELCA entered into full communion with the Presbyterian Church (U.S.A.), the Reformed Church in America and the United Church of Christ. In 1999, it entered into full communion with the Moravian Church and the Episcopal Church.

The *Lutheran Church-Missouri Synod* (www.lcms.org), with about 2.5 million members in 2005, is the second-largest U.S. Lutheran body. Its headquarters is in St. Louis. It does not permit ordination of women and is oriented toward strict literal interpretation of Scripture. It does not have bishops, and polity is strictly congregational. Its highest governing body is the national convention, a meeting every three years of representatives of the synod's 35 districts. The convention elects a president, who oversees the synod's institutional and mission programs. Many Missouri Synod Lutherans are of German background. It is the largest Lutheran body that does not belong to the Lutheran World Federation.

There are more than a dozen smaller Lutheran groups in the United States, most of them formed by congregations that split from a parent body because of doctrinal differences.

BELIEFS: Luther's emphasis on the sinfulness of human nature and his teaching on justification by faith alone are central to Lutheran belief. His other most significant teaching, adopted with different nuances by many non-Lutheran Reformation movements as well, was that Scripture is the only ultimately normative standard for judging faith and doctrine. Lutherans believe in the Trinity and the divinity and humanity of Jesus. They accept only the two sacraments, baptism and Eucharist, for which there is clear biblical evidence of establishment by Christ. Luther's insistence on Scripture alone as a rule of faith has led to strong emphasis in Lutheran worship on proclamation of the word and preaching. At the same time his insistence on the real presence of Christ in the Eucharist led to Lutheran retention of the eucharistic service as the central element of worship. Most U.S. Lutherans call the worship service itself *Holy Communion.* See **church services** and **holy Communion.**

RELATIONS WITH CATHOLICS: The Lutheran World Federation, based in Geneva, maintains an official international dialogue with the Catholic Church. In the United States, the Evangelical Lutheran Church in America is in dialogue with the Catholic Church, with participation by representatives of the Lutheran Church-Missouri Synod. In 1999 the Holy See and Lutheran World Federation signed a "Joint Declaration on the Doctrine of Justification," declaring that their churches "are now able to articulate a common understanding of our justification by God's grace through faith in Christ ... (and) the remaining differences in its explication are no longer the occasion for doctrinal condemnations."

CLERGY: Members of the clergy are known as *ministers*. *Pastor* applies if a minister leads a congregation. Some Lutheran churches have *bishops*. See **religious titles.**

M

MacBride Principles Named for Nobel laureate Sean MacBride, they are a set of nine standards addressing aspects of job discrimination in Northern Ireland.

See **Sullivan Principles.**

Madonna Capitalize when it is used as a title for Mary or substitute for her name, but ordinarily it should not be used except in direct quotes. See **Mary.**

Use of *Madonna* in various devotional titles for Mary is common in Italian, but English usage tends to parallel French and Spanish, in which *Our Lady* is the more common form used: *Our Lady of the Lake, Our Lady of the Snows,* etc. Note, however, that the smoke-darkened image widely revered in Poland, *Our Lady of Czestochowa,* is also popularly known as the *Black Madonna.*

Madonna House (www.madonnahouse.org) An association of Catholic laymen, laywomen and priests founded by the late Catherine de Hueck Doherty in Combermere, Ontario. In 2005 it included some 200 members, as well as 125 associates, and had 20 "field houses" on five continents.

magazine names Consult the Catholic Press Directory published by the Catholic Press Association for the official names of U.S. and Canadian Catholic magazines.

Magi, the Also, the *Wise Men.* The sole Gospel account (Matthew) of their visit to the infant Jesus does not name or number them or call them kings. The popular tradition in the West that there were three seems to have grown from the number of gifts, but there is a tradition in the East that there were 12. There is no historical basis for the popular tradition that they were kings or for the names Melchior, Balthasar and Gaspar given to them in the West about the eighth century. They have been given different names in some Eastern traditions.

magisterium Lowercase in all uses. Ordinarily its meaning should be explained on first use. While *the church's teaching authority* is almost always an adequate explanation, be aware that in Catholic thought the term can refer both to the authority that the pope and bishops have to teach and to the content of what is authoritatively taught.

major archbishop Among the Eastern Catholic churches, three — the Syro-Malabar, Syro-Malankara and Ukrainian — are headed by a *major archbishop.* A *major archiepiscopal church* is similar to a patriarchal church in terms of its relative autonomy in internal governance, especially in its home territory. The chief see of a major archiepiscopal church is called a *major archbishopric,* but apart from some technical references where that status is important to the story, it is sufficient to use *archdiocese: the Ukrainian Catholic Archdiocese of Kiev-Halych, Ukraine; the Kiev-Halych Archdiocese; the Syro-Malabar Archdiocese of Ernakulam-Angamaly, India; the Ernakulam-Angamaly Archdiocese.*

The Code of Canons of the Eastern Churches devotes only four canons, Nos. 151-154, to the differences between patriarchal churches and major archiepiscopal churches. The most significant difference is that when a new major archbishop is elected by a synod of the bishops of that church, his election must be confirmed by the pope. If the pope denies it, a new election must be held. When a synod of bishops of a patriarchal church elects a new patriarch, his election need not be confirmed by the pope. The new patriarch is to submit a request to the pope for ecclesial communion as soon as possible, and he is not to convoke a synod or ordain bishops before he receives ecclesial communion from the pope.

See **Eastern Catholic churches; patriarch; "sui iuris"; and synod.**

man, mankind See **inclusive language.**

March for Life (www.marchfor life.org) The march marks the anniversary of the 1973 Supreme Court decisions that legalized abortion in the United States. Capitalize in references to the annual march — held each Jan. 22, or when Jan. 22 falls on a weekend, the following Monday, in Washington — and to the national office in Washington that organizes it.

Mardi Gras This term, French for "Fat Tuesday," has largely replaced the English terms *Shrovetide* and *Shrove Tuesday* in American references to the Tuesday before Ash Wednesday and to the parades and other festivities that take place, especially in traditionally Catholic countries, during the days preceding Lent. The festive period is called *carnival* in many Latin American and European countries.

marginalize The proper term when you mean *to exclude or ignore, especially by relegating to the outer edge of a group.* The adjective is *marginalized.*

Do not use the words *emarginate* or *emarginated.* They have completely different meanings. See **emarginate, emarginated.**

Marian Capitalize in all uses: *Marian year, Marian devotions.*

Marian Movement of Priests (www.mmp-usa.net) U.S. headquarters is in St. Francis, Maine.

Mariological Society of America (www.udayton.edu/mary/outdev/msa.html) Headquarters is in Dayton, Ohio.

Mariology, Mariological, Mariolatry Compounds formed from the proper name *Mary.* Capitalize in all uses.

marital status Use the same guidelines for men and women in determining whether their marital status is relevant to a story.

See **annul; divorce;** and **sexism, sexist language.**

marriage See **matrimony.**

Marriage Encounter, National (www.marriage-encounter.org) Headquarters is in Orlando, Fla.

Marriage Encounter, Worldwide (www.wwme.org) Headquarters is in San Bernardino, Calif.

Mary In general, avoid titles such as *the Blessed Virgin, Star of the Sea, Queen of Peace, Our Lady,* etc., except in direct quotes. When it is necessary to use honorific or devotional titles that stand for Mary's name, capitalize them.

Do not, however, capitalize descriptive references in sentences which use Mary's name or a pronoun referring back to her: *Catholics believe that Mary, the mother of Jesus, was a virgin. They consider her the spiritual mother of the church.* See **Jesus** for comparison.

For apparitions or miracles attributed to Mary, see **miracles, apparitions.**

For capitalization of events in Mary's life, see **biblical events.**

Maryheart Crusaders Headquarters is in Meriden, Conn.

Maryknoll (www.maryknoll.org) The center of the Maryknoll Fathers and Brothers, formally known as the Catholic Foreign Mission Society, and the Maryknoll Sisters, it is acceptable in datelines. The form: *MARYKNOLL, N.Y. (CNS) —.*

See **datelines.**

Masons Members of those fraternal organizations that follow the principles, usages and rites known as *Freemasonry.* In 2005, there were an estimated 5 million Masons worldwide, 3 million of them in the United States.

Before its new Code of Canon Law in 1983 the Catholic Church had a strict legal prohibition against Catholic membership in the Masons. Since 1983, that prohibition has been moral and doctrinal, not legal.

A 1983 declaration by the Vatican Congregation for the Doctrine of the Faith said the new code no longer invokes excommunication for belonging to the Masons, but Masonic principles "have always been regarded as irreconcilable with the church's doctrine." The declaration added, "Catholics enrolled in Masonic associations are involved in serious sin and may not approach holy Communion."

In an April 1985 report, the U.S. bishops' Committee on Pastoral Research and Practices expanded on the Vatican declaration, saying Masonic principles and rituals "embody a naturalistic religion" that is "incompatible with Christian faith and practice. Those who knowingly embrace such principles are committing serious sin."

Mass The common name for the eucharistic liturgy in the Latin Church. It is also used by Old Catholics, Lefebvrites and sometimes by Anglicans and Armenian Catholics.

The priest *celebrates* or *says* Mass. He does not *read, recite, conduct* or *perform* it. See **celebrant** and **president, presiding.** Always capitalize when referring to the rite, but lowercase any preceding adjectives: *nuptial Mass, funeral Mass, chrism Mass.* Exceptions: *Red Mass,* the traditional name for a special Mass celebrated for members of the legal profession, and, in some places more recently, *White Mass* for health care workers and *Blue Mass* for those in law enforcement.

Generally lowercase names of parts of the Mass if the name is descriptive of the rite or prayer. For example: *opening procession, entrance hymn, penitential rite, readings, first (second, third) reading, homily, profession of faith, prayer of the faithful, petitions, offering of gifts, offertory procession, offertory hymn, prayer over the gifts, preface, eucharistic prayer, kiss of peace, blessing, dismissal.*

Capitalize the formal names, however, of the two major parts of the Mass: *Liturgy of the Word, Liturgy of the Eucharist.*

Also capitalize the names of specific prayers within the Mass which are unchanging. Preferred titles for the main prayers are: *Kyrie, Gloria, Nicene Creed* (or, at times: *Apostles' Creed), Sanctus, Lord's Prayer, Lamb of God.* Acceptable variations are: *Our Father* for *Lord's Prayer, Agnus Dei* for *Lamb of God.* Since hymnals often replace *Kyrie, Gloria* and *Sanctus* with the English titles *Lord, Have Mercy, Glory to God* and *Holy, Holy, Holy,* these English prayer names are also acceptable, particularly when referring to a sung version.

For the specific eucharistic prayers of the *Roman Canon,* use capitals and Arabic numerals: *Eucharistic Prayer 1, Eucharistic Prayer 2,* etc., or lowercase for alternative references: *the first eucharistic prayer,* etc.

Note: Terminology for the eucharistic liturgy and its parts varies among denominations and among Eastern Catholic churches. For example, the service is called the *Divine Liturgy* by many Eastern Catholics; the *Divine Service of the Holy Mysteries* by Maronite Catholics; the *Lord's Supper* by some Protestant denominations; *Holy Eucharist* by Anglicans; *Holy Communion* by Lutherans; the *Service of the Lord's Day* by Presbyterians. Check with denominational officials for current official usage.

See **Catholic Church** and **liturgy, devotions.**

Massgoer

Mass offering See **stipend.**

matrimony The Catholic, Orthodox and Old Catholic churches consider matrimony a sacrament. Most others do not. In the Latin Church, the man and woman who marry are considered the ministers of the sacrament; the priest or deacon is the chief official witness of the church. The priest is generally considered the minister of the sacrament in the theology of the Orthodox, Old Catholic and Eastern Catholic churches. See **sacraments.**

In the Latin Church, Canons 1055-1165 of the Code of Canon Law spell out the requirements and conditions for marriage, impediments to it, norms for celebration of the sacrament, rules for mixed marriages and other matters such as separation of spouses and validation of marriages. Canons 1671-1707 spell out special processes in church courts for matrimonial cases. In the Code of Canons of the Eastern Churches, legislation on marriage is found in Canons 776-866. Canons 1357-1400 of that code spell out special matrimonial procedures in church courts.

Because of the pervasive impact of marriage on most people's lives, the laws, policies and pastoral care concerns of church bodies concerning marriage and family life are complex and highly nuanced. In dealing with the laws and policies of different churches, consult with authorities of the denomination in question to assure that its beliefs and practices are accurately characterized.

See **annul; Cana conference, pre-Cana conference;** and **divorce.**

me, my Lowercase personal pronouns referring to God.

See **God, god(s).**

Mecca, mecca Capitalize only when referring to the Saudi Arabian city in which the holiest shrine of Islam, the Kaaba, is located. See **Islam.**

Lowercase in metaphorical uses: *Hollywood is still a mecca for aspiring actors and actresses.*

medical schools, Catholic In 2005 the only Catholic medical schools in the United States were: New York Medical College in Valhalla, N.Y.;

Loyola University Stritch School of Medicine in Maywood, Ill.; and the schools of medicine of Georgetown University in Washington, St. Louis University in St. Louis and Creighton University in Omaha, Neb.

Melkite Church See **Eastern Catholic churches.**

Memores Domini See **Communion and Liberation.**

memorial of In the general liturgical calendar of the Latin Church, many days popularly called *feast days* are technically classified in the lower rankings of *obligatory memorial* or *optional memorial.* In most news stories the technical liturgical ranking of an observance is not relevant to the story. Use *feast of* unless the ranking is relevant.

See **feast of.**

mercy killing Avoid its use as a synonym for euthanasia.

See **euthanasia.**

Messiah, messiah From the Hebrew word meaning *the anointed one.* Capitalize only when it refers to the divinely promised individual still expected by Jews as their deliverer or when it is used as a name for Jesus, whom Christians recognize as the promised deliverer.

The alternative name for Jesus that Christians use most often, *Christ,* is from the Greek word meaning *the anointed one.*

Lowercase *messiah* when it is applied to any other savior or liberator, religious or secular.

See **God, god(s); Jesus;** and **Judaism.**

messianic Lowercase in all uses.

Methodist churches They trace their origins to an early 18th-century spiritual revival movement, led by John Wesley, within the Church of England. The main branches of Methodism are notable for their combination of personal spirituality, social ministry and evangelical outreach as a Christian ethic.

In Methodist teaching, Scripture contains all the knowledge needed for salvation. Apart from central Christian beliefs, they stress doctrinal freedom but look to the teachings of John Wesley as important guidelines for interpreting Scripture. Central to his teachings were the universality of Christ's redemption, the freedom of every person through faith to be saved, and the importance of interior holiness and of loving service to others.

Methodists recognize the two dominical sacraments, baptism and the Lord's Supper, which they view as a memorial of Jesus' passion and death.

They view themselves as part of the one church of Christ and are ecumenically active.

While the main U.S. Methodist bodies have bishops, the Methodist Church in England has no episcopacy. That lack led Anglicans in 1969 to reject a long-planned reunion of the Church of England and the Methodist Church in England.

The World Methodist Council (www.worldmethodistcouncil.org), with headquarters in Lake Junaluska, N.C., is a cooperative federation of Methodist bodies in 108 countries. There are some 15.5 million Methodists in the United States and some 33 million worldwide.

The *Social Creed,* adopted in 1908 by one of the U.S. Methodist bodies that later formed the United Methodist Church, articulated the commitment of many Methodist churches to social service. It served as the model for the *Social Creed of the Churches* adopted in 1912 by the Federal Council of the Churches of Christ in America, forerunner of the National Council of Churches.

The United Methodist Church (www.umc.org), chief U.S. Methodist body today, reported in 2005 that it had 8.2 million members in 2003. Created in 1968 by the merger of the Methodist Church and the Evangelical United Brethren Church, its Office of Public Information is in Nashville, Tenn.

The highest authority in the United Methodist Church is the General Conference, which meets every four years. It is composed of clergy and laity elected by geographic units called annual conferences, which generally follow state lines.

There are also three major black Methodist denominations in the United States: the African Methodist Episcopal Church (www.ame-church.com), the African Methodist Episcopal Zion Church and the Christian Methodist Episcopal Church (www.c-m-e.org).

All four of these bodies are members of the *Churches Uniting in Christ.* See that entry.

RELATIONS WITH CATHOLICS: The World Methodist Council maintains an official dialogue with the Catholic Church. In the United States the United Methodist Church and the Catholic Church have been in dialogue since 1966. In 2001, the U.S. dialogue team published results of some 30 years of international and national dialogue as resource materials for grass-roots dialogues among members of local Catholic and Methodist congregations.

See **religious titles.**

metropolitan (n., adj.) In Latin-rite ecclesiastical usage, a *metropolitan see* is an archdiocese that is the chief diocese of an ecclesiastical province. Only a few archdioceses are not metropolitan sees. A *metropolitan tribunal* is the first appellate court for diocesan courts in the province. The local court of the archdiocese is distinct and is called the archdiocesan tribunal. A *metropolitan archbishop* is one who heads a province. See **province.**

Unless the status of provincial leadership is a significant element of the story, the term *metropolitan* ordinarily is irrelevant and should not be used.

Used as a noun, *metropolitan* means *metropolitan archbishop.* Use it as a personal title before a name for Orthodox and Eastern Catholic archbishops who use it as their ordinary title: *Russian Orthodox Metropolitan Filaret of Kiev.* For all others, use *archbishop.*

Among the Eastern Catholic churches, use of the term *metropolitan* in reference to an archdiocese or archbishop is more common than in the Latin Church. In Eastern Catholicism, certain metropolitan churches have the status of a *metropolitan church "sui iuris" (of its own right).* Such a church is governed by a council of hierarchs, which enjoys significantly greater legislative power than a province of bishops in the Latin Church. Canons 155-176 of the Code of Canons of the Eastern Churches deal with metropolitan churches and other churches "sui iuris." In stories where the distinctive character of a metropolitan church of an Eastern rite is relevant, use of the term *metropolitan* is appropriate, but its meaning should be explained.

See **archbishop; archeparch, archeparchy; Eastern Catholic Churches;** and **"sui iuris."**

Mexican American Cultural Center (www.maccsa.org) A pastoral institute devoted to ministry within the Hispanic community, focusing on the evangelization of Hispanics in the United States. It is in San Antonio.

Migration and Refugee Services *MRS* is acceptable on second reference for this U.S. Catholic agency. Headquarters is in Washington.

See **Appendix F: U.S. Conference of Catholic Bishops.**

military ordinariate A national ecclesiastical jurisdiction established to assure the spiritual assistance of Catholics who are in military life or involved in work closely linked to the armed forces. Before the Vatican modified norms for them in 1986, these jurisdictions were called *military vicariates.*

More than 30 countries have military ordinariates. They are listed in the Annuario in the section on ecclesiastical jurisdictions other than dioceses.

When the Vatican modified the norms, the U.S. Military Vicariate changed its name to *Archdiocese for the Military Services, United States of America.* In all references *Archdiocese for the Military Services* or *U.S. Archdiocese for the Military Services* is acceptable as a proper name. On second reference *the military archdiocese* or *the archdiocese* is acceptable. Headquarters is in Washington.

Unless a different proper name is used in the story, capitalize *military ordinariate* when it is joined with the name of the country in the form of a title: *The Military Ordinariate of Brazil, the New Zealand Military Ordinariate, the Dutch Military Ordinariate.* Lowercase *military ordinariate* when it stands alone or is used in the plural: *the military ordinariate, the military ordinariates of France and Spain.* In all cases *ordinariate* is acceptable on second reference.

Military Services, Archdiocese for the See **military ordinariate.**

military vicariate See **military ordinariate.**

Militia of the Immaculata (www.consecration.com) A worldwide evangelization movement founded by St. Maximilian Kolbe. U.S. headquarters is in Libertyville, Ill. International headquarters is in Rome.

millennium, millenary *Millennium* and its variants *(millennial, millennialism, millennialist)* are spelled with a double *l* and a double *n.*

Millenary and its variants *(millenarian, millenarianism, millenarianist, premillenarianist, postmillenarianist,* etc.) have a double *l* but a single *n.*

Millenarianism is the belief, espoused by some Christian denominations, that Christ will establish a kingdom on earth for 1,000 years.

See **Jehovah's Witnesses** and **Seventh-day Adventist Church.**

milliard It means *1,000 million:* the amount that is referred to in the United States and Canada as a *billion: 1,000,000,000.*

In the British, French, German, Spanish and Italian counting systems, a *billion* usually refers to what people in the United States and Canada would call a *trillion,* that is, a *million million: 1,000,000,000,000.*

When reporting from a country that uses the British system of expressing large numbers, use the U.S. forms, not the local ones, for figures with 10, 11 or 12 digits before the decimal point:

WRONG: *It cost 15,000 million lire.*

WRONG: *It cost 15 milliard lire.*
RIGHT: *It cost 15 billion lire.*

minister, ministry Never use *minister* as a formal title before the name of a religious leader. It may be used as part of a formal title before the names of certain government officials: *Prime Minister Tony Blair, Foreign Minister Ariel Sharon.* Most Protestant denominations describe their clergy as *ministers.* In most denominations that use this description, the proper formal title before the name is *the Rev.* on first and *Rev.* on subsequent references. See **religious titles.**

In many denominations, including the Catholic Church, the term *lay minister* is used to describe individuals engaged in certain religious activities. Formally recognized lay ministries throughout the Latin rite of the Catholic Church are *acolyte* and *lector.* In the United States, Canada and some other countries, laypeople serve as *extraordinary ministers of holy Communion.* No formal title before a name is used for holders of these offices. See **altar server; extraordinary minister of holy Communion; lay ecclesial ministers;** and **lector.**

Other liturgical and charitable or social-service activities often are described as ministries, whether done by clergy or laypeople. For example: *prison ministry, catechetical ministry, youth ministry, hospital ministry.* Treat all terms for people engaged in these activities as occupational or vocational descriptions, not as formal titles. Many such uses of *ministry* are acceptable, but avoid applying the term so broadly that it loses all definition. Use *service, assistance* or other appropriate terms, for example, to describe paid or volunteer support services for parishes such as printing bulletins, cleaning altar linens, organizing bake sales, answering the office telephone or handling parish finances.

In recent years the church has begun to use the phrase *lay ecclesial ministers* to describe lay ministers who collaborate more substantially or extensively with the pastoral ministry and leadership of the ordained, to the extent that they are regarded as part of the parish or diocesan staff or leadership team.

miracles, apparitions In religious language a *miracle* is a supernatural event. The New Catholic Encyclopedia describes it more technically as "an extraordinary event, perceptible to the senses, produced by God in a religious context as a sign of the supernatural."

Generally *miracle* is used to refer to physical phenomena that defy natural explanation, such as medically unexplainable cures.

When Catholic Church officials investigate alleged *miracles,* they require extensive factual evidence and scientific study before they judge a miracle to be authentic. Proof of two miracles usually is required as a condition for official recognition that someone is a saint. See **canonization.**

An *apparition* is a supernatural manifestation of God, an angel or a saint to an individual or a group of individuals. Often others who are present do not see or hear the apparition.

When Catholic Church officials investigate alleged *apparitions,* the study focuses on the moral, spiritual and psychological character of the visionary, the consistency of any messages with church teachings and other spiritual effects connected with the event. Sometimes — as in the recognized appearances of Mary in Lourdes, France, and in Fatima, Portugal — claims of miracles in conjunction with apparitions are investigated as possible corroboration of the alleged apparitions.

If the church makes an affirmative judgment on an alleged apparition, it says that it is "worthy of belief," but it does not require Catholics to accept any such private revelations as a matter of faith.

A good rule of thumb in reporting on alleged miracles or apparitions is to be skeptical but not cynical.

If church authorities have made no judgment on an event, it should be referred to as an *alleged, claimed* or *reported* apparition or miracle.

If church authorities are investigating a claimed apparition or miracle or have made a judgment on it, those facts should be reported as an essential part of the story.

Miraculous Medal The first medals were made in 1832 and distributed in Paris, after St. Catherine Laboure saw Our Lady standing on a globe, with rays of light streaming from her outstretched hands. Framing the figure was an inscription: O Mary, conceived without sin, pray for us who have recourse to thee." Mary then told Catherine: "Have a medal struck upon this model. Those who wear it will receive great graces, especially if they wear it around the neck." On the reverse of the medal appears the letter M surmounted by a cross with a bar at its base; below this monogram appear the Sacred Heart of Jesus crowned with thorns, and the Immaculate Heart of Mary pierced with a sword.

Misereor (www.misereor.org) A German Catholic foreign relief and development agency similar to *Catholic Relief Services* in the United States, it is funded by an annual collection in Catholic parishes.

MISNA (www.misna.org) Its full name, Missionary International Service News Agency, does not need to be given in stories, but use a descriptive phrase such as *MISNA, a Rome-based missionary news service.*

missal Lowercase unless it is part of the title of a published work: *the Roman Missal, the St. Andrew's Missal.* Do not use quotations around the titles of such resource works.

mission (n., adj.) In Catholic usage *mission* can have many meanings, among them:
— The *mission of the church* refers to its mandate from Christ to preach the Gospel to all people.
— A *mission territory (nation, diocese,* etc.) refers to an area in which the church is not yet firmly established and needs outside assistance.
— A local *mission* or *mission church* is a congregation too small or too new to be established as a separate parish.
— A *mission statement* by a parish, religious order, etc., is a statement of its basic purpose.
— A *parish mission* is an evangelization or renewal technique in which a priest, often a religious priest, visits a parish for a set period of time to preach on matters such as holiness and personal conversion.

Ordinarily the meaning of *mission* within any particular context is clear from the context. Because of the numerous meanings of the word, however, care sometimes is needed to avoid ambiguous language that may be misunderstood.

Do not use *mission* as a verb. Use *commission* for the act of sending a person on a mission or giving a person a mission.

Missionaries of Charity The name of both the male and female orders founded by Blessed Teresa of Calcutta. *Missionary Sisters of Charity* is acceptable if necessary to distinguish between female and male religious orders founded by her, but do not use *Sisters of Charity.*

Missionary Union of Priests and Religious (www.worldmis sions-catholicchurch.org/mu) Promotes missionary awareness. It is one of four *pontifical missionary societies* under the jurisdiction of the Vatican Congregation for the Evangelization of Peoples.

U.S. headquarters is in New York.

See **pontifical missionary societies.**

Missionary Vehicle Association (www.miva.org) Headquarters is in Washington.

mission "sui iuris" A mission territory that is not part of any vicariate or apostolic prefecture, it is headed by an ecclesiastical superior who need not be ordained a bishop. *"Sui iuris"* means *of its own right* and signifies that it is not part of another local ecclesiastical jurisdiction.

miter Not mitre. The tall, pointed ceremonial cap worn as part of liturgical dress by a pope, bishop or abbot in the Latin Church and some Eastern churches. The *miter* and the *pastoral staff,* or *crosier,* are symbols of the office of bishop. In some Catholic and Orthodox churches the liturgical cap, modeled after the Byzantine imperial crown, is more commonly called a *crown.* Some Eastern Catholic and Orthodox bishops and monks also wear a brimless, cylindrical black hat called the *kamelaukion.*

See those entries and **liturgical dress.**

modernism Condemned in 1907 by Pope Pius X, *modernism* in Catho-

lic theological usage does not refer to a single heresy but to a collection of different theories and methods of approach to Scripture and church teaching, each of which was judged to deny some important aspect of Catholic belief.

The *Oath Against Modernism,* instituted in 1910 and dropped in 1967 when a new profession of faith was adopted, was required of all clerics, seminary professors, religious superiors and certain other church officials. The Vatican issued a revised profession of faith in 1989.

In recent decades a number of theologians, religious educators and church officials have been labeled *neomodernists* by some critics who accuse them of reviving modernist views. Neomodernism is neither defined nor condemned by the church.

Mohammed The spelling for the founder of Islam. See **Islam.** For other individuals, follow the spelling the individual uses.

Muslims often refer to Mohammed simply as *the Prophet.* Capitalize *prophet* when it is used as a substitute name. Lowercase when *Mohammed* or a pronoun referring back to him appears in the same sentence, as is done with alternate names used for *Jesus* and *Mary.* See those entries.

monastery A relatively autonomous community house of a religious order, possibly but not necessarily a monastic order. In the Orthodox and Eastern Catholic churches, most religious communities are monastic.

The term may be used as a synonym for *abbey* (a monastery headed by an abbot or abbess) or *priory* (a monastery headed by a prior or prioress). It may not be interchanged freely, however, with *friary, convent, motherhouse, generalate, provincial-*

ate, etc. Some such institutions may be monasteries, but most are not.

Capitalize *monastery* only when it is part of the formal name of a residence: *Emmanuel Monastery in Lutherville, Md.* But: *the Trappist monastery in Spencer, Mass.* (The name of the Spencer institution is *St. Joseph's Abbey.*)

monk A man who belongs to one of the monastic orders in the church, such as Basilians, Benedictines, Cistercians and Carthusians. Do not use interchangeably with *friar.* Do not use as formal title before a name. A monk who is ordained has the title *Father.* One who is not ordained has the title *Brother.* Monastic women are called *sisters* or *nuns.*

monophysite See **Oriental Orthodox churches.**

monsignor An honorary title conferred on some diocesan priests by the pope. It is not given to priests in religious orders. Always abbreviate as *Msgr.* when used before the name. Spell out and lowercase in all other uses. The preferred plural is *monsignors,* not the Italian *"monsignori."*

The Annuario's alphabetical index of names lists many monsignors and the date they received the title. Many priests who have been monsignors for years are not listed, however.

In certain countries, notably England, France and Spanish-speaking nations, it is customary to use *monsignor* (variously abbreviated: *Msgr., Mgr., Mons.*) as a formal title before the names of bishops and archbishops as well. When quoting directly from an English-speaking source, follow the title with the appropriate U.S. form in parentheses: *"Msgr. (Archbishop) Lefebvre is in schism,"* the *British theologian said.* In narrative, indirect discourse or quotations from other languages, always translate the foreign form of the courtesy title into the standard American form: *Archbishop Lefebvre; Bishop Smith.*

The title *Rt. Rev.* refers to a monsignor. If the title *Very Rev.* is used by a source, however, it does not necessarily refer to a monsignor. *Very Rev.* often is used for priests who hold certain church posts, such as seminary rector or diocesan vicar general, whether they are monsignors or not.

See **religious titles.**

monstrance An exposition case and stand, generally large and ornate, used to display the Eucharist for certain processions and devotions. It is sometimes called an *ostensorium.* Do not confuse with the *pyx,* a small case used to bring Communion to people outside Mass.

Morality in Media (www.moralityinmedia.org) A national interfaith organization founded by a Catholic priest. Headquarters is in New York.

Mormon Use with caution in references to members of the *Church of Jesus Christ of Latter-day Saints.* See that entry.

morning-after pill A high dosage of a birth control pill, it is taken up to 72 hours after intercourse to prevent pregnancy. Do not use *emergency contraception* as an equivalent term, except as necessary in quoted material, since the pill can inhibit or delay ovulation, thus acting as a contraceptive, or prevent a fertilized egg from implanting in the uterus, causing an early abortion. In mid-2005, seven U.S. states allowed over-the-counter sales of the morning-after pill, and the Food and Drug Administration had delayed a decision about a similar change in federal law.

Moslem Do not use. Use *Muslim*.

See **Islam** and **Muslim(s).**

"motu proprio" This Latin phrase, which appears at the top of some papal documents, means "on one's own initiative." Popes use it to signal a special personal interest in the subject.

When possible, avoid using the Latin phrase. If it is relevant to the story that the pope issued the document *on his own initiative,* simply say so in English.

If *"motu proprio"* must be used, lowercase it, place it in quotes and follow it with the translation in parentheses. Use it as an adverbial phrase modifying a word such as *issued* or *published.* Do not use it as a noun or adjective or as the title of the document.

WRONG: *In the "Motu Proprio" Pope John Paul II said ...*

WRONG: *According to the "motu proprio" letter ...*

RIGHT: *In the document, issued "motu proprio" (on his own initiative), the pope said ...*

movie classifications and ratings The categories into which the U.S. Conference of Catholic Bishops places films are known as *classifications.* Those of the Motion Picture Association of America are called *ratings.*

These are the USCCB symbols and their meanings:

A-I — general patronage.

A-II — adults and adolescents.

A-III — adults.

L — limited adult audience, films whose problematic content many adults would find troubling.

O — morally offensive.

A formerly used classification, A-IV, designated certain films that, while not morally offensive in themselves, required caution and some analysis and explanation as a protection to the uninformed against wrong interpretations and false conclusions. It was replaced by the L classification in 2003.

These are the MPAA symbols and their meanings:

G — general audiences. All ages admitted.

PG — parental guidance suggested. Some material may not be suitable for children.

PG-13 — parents strongly cautioned. Some material may be inappropriate for children under 13.

R — restricted. Under 17 requires accompanying parent or adult guardian.

NC-17 — no one 17 and under admitted.

When the classifications or ratings are used in news stories or reviews, use these forms as appropriate: *an A-III classification, classified A-II — adults and adolescents — by the USCCB, a PG rating, an NC-17-rated movie, rated R.*

Muhammad The preferred spelling for the founder of Islam is *Mohammed.* See that entry. For all others follow the individual's preference.

Muslim(s) The preferred spelling for followers of Islam. Do not use *Moslem(s).*

Do not use *Black Muslim* (with a capital *B)* except in quoted matter or historical references. There is no major U.S. group that uses this as a formal name today, and many members of the sect once known as *Black Muslims* consider the term derogatory. They simply call themselves *Muslims.*

The predominantly black Islamic sect in the United States that was widely known in the 1960s as the *Black*

Muslims was the *Nation of Islam,* then headed by Elijah Muhammed. After his death in 1975, under the leadership of his son, Wallace D. Muhammad (note the different spelling), it was renamed the *World Community of Islam in the West* and then, in 1980, the *American Muslim Mission.* Wallace Muhammad gradually moved the group toward more orthodox Islamic belief and practice. In 1985 he disbanded the national organization of the American Muslim Mission, in keeping with the traditional Islamic practice of local congregational autonomy.

The name *Nation of Islam* was revived by Louis Farrakhan in 1978 when he broke from the World Community of Islam in the West because he opposed its movement toward more universal Islamic practice and away from distinctive characteristics of the earlier Nation of Islam.

See **Islam** and **Mohammed.**

Muslim World League An Islamic organization formed in the 1960s to represent Muslim people around the world. It has U.N. membership as a nongovernmental organization. Headquarters is in Mecca, Saudi Arabia.

names Unless it would entail a breach of confidentiality, the reader has a right to clear identification of people in stories. Use pseudonyms or other means to hide the identity of a source only if the source, for good reason, must be protected or requires such confidentiality as a condition of providing the information or comment. If a pseudonym is used, inform readers that it is not the person's real name. While hiding an identity is occasionally necessary, in general it should be resisted. Often it is better to ignore the source's information or comments rather than publish them without identifying the source.

Those identified in a story have a right to determine the name by which they are known. When a person changes his or her name — as when Cassius Clay became Muhammad Ali or Jacqueline Kennedy became Jacqueline Onassis — immediately start using the new name as the primary form of reference, but also give the former name in all stories until the public becomes familiar with the new name. After that, include the former name only if there is a specific reason to do so.

In some cases the new name may never become known well enough to allow its use alone. Few people, for example, would recognize *Sister Teresa Benedicta of the Cross* as the religious name of St. Edith Stein, or *Father Louis* as the religious name of Thomas Merton. In such cases, use the better-known name primarily. Mention the lesser-known name if it is relevant to the story.

For personal names of church officials and Vatican employees, the definitive source for spelling is the Vat-

ican's Annuario Pontificio, if the person is named in that book. Do not use the Annuario, however, as a source for the spelling of foreign place names. See **Appendix H: Use of the Annuario.**

Ignore all diacritical marks. Do not add *e* after a vowel with an umlaut in Germanic words and names: *Father Hans Kung (not Kueng), Cardinal Christoph Schonborn (not Schoenborn).*

See **Asian names** for guidelines on family names on that continent and **Spanish and Portuguese names** for guidelines on double last names in those languages.

National Advisory Council The U.S. bishops' *National Advisory Council* is a group of lay men and women, religious men and women, diocesan priests and bishops from around the country selected to advise the U.S. Conference of Catholic Bishops on issues facing the church in the United States. On second reference *the advisory council* or *the council* is acceptable.

National Apostolate for Inclusion Ministry (www.nafim.org) Formerly called the National Apostolate With People With Mental Retardation. Supports the inclusion of people with mental retardation in the Catholic Church. Headquarters is in Riverdale, Md.

National Association for an Inclusive Priesthood (www.corpus. org) Formerly known as CORPUS, this is a membership organization of resigned, married Catholic priests and their spouses. When it was created in 1974, the acronym *CORPUS* stood for *Corps of Reserve Priests United for Service.* The association no longer uses that full name but retains the acronym in its Web address and on its publication, CORPUS Reports. Originally formed to seek a change in the church law of mandatory celibacy and the restoration to active service of priests who had married, it has since expanded its purposes to include advocacy for the ordination of women. In 2005 it had no permanent headquarters but member services were based in Raynham, Mass.

National Association for Lay Ministry (www.nalm.org) Promotes lay ministry. Headquarters is in Washington.

National Association for Parish Catechetical Directors (www.ncea. org/departments/npcd) Headquarters is at the National Catholic Educational Association in Washington.

National Association of African-American Catholic Deacons No permanent headquarters. Check online at www.usccb.org/deacon/organizations.shtml for latest officers.

National Association of Asian-Pacific American Deacons (www. permanentdeacons.org) No permanent headquarters.

National Association of Boards, Commissions and Councils of Catholic Education (www.ncea. org/departments/nabccce) Headquarters is at the National Catholic Educational Association in Washington.

National Association of Catholic Chaplains (www.nacc.org) Headquarters is in Milwaukee.

National Association of Catholic Family Life Ministers (www.nacflm.org) Headquarters is in Dayton, Ohio.

National Association of Catholic Homes & Educators (www.nache. org) Formerly called National Association of Catholic Home Educators. Headquarters is in Elkton, Md.

National Association of Catholic School Teachers (www.nacst. com) Headquarters is in Philadelphia.

National Association of Catholic Youth Ministry Leaders (www. nacyml.org) Operates out of the National Federation for Catholic Youth Ministry in Washington.

National Association of Church Personnel Administrators (www. nacpa.org) Headquarters is in Cincinnati.

National Association of Deacon Organizations (www.nado.us) No permanent headquarters.

National Association of Diaconate Directors (www.nadd.cc) Headquarters is in Rockford, Ill.

National Association of Diocesan Directors of Campus Ministry No permanent headquarters or Web site but chairwoman was in Detroit in 2005.

National Association of Diocesan Ecumenical Officers (www. nadeo.org) No permanent headquarters.

National Association of Evangelicals (www.nae.net) An interdenominational association founded in 1942, consisting of approximately

47,000 congregations nationwide from 52 member denominations and fellowships, as well as a network of several hundred independent churches. The association says it "directly and indirectly benefits over 30 million people." Its Office of Government Affairs is located in Washington and the Office of the President is in Colorado Springs, Colo.

National Association of Hispanic Deacons No permanent headquarters. Check online at www.usccb.org/deacon/organizations.shtml for current officers.

National Association of Hispanic Priests in the United States (www.ansh.org) *National Association of Hispanic Priests* is acceptable in all references. Known in Spanish as *Asociacion Nacional de Sacerdotes Hispanos, EE.UU.* Headquarters is in Lubbock, Texas.

National Association of Independent Colleges and Universities (www.naicu.edu) Headquarters is in Washington.

National Association of Pastoral Musicians (www.npm.org) Headquarters is in Silver Spring, Md.

National Association of Priest Pilots Headquarters is in Cedar Falls, Iowa.

National Association of Religious Brothers See **Religious Brothers Conference.**

National Association of State Catholic Conference Directors (www.nasccd.org) No permanent headquarters.

National Association of the

Holy Name Society See **Holy Name Society, National Association of the.**

National Black Catholic Clergy Caucus (www.bcimall.org/nbccc/index.htm) Headquarters is in New York.

National Black Catholic Congress (www.nbccongress.org) Headquarters is in Baltimore.

National Black Sisters' Conference Headquarters is in Washington.

National Catholic AIDS Network (www.ncan.org) Headquarters is in Chicago.

National Catholic Band Association (www.catholicbands.org) Headquarters is in Chicago.

National Catholic Bioethics Center (www.ncbcenter.org) Located in Philadelphia, it was formerly known as the Pope John Center, the Pope John Center for the Study of Ethics in Health Care, or the Pope John XXIII Medical-Moral Research and Education Center.

National Catholic Cemetery Conference (www.ntriplec.com) Headquarters is in Des Plaines, Ill.

National Catholic Church of America This church with headquarters in Albany, N.Y., is not part of the Roman Catholic Church.

National Catholic Committee on Scouting (www.nccs-bsa.org) Coordinates the Catholic program of the Boy Scouts of America. Headquarters is in Irving, Texas.

For *Catholic awards,* see that entry.

National Catholic Community Foundation (www.nccfcommunity. org) Established in 1997 to help individuals or organizations make a lasting contribution to religious or charitable activities even if they lack the financial or other resources to form their own private foundations. It is located in Annapolis, Md.

National Catholic Council for Hispanic Ministry (www.ncchm. com) Headquarters is in Phoenix.

National Catholic Council on Alcoholism and Related Drug Problems (www.nccatoday.org) Headquarters is in Lake Orion, Mich.

National Catholic Development Conference (www.ncdcusa. org) Headquarters is in Hempstead, N.Y.

National Catholic Educational Association (www.ncea.org) *NCEA* is acceptable on second reference. Do not capitalize the names of departments which fall under its jurisdiction: *secondary education department, seminary department*, etc. But capitalize names of the national organizations connected with some of those departments: *Association of Catholic Colleges and Universities, Chief Administrators of Catholic Education, National Association for Parish Catechetical Directors, National Association of Boards of Catholic Education.* Headquarters is in Washington.

National Catholic Ministry to the Bereaved (www.griefwork.org) Headquarters is in St. Louis.

National Catholic News Service Former name of *Catholic News Service.* See that entry.

National Catholic Office for Persons With Disabilities See **National Catholic Partnership on Disability.**

National Catholic Office for the Deaf (www.ncod.org) Headquarters is in Landover Hills, Md.

National Catholic Partnership on Disability (www.ncpd.org) Formerly called National Catholic Office for Persons With Disabilities. Located in Washington.

National Catholic Rural Life Conference (www.ncrlc.com) Headquarters is in Des Moines, Iowa.

National Catholic Society of Foresters (www.ncsf.com) A fraternal insurance society. Headquarters is in Mount Prospect, Ill.

National Catholic Student Coalition (www.catholicstudent.org) Headquarters is in Newark, Del.

National Catholic Vocation Council See **National Coalition for Church Vocations.**

National Catholic War Council Formed by the U.S. bishops in 1917 to coordinate Catholic service and welfare activities during World War I. Following the war it was restructured as the *National Catholic Welfare Conference.* See that entry.

National Catholic Welfare Conference Established by the U.S. bishops in 1919 as a forum of discussion among themselves and a means of fostering Christian principles at the national level, particularly in the fields of education and social action. It succeeded the *National Catholic War Council* and was itself restructured in

1967 and renamed the *U.S. Catholic Conference.* It became the *U.S. Conference of Catholic Bishops* in 2001. See that entry and **Appendix F: U.S. Conference of Catholic Bishops.**

National Catholic Young Adult Ministry Association (www.ncyama. org) Headquarters is in Washington.

National Center for Catholic Youth Sports (www.nccys.org) Operates out of National Federation for Catholic Youth Ministry in Washington.

National Center for Pastoral Leadership (www.ncpl.org) Formerly Time Consultants. It is located in Severna Park, Md.

National Center for the Laity Founded in 1978 to help U.S. Catholics "link their faith with their work around the home, in the neighborhood and on the job." Headquarters is in Chicago.

National Center for Urban Ethnic Affairs It is based at The Catholic University of America in Washington.

National Christ Child Society (www.nationalchristchildsoc.org) Headquarters is in Bethesda, Md.

National Coalition for Church Vocations (www.nccv-vocations.org) Formerly National Catholic Vocation Council. Headquarters is in Chicago.

National Coalition of American Nuns Headquarters is in Chicago.

National Coalition to Abolish the Death Penalty (www.ncadp.org) It is based in Washington.

National Committee for a Human Life Amendment (www.nchla. org) A Catholic grass-roots pro-life organization. It is located in Washington.

National Conference for Community and Justice (www.nccj.org) Formed in 1927 as the National Conference of Christians and Jews and dedicated to fighting bias, bigotry and racism in America. Local activities are coordinated by 55 regional offices. Do not confuse with the *National Workshop on Christian-Jewish Relations.* See that entry. The national office is located in New York.

National Conference of Catechetical Leadership (www.nccl. org) Formerly called National Conference of Diocesan Directors of Religious Education-CCD. Headquarters is in Washington.

National Conference of Catholic Airport Chaplains Headquarters is at the headquarters of the U.S. Conference of Catholic Bishops in Washington.

National Conference of Catholic Bishops See **U.S. Conference of Catholic Bishops.**

National Conference of Catholic Charities See **Catholic Charities USA.**

National Conference of Diocesan Directors of Religious Education-CCD See **National Conference of Catechetical Leadership.**

National Conference of Diocesan Vocation Directors (www. ncdvd.org) Headquarters is in Neillsville, Wis.

National Conference of Religious Vocation Directors See **National Religious Vocation Conference.**

National Council of Catholic Women (www.nccw.org) *NCCW* is acceptable on second reference. Headquarters is in Arlington, Va.

National Council of Churches (www.ncccusa.org) Acceptable in all references for the *National Council of the Churches of Christ in the U.S.A.* On second reference *NCC* is acceptable, but generally *the council* is preferable.

The NCC was formed in 1950 as a single successor to the Federal Council of Churches and several smaller councils with basically the same goals of bridging denominational differences and furthering cooperation and fellowship. Its members include most major Protestant, Orthodox and Old Catholic denominations in the United States. The Yearbook of American and Canadian Churches lists its members.

The Catholic Church in the United States is not a member but maintains a cooperative relationship with the council. Headquarters is in New York.

See **World Council of Churches.**

National Diaconate Institute for Continuing Education (http://ndice.org) National center for continuing education and spiritual formation of deacons and their wives. Located at the University of Notre Dame in Indiana.

National Evangelization Teams (www.netusa.org) Headquarters is in West St. Paul, Minn.

National Federation for Catholic Youth Ministry (www.nfcym.org) Successor to the National CYO Federation, it fosters ministry by and to Catholic youth through diocesan, regional and national structures.

Among its activities is coordination of the Catholic national religious awards for girls' organizations. Headquarters is in Washington.

See **Catholic awards.**

National Federation of Catholic Physicians' Guilds See **Catholic Medical Association.**

National Federation of Priests' Councils (www.nfpc.org) Headquarters is in Chicago.

National Fellowship of Catholic Men (www.catholicmensresources.org) Not a membership organization but provides resources, training and conferences for Catholic men. Located in Gaithersburg, Md.

National Foundation for Catholic Youth See **Catholic Youth Foundation USA.**

National Hispanic Priests Association See **National Association of Hispanic Priests.**

National Institute for the Word of God (www.wordofgodinstitute.org) Founded to "further effective communication of the revealed word of God as the primary pastoral work of the church." It is located in Washington.

National Leadership Roundtable on Church Management (www.nlrcm.org) Founded in 2005 by a group of Catholic laypeople to assist bishops, pastors and other church leaders in improving the effectiveness of church leadership and managing and developing the church's human and financial resources more effectively. On second reference use *the round table* or *the organization.* Its national office is in Washington.

National Opinion Research Center (www.norc.uchicago.edu) A research center at the University of Chicago. It is noted in religious circles for its studies of religious attitudes and practices in the United States, especially its studies of U.S. Catholics under researchers Father Andrew M. Greeley and William H. McCready.

On second reference, use *the center* or *the research center,* not *NORC.*

National Organization for Continuing Education of Roman Catholic Clergy (www.nocercc.com) Headquarters is in Chicago.

National Pastoral Life Center (www.nplc.org) It is in New York.

National Religious Retirement Office Formerly called the Tri-Conference Retirement Office, it took this new name when the bishops voted in 1994 to add the Council of Major Superiors of Women Religious to the previous members — National Conference of Catholic Bishops (now U.S. Conference of Catholic Bishops), Leadership Conference of Women Religious and Conference of Major Superiors of Men. It was formed in 1986 to address a financial crisis created by rising health care costs, declining membership in religious orders and the inability of religious who served in past decades to save for retirement because they were unsalaried or received only small stipends. The office sponsors the annual collection in U.S. parishes, usually the second weekend in December, for the Retirement Fund for Religious and distributes the funds raised.

See **Support Our Aging Religious.**

National Religious Vocation Conference (www.nrvc.net) Note the singular *Vocation.* Formerly the National Conference of Religious Vocation Directors. Headquarters is in Chicago.

National Review Board Established in 2002 under the terms of the "Charter for the Protection of Children and Young People," it is responsible for monitoring dioceses for compliance with the charter.

National Service Committee of the Catholic Charismatic Renewal (www.nsc-chariscenter.org) It is located in Locust Grove, Va.

National Workshop on Christian-Jewish Relations Begun in 1973 by the U.S. bishops' Committee on Ecumenical and Interreligious Affairs, it gained sponsorship of a number of Christian and Jewish organizations and met every 18 months to two years until 1996.

National Workshop on Christian Unity (www.nwcu.org) An annual workshop begun by Roman Catholics in 1963 to prepare Catholic leadership for the task of ecumenism, it was under the auspices of the dioceses where it met from 1964 to 1969. In 1969 it invited leaders of other Christian churches and ecumenical groups to join as planning and sponsoring partners and formed a national planning committee of about 25 people, representing various U.S. churches, national ecumenical bodies and national associations of ecumenical officers, who plan the next workshop.

native While it is acceptable in most contexts to describe where a person was born, many people from African nations find the word *native* highly offensive because of a long history of derogatory uses of the term on that continent. Use *born in* or similar alternatives to refer to the place of origin of anyone from Africa: *Cardinal Francis Arinze, who was born in Nigeria,* or: *... who comes from Nigeria,* or: *... a Nigerian,* but not: *... a native of Nigeria.*

native American See **Indians** and **Inuit.**

Native American Deacons Association Founded in 1988 in Great Falls, Mont. Check online at www. usccb.org/deacon/organizations.shtml for current officers.

Nativity Capitalize the name of the feast celebrated Dec. 25, *the Nativity of the Lord,* and stand-alone references to the unique historical event of Christ's birth: *a Nativity scene.*

See **biblical events** for guidelines on lowercasing such terms when they are used in their common meaning, but in most cases *birth* is preferable to *nativity* to express the common meaning.

natural family planning Lowercase. It refers to forms of birth regulation which, in conformity with Catholic teaching, do not involve use of any artificial means of contraception. The different methods of natural family planning all share two basic elements: monitoring of the woman's monthly fertility cycle and abstinence during her fertile period except when the couple wants to have a baby.

See **abortion; artificial contraception; birth control;** and **contraceptive sterilization.**

Navajo Not *Navaho*

NCCB-USCC See **U.S. Conference of Catholic Bishops.**

NC, NC News See **Catholic News Service.**

Neocatechumenal Way (www. camminoneocatecumenale.it) Also called the *Neocatechumenate,* this spiritual renewal movement in the Catholic Church began in Spain in 1964 and now has members in 105 countries on five continents. The local Neocatechumenal communities are parish-based and operate as small communities of renewal within the parish. In 1990, in appointing a Vatican official as moderator of the Neocatechumenal Way, Pope John Paul II described it as "an itinerary of Catholic formation valid for our society and for our times." Its statutes were approved by the Vatican in 2002.

The terms *Neocatechumenate* and *Neocatechumenal* were coined by the members of the movement to refer to themselves. They are not used in reference to the modern revival of the catechumenate to prepare unbaptized adults for baptism in the Catholic Church, and they should not be lowercased or used in that way. See **Rite of Christian Initiation of Adults.**

neo-Pentecostal movement See **charismatics.**

neophyte A term used in the Rite of Christian Initiation of Adults for someone who is newly baptized. Avoid its use when possible, substituting phrases such as *newly baptized* or *recently baptized,* or explain its meaning when it is used.

See **Rite of Christian Initiation of Adults.**

Network (www.networklobby. org) A Catholic social-justice lobby. It is not an acronym: Capitalize the first letter only. It is located in Washington.

New Age A term that began to be applied in the 1970s to a wide range of unconventional spiritual quest and personal transformation movements that were then emerging. No single description can be applied to the diverse religious and quasi-religious movements encompassed by the term, but many of them were connected with revived interest in spiritualism or the metaphysical techniques of Eastern religions, identification of the individual person with the essence of the divine, a departure from the Jewish or Christian mainstream from which many adherents came, and expectations that cooperative, environmentally conscious, healthy lifestyles would help bring a golden age of peace and light. When the term is used in a story, the reader should be informed what the speaker means by it.

new evangelization A term first used by Pope John Paul II in 1983 to call for the "re-evangelization" of formerly Christian areas or areas that had turned away from Christian ideals because of cultural influences. Do not capitalize or put in quotes, unless quoting the late pope directly.

New Right But *religious New Right.*

newspaper names Consult the Catholic Press Directory for the official names of U.S. and Canadian Catholic newspapers. Capitalize *the* in a newspaper's name if that is the way the publication is published.

Where location is needed within a name but is not part of the official name, use parentheses: *The Providence (R.I.) Visitor.* Geographic names and adjectives that are part of a newspaper's full name may be dropped on second reference if no confusion would result: *The Vermont Catholic Tribune, the Tribune.* But not: *the South Texas Catholic, the Catholic.*

New Ways Ministry An unofficial resource center and advocacy group for gay and lesbian Catholics based in Mount Rainier, Md., it also seeks changes in church teaching or practice in other areas such as selection of bishops and the ordination of women and married priests.

Nicene Creed A profession of faith considered the primary rule of faith in the Eastern churches and widely held as an authoritative expression of faith in Western churches. In the Catholic Church it is recited at Mass on Sundays and certain other feasts.

Although this is commonly known as the Nicene Creed, scholars refer to it as the *Niceno-Constantinopolitan Creed* because it is not the original creed of the Council of Nicaea in 325. It is an expanded version which the Council of Chalcedon, held in 451, attributed to the Council of Constantinople in 381.

See **Apostles Creed; Creed, creed; "filioque"; and Orthodox churches.**

"nihil obstat" See **imprimatur, "nihil obstat."**

nondenominational A term used especially among North American Protestants to describe Christian organizations or activities not sponsored by or linked to any specific *denomination.* See that entry.

The *Young Men's Christian Association* and *Young Women's Christian Association* are examples of nondenominational organizations. See those entries.

If joint sponsorship or participation by several Christian bodies is meant, the correct term may be *inter-*

denominational, ecumenical or *interfaith,* but not: *nondenominational.* If non-Christian bodies are among sponsors or participants, the proper term may be *interreligious* or *interfaith.*

See **ecumenical, interreligious** and **interdenominational, interfaith.**

North American Academy of Liturgy (http://naal-liturgy.org) It is located in Valparaiso, Ind.

North American College See **Pontifical North American College.**

North American Conference of Associates and Religious (www.catholic-church.org/nacar) Headquarters is in Englewood Cliffs, N.J.

North American Conference of Separated and Divorced Catholics (www.nacsdc.org) Central office is in Hancock, Mich.

North American Forum for Small Christian Communities (www.nafscc.org) A U.S.-Canadian organization of Catholic diocesan directors of *small Christian communities.* See that entry.

North American Forum on the Catechumenate (www.naforum.org) Headquarters is in Washington.

Northeast Hispanic Catholic Center It is located in New York.

Notre Dame This Indiana site of the University of Notre Dame is acceptable in datelines. The form: *NOTRE DAME, Ind. (CNS) —.*
See **datelines.**

novena Any nine-day series of prayers or devotions. Any use for a longer or shorter period is incorrect. Lowercase: *a novena to the Sacred Heart.*

"nullius" See **territorial abbeys.**

nuncio See **papal nuncio.**

nuns, sisters In everyday language the distinction between *nuns* and *sisters* has been ignored to the point that either word may be used as a synonym for the other in references to women religious. The technical distinction, when it is relevant, is that *nuns* belong to *orders* and take *solemn vows* of consecrated life, while *sisters* belong to *congregations* and take *simple vows* of consecrated life.

Both simple and solemn vows may be permanent, and both orders and congregations require periods of postulancy, novitiate and temporary vows before a woman may take permanent vows.

Lowercase *nun* in all uses. Lowercase *religious* unless it is used as part of the proper name of a religious order or congregation. Lowercase *sister* when it stands alone, but capitalize it when it is used as a title before a name or as part of the proper name of a religious order or congregation: *She became a sister in 1978.* But: *Sister Janice Smith, a Religious Sister of Mercy, a member of the Sisters of St. Joseph.*

See **order, congregation, society; religious; religious titles; sister;** and **Appendix E: Religious Orders, Women.**

nuptial Lowercase in all uses: *nuptial blessing, nuptial Mass.*
See **Mass** and **matrimony.**

O

obituaries When writing for the religious press about a death, provide information on the principal funeral service and the date and place of committal of the remains whenever it is relevant and available.

When referring to the principal Catholic Mass celebrated for a dead person prior to burial or entombment of the remains, use *funeral Mass,* even if the body is not present. Any additional Masses celebrated before committal of the remains should be called *memorial Masses.*

Mass for the Dead or *memorial Mass* is used for any later commemorative Masses such as those on the anniversary of someone's death.

In the liturgical laws of the Eastern Catholic churches there is no mention of cremation. In the Latin Church, general liturgical norms forbid the presence of cremated remains at a funeral Mass, but since 1997 each U.S. bishop heading a Latin-rite diocese has had the authority to determine whether cremated remains may be present at funeral Masses in his diocese. In the Latin Church, the rite of committal can be used with a body or with cremated remains. See **cremation.**

The term *Requiem Mass* is no longer appropriate for a funeral or memorial Mass. *Mass of the Resurrection,* a term used briefly in the 1970s for funeral Masses, was abandoned when it was found to be confusing.

Use *Mass of Christian Burial* only in quoted matter. This was the official liturgical name used in many English-speaking countries for the funeral Mass until 1986. At that time the International Commission on English in the Liturgy dropped the term in favor of *funeral Mass* because *Mass of Christian Burial* suggested that burial followed immediately, which was not always the case in practice.

If the liturgy at the church is not a Mass, use *funeral liturgy, funeral rites* or *funeral service.*

The Catholic service at a cemetery chapel, mausoleum or grave site immediately preceding burial or entombment of the remains is called the *rite of committal.*

Devotions or prayer services for the dead person before the funeral Mass may be variously described, but in general they are all *vigil services.* Information on them may be important locally, but it is rarely relevant in national news stories.

Avoid euphemisms for death except in direct quotes.

obscenities See **offensive language** in **Appendix A: Special Style Considerations.**

Oceania As used by the Vatican, this geographical region includes Australia, New Zealand and Papua New Guinea as well as the three major Pacific island regions of Melanesia, Micronesia and Polynesia. It does not include the Philippines or Indonesia.

For a complete list of church jurisdictions in Oceania, see the "Geographic Distribution of Sees" section in the Annuario Pontificio. See **Appendix H: Use of the Annuario.**

When *Oceania* must be used, as in stories about church statistics around the world, explain that it refers to *Australia and the islands of the Pacific.* Give additional details only if the context requires greater precision.

octave In religious usage, the eighth day following a major feast or the period from the feast to its eighth day. Since the feast itself is one of the days counted, the octave day falls on the same day of the week as the feast.

offensive language See **Appendix A: Special Style Considerations.**

offline See **online.**

Old Catholic churches (www. utrechter-union.org) An association or communion of national churches brought together in 1889 by the Union of Utrecht. Composed of small church groups that broke with Rome, mainly in the 19th century and mainly out of nationalist concerns or opposition to Vatican I definitions of papal primacy and infallibility, Old Catholics maintain most central Catholic beliefs and are led by bishops validly ordained in apostolic succession.

NOTE: Scores of churches, many consisting of very few congregations, call themselves *Old Catholic* although they do not belong to the Union of Utrecht. When writing about those churches clarify to readers that they are not part of the union. In 2005, there were no churches belonging to the union in the United States and Canada.

Among the bishops of the autonomous churches of the union, the archbishop of the Little Church of Utrecht is considered first among equals. He is president of the *International Bishops' Commission,* composed of all the bishops of all member churches. The commission, which meets annually, gives the union overall direction.

Until its separation in 2003 the largest denomination in the union had been the *Polish National Catholic Church* in the United States and Canada.

Members in 2005 were the Old Catholic churches of the Netherlands, Germany and Switzerland — the union's three founding members — and those of Austria, the Czech Republic and Poland. Churches or missions in Croatia, France, Italy, Sweden and Denmark are governed by a bishop-delegate from one of the six countries where dioceses are established.

Intercommunion, or sharing in the sacramental life of one church by members of the others, is practiced among all member churches of the union. In addition, since 1931 they have had an intercommunion agreement with Anglicans. The Polish National Catholic Church joined in that agreement in 1946 but terminated it in 1978 after the U.S. Episcopal Church began ordaining women. In 1996 the PNCC broke communion with the German Old Catholic Church when the German church ordained two women priests. Two years later the PNCC did the same with the Austrian Old Catholic Church when that church ordained a woman priest and approved the blessing of homosexual unions. The PNCC-Old Catholic separation was finalized in 2003.

BELIEFS: The Declaration of Utrecht, which accepts the first seven ecumenical councils, serves as a basis of doctrinal unity, although not all members adhere fully to it. They accept seven sacraments but generally do not require auricular confession and generally do not use transubstantiation as a formulation for expressing Christ's real presence in the Eucharist. Their liturgy resembles the Roman liturgy but has been celebrated in local languages since the 19th century.

STRUCTURE: Each bishop governs his diocese autonomously in accord with the laws established by clerical and lay members of synods, which are the highest authority in each church. Bishops are elected by the synods. Priests govern parishes.

CLERGY TITLES: Clergy offices and titles parallel those used in the Catholic and Anglican churches: *archbishop, bishop, father.*

ECUMENICAL RELATIONS: Old Catholic churches have been in dialogue with the Orthodox and Anglican churches for many years and hold membership in the World Council of Churches.

For more about the PNCC and its distinctive ecumenical relations with the Catholic Church, see **Polish National Catholic Church.**

Old City Capitalize when referring to the portion of modern Jerusalem contained within the ancient city walls.

See **Jerusalem.**

online The condition of a computer (or by extension its user) when it is connected to a network, especially the Internet. One word in all uses.

Opus Dei (www.opusdei.org) Founded in 1928 in Madrid by St. Josemaria Escriva de Balaguer, its aim is to spread throughout all sectors of society a profound awareness of the universal call to holiness and apostolate in the ordinary circumstances of life and through one's professional work. In 1982, Pope John Paul II designated it a personal prelature, formally known as the *Prelature of the Holy Cross and Opus Dei.*

In 2005 it reported membership of about 86,000 in 60 countries. Included are about 3,000 in the United States and about 1,750 priests worldwide. Its U.S. press office is in New York.

See **personal prelatures.**

ordain, ordination These are the proper terms in Catholic usage for references to the conferral of the sacrament of orders on a deacon, priest or bishop.

See **consecrate, consecration** and **ordination of women.**

order, congregation, society
A *religious order* or *religious congregation* in the Catholic Church refers to an institute of men or women who take vows of poverty, chastity and obedience, living under a common rule in what the church calls a consecrated life. In general news reporting these usually can be referred to as *religious orders* without reference to technical distinctions between orders and congregations.

The basic technical distinction, if it must be made, is this: Members of an *order* take solemn vows. Members of a *congregation* take simple vows. See **brother; celibacy, chastity; nuns, sisters; sister;** and **vow, promise.**

For the use of *order* relating to members of *third orders secular,* see **third order.**

Societies of priests are organizations formed for a particular apostolate, often foreign missionary work. Most of these are not properly called religious orders or congregations because their members do not profess vows, even though many follow a pattern of life similar to religious and are governed by many of the same general church laws. Although they are not religious orders, their major superiors can hold membership in national conferences of religious superiors.

Two priestly societies with U.S. members that are often in the news are:

— *The Society of St. Sulpice (Sulpicians),* a society of diocesan priests released from diocesan duties to work in seminaries run by the society.

— *The Catholic Foreign Mission Society of America (Maryknoll),* a society devoted to missionary work.

As a rule, avoid referring to such societies individually as religious orders. In stories in which they are referred to along with congregations or orders, however, because of the similarities all may be included in collective references to *religious orders.*

EXCEPTIONS: Several orders or congregations have *society* in their name but are orders or congregations whose members profess vows. These include the *Society of Jesus (Jesuits),* which is a religious order, and the *Society of Mary (Marists), Society of St. Edmund (Edmundites)* and *Society of the Divine Word (Verbites),* which are congregations.

See **Appendix D: Religious Orders, Men** and **Appendix E: Religious Orders, Women.**

Order of Alhambra See **International Order of Alhambra.**

orders An acceptable term, if no confusion would result, for referring to the sacrament known more fully as *holy orders* or *the sacrament of orders.*

See **holy orders.**

ordinary (n., adj.) In Catholic ecclesiastical usage *ordinaries* are diocesan bishops or their equivalent, their vicars general and episcopal vicars, and major superiors of clerical religious orders, congregations or societies. Lowercase. Always treat as a job description, never as a title before a name. See **archbishop** and **bishop.**

Before the new Code of Canon Law was issued in 1983, *ordinary* often was used to refer exclusively to those who were heads of dioceses or major superiors of religious orders. The new code redefined the term, extending its meaning to cover vicars general and episcopal vicars. The proper term now for the chief bishop of a diocese is the *diocesan bishop* or *residential bishop.* See **residential bishop.**

When *ordinary* must be used as a noun in its ecclesiastical sense in a news story, give the reader a definition or explanation appropriate to the context. Some examples: *Only ordinaries — bishops, religious superiors and certain other diocesan authorities — are eligible. "You need the permission of your ordinary (bishop or episcopal vicar)," the pastor said. "I've been transferred by my ordinary (religious superior)," Father Jones said.*

The ecclesiastical usage of *ordinary* as an adjective means having jurisdiction or power by virtue of ordination or office, not by delegation. For example, in the Latin Church, any bishop, priest or deacon is an ordinary minister of Communion, but laypeople are not; they are not to distribute Communion without authorization from a competent authority. See **extraordinary minister of holy Communion.** In Eastern Catholic churches, any priest is an ordinary minister of chrismation. In the Latin Church the ordinary minister of confirmation is the bishop; a Latin-rite priest must be authorized by law or the competent authority to administer confirmation. This ecclesiastical usage of *ordinary* as an adjective is closely akin to its standard use in English in the sense of *usual, regular, normal.* Unless there is special reason to clarify its technical meaning, usually it can be used in this way without additional explanation.

ordination of women In a 1976 declaration the Vatican Congregation for the Doctrine of the Faith said that "the church, in fidelity to the example of the Lord, does not consider herself authorized to admit women to priestly ordination." In a 1994 apostolic letter

Pope John Paul II said, "I declare that the church has no authority whatsoever to confer priestly ordination on women and that this judgment is to be definitively held by all the church's faithful." In 1995 the doctrinal congregation said the church's teaching on this matter pertains to the deposit of faith and is taught infallibly.

Catholic officials have termed the admission of women to priesthood and episcopal orders in the Anglican Communion an obstacle to restoration of church unity. The Orthodox churches do not admit women to priestly ordination. Within the communion of autonomous Old Catholic churches, ordination of women to the priesthood in the German and Austrian churches in the 1990s led the U.S.-Canadian member, the Polish National Catholic Church, to break off communion with those two churches.

In writing about this issue, make it clear high in the story that the Catholic Church's teaching concerns *priestly ordination* or *ordination to the priesthood.* In 2005 it was not definitively settled whether the nonadmission of women to the diaconate would remain in force in the Catholic Church, but the diaconate issue was recognized as a distinct issue doctrinally and historically, and the authoritative teachings cited above clearly refer only to *priestly* (and a fortiori *episcopal*) ordination. In 2001, however, three Vatican congregations ordered the discontinuation of any courses that "directly or indirectly" appear to be preparing women for ordination as Catholic deacons, and in 2002 a study by the International Theological Commission concluded that the role of women deacons in the early church cannot be considered equivalent to that of ordained male deacons.

See **ordain, ordination.**

For references to women ordained as deacons, priests or bishops in those churches that permit the practice, see **religious titles.**

ordo, "ordo" A Latin word meaning *order,* its English-language usage given in dictionaries, as the Catholic Church's official annual calendar of feasts, has largely disappeared. Refer to such calendars simply as *liturgical calendars.* If it must be used as the Latin word for *order* in other senses, as in the orders of diaconate, priesthood and episcopate or as part of the title of various liturgical books in Latin, place it in quotes as a foreign word and provide a translation. In most cases, except in direct quotations it is better simply to substitute the normal English translation (or official English title) in place of the Latin version. For example: *Order of Religious Profession,* not: *"Ordo Professionis Religiosae"*; *Rite for the Dedication of a Church or Altar,* not: *"Ordo Dedicationis Ecclesiae et Altaris."* Capitalize *"ordo"* only when it occurs as part of the formal title of a book or document.

See **liturgical books** and **liturgical calendar.**

organizations and institutions Capitalize the formal names of departments and offices of the USCCB and of the congregations and other bodies of the Roman Curia, the church's central administrative offices. Lowercase flip-flopped or shortened versions of those names. See **Appendix F: U.S. Conference of Catholic Bishops** and **Appendix G: Vatican Agencies.**

Capitalize formal names of religious orders and flip-flopped or informal proper names by which they are commonly known. For example: *the Order of the Holy Cross, Crosier Fathers, Crosiers.* See **Appendix D: Re-**

ligious Orders, Men and **Appendix E: Religious Orders, Women.**

Many organizations and institutions use extensive capitalization of common nouns and adjectives when referring to their own internal divisions and structures. For consistency, lowercase the names of such internal elements if they are widely used generic terms: the *general chapter* of the Sisters of Mercy, the *board of trustees* of Georgetown University, the *communications office* of the Detroit Archdiocese, the University of Notre Dame's *theology department.*

Uppercase such elements only when they are unique proper names or are not widely used as generic terms: Catholic University's *National Catholic School of Social Service,* the *General Assembly* of the World Council of Churches, the *House of Delegates* of the National Federation of Priests' Councils, the *House of Bishops* and *House of Deputies* of the Episcopal Church.

Oriental Use *Eastern,* not *Oriental,* in references to the Catholic churches which have their origins in the East: *the Eastern Catholic churches, the Vatican Congregation for Eastern Churches.*

See **Eastern Catholic churches** and **Oriental Orthodox churches.**

Oriental Orthodox churches The Oriental Orthodox churches, also known as ancient Oriental churches or pre-Chalcedonian, are the Armenian, Coptic, Ethiopian, Syrian, Malankara Orthodox Syrian and Eritrean (made independent from the Ethiopian by mutual agreement in 1994, following Eritrea's political independence from Ethiopia). They trace their roots to apostolic times, and, like the Orthodox churches, they accept seven sacraments and allow ordination of married men to the priesthood but choose their bishops only from among celibate priests. They are in communion with one another, but not with the Catholic Church or the Orthodox churches that split with Rome in the 11th century. Worldwide membership totals about 30 million.

Do not use *monophysite* to describe the Oriental Orthodox churches except in historical references to the origins of their split with the rest of Christianity.

Monophysitism refers to a heresy that generally is no longer ascribed to these churches. For centuries they were considered heretical because they insisted that Christ has only *one nature.* They broke with the rest of Christianity over the *two natures in one person* terminology adopted in 451 at the Council of Chalcedon. Most scholars today conclude, however, that the differences were semantic rather than doctrinal. In 1971 Pope Paul VI and Syrian Patriarch Mar Ignatius Yakoub III jointly declared that "there is no difference in the faith" of their churches concerning Christ. Similar official joint declarations with heads of Oriental Orthodox churches followed: Catholic-Coptic in 1973, Catholic-Malankar Syrian in 1983 and Catholic-Armenian in 1996.

Catholic-Oriental Orthodox dialogue in the United States began in 1976.

original sin

orthodox, Orthodox Lowercase in nonreligious and generic religious uses: *orthodox Republicans, orthodox Catholic beliefs.* Capitalize in references to Eastern Orthodox or Oriental Orthodox churches and their members and in references to the Orthodox branch of Judaism. See **Judaism; Oriental Orthodox churches;** and **Orthodox churches.**

When referring to groups which describe themselves as defenders of *orthodox Catholic teaching,* avoid using *orthodox* in a loaded or judgmental way that suggests that all those persons with whom such groups disagree are heterodox or heretical.

Orthodox churches The collective term for those churches originating in Eastern Europe and the Mediterranean region that separated from Rome in the 11th century. They maintain a unity of doctrine and an ordained hierarchy that traces its roots back to the original apostles.

They also are called *Eastern Orthodox churches. Eastern* may be dropped in most references, except where there could be confusion with the *Oriental Orthodox churches.* See that entry.

NOTE: There are many small independent church bodies that use *Orthodox* in their name but are not in communion with the canonical Orthodox churches. When writing about any of them, clarify to the reader that they are not part of the Orthodox Communion.

The Orthodox churches were part of the main body of Christendom that remained undivided until 1054, when the patriarch of Constantinople and a papal delegation from Rome excommunicated each other in a dispute over papal primacy. The schism gradually hardened because of political divisions, Orthodox objections to the "filioque" addition to the Nicene Creed in the Catholic Church, and atrocities committed by partisans on both sides. See "**filioque**" and **Nicene Creed.**

ORGANIZATION: Orthodox churches are self-governing and are generally defined by the national or ethnic identity of their region of origin. Within a church there are archdioceses and dioceses, each governed by a bishop. The chief archbishop of the church governs along with the synod of that church's bishops. Synods elect new bishops and resolve any major issues of faith and order facing the church.

All the churches give special honor to the Orthodox patriarch of Constantinople, who is called the *ecumenical patriarch.* The section of Istanbul, Turkey, where he resides is called *the Phanar.* He has power to propose a pan-Orthodox synod of bishops and to invite the other Orthodox churches to join in common action, but among all Orthodox bishops he is considered the "first among equals." His primacy does not entail direct or ultimate jurisdiction over other Orthodox churches.

With a combined total of about 219 million members, the Orthodox form Christianity's second-largest faith family, after the Catholic Church.

There are 14 Orthodox churches that are generally accepted as "autocephalous," which in Greek means "self-headed." These include: the four ancient Eastern patriarchates (Constantinople, Alexandria, Antioch and Jerusalem); five other patriarchates (Russia, Serbia, Romania, Bulgaria and Georgia); and five churches headed by an archbishop or metropolitan (Cyprus, Greece, Poland, Albania and the Czech and Slovak Republics, as one church). The Orthodox Church in America was given independence in 1970 by the patriarch of Moscow, but the patriarch of Constantinople and most other Orthodox churches refused to recognize it as autocephalous.

The autonomous Orthodox churches, which are canonically dependent on another Orthodox church, include those of Sinai, Finland, Japan, China and Estonia. Another group of churches is under the canonical protection of the Ecumenical Patriarchate because of special circumstances or political turmoil in their countries of origin. These include the American Carpatho-Russian Orthodox Greek Catholic Diocese of the USA, based in Johnstown, Pa.; the Ukrainian Orthodox Church of the USA and Diaspora, with headquarters in South Bound Brook, N.J.; the Russian Orthodox Archdiocese in Western Europe, based in Paris; the Albanian Orthodox Diocese of America, with headquarters in Las Vegas; the Belarusan Council of Orthodox Churches in North America, based in South River, N.J.; and the Ukrainian Orthodox Church of Canada, based in Winnipeg, Manitoba.

The largest Orthodox body in the United States is the Greek Orthodox Archdiocese of America, with headquarters in New York. The second-largest U.S. body is the Orthodox Church in America, based in Syosset, N.Y. Heads of Orthodox jurisdictions in the Americas cooperate through the Standing Conference of Canonical Orthodox Bishops in the Americas, often abbreviated in Orthodox circles as SCOBA. Its headquarters is in New York. In writing for non-Orthodox audiences, *SCOBA* is acceptable on second reference, but alternate forms of reference such as *the conference* are preferred. Most of the Orthodox churches are members of the World Council of Churches.

RELATIONS WITH CATHOLICS: The Orthodox churches maintain an official dialogue with the Catholic Church, and leaders on both sides have engaged in numerous exchanges and symbolic acts to overcome old enmities and restore mutual understanding. In 1965 Pope Paul VI and Patriarch Athenagoras I annulled the mutual excommunications that had divided Constantinople and Rome since 1054. In 1979 Pope John Paul II and Patriarch Dimitrios jointly created the International Commission for Theological Dialogue Between the Catholic Church and Orthodox Churches. As of mid-2005 the dialogue had not met since 2000, when it was unable to reach agreement regarding the church unity model represented by the union with Rome of the Eastern Catholic churches. In the United States, a Catholic-Orthodox theological consultation has been going on since 1965 and a joint committee of bishops has met annually since 1981. The Catholic Church recognizes the validity of all Orthodox ministry and sacraments.

BELIEFS: The term orthodox (Greek for "right-thinking") derives from the adherence of these churches to the teachings of the seven ecumenical councils held before the schism of 1054.

Aside from the questions of papal primacy and infallibility, beliefs generally are the same as those described in the Catholic Church entry. Theological, artistic and prayer traditions reflect an emphasis on the Holy Spirit, on mystery, and on Christ's redemption of the whole cosmos, not just of humanity.

Liturgies reflect cultural heritage. The principal eucharistic worship service is called the Divine Liturgy. Communion ordinarily is given under both forms, and the bread ordinarily is leavened. The Orthodox have seven sacraments. The three sacraments of initiation — baptism, chrismation and first Communion — usually are given together in infancy.

CLERGY: Married men may be ordained priests, but an ordained man may not marry after ordination. Celibacy is required of monks. Because only celibates are permitted to become bishops, bishops are usually chosen from among monks rather than from the diocesan clergy. Women cannot be ordained. Many Orthodox archbishops and bishops follow the custom of using only a first name after the title. If a patriarch uses a Roman numeral after his name to indicate succession, it may be dropped in subsequent references. If a patriarch is the first of that name, however, drop the number on first reference as well. If a bishop uses only a first name, use the title and first name in all references: *Orthodox Patriarch Bartholomew of Constantinople, Patriarch Bartholomew; Greek Orthodox Archbishop Demetrios of America, Archbishop Demetrios.* Use *Father* as the standard title before the name of an Orthodox priest. See **religious titles.**

See **Eastern Catholic churches** and **Oriental Orthodox churches.**

Our Father Also, the *Lord's Prayer.*

Our Lady, Our Lord Capitalize *Our.* As in other phrases such as *His Holiness* or *Your Majesty,* the pronominal adjectives preceding these honorific titles for Mary and Jesus have come to be treated as part of the titles themselves.

Our Lady's Rosary Makers (www.olrm.win.net) Headquarters is in Louisville, Ky.

pagan (n., adj.) Use of this term, once commonly employed by Christians to refer to nonmonotheistic people — anyone who was not Christian, Jewish or Muslim — today should be avoided in news reporting except in direct quotations or historical references, especially to the ancient polytheistic peoples of the Greek and Roman worlds or their beliefs or practices. Use *non-Christian* or other descriptions appropriate to the specific individual, group or set of groups to which you are referring. For example: *Buddhists, Hindus, members of traditional tribal religions, nonbelievers* (for those who reject all religious belief), *animists.*

Palestinian Authority Acceptable in all references for *Palestinian National Authority*, created in 1994 to administer Palestinian areas of the West Bank and Gaza Strip. It is headed by a president. Do not confuse with the *Palestine Liberation Organization*, a coordinating council for Palestinian organizations, which was founded in 1964 and is headed by a chairman.

pall A small square of stiffened linen, or cardboard covered with linen, used to cover the chalice at Mass.

pallium A circular white woolen band with pendants front and back, featuring six black crosses. Worn around the neck atop the outer vestments in liturgical ceremonies, it is given by the pope to Latin-rite archbishops who head metropolitan sees as a symbol of their authority over the ecclesiastical province and their unity with the pope. If an archbishop is transferred from one metropolitan see to another, he receives a new pallium.

In the Eastern Catholic churches, patriarchs and major archbishops do not receive a pallium, but the head of a metropolitan church "sui iuris" cannot ordain bishops or convene his council of hierarchs before he receives the pallium from the pope.

Use *palliums,* not *pallia* for the plural.

See **liturgical dress.**

Palm Sunday See **Passion Sunday.**

pantheism, panentheism *Pantheism* is a belief that the whole universe is God. It is alien to Christian belief.

Panentheism is a belief that God is present in everything. In some forms it is compatible with Christian belief.

Papal Foundation (www.thepapalfoundation.com) Headquarters is in Philadelphia.

papal honors Two decorations and five orders of chivalry are listed in the Annuario as honors conferred directly by the pope.

The decorations are the *Pro Ecclesia et Pontifice Cross* and the *Benemerenti Medal.*

Of the five equestrian orders, only the two of lowest rank are widely known because of the number of recipients. The orders are, in descending rank:

— The *Supreme Order of Christ,* or *Knights of Christ:* reserved mainly to heads of state.

— The *Order of the Golden Spur,* or *Knights of the Golden Spur.*

— The *Order of Pius,* or *Knights of Pius.*

— The *Order of St. Gregory the Great.* See **Knights of St. Gregory.**

— The *Order of St. Sylvester the Pope.* See **Knights of St. Sylvester.**

Another equestrian order, the *Knights of the Holy Sepulcher,* is under the patronage of the Holy See but is governed by a cardinal, called the grand master, who is appointed by the pope. See **Knights of the Holy Sepulcher.**

papal nuncio A Vatican diplomatic representative with the rank of ambassador. He is responsible for the Holy See's relations with the church where he is stationed as well as its diplomatic relations with the state.

The title of nuncio was given formerly only to a papal envoy who automatically held the rank of dean of the diplomatic corps in the nation. One who was not dean of the diplomatic corps was called a *papal pro-nuncio.* In the 1990s the Vatican began to phase out the title *pro-nuncio* by calling all its new ambassadors nuncios. Only those appointed as pro-nuncio before the phaseout retained that title. By 2004 no pro-nuncios remained. The Vatican yearbook designates nuncios who are not diplomatic corps deans with an asterisk.

A nuncio or a pro-nuncio can also be described as a *Vatican ambassador, papal ambassador* or *ambassador of the Holy See.*

An *internuncio* is a papal envoy with the rank of minister rather than ambassador.

The forms *apostolic nuncio, apostolic pro-nuncio* and *apostolic internuncio* also are acceptable.

In historical references to former pro-nuncios, as in giving biographical background of someone who was a pro-nuncio before the decision to phase that title out, use *pro-nuncio* but explain briefly with a phrase such as: *a title then given to Vatican ambassadors to some countries.*

Since all papal representatives to nations are clergy, the religious title takes precedence over the diplomatic title: Lowercase the diplomatic title and do not use it as a formal title before the name.

Do not confuse the office of nuncio with that of *apostolic delegate,* a papal representative to the church in a country who is not an accredited envoy to the country itself. See **apostolic delegate.**

parable See **Bible.**

paradise

paraliturgical A term describing communal prayer services or communal devotional practices that are not part of the official worship, or liturgy, of a church. In the Catholic Church there are numerous popular devotions that are paraliturgical. Explain the term if it must be used in a story. Do not use the noun form, *paraliturgy;* instead, use an appropriate descriptive term for the particular devotion or service being discussed, such as *novena, rosary* or *prayer service.* See **liturgy.**

paraliturgy Do not use this term to describe a ceremony that includes elements of the Mass. Use *ceremony, celebration* or a similar term instead.

parish In Catholic usage, most parishes are territorial: Their membership consists of Catholics within the parish's geographic boundaries.

Some parishes are formed on a different basis. A *national* or *ethnic* parish may be established to care for people of a particular nationality. A parish established for the faculty and students of an educational institution may be called a *campus* or *university* parish.

The canonical head of a parish is a *pastor.* See that entry. If a parish has no pastor or is served by a nonresident pastor, it may be governed in many matters by an *administrator.* See that entry.

Capitalize as part of a formal name: *St. Anne Parish, Resurrection Parish.* Lowercase in other uses. Generally it is preferable to use *parish* when referring to the organization or congregation, reserving *church* for the building used for worship. See **church.**

For proper use of the possessive form when a parish is named after a saint, see **saint.**

Parish may be used to designate a local organization or its membership in Orthodox, Old Catholic and Anglican bodies. Many Protestant denominations prefer to use *congregation.*

In Louisiana, *parish* is also used as a term for a civil division, corresponding to a county in other states. For readers outside Louisiana explain the civil meaning when using *parish* in this sense.

parish council See **pastoral council.**

parish life coordinator A deacon, layperson or religious sister or brother who administers a Catholic parish that does not have a resident pastor. Do not use as a title before a name. See **pastor** and **administrator.**

parish school of religion A term used in some places for Catholic parish religious education or catechetical programs for school-age children who are not in Catholic schools. If the term is used, explain its meaning. Do not capitalize unless it is used as part of a formal name. On subsequent references, repeated use of *school* could mislead a reader into thinking it includes a full academic program, like a parochial school. Use more commonly understood alternative descriptions, such as *catechetical program* or *religious education program* to clarify what it is.

parishioner Not *parishoner.*

parochial schools Except in direct quotations do not use as a synonym for *Catholic schools* or *religiously sponsored* schools. A *parochial school* is a school owned or run by a *parish.* Within the Catholic Church there are also *interparish, regional* and *diocesan* schools and schools run by religious orders or by private lay groups.

partial-birth abortion A procedure used in late-term abortions in which an unborn child is partially delivered, feet first, and an incision is made at the base of the skull, so that the child's brain may be removed by suction, allowing for easier delivery of the collapsed head.

As of mid-2005, a federal ban on the partial-birth abortion procedure was not being enforced because of several court challenges.

See **abortion.**

Pasch, paschal Note the *h.* Capitalize the noun but lowercase the adjective. In Jewish use it refers to *Passover.* In Christian use it refers more commonly to *Easter.*

See **Easter** and **Passover.**

Pascha The Orthodox churches' term for *Easter.* See that entry.

Passion play A religious drama focusing on the suffering, death and resurrection of Christ. The most famous is that performed every 10 years in Oberammergau, Germany. *Passion* is capitalized because it refers to the biblical event.

Some of those plays have given rise to controversies between Jews and Christians because of their interpretation of Scripture or because of their use of extraneous material. See the U.S. bishops' 1988 guidelines for a fuller discussion.

Passion Sunday The Sunday before Easter. Also popularly known as *Palm Sunday* because of the blessing and distribution of palms on that day, its proper name as a liturgical feast in the Latin Church is *Passion Sunday.* Either form is correct, but the liturgical name is preferred in most contexts of religious news reporting. Many Orthodox and Eastern Catholic churches call the feast the *Sunday of the Triumphal Entry Into Jerusalem.*

Passover The Jewish holiday, celebrated for eight days, commemorating the deliverance of the ancient Hebrews from slavery in Egypt. It occurs in March or April.

For the religious observance at the start of Passover, see **Seder.**

See also **Pasch, paschal** and **Pesach.**

pastor The priest or minister who is in charge of a congregation.

In Catholic parishes only a priest can hold the office of pastor. Other priests who work under the pastor usually are called *associate pastor* or *assistant pastor.* These terms also are reserved to priests. A layperson who is part of a parish ministry team usually is called a *pastoral associate.* If a pastor resides in the parish he is the *resident pastor.* A priest assigned as pastor of a parish where he does not live is a *nonresident pastor.* Do not note the distinction about *resident* or *nonresident* unless it is necessary to the story. For administration of parishes by someone other than a pastor, see **administrator** and **parish life coordinator.**

Treat *pastor* and related titles as occupational descriptions, not as formal titles before names. Lowercase.

See **religious titles** and the entry for the individual's denomination.

pastoral council A parish or diocesan body which the pastor or bishop consults concerning policies and major decisions in the governance of the local church. The term *pastoral* ordinarily is not used in parish references: *diocesan pastoral council, parish council.*

Canon law contains some norms for the establishment and structure of such bodies, but details concerning their composition and function are largely left to local authorities. Their role is consultative and always subject to the final authority of the pastor or bishop. Parish councils are composed chiefly of lay parishioners; diocesan councils of various significant segments in the diocese, including laity especially, but also clergy and religious.

Capitalize only when you are giving the proper name of a particular body: *the Brooklyn Diocesan Pastoral Council, the Diocesan Pastoral Council, the St. John Parish Council, the Parish Council.* But: *the pastoral council, the council, the San Diego and Oakland diocesan pastoral councils.*

See **priests' council.**

pastoral letter Lowercase except when using as part of a formal title. *Pastoral* is acceptable on second reference. A pastoral letter is a letter about Catholic teaching or practice from a bishop to his people. It also may be a joint letter by a group of bishops: the bishops of a nation, region, state or ecclesiastical province, black bishops, Hispanic bishops, bishops of rural dioceses, etc.

A pastoral letter by the pope usually carries its own special designation. *Apostolic exhortation* and *encyclical* are among the most common forms. See those entries.

Place formal title in quotes: *the U.S. bishops' peace pastoral, "The Challenge of Peace: God's Promise and Our Response."*
See **composition titles** in **Appendix A: Special Style Considerations.**

pastoral workers A term used in many countries, especially in Europe and Latin America, for unordained people engaged in church ministries or apostolates: catechists, schoolteachers, social workers, lay liturgical ministers, administrators of priestless parishes, etc.

paten A metal disk or plate, especially one of precious metal, for holding the bread in a eucharistic service.

patriarch Capitalize only when used as a formal religious title before a name: *Russian Orthodox Patriarch Alexy II, Patriarch Alexy II, the patriarch of Moscow and all Russia; Ecumenical Patriarch Bartholomew of Constantinople, Patriarch Bartholomew, the Greek Orthodox patriarch.*

Orthodox patriarchs usually are identified only by their first name or first name and a Roman numeral. Catholic patriarchs usually are identified by their last name as well. Watch for Roman numerals that may appear to be middle initials: *Patriarch Maximos V Hakim.* (No period after *V:* It is a numeral, not a middle initial.) Whenever the last name is given, use it on second reference: *Latin Patriarch Michel Sabbah of Jerusalem, Patriarch Sabbah.*

If a Catholic patriarch is also a cardinal, use *cardinal,* not *patriarch,* as his title: *Cardinal Nasrallah P. Sfeir, patriarch of the Maronite Catholic Church; Cardinal Sfeir.* Among the Eastern Catholic churches, only those headed by patriarchs or by major archbishops have synods of bishops, which have the power to elect bishops, including a new patriarch or major archbishop. A newly elected Eastern Catholic patriarch does not have his election confirmed by the pope, but he requests and receives ecclesial communion from the pope. See **cardinal.**

In the Latin Church, use of *patriarch* as a personal title before a name has fallen into disuse except for the Latin patriarch of Jerusalem. The patriarch of the West, who is bishop of Rome, is called *pope;* those of the East Indies, Lisbon and Venice are called *archbishop* or *cardinal;* the Patriarchate of the West Indies exists only in name.

If the civil name of a patriarchal see has changed or if the patriarch does not reside in the original see city, often it is better to give a functional description of his jurisdiction than to identify him by his see: *Patriarch Jean Pierre XVIII Kasparian, head of Armenian Catholics;* not: *Patriarch Jean Pierre XVIII Kasparian of Cilicia of the Armenians.*
See **Catholic Church; Eastern Catholic churches; Oriental Orthodox churches; Orthodox churches; patriarchate;** and **religious titles.**

patriarchate A Catholic, Orthodox or Oriental Orthodox see headed by a patriarch. Capitalize when part of a proper name: *the Moscow Patriarchate, the Ecumenical Patriarchate of Constantinople, the Syrian-rite Patriarchate of Antioch.* Lowercase in other uses: *Venice and Lisbon are Latin-rite patriarchates.* See **patriarch.**

Although Rome is a patriarchal see, it is called the *Diocese of Rome,* not: the *Patriarchate of Rome.* See **Rome, Diocese of.**

Paul VI audience hall

Paulist National Catholic Evangelization Association (www.pncea. org) Headquarters is in Washington.

Pax Christi USA (www.paxchristiusa.org) No hyphen. National branch of the international Catholic peace movement. *Pax Christi* is acceptable on second reference.

U.S. headquarters is in Erie, Pa., with a national office also in Washington. Headquarters of Pax Christi International (www.paxchristi.net) is in Brussels, Belgium.

Pax Romana (www.paxromana. org) An international Catholic organization for students, intellectuals and professionals, divided into two main branches. One branch, the *International Movement of Catholic Students,* with headquarters in Paris, is for undergraduates. The other branch, the *International Catholic Movement for Intellectual and Cultural Affairs,* with headquarters in Geneva, is for intellectuals and professionals.

The U.S. affiliate of the first branch is the *National Catholic Student Coalition.* (www.catholicstudent. org) The U.S. affiliate of the second branch is the *Catholic Movement for Intellectual and Cultural Affairs of Pax Romana.*

penance Recognized as a sacrament in the Catholic and Orthodox churches. Anglicans have a rite of penance called a *service of reconciliation.*

In the Catholic Church penance is also called the *sacrament of reconciliation.* It can be administered according to three different rites: individual confession and absolution, a communal penance service with individual confession and absolution or a communal penance service with generic confession and general absolution. Use of the third rite is permitted only when certain strict conditions are met.

See **absolution; confession;** and **sacraments.**

penitential days The days of Lent and Fridays are the main penitential days of Christian tradition. Do not write about penitential activity as if it referred only to acts of self-denial. Prayer and works of charity are an integral part of penitential practice. See **abstinence, days of** and **fasting.**

penitentiary The Vatican's *Apostolic Penitentiary, major penitentiary* and *minor penitentiaries* are not prisons.

See **Apostolic Penitentiary.**

Pentecost Not *Pentacost.* The Christian feast commemorating the outpouring of the Holy Spirit on the apostles, which marked the start of the church's mission on earth. It is observed on the seventh Sunday after Easter. Because of the different methods of reckoning Easter in the East and West, the Orthodox usually observe Pentecost one, four or five weeks after it is observed by the Catholic and Protestant churches.

Pentecostal churches Not *Pentacostal.* Churches which were formed out of the revivalist movement that began in the United States in the early 20th century. They receive their name from their emphasis on the visible manifestations of the Holy Spirit, such as healing and speaking in tongues, which marked the start of the church at the first Pentecost.

Total membership in various Pentecostal churches in the United States was estimated at 24 million in 2005.

The largest Pentecostal church is the *Assemblies of God* (www.ag.org), formed in 1914, which has more than 12,000 churches and more than 2.7 million members. Assemblies of God members emphasize baptism in the Spirit through acceptance of Jesus as one's savior. They believe that the Bible is God's infallible word and the sole rule of faith, that salvation is available only through Jesus Christ, that divine healing is made possible through Christ's suffering and that Christ will come again to those who love him.

They observe baptism and the Lord's Supper as divine ordinances. Worship is informal and centers on preaching. Baptism is administered by immersion.

Other Pentecostal churches include the *United Pentecostal Church International* (www.upci.org), *Pentecostal Church of God* (www.pcg.org), *The Vineyard* community of churches (www.vineyardusa.org), *Church of God in Christ* (www.cogic.org) and *Full Gospel Baptist Church Fellowship* (www.fullgospelbaptist.org). Despite differences, all are similar in their emphasis on conversion to Jesus, spiritual baptism, preaching and the Bible literally interpreted as their rule of faith.

Pentecostals have an official dialogue with the Catholic Church.

While the Pentecostal movement of the early 20th century was marked by the formation of new denominations, the *neo-Pentecostal* or *charismatic* movement that grew rapidly in the 1960s and '70s was distinctive as a movement that took place within Catholic and mainline Protestant churches. See **charismatics.**

people of God

peritus The plural is *periti.* No quotes around these Latin terms now taken over into English. If you use either term explain its meaning. It refers to an expert consultant (usually a theologian) at a church meeting such as a council or synod, especially one held in Rome. In most cases it is preferable to say *expert, theological expert* or *theological adviser.*

An expert brought in by the church authority that convenes the meeting is an adviser to the whole gathering and usually attends the meeting. An expert brought in by an individual participant or group of participants is only a personal adviser to the individual or group and ordinarily does not attend the meeting.

Since the English definition makes no gender distinction, use *peritus* and *periti* for all individuals and groups regardless of sex.

perpetual adoration A practice in some Catholic parishes and religious communities of exposing the Eucharist 24 hours a day in a chapel for continuous adoration by members of the community. Communities that establish perpetual adoration of the Eucharist are expected to assure that there are always some members present in prayer before the exposed Blessed Sacrament. Do not capitalize unless it is part of the formal name of a religious order or an organization: *Dominican Nuns of Perpetual Adoration, Perpetual Adoration Society of St. Peter Parish.*

See **Forty Hours devotion** and **liturgy, devotions.**

-person, -people Do not substitute these compound endings as gender-neutral replacements for the endings *-man, -men* or *-woman, -women* without first checking style and dictionary resources. Some recent coinages have become acceptable words; others have not.

See **inclusive language.**

personal prelatures Church jurisdictions without geographic boundaries, erected by the Holy See to carry out particular pastoral initiatives at the regional, national or international level without infringing on the rights of the local bishops. The head of such a jurisdiction, called a *prelate,* is appointed by the pope.

In 2005 the only personal prelature was *Opus Dei.* See that entry.

Pesach The Hebrew word for *Passover.* See that entry.

photos See **Appendix B: Photo Guidelines.**

physician-assisted suicide See **assisted suicide.**

"placet" For consistency, retain the quotes around this and related phrases when writing about some Catholic meetings, especially those called by the Holy See or one of its departments, in which formal votes may be recorded in Latin. Although Webster's New World now recognizes *placet* as an English word, it does not recognize the related forms as English.

The three main types of vote are: *"placet," "non placet"* and *"placet iuxta modum."* These mean, respectively: *yes, no* and *yes with reserva-*tions (or: *yes, if amended).*

Translated literally, the three phrases are: *it pleases me; it does not please me; it pleases me after a fashion.* Ordinarily it is better to ignore the literal translations in favor of commonly understood English terms such as *voted for, voted against; approved, rejected; agreed, disagreed, agreed in part but suggested amendments,* etc.

A "placet iuxta modum" vote is permitted only during drafting stages of a document, when it can still be changed. Such a vote means that an individual agrees with the basic idea of a proposal but wants something added, deleted or changed.

The individual is expected to submit his or her "modus," generally in the form of a suggested amendment to the original language. The plural of *"modus"* is *"modi."* The "modi" usually can be characterized in English as *amendments.*

plainchant, plainsong See **Gregorian chant.**

plenary council A council of the bishops of a nation, convoked by the conference of bishops but with lay, religious and clerical participation. It has legislative power, subject to approval by the Holy See. The general norms for such councils are contained in the Code of Canon Law. Capitalize as part of a council's formal name.

podium See **dais, podium, rostrum** and **lectern, ambo.**

Polish National Catholic Church (www.pncc.org) This church had its origins in a series of pastoral and administrative conflicts between Catholic Polish immigrant parishes and their bishops in the late 19th and early 20th centuries. In 2005 it claimed 25,000 members in the United States and Canada. *PNCC* is acceptable on second reference.

The PNCC began with the establishment of an independent parish of Polish Catholics in Scranton, Pa., by Father Francis Hodur in 1897. In 1904 he convened the first synod of representatives of Polish independent parishes, which formally voted to break with the Roman Catholic Church, adopted a constitution and elected him as first bishop of the new church. In 1907 he was ordained a bishop by three bishops of the Union of Utrecht. The PNCC was a member of that union from 1907 until 2003, when PNCC opposition to the ordination of women in the German and Austrian Old Catholic churches and to the blessing of same-sex unions in the Austrian church led to separation. See **Old Catholic churches.**

The Polish National Catholic Church is organized into five dioceses in the United States and Canada. It is headed by a *prime bishop,* who is elected by the church's highest governing body, the General Synod. The synod meets every four years. Headquarters is in Scranton, Pa.

The PNCC recognizes seven sacraments and uses Polish and English for its liturgies. It requires auricular confession up to the age of 16, but after that general absolution in a communal penance service is the ordinary way of receiving the sacrament. It permits married clergy.

ECUMENICAL RELATIONS: The PNCC is a member of the National Council of Churches and has been in formal dialogue with the Catholic Church since 1984. In 1985 the Vatican recognized as already validly ordained a PNCC priest who had entered the Roman Catholic Church. In 1993, in response to a request originating with the PNCC, the Vatican said Polish National Catholics should be accorded the same treatment as Orthodox Christians if they seek access to Eucharist, penance or anointing in the Roman Catholic Church. At PNCC centenary observances in 1997, Roman Catholic Bishop James C. Timlin of Scranton, Pa., asked PNCC "forgiveness for every offense, misunderstanding, unkind act, mistaken judgment, or any thought, word or deed ever committed against you on the part of anyone in the Roman Catholic community." Later that year the PNCC bishops and clergy called for the dialogue to be directed toward restoration of full unity.

Note: A missionary diocese in Poland, founded by the Polish National Catholic Church in 1924, broke from the parent church in the 1950s and became a separate denomination called the *Polish Catholic Church.*

pontiff Although it can mean a *bishop* or *high priest,* in practice it is now used almost exclusively as an alternative form of reference to the *pope.* It is acceptable in news writing, but do not overuse it and never use it as a formal title before a name. Always lowercase.

See **Holy Father** and **pope.**

pontifical In most uses *pontifical* means *papal, having to do with the pope.* See entries that follow for certain specific uses.

In some uses *pontifical* means *episcopal, having to do with bishops.* The *Roman Pontifical* is the official collective name in the Latin Church for liturgical ceremonies celebrated by bishops. A *pontifical Mass* is a Mass celebrated by a bishop.

pontifical degrees The preferred term is *ecclesiastical degrees.* See that entry.

Pontifical Gregorian University The Gregorian is acceptable on second reference. See **pontifical universities.**

pontifical missionary societies Collective term for four missionary awareness and mission-funding agencies coordinated under the jurisdiction of the Vatican Congregation for the Evangelization of Peoples. Each agency has a general secretariat in Rome and a system of national and diocesan directors who coordinate fundraising and mission awareness in various countries and dioceses.

They are coordinated in Rome by the *Supreme Committee of the Pontifical Missionary Societies of the Propagation of the Faith, of St. Peter Apostle, of the Holy Childhood and of the Missionary Union,* which is headed by the prefect of the evangelization congregation.

The agencies are known individually in the United States as: *Holy Childhood Association, Missionary Union of Priests and Religious, Society for the Propagation of the Faith* and *Society of St. Peter Apostle.* See separate entries for each.

Pontifical Mission for Palestine See **Catholic Near East Welfare Association.**

Pontifical North American College (www.pnac.org) The U.S. seminary program in Rome. But the USCCB committee that monitors the college is the *Committee on North American College Rome.*

pontifical right, pontifical rite A religious order or other church association or community is said to be *of pontifical right* when its constitution is approved by the Holy See and it no longer depends upon a particular diocese or bishops' conference for its legal establishment. New orders or institutes usually begin as institutions of *diocesan right.* The term *right* refers to *legal basis.*

Pontifical rites are certain liturgical ceremonies led by a pope, bishop or abbot. In the Latin Church these ceremonies basically are contained in the official liturgical collection called the Roman Pontifical. There are comparable ceremonies in the Eastern Catholic churches as well. See **liturgy, devotions.**

Do not use *pontifical rite* when speaking of the Vatican-based legal status of ecclesiastical organizations.

pontifical universities Do not drop *pontifical* from the names of the ecclesiastical universities, academies and national seminaries in Rome that operate under papal charter: *Pontifical Gregorian University, Pontifical Oriental Institute, Pontifical North American College.* On second reference, use the shorter version of the name, without *Pontifical.* Only papally chartered universities or faculties can confer *ecclesiastical degrees.* See that entry.

Pontifical Urbanian University (www.urbaniana.edu) A pontifical university in Rome, directed by the Congregation for the Evangelization of Peoples, for the education of seminarians from mission countries. Do not call it *Urban University.* From 1605 to 1962 its name referred to the city: *Urban College of the Propagation of the Faith ("Collegium Urbanum de Propaganda Fide"),* but in 1962 Pope John XXIII proclaimed it a pontifical university and renamed it in honor of its founder, Pope Urban VIII: *"Pontificia Universitas Urbaniana."*

See **pontifical universities.**

pope The religious title given to the head of the Catholic Church and the head of the Coptic Orthodox Church. Lowercase except when it is used as a formal title before a name: *Pope John Paul II, Pope Shenouda III, the pope.*

See **Catholic Church; Holy Father; pontiff;** and **religious titles.**

pornography *Porn* and *porno* are slang terms. Do not use them except in quoted matter.

Portuguese names See **Spanish and Portuguese names.**

postconciliar No hyphen. An exception to Webster's New World, based on widespread Catholic usage. The term should not be used in a story without a reference, either beforehand or soon afterward, to the council to which it refers — generally the *Second Vatican Council.* See that entry.

postsynodal No hyphen.

practitioner See **Church of Christ, Scientist** and **religious titles.**

prayers Capitalize only proper names of fixed prayers: *Our Father, Lord's Prayer, Hail Mary, Act of Faith, Sign of the Cross,* etc.

Some Latin names of prayers and hymns have become part of the English language and do not need quotation marks. For example: *Angelus, Agnus Dei, Ave Maria, Pater Noster, Magnificat.* Use quotation marks if the name is not listed in Webster's New World or is given there as a foreign word or phrase. For example: *"Regina Coeli," "Dies Irae," "Memorare," "Nunc Dimittis," "Salve Regina."*

If a prayer name must be placed in quotes, it generally needs to be translated or explained as well: *The pope addressed the crowd gathered for the "Regina Coeli," a noontime prayer to Mary recited during the Easter season. The bishops ended the meeting by singing the "Salve Regina," a Latin hymn to Mary.*

Lowercase generic terms which do not describe a unique prayer, but rather refer to a type of prayer, a group of prayers or a set of variable prayers: *bedtime prayers, grace before meals, an act of contrition, a prayer of thanksgiving, the prayer of the faithful, a novena to the Sacred Heart.* For consistency, always lowercase *rosary,* whether referring to the set of beads or the set of prayers said on it. Lowercase *sign of the cross* except when referring to the specific prayer: *The pope urged Catholics to learn the Sign of the Cross in Latin.* But: *He made the sign of the cross as he entered the church.*

See **liturgy, devotions; Mass;** and **rosary.** For prayers set to music, see **hymns.**

preacher Not a religious title. Never capitalize.

See **religious titles.**

prefect In Catholic ecclesiastical usage, the occupational title given to those who head Vatican congregations and occasionally to certain authorities in seminaries: *prefect of the Congregation for Bishops, prefect of studies.* If the head of a Vatican congregation is not a cardinal, he formerly was called a *pro-prefect,* but Pope John Paul II ended that practice. Always lowercase. Do not use as a formal title before a name.

prelate Specifically, someone who heads a territorial or personal prelature. However it is acceptable in a general sense to describe monsignors, who are *prelates of honor,* or any group of higher-ranking church leaders, especially bishops. Do not capitalize.

Do not use as a religious title before a name. A prelate is always referred to by another personal title, such as *monsignor, bishop,* etc.

prelature See **personal prelatures** and **territorial prelatures.**

presbyter, presbyterate, presbyterial, presbytery In Catholic usage:

— *Presbyter* is a synonym for *priest.* Use it only in quoted matter or technical theological references (as in New Testament references to church elders, who were called presbyters) and explain the term when it is used.

— *Presbyterate* or its alternative Latin form, *"presbyterium,"* may be a synonym for *priesthood* or may refer to the collective body of priests of a diocese or similar ecclesiastical jurisdiction. Usually it is preferable to use *priesthood* or *priests*: *He was ordained to the priesthood. He called a meeting of the priests of the diocese.*

— *Presbyterial* or its alternative form, *presbyteral,* is a synonym for *priestly* or *of priests.* Use it only in quoted matter or technical references and explain the term when it is used. See **priests' council.**

— *Presbytery* may mean the same as *presbyterate* or may be a synonym for *rectory* or *pastor's residence.*

For usage in non-Catholic denominations, check other entries in this book or contact officials of the denomination in question. See **Presbyterian churches.**

Presbyterian churches *Presbyterian* is lowercased when it refers simply to a form of church governance in which authority lies primarily in the elected *elders* of a congregation. It is capitalized when it refers to any of those branches of the Calvinist or Reformed churches that have adopted *Presbyterian* as part of their name. These have their origins chiefly in Great Britain and North America. In Scotland the established church, the Church of Scotland (www.churchof scotland.org.uk), is Presbyterian.

Most Presbyterian and Reformed churches are members of the *World Alliance of Reformed Churches,* which since 1969 has engaged in formal dialogue with the Roman Catholic Church. See **World Alliance of Reformed Churches.**

Presbyterian beliefs are based heavily on the teachings of 16th-century theologian John Calvin, who emphasized the supremacy of God and his word and taught that any form of church government is purely human.

After Scripture, which is the supreme rule of faith and life, important subordinate standards of doctrine are the early creeds, apostolic preaching and teaching, and the Westminster Confession of Faith, a document drawn up by an assembly of leaders who met from 1643 to 1648 in England.

Presbyterians recognize only two sacraments: baptism, which is administered to infants, and the Lord's Supper, which is the supreme act of worship.

The distinctive character of Presbyterian church organization lies in the interpretation of *presbyter* or *elder* in the New Testament as a single order within which are two differentiated roles: that of minister of the word and sacraments and that of the ruling elder, who assists in the administration of sacraments, pastoral care and church government.

At each level of authority in Presbyterian churches — session, presbytery, synod and general assembly —

pastors and ruling elders govern together. The session, consisting of the pastor and elected elders, governs the local church. The ruling elder and the pastor from each church in a district form the presbytery. Both regional synods and the general assembly are composed of elected delegates from each presbytery.

The general assembly meets yearly. In addition to deciding major matters of church policy and administration, it chooses the denomination's *moderator,* who serves a one-year term as chief presiding officer, and the *stated clerk,* who ordinarily serves for a longer period as principal administrative officer.

The *Presbyterian Church (U.S.A.)* (www.pcusa.org), which had about 2.4 million members in 2005, is the chief U.S. Presbyterian body. It was created in 1983 by the merger of the main northern and southern Presbyterian churches. Its headquarters is in Louisville, Ky. Strongly ecumenical, it is a member of *Churches Uniting in Christ.* See that entry.

Another branch, with more than 250,0000 members, is the *Presbyterian Church in America* (www.pcanet. org). Its headquarters is in Lawrenceville, Ga..

See **religious titles.**

president, presiding Reserve *president* for one who holds that title as head of a nation or organization. Capitalize and use as a formal title before a name only if the post is a full-time job. Lowercase and treat as a functional description in other uses: *President George W. Bush* but *parish council president Joan Johnson.*

While the celebrant or chief concelebrant of Mass is sometimes described as *presiding* over a eucharistic celebration, do not refer to him as the *president* or *presider.* The proper litur-

gical term is *celebrant* or, when other priests or bishops are concelebrating, *chief concelebrant.*

When a bishop is present at Mass but not concelebrating, liturgical norms say he "should preside at least by celebrating the Liturgy of the Word and by blessing the people at the end. In such cases he may be referred to as the *presiding bishop.*

See **celebrant** and **Mass.**

presidents, U.S. Use full names for all U.S. presidents, current and former, on first reference.

priest A term used for certain ordained ministers in the Catholic, Old Catholic, Orthodox and Anglican traditions and a few other Christian denominations. It is used to describe a leader of worship or ritual in some non-Christian religions as well. Never capitalize it or use it as a formal title before a name.

See **Father; religious titles** and the entry for an individual's denomination.

priests' council Capitalize as part of a formal name: *Dubuque Archdiocesan Priests' Council.* Lowercase when used alone or in plural uses: *the priests' council, the Dubuque and Des Moines priests' councils.*

Avoid using *presbyteral council* outside quoted matter. If the term must be used, explain that it means a *council of priests.*

For dioceses that use *presbyteral council* as the formal title, generally it is better to use *priests' council* (lowercase) than to use the proper title and interrupt the story to explain to the reader what it means.

See **pastoral council** and **presbyter, presbyterate, presbyterial, presbytery.**

Priests for Life (www.priests-forlife.org) Headquarters is in Staten Island, N.Y.

primacy In Catholic teaching, *papal primacy* refers to the direct authority of the pope over the whole church. It is defined in canon law as "supreme, full, immediate and universal ordinary power in the church, which he can always freely exercise." See **Catholic Church.**

In the Orthodox and Anglican churches the primacy of the chief bishop is that of a *first among equals,* often referred to as a *primacy of honor.* The authority of these primates outside their own diocese is basically that of prestige and persuasion, not of jurisdiction.

See **primate, primatial see.**

primate, primatial see *Primatial sees* are generally the original bishoprics of a particular rite or church or, in the Latin Church, the first diocese formed in a nation.

The bishop who holds such a see is the *primate* of that church, rite or nation. Do not capitalize *primate* or use it as a personal title before a name. Do not refer to someone as a primate or to his diocese as a primatial see unless it is relevant to the story — to indicate, for example, a bishop's special standing to speak for the hierarchy of his nation.

The term ordinarily is not used in the Orthodox or Eastern Catholic churches.

The primatial see of the Anglican Communion is the Archdiocese of Canterbury. Its archbishop often is called *primate of the Anglican Communion* or *primate of the world's Anglicans.* See **archbishop of Canterbury.** National churches of the Anglican Communion, such as those in the United States and Canada, may refer to their elected presiding bishop as their primate. The office is not connected with a particular diocese.

In the Latin Church, the Code of Canon Law says the office of primate is "a prerogative of honor" with "no power of governance" except in a few cases where clearly established custom or papal privilege provides otherwise.

In the United States the Archdiocese of Baltimore sometimes is referred to as the primatial see because it was the first diocese formed in the nation. The title is unofficial, however, and the archdiocese holds no primatial privileges.

As bishop of Rome, the pope is primate of Italy and primate of the West. His primacy over the Western church includes jurisdictional powers unique to that office. See **primacy.**

prior, prioress In religious orders, the title sometimes given to the head of a local community, especially a monastic community. In abbeys the next person in charge after the abbot may be called a prior. See **abbey, abbess, abbot.**

Treat as a job description, not a personal title. Do not capitalize. Use *Father* or *Sister* as the personal title before the name of a prior or prioress. See **religious titles.**

pro- In general, use a hyphen after the prefix *pro-* only when it is used to coin words that mean *in support of* something. For example, *pro-labor, pro-union.*

Before the 1990s, there were three exceptions, peculiar to Catholic usage. The Vatican used *pro-nuncio* as a title of its ambassador to a country when he was not dean of the diplomatic corps in that country. In 1990, it started using *nuncio* as the title for all newly appointed ambassadors. See **papal nuncio.** The Vatican also used *pro-prefect* and *pro-president* as titles for Vatican department heads who would be called *prefect* or *president* if they were cardinals. In the 1990s, it dropped the distinction and began to use *prefect* or *president* immediately from the time of appointments even if the official was not yet a cardinal. Hyphenate these three *pro-* terms if they occur.

pro-choice See **abortion.**

Pro Ecclesia et Pontifice Cross See **papal honors.**

profanity See **offensive language** in **Appendix A: Special Style Considerations.**

pro-life See **abortion.**

promise See **celibacy, chastity; order, congregation, society;** and **vow, promise.**

pro-nuncio See **papal nuncio** and **pro-.**

prophecy (n.), **prophesy** (v.) An element of predicting the future is almost always contained in these terms. See **prophet, prophetic.**

prophet, prophetic While these terms usually connote an element of predicting the future when used in general language, in religious language they refer to speaking in the name of God or expressing a faith message, often a countercultural one.

pro-prefect, pro-president See **pro-.**

Pro Sanctity Movement (www. prosanctity.org) U.S. addresses in Fullerton, Calif., Brooklyn, N.Y., Omaha, Neb., and Elkhorn, Neb.

proselytize Originally a neutral term, it now generally carries negative connotations of divisive competition among the churches or unscrupulous methods of persuasion — such as psychological pressure, spiritual threats or material inducements — to win converts. The Second Vatican Council used it in this pejorative sense. *Proselytize* should not be used as a synonym for *evangelize.* See **evangelize, evangelization.**

In some nations with non-Christian majorities — especially Islamic and Hindu nations — all efforts to convert members of the prevalent religion to another faith are considered proselytism and may be forbidden by law.

Protestant The proper term for the new churches of Western Christianity formed during the Reformation, for their subsequent branches or for their members. The main branches of Protestantism include Baptist, Congregational, Lutheran, Methodist, Quaker and Presbyterian and Reformed denominations.

Since the initial Anglican break with Rome was jurisdictional rather than doctrinal, when Anglican bodies are referred to alone they should not be described as *Protestant.* They may, however, be included in the term *Protestant* in general references or listings in which the distinction is insignificant.

The Protestant Church in Germany is a federation of the Lutheran, Reformed and United churches.

Groups that have separated from the Roman Catholic Church more recently, such as the Old Catholics, Polish National Catholic Church and members of the Lefebvre movement, are not considered *Protestant.*

Protestant is not applied to Jehovah's Witnesses, Latter-day Saints or the Unification Church, all of which are based on claims of new revelations.

Never use *Protestant* to describe any Orthodox or Oriental Orthodox church or any member of those churches. Use a phrase such as *Orthodox Christian* instead.

For guidelines on personal titles in Protestant denominations, see **religious titles.**

Protestant Episcopal Church in the U.S.A. See **Episcopal Church.**

Protestant Reformation See **Reformation.**

protosyncellus The equivalent in the dioceses of Eastern Catholic churches to *vicar general* in Latin-rite dioceses. Apart from direct quotations or technical uses, the more readily understood term *vicar general* should be used. If *protosyncellus* is used, explain its meaning. Use it as a job description, not as a formal title before a name. See **vicar.**

The Code of Canons of the Eastern Churches says that if there is a coadjutor bishop, he must be named protosyncellus. If there are auxiliaries but no coadjutor, one auxiliary is to be named protosyncellus, the others are to be named syncelli. Outside of quotes or technical uses, use *vicar* or *episcopal vicar*, not *syncellus,* for the job description for that post. If a diocese has no auxiliary bishops, a priest is named protosyncellus. In the Maronite Church, the protosyncellus automatically receives the title of *chorbishop* even if he has not been ordained a *chorbishop*. See that entry.

province In Catholic ecclesiastical usage, *province* may refer to:

— A grouping of an archdiocese, called the *metropolitan see,* and the dioceses under it, called *suffragan sees.* The Code of Canon Law spells out certain limited obligations and authority that the metropolitan archbishop has with respect to the dioceses within his province. The province takes its name from the metropolitan see. About half the ecclesiastical provinces in the United States are coextensive with state boundaries; about half are multistate; California and Texas are the only states with two provinces. Except in lists of provinces, generally if a province is mentioned in a story, its geographic scope should be indicated. See **metropolitan** and **suffragan**.

— A grouping of communities of a religious order. The superior of such a group is called a *provincial* or a *provincial superior.* Often the provincial headquarters is called the *provincialate.*

Do not capitalize *province* when used alone or attached to a geographic reference: *the province of St. Paul-Minneapolis, the Detroit province of Jesuits, the Jesuits' Wisconsin province, the Eastern province of the Servites.*

Capitalize *province* when it is part of a religious province's formal name if the formal name is religious rather than geographic in nature. For example: *Province of St. Joseph* for the Chicago-based province of Capuchins, *Immaculate Conception Province* for the province of Felician Sisters based in Lodi, N.J.

provincial (n.) In Catholic ecclesiastical usage, the superior of a province of religious men or women. Treat it as a job description. Do not capitalize it or use it as a formal title before a name: *Father Robert J. Scullin, provincial of the Detroit province of Jesuits,* not *Provincial Robert J. Scullin.*

provincial council In Catholic ecclesiastical usage this term may refer to:

— An assembly of the bishops of an ecclesiastical province under the metropolitan archbishop.

— The organization, composed of the provincial superior and his or her chief advisers, which governs a province of a religious order of men or women.

See **province.**

psalms, Psalms Capitalize when used as a shortened form for the entire Book of Psalms; lowercase when used in reference to the compositions within the collection rather than the entire collection. *Among different kinds of psalms found in the Book of Psalms are royal psalms, lamentations, hymns and prophetic psalms.* In the singular, capitalize proper names, consisting of the psalm with its number; lowercase otherwise: *The 21st Psalm describes God's care for his people. His favorite psalm is Psalm 21.* See **Appendix C: Endnotes** for an explanation of the differences in how psalms are numbered.

See also **Bible** and **Psalter.**

Psalter It can mean simply the Book of Psalms published in numerical sequence in book form or a published collection of the psalms, often along with other hymns or canticles from Scripture, arranged for use in prayer, especially such an arrangement for the Liturgy of the Hours. A Psalter arranged for use in prayer may also include musical arrangements. Use *Psalter* only for such separate published works. When referring to the collection of psalms as a part of Scripture, the correct name is the *Book of Psalms* or, especially in lists or parenthetical or footnote references, *Psalms.*

See **Bible.**

pulpit Most Latin Catholic churches no longer have a pulpit. The place for the Scripture readings is called an *ambo* or *lectern.* The place for preaching can be the *ambo* or *lectern* or the *president's chair.*

In Catholic references *pulpit* should be used in a literal sense only for those raised, partially enclosed areas for preaching that still exist in some Catholic churches: *He climbed into the 75-year-old cathedral's ornately railed pulpit to preach the homily.*

Pulpit also may be used in a metaphorical way to mean any *preaching within a religious service,* as: *He was accused of using the pulpit for politics.* The cliché, *... mounted the pulpit to ...* is probably best avoided in all contexts, but especially if there were no steps to climb.

See **dais, podium, rostrum** and **lectern, ambo.**

purgatory

purificator A small linen cloth used by the priest at Mass to dry his fingers and the chalice, and by ministers of holy Communion to wipe the Communion cups.

Purim A Jewish holiday, the Feast of Lots, celebrated in February or March. It commemorates the deliverance of the Jews living in Persia by Esther from a general massacre plotted by Haman.

pyx A small case used to bring Communion to people outside Mass. Do not confuse with the *monstrance,* an exposition case and stand used to display holy Communion for certain processions and devotions.

Quakers This popular name is acceptable on all references for members of the *Religious Society of Friends.* Members are also called *Friends,* and the denomination is also known as the *Society of Friends* or *Friends Church* (but not *Quaker Church*). When writing primarily about the structure or activities of the denomination, always include its full name in the story. Of nearly 340,000 Quakers worldwide, about 94,000 are in the United States and Canada. An estimated 154,000 — about 45 percent of the worldwide population of Quakers — are in Africa.

Originally *Quaker* was used as a scornful term for its founder's intense preoccupation with religious matters, but it is no longer used derisively and is not offensive to Friends.

BELIEFS: George Fox, an English preacher, formed the Quakers in the middle of the 17th century. His teaching centered around a doctrine he called *Inner Light:* that the source of all religious truth and life is the voice of God, the light of Jesus, experienced within each person. Since each person's relationship with God is immediate in Fox's teaching, external ecclesiastical structures, creeds, doctrines or rituals of worship have no binding force.

Quakers faced legal and popular oppression in England for their opposition to religious laws, military service and oaths. Many found refuge in Pennsylvania after 1680, when Quaker leader William Penn was given proprietary governorship of the colony as payment of a royal debt to his father.

Many meetings of worship involve silent meditation, in which any participant may speak when spiritually moved to do so. In others, there is a service of prayer and preaching. Quaker spirituality has a strong element of meditation and mysticism.

Since all people can share equally in the Inner Light according to Quaker belief, there is an emphasis on the radical equality and dignity of each person that has led to deep sensitivity to social inequalities. Quakers have been noted for their opposition to slavery, war and conscription and for their support of education, prison reform, social equality and humane treatment of the insane.

ORGANIZATION: Quakers call both their gatherings and their basic organizational structures *meetings.* The local congregation, which meets every week for worship but once a month for business, is called a *monthly meeting. Quarterly meetings* and *yearly meetings* embrace successively wider geographical areas. Capitalize these terms only when they are part of a proper name.

Some yearly meetings are unaffiliated with any others, but others are members of one or more associations. The largest association of yearly meetings is the *Friends United Meeting* (www.fum.org), with headquarters in Richmond, Ind. The *Evangelical Friends International—North American Region* (www.evangeli cal-friends.org), which resulted from the restructuring of the *Evangelical Friends Alliance* in 1990, is based in Canton, Ohio. The *Friends General Conference* (www.fgcquaker.org) is based in Philadelphia.

See **religious titles.**

 question-answer format should be used rarely and judiciously. If the transcript of a news conference, interview or hearing is so important that the text itself should be published, it also deserves a separate news story. Occasionally a verbatim excerpt from an exchange, placed within a story in a clearly defined way, can be used as a literary device to give readers a feel for the event which could not be conveyed as effectively in narrative form.

When using the question-answer format, follow these guidelines:

— Do not use quotation marks around each speaker's words.

— Use a new paragraph for each new speaker. Begin the paragraph with an identification of the speaker (usually his or her name) followed by a colon. For example:

CNS: Where were you in April?

Smith: I spent most of the month in Italy.

CNS: What did you do there?

Smith: I spent a week touring around northern Italy. Then I went to Rome for a series of meetings....

— If long questions or answers require breaking a speaker's words into two or more paragraphs several times in the course of a Q-and-A text, insert a blank line before each new speaker throughout the text in order to signal each change in speakers more clearly.

— Correct errors in grammar or usage that may go unnoticed in speech but are embarrassing in print. Ignore meaningless interjections such as *er* or *umm.* Such interjections become meaningful only if they convey hesitancy or uncertainty by the speaker that is a significant element in the exchange.

— Use ellipses sparingly. If more than two or three ellipses are needed to eliminate extraneous matter, the text probably should be introduced as *excerpts,* not as a *text.* Frequent ellipses may signal that the Q-and-A format is not an appropriate vehicle for reporting that event.

— It is preferable to use the names of the speakers or the organizations they represent, rather than *Q* and *A,* to identify each speaker.

— Identify a speaker fully either in the introduction to the transcript or in the first reference within the transcript; in subsequent references use only the last name, preceded by a title if needed.

— If each questioner cannot be identified, as may happen at a news conference or when a panel of investigators is questioning a witness, *Q* may be used as a substitute for identification of each questioner. The person who answers ordinarily should be identified by name, however, whether one is dealing with a single respondent or several.

In transcripts of interviews conducted by a Catholic News Service reporter, the reporter's name and *Catholic News Service* should be identified in the introduction. Questions can then be introduced by *CNS.*

To avoid long identifications that may obstruct the flow of a news conference transcript, it may be preferable to use only *Q* or only the name of the news organization to identify questioners. At times, however, the nature of some questions makes identification of the questioner an important aspect of the news.

"quinceanera" The Spanish word for the celebration among Hispanics marking a girl's 15th birthday. If it is used, it should be placed in quotes and its meaning explained.

quinquennial It means *five-year* or *every five years.* When possible, use the simpler terms rather than *quin-quennial* when referring to the five-year reports that bishops give when they make their "ad limina" visits to Rome.

See **"ad limina."**

Quran For news writing use this spelling, not *Koran* or *Q'uran*, for the sacred book of Islam. It contains the fundamental beliefs, practices and law of Muslims. They consider it divinely inspired in a literal sense: the words of Allah himself dictated to Mohammed through the Angel Gabriel.

See **Islam** and **Shariah.**

rabbi Capitalize when used as a formal title before a name. Repeat the title before the last name on second reference. Lowercase when it stands alone. Do not say *Jewish rabbi:* It's redundant.

A rabbi may lead worship, but that is not his chief function in the Jewish community. He is a religious scholar, teacher or interpreter of the law.

See **Judaism** and **religious titles.**

racial slurs See **offensive language** in **Appendix A: Special Style Considerations.**

Rainbow Sash (www.rainbowsashmovement.com) Describes itself as "an organization of gay, lesbian, bisexual, transgender Catholics, with their families and friends, who are publicly calling the Catholic Church to conversion of heart around issues of human sexuality." As of mid-2005, the U.S. bishops were split over whether to give Communion to those wearing the sashes at Mass; a Vatican official under Pope John Paul II said in February 2005 that those wearing the sashes disqualify themselves from Communion because they are demonstrating opposition to church teaching on homosexuality. Do not capitalize the *M* in *Rainbow Sash movement.*

See **homosexuality.**

Ramadan A month of fasting in the Islamic calendar.

See **Islam.**

Raskob Foundation for Catholic Activities (www.rfca.org) Headquarters is in Wilmington, Del.

RCIA See **Rite of Christian Initiation of Adults.**

reader Interchangeable with *lector* to describe the person who reads Scripture readings, except for the Gospel, at Catholic liturgical ceremonies. In the *Church of Christ, Scientist,* it is the term for the leader of Sunday worship. In all uses treat it as a job description, not as a title before a name.

See **Church of Christ, Scientist** and **lector.**

real presence Capitalize only when used without the words *Eucharist* or *Christ: He believes in the real presence of Christ in the Eucharist.* But: *Fewer Catholics now believe in the Real Presence.*

Real Presence Association (www.therealpresence.org) Headquarters is in Chicago.

rector In Catholic practice, a term generally used to describe the chief administrator of a seminary and sometimes used for a priest in charge of a cathedral, shrine or religious house. In Episcopal practice it is used to describe the priest in charge of a parish. Treat as a job description, not a religious title. Lowercase.

See **religious titles.**

Red Cross Capitalize in all references to the Swiss-based international humanitarian organization or any of its national affiliates. Affiliates in Islamic countries use the name *Red Crescent.*

The International Red Cross and Red Crescent Movement (www.

redcross.int) (formerly called International Red Cross) consists of the International Committee of the Red Cross (www.icrc.org), the International Federation of Red Cross and Red Crescent Societies (www.ifrc.org) (formerly the League of Red Cross and Red Crescent Societies) and more than 175 national Red Cross and Red Crescent societies around the world. The U.S. affiliate is called the *American Red Cross* (www.redcross.org).

Red Mass An annual Mass celebrated in many places for members of the legal profession, usually with a bishop presiding, usually marking the start of the court year or academic year. The tradition dates back to the 13th century. The name stems from the red vestments of the presiding clergy and, in England, the scarlet robes of the high judges and law professors in attendance. The first Red Mass in the United States was celebrated in New York in 1928.

By analogy, the more recent customs of a Blue Mass for those in law enforcement and White Mass for those in health professions draw their names from the traditional uniform colors associated with those professions.

See **Mass.**

reference works For the chief reference works for spelling and usage employed by Catholic News Service, see the Introduction.

In a story, when citing a standard reference work — an almanac, dictionary, directory, encyclopedia, gazetteer, handbook, manual, yearbook, etc. — capitalize its proper name but do not use quotation marks around it. In religious usage, this includes the Bible and its individual books, official liturgical books, church yearbooks and directories, law codes and established descriptive names of major church documents. Some examples: *the Augsburg Confession, the Sacramentary, the Second Vatican Council's Constitution on the Sacred Liturgy, the Code of Canon Law, the Catholic Press Directory, the Catechism of the Catholic Church.*

The rule against quotation marks does not apply to creative names given as unique titles to such works.

Note that Vatican II documents have both proper descriptive names, without quotation marks, and unique titles formed by the first two or three Latin words of each document, which are placed in quotation marks. See **Appendix I: Vatican II Documents.** Also note that proper names of encyclicals and similar papal documents are placed in quotes. See **encyclical.**

See also **Bible** and **liturgical books.**

Reformation Acceptable in all references to the 16th-century *Protestant Reformation.* The symbolic date of its start is Oct. 31, 1517, when Martin Luther posted his 95 Theses on the door of All Saints Church in Wittenberg, Germany. Lutheran churches commemorate that date each year as *Reformation Day* and may observe the preceding (or in some cases the following) Sunday as *Reformation Sunday.*

See **Counter-Reformation; Lutheran churches** and entries for individual Protestant denominations.

Reformed churches Those bodies that share a religious and theological heritage derived mainly from the circle of Protestant reformers having John Calvin as its chief spokesman. They include both Reformed and Presbyterian denominations. The *World Alliance of Reformed Churches* maintains an official dialogue with the Catholic Church.

See that entry and **Presbyterian churches.**

Reform Judaism Not *Reformed.* See **Judaism.**

refugee Any individual forced to flee home or country because of war, political or religious persecution, natural disaster or economic necessity.

Only certain individuals or groups, however, are officially recognized as refugees by the U.S. government for purposes of receiving asylum in the United States.

"Regina Coeli" This prayer to Mary, celebrating the Resurrection, replaces the *Angelus* as a daily noontime prayer during the Easter season. Note that *Angelus,* a Latin prayer title that has become part of standard English, has no quotation marks, but *"Regina Coeli"* is placed in quotes.
See **Angelus.**

Regnum Christi (www.reg numchristi.org) A predominantly lay ecclesial movement founded in 1959 by Father Marcial Maciel, who also founded the Legion of Christ. Latin for "kingdom of Christ," the group also includes deacons and priests who are not members of the Legion of Christ. Regnum Christi members, under the spiritual direction of the Legion of Christ, are to serve as "missionaries to a secularized world," according to Father Maciel. Regnum Christi also includes young volunteers called "co-workers," who dedicate two or three years to full-time service and formation.

reign (papal) While *reign* is certainly appropriate in historical references to popes during the centuries when they were temporal rulers, other terms such as *papacy* or *pontificate* are generally more appropriate to describe the terms in office of modern-day popes, whose authority is usually conceived in more religious and spiritual terms.

Pope John XXIII eliminated many of the regal trappings of the papacy. Pope Paul VI set aside the papal tiara after his coronation and further simplified papal ceremonies. When Popes John Paul I, John Paul II and Benedict XVI were installed in the papacy, there was no coronation. Each one's installation ceremony was called an inauguration of his pastoral ministry.

However, the period between two papacies is still described as an *interregnum.* See that entry and **tiara.**

Religion Communicators Council (www.religioncommunicators.org) Formerly the *Religious Public Relations Council,* it is an interfaith association of religion communicators working in print and electronic communication, marketing and public relations. Its national office is in New York.

Religion News Service (www. religionnews.com) Formerly *Religious News Service.* Owned by Newhouse News Service and located in Washington, it provides news and photos for use in secular and religious publications.

Religion Newswriters Association (www.rna.org) A membership organization aimed at promoting excellence in religion reporting in the secular media. Headquarters is in Westerville, Ohio.

religious Lowercase the word *religious* when used as an adjective or a noun referring to communities of people in consecrated life or the members of those communities: *men religious,* *women religious, a religious order, a religious congregation, religious superior, a group of religious.* Be sure, however, that the story is sufficiently clear and free of jargon to avoid confusing readers about whether the word is being used to refer to sisters, brothers and religious order priests or is being used in the larger sense.

Identify religious by their religious order or community, generally on first reference, but do not use initials: *Jesuit Father John Smith; Father John Smith, a Jesuit;* or *Father John Smith, a member of the Society of Jesus;* but not: *Father John Smith, S.J.* If the order's name is more than one or two words, do not use before the name. Identification by affiliation with an order or community may be deferred to second reference in order to avoid a cumbersome lead.

See **brother; congregation; nuns, sisters; order, congregation, society; religious titles; sister; Appendix D: Religious Orders, Men;** and **Appendix E: Religious Orders, Women.**

religious affiliation If a person in the news expresses opinions about religious or moral issues from a particular denominational perspective, is engaged in activities based on religious conviction or holds an official position in a denomination, his or her religious affiliation generally is pertinent to the story.

The religious affiliation of public officials speaking or acting in their civil capacity generally is not pertinent to a story unless some specific aspect of the news, such as religious groups taking sides on an action, makes it relevant.

Do not give a person's religious affiliation unless it is pertinent to the story. Let the context determine whether a general identification is suf-

ficient or more specific information is needed. For example: *Muslim* or *Shiite Muslim; Jewish* or *Orthodox Jewish; Orthodox* or *Russian Orthodox, Greek Orthodox,* etc.; *non-Catholic* or *Methodist, Presbyterian, Baptist,* etc.; *Lutheran* or *Missouri Synod Lutheran; evangelical* or *Baptist, Southern Baptist,* etc.

For affiliation of Catholic professed religious with their orders or communities, see **religious.**

Religious Brothers Conference (www.brothersonline.org) Formerly the National Association of Religious Brothers. Headquarters is in Chicago.

Religious Formation Conference (www.relforcon.org) Headquarters is in Silver Spring, Md.

religious institutes See **institute** and **order, congregation, society.**

religious movements Also called *new religious movements.* These terms often are used among mainline Christian denominations to describe new religious groups nonjudgmentally. Many of the groups so described may have characteristics of *sects* or *cults,* but they object to the negative connotations of those terms. In Europe such movements often are called *alternative religious movements.*

See **cult** and **sect.**

Religious News Service See **Religion News Service.**

Religious Society of Friends See **Quakers.**

religious titles In general, every cleric and religious, Catholic and non-Catholic, should have a title before the name on first and subsequent references.

JOB TITLES: Specifically religious titles take precedence over job titles if a person has both. When a person has a formal religious title such as *Bishop, Father or Sister,* for example, positions such as *chancellor, episcopal vicar, papal nuncio, pastor, patriarchal vicar, prefect, president, professor, provincial* or *rector* should be treated as job descriptions.

CATHOLIC TITLES:

ABBESS: Use *abbess* before the name only if the individual prefers it. Most use the title *mother* before their names. Ordinarily identify by the religious community on first reference. On second reference, use the first name: *Benedictine Mother Jane Smith; Mother Jane* (or, if she prefers: *Mother Smith, Abbess Smith* or *Abbess Jane); the abbess.* Do not use *Mother Abbess* outside direct quotes.

ABBOT, ARCHABBOT: *Benedictine Abbot Joel P. Macul, Abbot Macul; Benedictine Archabbot Justin DuVall; Archabbot DuVall; the archabbot.* Do not use *Father Abbot* outside direct quotes.

ARCHBISHOP: *Archbishop John G. Vlazny of Portland, Ore.; Archbishop Vlazny; the archbishop.* Generally include the name of a residential archbishop's see in the first reference. Most residential archbishops also are *metropolitans* — heads of ecclesiastical provinces — but that term should never be used as a personal title in stories about archbishops of the Latin Church. See **archbishop** and **metropolitan.**

AUXILIARY, CHORBISHOP, COADJUTOR: *Auxiliary Bishop Michael F. Burbidge of Philadelphia; Bishop Burbidge; the bishop.* Use the same form for *coadjutor.* A coadjutor may have the title of bishop or archbishop. For a chorbishop, use *chorbishop* as the title in all references. See **auxiliary; chorbishop;** and **coadjutor.**

BISHOP: Use the same form as for archbishops, with diocese or other jurisdiction included. For bishops who head a jurisdiction of lower rank than a diocese, use the form: *Bishop Leonardo Mario Bernacchi, apostolic vicar of Camiri, Bolivia.* See **bishop.**

BROTHER: Generally identify by religious community on first reference: *Franciscan Brother John J. Smith; Christian Brother Joseph F. Jones.* On second reference, use the first name: *Brother John, Brother Joseph* (or, if he prefers, *Brother Smith, Brother Jones).* See **brother** and **religious.**

CARDINAL: *Cardinal Francis E. George* (not: *Francis Cardinal George) of Chicago; Cardinal George; the cardinal.* Generally include the name of the see of a residential cardinal in first reference. For curial cardinals, use: *Cardinal Angelo Sodano, Vatican secretary of state; Cardinal Zenon Grocholewski, prefect of the Vatican Congregation for Catholic Education.* If an Eastern Catholic patriarch or major archbishop is a cardinal, use *cardinal* as his title. See **cardinal** and **patriarch.**

DEACON: *Deacon John M. Bresnahan; Deacon Bresnahan; the deacon.* See **deacon, diaconate.**

EASTERN CATHOLICS: Indicate the specific rite of Eastern Catholic clergymen in first reference. Use *-rite* after the name of a specific rite only if it is needed to clarify to the reader that you are referring to a liturgical or canonical affiliation, not simply to the person's nationality.

Coptic Patriarch Stephanos II Ghattas of Alexandria, Egypt; Patriarch Ghattas; the patriarch; Cardinal Nasrallah P. Sfeir, patriarch of Maronite Catholics. See **patriarch.**

Ukrainian-rite Archbishop Michael Bzdel of Winnipeg, Manitoba; Ruthenian Bishop Basil M. Schott of

Parma, N.J.; Maronite Father John L. Smith. Do not use *archeparch, archimandrite, eparch, exarch* or *metropolitan* as personal titles before names of Eastern Catholic clergy. See individual entries for those terms.

MONSIGNOR: An honorary title given to some priests: *Msgr. John Smith; Msgr. Smith; the monsignor.* Always abbreviate as *Msgr.* when used as a title before a name. CAUTION: In many other countries and in several foreign languages, *Msgr.* (or alternative abbreviations, *Mgr.* or *Mons.)* are used as a title of respect before the names of bishops and archbishops as well as before the names of priests who hold the honorary title of *monsignor.* Use *bishop* or *archbishop* as the title of anyone ordained a bishop. See **monsignor.**

MOTHER: Use *mother* before the name of a woman religious superior if she prefers to be known that way, but do not use it alone: *Mother Maria Martin; Mother Maria* (or *Mother Martin* if she prefers). But: *the superior; the nun; the sister.* Many superiors prefer to continue using the title *sister.*

POPE: *Pope Benedict XVI, Pope Benedict, the pope* or *the pontiff.* Do not use *Holy Father* or *His Holiness* except in direct quotes. See **pontiff** and **pope.**

PRIEST: *Father John L. Smith; Father Smith; the priest.* Never abbreviate *Father.* Do not use *Father* alone without the last name. Identify the religious community of an order priest in the first reference, if possible: *Jesuit Father John L. Smith, Father Smith, the priest, the Jesuit.* If the name of the religious order is more than one or two words, however, give the name of the order after the name or somewhere else high in the story: *Father Tullio Favali, a member of the Pontifical Institute for Foreign Missions.* See **priest** and **religious.**

SISTER: Use the religious and family name on first reference and identify by religious community: *Sacred Heart Sister Jane M. Jones; Dominican Sister Regina C. Smith.* On second reference, use the first name: *Sister Jane, Sister Regina (*or, if she prefers, *Sister Jones, Sister Smith).* Never abbreviate *Sister.* Do not use *Sister* alone without the first or last name. If the name of the religious order is more than one or two words, however, give the name of the order after the name or somewhere else high in the story. *Sister Jean R. Abbott, a member of the Sisters of St. Joseph of Carondelet.* See **nuns, sisters; religious;** and **sister.**

NON-CATHOLIC TITLES:

In general, Protestant ministers, including Anglicans and Episcopalians, should be identified as *the Rev.* on first and *Rev.* on subsequent references: *the Rev. Jesse Jackson, Rev. Jackson; the Rev. Joan Brown Campbell, Rev. Campbell.* Where exceptions to the general rule apply, they are noted below or in the separate entry for the denomination in question.

Some denominations and non-Christian religions prefer no clergy titles. These include the Church of Christ, Scientist, the Church of Jesus Christ of Latter-day Saints, Jehovah's Witnesses, many Quakers, the Seventh-day Adventists and Buddhists. Treat leaders of these denominations as laity, but identify them by religious affiliation high in the story.

For Orthodox clergy, the title Father is acceptable in all references, but avoid for all other denominations. Titles for higher clergy generally parallel Catholic usage, but see below.

For Jewish leaders, use *rabbi* in all references, never *Mr., Miss, Ms.* or *Mrs.: Rabbi A. James Rudin, Rabbi Rudin, the rabbi.* Do not use *Jewish rabbi.* It is redundant.

Some other examples for non-Catholics:

Patriarch Bartholomew of Constantinople (Istanbul) or *Ecumenical Patriarch Bartholomew of Constantinople; Patriarch Bartholomew; the patriarch.*

Greek Orthodox Archbishop Demetrios of America; Archbishop Demetrios; the archbishop.

Russian Orthodox Metropolitan Vladimir of St. Petersburg; Metropolitan Vladimir; the metropolitan.

Anglican Archbishop Rowan Williams of Canterbury or *Archbishop Rowan Williams of Canterbury, Anglican primate; Archbishop Williams; the archbishop.*

The Rev. John Smith, an Episcopal priest, Rev. Smith, the priest. The Rev. Jane Doe, an Episcopal priest, Rev. Doe, the priest.

For Episcopal priests who hold titles such as *rector* (head of a parish), *dean* (head of a cathedral parish), *canon, curate* or *archdeacon,* treat these as job titles and do not use them before names.

For clergy titles in *Presbyterian churches*, see that entry.

For leaders of non-Christian faiths:

Swami Sivananda, the swami (Hindu).

Muruttetuwe Ananda, a Buddhist monk; Ananda; the monk. See **dalai lama.**

Sheik Mohammed Zafzaf, Sheik Zafzaf, the sheik (Muslim).

While *sheik* is the most commonly used title among Muslim clergy, several others also are used. These include *grand mufti, ayatollah, hojatoleslam, mullah* and *imam.* Capitalize if used before a name. See **imam.**

Renew (www.renewintl.org) A parish-level Catholic faith renewal program begun in 1978 in Newark, N.J. The organization uses *RENEW,* but the name is a proper noun, not an acronym. Capitalize only the first letter. The International Office of Renew is in Plainfield, N.J.

Reorganized Church of Jesus Christ of Latter Day Saints See **Community of Christ.**

residential bishop This, not *ordinary,* is the correct term to specify a bishop who is head of a diocese or similar ecclesiastical jurisdiction of the Catholic Church. If the jurisdiction is a diocese, *diocesan bishop* is also correct.

See **bishop** and **ordinary.**

retired See **emeritus, retired.**

Retreats International (www.retreatsintl.org) Headquarters is in Notre Dame, Ind.

Retrouvaille (www.retrouvaille.org) A ministry to marriage partners who are hurting.

revelation In theological terms, revelation is the manifestation of divine will or truth. Lowercase in this usage. Capitalize only in reference to the Book of Revelation in the New Testament.

reverend For most Protestant clergy, *the Rev.* is the form used as a title before the name on first reference: *the Rev. John Smith, the Rev. Jean Jones.* On second reference, use only the last name preceded by Rev.: *Rev. Smith, Rev. Jones.*

The plural form may be used preceding a list of two or more clergy who use the same title: *the Revs. John Smith and Jean Jones.*

Use *the minister, the pastor, the clergyman,* etc., not: *the reverend,* in references that do not use the person's name. Use of *reverend* as a noun is colloquial.

Except in quoted matter, do not use *Dr.* in place of or in combination with *Rev.* as a formal title before a name: *the Rev. Billy Graham, Rev. Graham,* not: *the Rev. Dr. Billy Graham, Dr. Graham.*

Protestant clergy generally link their title to a ministerial post within their church. If a minister has a secular post carrying its own title, such as *Mayor* or *Rep.,* use whichever is appropriate to the context.

See **religious titles** and the entry for the denomination of the individual in question.

right, rite *Rite* has to do with liturgy, ceremony or liturgical family.

Do not confuse it with *right,* which has to do with justice, law and morality.

See **pontifical right, pontifical rite** and **rite of...**.

rite, -rite Use sparingly in references to the distinct national or liturgical traditions within the Catholic Church which are called *rites.* In most cases the more appropriate form of reference is *church,* although *rite* is needed at times to clarify that the writer is referring to a particular ecclesial patrimony and culture, not simply to a language, nation or geographical region. The Code of Canons of the Eastern Churches emphasizes the character of the Eastern churches as churches and does not call the churches *rites.* Canon 28 of that code defines a rite as "the liturgical, theological, spiritual and disciplinary patrimony, culture and circumstances of a distinct people, by which its own manner of living the faith is manifested in each church 'sui iuris.'"

When *rite* is used in a story, capitalize the proper name associated with it but lowercase *rite.* If *rite* is used as a noun, do not hyphenate; if it is used as an adjective, hyphenate: *a member of the Melkite rite* (but *a Melkite Catholic* or *a member of the Melkite Catholic Church* might be better), *a Latin-rite Mass, in the Ukrainian rite* (but *in the Ukrainian Catholic Church* might be better).

See **Catholic Church** and **Eastern Catholic churches.**

rite of... Lowercase when referring to a ritual event: *They celebrated the rite of baptism during Mass.* Uppercase when referring to an official liturgical book containing the words and actions of the rite and regulations concerning its use: *The bishops approved a revised version of the Rite of Baptism for Children.* As reference works, such liturgical books are not enclosed in quotes. See **liturgical books** and **reference works.**

Note that *Rite of Christian Initiation of Adults* is always capitalized. See that entry.

Rite of Christian Initiation of Adults The liturgical book containing the norms and rituals of the Catholic Church for people who wish to become Christians in the Catholic Church. Although the RCIA is aimed chiefly at preparing and initiating the unbaptized, one chapter is intended for baptized members of other Christian churches who wish to become Catholics, and other elements of the ritual may be adapted for those situations. Always capitalize when the full name is used: It refers to the whole set of norms and rituals, not a single ritual event. RCIA is acceptable on second reference. Also acceptable are shorter forms such as the initiation rite, the rite.

Use *catechumen* or *catechume-*

nate, not *RCIA,* to refer to the person's formation period before baptism: *She is a catechumen.* Or: *She is in the catechumenate.* Not: *She is in the RCIA.* One who is already baptized and going through an adapted version of formation for entry into full communion with the Catholic Church is called a *candidate*, not a *catechumen.* See **catechumen.**

Roman Catholic Church Technically this term refers only to the *Latin* Church, although sometimes it is used loosely in ways that include the *Eastern Catholic churches.* See those entries and **Catholic Church.**

Roman Curia *Curia* is acceptable on all references. The adjective is *curial.*

See Catholic Church and **Appendix G: Vatican Agencies.**

Romanian Orthodox Church Recognized by the patriarch of Constantinople as an autocephalous church in 1885 and established as a patriarchate in 1925, with Bucharest as the patriarchal see. The communist government after World War II did not separate church and state but held the church under tight controls. It forcibly incorporated Romanian-rite Catholics into the Orthodox Church. The government was overthrown by popular revolution in December 1989. With about 19 million members the Romanian Orthodox Church is the second-largest autonomous body in Orthodoxy, after the Russian Orthodox Church.

There are two Romanian Orthodox bodies in the United States.

The Romanian Orthodox Church in America, established in 1929 and based in Detroit, is an autonomous archdiocese with canonical ties to the Patriarchate of Bucharest.

The Romanian Orthodox Episcopate of America was formed in 1951 by about 40 parishes that severed their ties with the patriarchate and subsequently became an autonomous diocese within the Orthodox Church in America. Headquarters is in Grass Lake, Mich.

See **Orthodox churches.**

Roman Missal The entire book of Mass prayers and readings approved by the Holy See for use throughout the church of the Latin rite. Before the liturgical reforms of the Second Vatican Council, these were all contained in one large volume. Since then, however, in practice the Roman Missal has been divided into a volume of Mass prayers called the *Sacramentary* and two or more volumes of readings called, individually or collectively, the *Lectionary.* See those entries. As of 2005, there were indications, however, that for several years the Vatican has wanted *Roman Missal* restored as the name for any future national editions of the Sacramentary.

Roman numerals In addition to their use for sequence of wars and personal sequence for people and animals, Roman numerals are used to express sequence of Catholic ecumenical councils in shortened forms of reference. Use the shortened form only on second reference: *the Second Vatican Council, Vatican II; the First Council of Nicaea, Nicaea I*

Traditionally the first in a potential sequence of people is not identified by a numeral until a second of the same name has appeared, creating an actual sequence: *Queen Beatrix of the Netherlands, Patriarch Bartholomew of Constantinople.* There are exceptions, however: *King Juan Carlos I of Spain.* Do not use *I* after the name of a current hereditary monarch or holder of ecclesiastical office unless the person consistently uses it as an official part of his or her name.

On second reference to people or animals, the Roman numeral need not be repeated unless confusion may result, e.g., because another individual in the sequence is referred to in the same story.

Roman Rota, Tribunal of the See **ecclesiastical courts.**

Rome, Diocese of Despite its unique position as the diocese of the pope and center of Catholicism, the Rome Diocese is known simply as a diocese in references to it as a local church jurisdiction.

In references to its position in relation to the whole church, however, it is generally called the *Holy See.* See **Catholic Church** and **Holy See.**

The Diocese of Rome encompasses the city and the region around it. It includes Vatican City State, an enclave within the city of Rome.

For purposes of local religious administration it is divided into two vicariates: the *Vicariate of Vatican City* and the *Vicariate of Rome.*

The Vatican City Vicariate is responsible only for the pastoral care and ecclesiastical administration governing those who live in Vatican City. It is headed by a bishop who is the pope's *vicar general of Vatican City.*

The Rome Vicariate is responsible for the governance of the rest of the diocese. It is headed by a bishop, usually a cardinal, who is the pope's *vicar general of Rome. Vicar of Rome* and *head of the Rome Vicariate* also are acceptable on all references.

For most news stories about local government of the church in the Rome Diocese, the administrative separation of Vatican City from the rest of the diocese is irrelevant. Unless the distinction is relevant to the story, it is acceptable to use *vicar of Rome* and *vicar of the Diocese of Rome* interchangeably.

Do not, however, call the vicar of Rome the *bishop of Rome.* The *bishop of Rome* is the pope.

The cathedral church of the pope and the Rome Diocese is *St. John Lateran Basilica.*

Another distinct ecclesiastical jurisdiction within the Rome Diocese is that of St. Peter's Basilica. It is governed by a papally appointed cardinal, who is called the *archpriest of St. Peter's Basilica.* St. Peter's is not a cathedral and should never be called one.

See **Vatican City State.**

rosary It is *recited, prayed* or *said,* never *read.* In many constructions it is difficult or impossible to tell whether *rosary* refers to the physical circlet of beads or the set of prayers said on them. For consistency, always lowercase.

The mysteries of the rosary are the joyful, sorrowful, glorious and luminous. The luminous mysteries, added by Pope John Paul II in 2002, may also be called the mysteries of light.

See **prayers.**

Rosh Hashana Preferred spelling for the Jewish new year, celebrated in September or October. It is one of the high holy days of Judaism.

roster, rostrum A *roster* is any list of members of a group or participants at an event, except a list of speakers.

A *rostrum* is a list of speakers at an event or the raised platform from which a speaker addresses a group.

See **dais, podium, rostrum** and **lectern, ambo.**

Roundtable (www.nplc.org/
roundtable.htm) National association
of Catholic diocesan social action directors. It is staffed by the National
Pastoral Life Center in New York.

RU-486 A drug originally produced by the French drug company
Roussel Uclaf that, when used in combination with a prostaglandin, induces
an abortion in the first seven weeks
of pregnancy. RU-486 is generically
known as mifepristone.

In 1994, Roussel Uclaf donated
the U.S. patent for RU-486 to the
nonprofit Population Council of New
York. In 1997, Roussel Uclaf and its
German parent company, Hoechst
AG, gave all other patent rights to Dr.
Edouard Sakiz, one of the drug's cre-
ators. Since its approval by the Food
and Drug Administration in September 2000, RU-486 has been marketed
in the United States under the names
Mifeprex and Early Option by Dan-
co Laboratories and the Population
Council. In mid-2005, the FDA delayed its decision on whether to allow
over-the-counter sales of the drug.

The Catholic Church views the
use of RU-486 as a chemical abortion,
equal in moral seriousness to a surgi-
cal abortion.

See **abortion.**

Russian Orthodox Church See
Orthodox churches.

Sabbath Capitalize whenever it is used for the weekly day set aside for religious observance by Jews or, by extension, Christians: *The Jewish Sabbath is Saturday but most Christians observe Sunday as their Sabbath.* It is better in most contexts, however, to refer to the Christian observance as *the Lord's day.* Lowercase to mean a period of rest in general: *She needs a sabbath when she finishes that project.*

A lengthy period of rest, particularly from one's professional routine, is more commonly called a *sabbatical.* In the academic world it is usually for one year unless otherwise specified.

sacerdotal Except in quoted matter, use *priestly.*

sacramentals The Second Vatican Council described sacramentals as sacred signs instituted by the church "which bear a resemblance to the sacraments. They signify effects, particularly of a spiritual kind, that are obtained through the church's intercession. By them, men (people) are disposed to receive the chief effects of the sacraments and various occasions in life are rendered holy." Signs regarded as sacramentals include liturgical prayers and rites used in administering the sacraments, funerals, exorcisms and blessings of persons and objects. The Holy See reserves to itself the establishment, interpretation, regulation and abolition of sacramentals. Church law once restricted the administration of all sacramentals to priests, but now it allows for administration of some sacramentals by deacons or laypeople. A layperson, for example, may administer blessed ashes on Ash Wednesday or a parent may bless a child.

See **sacraments.**

Sacramentary The book of prayers for Mass in the Catholic Church. Capitalize but do not place in quotes. As of 2005, there were indications that for several years the Vatican had wanted *Roman Missal* restored as the name for any future national editions of the Sacramentary.

See **Lectionary; liturgical books; Mass;** and **Roman Missal.**

sacraments Catholics and Orthodox recognize seven: *the Eucharist, baptism, confirmation, penance* (now often called *the sacrament of reconciliation), matrimony, holy orders,* and *the sacrament of anointing of the sick* (formerly *extreme unction).* Orthodox and Eastern Catholics usually call confirmation *chrismation.*

Many Protestant denominations recognize only the two commonly called the *dominical sacraments* because they are firmly established in Scripture as instituted and commanded by the Lord: *baptism* and *the Lord's Supper (Eucharist).* Other denominations recognize more or fewer. See entries for individual denominations.

In modern Catholic sacramental theology, *sacrament* is also used in a broader sense. Christ is often referred to as the first sacrament and the church as a sacrament. Protestant and Catholic theologians also speak of the sacramentality of the word of God.

Capitalize only *Eucharist* or similar proper names for that sacrament. Lowercase the names of the others.

See individual entries for each sacrament.

See **Mass** for guidelines on capitalization of worship services.

sacred, Sacred Lowercase in almost all uses: *sacred Scripture, the sacred liturgy.*

When combined with *heart,* however, it is capitalized because it forms the proper name of an object of devotion — the heart of Jesus, the heart of Mary, or the hearts of both: *the Sacred Heart, the Sacred Heart of Jesus, the Sacred Heart of Mary, the Sacred Hearts of Jesus and Mary.*

Note: The adjective *sacred* formerly was part of the formal names of the College of Cardinals, the Roman Rota, the Apostolic Penitentiary and all Vatican congregations. It has been dropped in all cases. Do not use it except when necessary for historical references to those agencies when *sacred* was part of their formal name. See **Apostolic Penitentiary; Catholic Church; ecclesiastical courts; Holy, holy;** and **Appendix G: Vatican Agencies.**

Sacred Heart League Parent organization of Sacred Heart Auto League and Apostolate of the Printed Word, based in Walls, Miss.

sacrilegious (adj.), **sacrilege** (n.)

saint Abbreviate as *St.* in proper names of saints and the places and institutions named after them: *St. Patrick, St. Anne Church, St. Jude League, St. Louis* (the city), *St. Croix River.*

Exceptions: Spell out *Saint* for the city of *Saint John* in New Brunswick, Canada, to help distinguish it from *St. John's, Newfoundland.* Use the abbreviation *Ste.* in *Sault Ste. Marie, Ontario.*

For use of alternate titles before the name of a saint, see **canonization.**

The standard plural form of the abbreviation is *Sts.: Sts. Peter and Paul died in Rome.* Use that form except in the names of institutions that use the abbreviated form *Ss.* or *SS.* as part of their formal name: *the Cathedral Basilica of SS. Peter and Paul* (in Philadelphia).

When an institution or organization has a saint's name as part of its formal name, use the possessive form only if that is the institution's or organization's official form of usage. For Catholic institutions in the United States, consult the Kenedy directory. In shortened references a possessive form is acceptable even if it is not used in the formal name: *St. Mary Church, the people at St. Mary's; St. Joseph Hospital, the staff of St. Joseph's.* See **church** and **parish.**

FOREIGN NAMES: In references to saints themselves, generally use names by which saints are known in English unless there is good reason, such as a local title of popular devotion, for using the name in a foreign language.

For names of famous churches, shrines or other institutions, use whichever form is widely known to U.S. Catholics. For example: *St. Peter's Basilica, St. John Lateran Basilica.* But: *Santa Susanna Parish* (the U.S. national parish in Rome).

If a foreign church or institution is not well known to U.S. Catholics, use whichever form is most appropriate or informative within the context. If a foreign name is used in these cases, two general guidelines apply:

— Translate common institutional words such as *church, cathedral, basilica, parish, school* or *hospital* into English, capitalizing them when linked immediately to the proper name: *San Saverio Parish, Santo Tomas Church,* not: *Parrocchia di San Saverio, Iglesia Santo Tomas.*

— Abbreviate the French masculine, which is identical with the English *(St.);* otherwise, spell out the foreign word for *saint.* Do not use a foreign abbreviation or substitute the English abbreviation: *Sao Joao,* not: *S. Joao* or *St. Joao.*

A caution: *Saint* is not always the proper translation of foreign words that ordinarily are translated *saint.* For example, *San Salvador* (Spanish) means *Holy Savior; St. Croix* (French) or *Santa Cruce* (Italian) means *Holy Cross; Santa Sofia* (Italian) or *Hagia Sophia* (Greek) means *Holy Wisdom* — a title of reverence for the Holy Spirit.

St. Anthony's Guild (www.hnp.org/guild/) Headquarters is in Paterson, N.J.

St. Bernadette Institute of Sacred Art Located in Albuquerque, N.M.

St. Januarius See **Januarius, St.**

St. Joan's International Alliance Headquarters is in Liege, Belgium.

St. Joseph Foundation (www.st-joseph-foundation.org) Founded by Charles M. Wilson in 1984 "to defend Catholic truth and uphold Catholic rights," it seeks to notify Catholics of their legal rights and to correct alleged abuses in the church through canonical processes. Headquarters is in San Antonio.

St. Jude League (www.stjudeleague.org) Headquarters is in Chicago.

St. Peter's Basilica Do not use *Basilica of St. Peter.* Do not call it a *cathedral:* The cathedral church of the pope, bishop of Rome, is *St. John Lateran Basilica.*

See **basilica.**

St. Peter's Square The elliptical piazza in front of St. Peter's Basilica. It is often used for outdoor papal Masses and is the place people gather on Sundays to pray the Angelus with the pope and receive his blessing.

Salvation Army (www.salvationarmy.org) Founded in England in 1865 by Methodist evangelist William Booth. He called it *The Christian Mission* until 1878, when he renamed it the *Salvation Army.* He originally intended it to be a nondenominational mission organized along military lines and devoted to Christian service and evangelization among London's poor. When the poor he worked with were unwelcome in class-conscious congregations of existing churches, he was gradually forced to form his own denomination.

Salvationists do not place much emphasis on theology but generally follow the beliefs of Methodism. They believe in the primacy of Scripture but emphasize the importance of personal conversion and the immediate inspiration of the Spirit in each believer. They remain most noted for their diversified program of religious and welfare services for the poor.

Religious services, held in halls, are informal and consist of free prayer, hymn singing, testimony, preaching and reading from Scripture. The sacraments of baptism and the Lord's Supper accepted by most Protestants are disregarded by Salvationists, but the Army has a ritual for the dedication of children.

Converts are expected to become soldiers, but those who do not wish to wear the uniform of the Army and devote their lives to the salvation of others may join other churches while remaining in the Army. Officers are drawn from the ranks of soldiers, without distinction of sex, and given a year of intensive training in an Officer Training College, after which they are given the rank of probationary lieutenant.

The equivalent of a parish or congregation is a *corps,* which is headed by a captain or lieutenant. The corps are grouped geographically into *divisions* headed by a colonel or major. Divisions are grouped into *territories* headed by a commissioner. Senior officers of the territories form the *High Council,* which can elect or depose the international commander in chief.

Capitalize the military titles when used before the names of officers, but make it clear they are titles used by the denomination.

At the end of 2004, the organization reported more than 449,000 Salvationists in the United States, including more than 5,400 officers. The U.S. organization (www.salvationarmyusa. org) has headquarters in Alexandria, Va. International headquarters is in London.

San Cristobal de las Casas Lowercase *las.* An exception to the National Geographic Atlas of the World.

sanctuary, shrine Use *sanctuary* for the area around the altar of a Catholic church or, more generally, for a place of refuge or asylum.

If a place of pilgrimage is meant, although many other languages may use a term that could be translated literally as *sanctuary,* the preferred term in English is usually *shrine: the Marian shrine in Loreto, Italy,* not: *the Marian sanctuary in Loreto.*

Sant'Egidio, Community of See **Community of Sant'Egidio.**

Satan Also capitalize *Lucifer,* but lowercase *devil.*

Capitalize *Satanism* and *Satanist,* terms referring to a religious cult of Satan or its adherents. Also capitalize *Satanic* when it is used specifically to describe cultic acts in the worship of Satan, but lowercase *satanic* when it is used generically to mean *wicked, evil* or *diabolical.*

savior Not *saviour.* See **Jesus.**

scapular This term may refer to the long, narrow outer cloak with a hole for the head, worn as part of the habit of many religious orders, or to one or two tiny patches of cloth, usually with devotional images, worn around the neck by some Catholics as a sign of devotion. The devotional kind is called a *small scapular.* The most widely known of these is the brown Carmelite scapular.

schema The plural in English, as in the original Greek, is *schemata.* This term, sometimes used by the Holy See to identify a preliminary version of a document that is still subject to revision, is usually best avoided in news writing in favor of the more familiar term, *draft: the first draft, the draft text, the draft document, the draft.*

See **"instrumentum laboris"** and **"lineamenta."**

schism In religion, an institutional division. It may or may not be accompanied or caused by significant doctrinal differences.

Schonstatt Fathers Not *Schoenstatt.* A secular institute comprised exclusively of priests and represented in 20 countries worldwide.

School of the Americas Located at Fort Benning, Ga., the school, now called the Western Hemisphere Institute for Security Cooperation, is a training facility for foreign military personnel. Since 1990, it has been the site of annual protests by demonstrators who link its graduates to human-rights abuses committed since the 1970s by government security forces in Latin America. The School of the Americas Watch (www.soaw.org), based in Washington, organizes the annual protests. SOA Watch is acceptable on second reference.

The U.S. Department of Defense, which runs the school, says its curriculum teaches Latin American military personnel democratic principles and respect for human rights.

Scripture, Scriptures Capitalize in references to the Hebrew or Christian Bible. Lowercase in references to sacred books of other religions.

Do not capitalize modifying adjectives: *sacred Scriptures, holy Scripture.*

See **Bible.**

season Always lowercase. *Christmas season, Easter season.*

See **liturgical year.**

second coming

second reference When this phrase is used in this book, it means any reference to an individual or organization after the first.

When a usage is described as *acceptable on second reference,* it does not mean that that form must be used after the first reference. It means only that this is a possible form of reference once the individual or organization has been identified more fully or formally.

If use of a form is *required* on all references after the first (for example: use of certain titles before names of individuals), the phrase *on second reference* is not preceded by the word *acceptable.*

Second Vatican Council *Vatican II* or *the council* is acceptable on second reference. It consisted of four sessions, approximately three months each, held in the years 1962-65.

See **Vatican councils** and **Appendix I: Vatican II Documents.**

secretary of state The secretary of state of the Holy See may also be called the *Vatican secretary of state.* In historical references, *papal secretary of state* is an acceptable alternative up to 1988, when that title was dropped in a reform of the Curia.

In other uses *secretary of state* is capitalized when used as a formal title before a name: *U.S. Secretary of State Condoleezza Rice.* The Vatican official, however, always holds a religious title that takes precedence: *the Vatican secretary of state, Cardinal Angelo Sodano.*

sect In religious usage, *sect* refers generically to any religious denomination, especially a small one, formed by breaking off from a larger, more established denomination. Sociologists of religion have proposed varying criteria for what constitutes a sect, however, and there is no agreed system or listing to determine which groups are properly described as sects.

In most uses *sect* is a judgmental term with negative connotations. It should not be applied to any specific group without attribution to a source.

See **cult, denomination** and **religious movements.**

secular institutes The Code of Canon Law defines a *secular institute* as "an institute of consecrated life in which the Christian faithful living in the world strive for the perfection of charity and work for the sanctification of the world especially from within." Canons 710-730 of the code contain the general church law governing such institutes. Laypeople who are members of secular institutes are not religious and do not use religious titles. A diocesan priest who is a member uses only the title he has as a priest.

secular orders See **third order.**

Seder Acceptable on all references for the *Passover Seder,* a meal-and-prayer service in Jewish homes on the eve of the first day of Passover (and on the eve of the second day as well by Orthodox Jews outside Israel).

Some Christian families and parish groups hold modified Seder observances because the Last Supper, at which Jesus instituted the Eucharist the night before his death, is traditionally believed to have been a Seder meal.

See **Passover.**

see (n.) Lowercase when referring to an archbishop's or bishop's jurisdiction, whether archdiocese, diocese, apostolic vicariate, territorial prelature or other.

Capitalize only *Holy See* and *Apostolic See,* unique references to the Diocese of Rome as chief diocese of the Catholic Church throughout the world. See those entries.

The *see city* of an archdiocese, diocese, etc., is the community in which the bishop resides and has his cathedral.

Apart from *Holy See* and *Apostolic See, see* should not be used as part of a formal name. Use the specific name of the jurisdiction instead: *Cincinnati Archdiocese, San Diego Diocese, Prelature of Itaituba, Brazil,* etc. Use of *see* is generally most appropriate in two contexts:

— In certain phrases such as *metropolitan see, suffragan see, patriarchal see* and *see city: Cincinnati is Archbishop Pilarczyk's see city. The Cincinnati Archdiocese is the metropolitan see for all the Latin-rite dioceses of Ohio. The Diocese of Toledo is one of its suffragan sees.* See **metropolitan** and **suffragan.**

—As an alternate form of reference to avoid excessive repetition of *diocese, archdiocese,* etc., or, especially in plural uses, as a generic term including both archdioceses and dioceses (and other jurisdictions if relevant): *The Cincinnati Archdiocese is only one of six Latin-rite sees in Ohio. The Archdiocese of Newark, N.J., was the first see in the nation to use the Renew program.*

sepulcher Not *sepulchre.* Capitalize *Holy Sepulcher,* the proper name of the tomb in Jerusalem in which Jesus is believed to have been buried.

Serra, Blessed Junipero Father Serra, a Franciscan priest, is credited with founding the first nine of the California missions. He was beatified in 1988.

Serra International (www.serra international.org) Promotes vocations to the priesthood and religious life. In 2005 it had about 19,000 members in 36 countries. Since 1986 it has admitted women. Members are called *Serrans.* Headquarters for Serra International's USA Council (www.serra us.org) is in Chicago.

Seven hills of Rome They are the Aventine, Caelian, Capitoline, Esquiline, Palatine, Quirinal and Viminal. All are east of the Tiber, across the river from the Vatican.

Vatican Hill, on which Vatican City is built, and the higher Janiculum Hill next to it are not among the seven.

Seventh-day Adventist Church Note the lowercase *d.* The denomination was organized in 1863 but had its origins in an interdenominational movement begun in 1831 by William Miller.

Miller used calculations from biblical texts to predict that Christ would come again and the world would end in 1843 or 1844. Millerites dispersed after 1844 except for a few small groups. The Seventh-day Adventist Church grew from one of these, strongly influenced by the visions of Ellen Harmon, later Ellen White, who believed that in 1844 Christ began a cleansing in preparation for his second coming.

The church calls itself *adventist* because of its emphasis on the need to prepare for Christ's second coming, inaugurating his 1,000-year reign. It is called *seventh-day* because it believes Christians are bound by the Old Testament prescription of Saturday as the Sabbath. Old Testament tithing and dietary laws are also considered binding. See **millennium, millenary.**

The Bible, interpreted literally, is considered the sole rule of faith, but Seventh-day Adventists also affirm the gift of prophecy as always present in their church. White's writings, in particular, are the basis for many doctrinal positions.

Baptism is by immersion and is given only to those old enough to understand its meaning. Baptism and the Lord's Supper are the only sacraments.

The church is governed by a General Conference, which meets every four years, and by a president who is head of the conference.

The conference oversees the church's worldwide evangelizing and publishing activities, a parochial school system that is the third-largest in the United States, and a network of medical institutions. Worldwide membership in 203 countries exceeded 13 million in 2005. Membership in the North American division — made up of the United States, Canada and Bermuda — is more than 1 million.

International headquarters and headquarters of the North American division are in Silver Spring, Md.

See **religious titles.**

sex abuse, sexual abuse No hyphen, even in compound modifiers.

sexism, sexist language In general, avoid words or phrases that suggest sexual stereotyping of people.

Do not describe a woman's physical or emotional attributes or her apparel in a story unless you would give comparable descriptions if the subject were a man. In contexts such as feature stories or personality profiles, where such descriptions may be an integral part of the story, avoid descriptive terms that suggest personality stereotypes. To say that a woman *has blond hair,* for example, is simply descriptive; to say that she *is a blonde* may suggest that she is defined by her hair color.

Entries in this stylebook that caution against use of certain words or constructions because they may have sexist connotations should be taken as constructive style guides for news writing, not as judgments that any individual who uses them is sexist.

See **fellow; inclusive language; layman, laywoman, layperson, laypeople;** and **-person, -people.**

SHARE Foundation (www.share -elsalvador.org) Acceptable on all references, but note in the story that it stands for Salvadoran Human Aid, Research and Education Foundation. National office is in San Francisco, with offices also in San Salvador and Washington.

Shariah The religiously based law of Islam, systematized in the second and third centuries of the Muslim era. Since Islam does not distinguish between religious and secular law, the Shariah encompasses the religious, political, social, domestic and private lives of Muslims. Christian leaders have objected to the incorporation of elements of the Shariah into civil laws of predominantly Muslim states because of the legal discrimination against non-Muslims that may result. See **Islam.**

Shavuot The Jewish Feast of Weeks, celebrated in May or June. Originally it was a spring harvest celebration, but later a commemoration of revelation of the law on Mount Sinai. The original Pentecost of Christianity coincided with Shavuot, but Christian tradition has found no particular theological or doctrinal significance in that fact.

she Except in quoted matter, use *it,* not *she,* to refer to the Catholic Church.
See **inclusive language.**

sheik See **religious titles.**

Shoah The Hebrew word for the Holocaust. Explain if used. Always capitalize.
See **Holocaust** and **Yom Hashoah.**

shrine See **sanctuary, shrine.**

Shroud of Turin (www.sindone. org) A linen shroud containing what looks like a photographically negative image of a man with wounds similar to those of the crucified Christ as described in the Gospels. The cloth was brought to Europe from the Holy Land during the Crusades. Capitalize *shroud* only in the full formal name, *Shroud of Turin.*

The shroud was owned for centuries by the House of Savoy, one of Europe's royal families, but for much of the time has been in the custody of the Archdiocese of Turin, Italy. The House of Savoy willed the shroud to the Vatican in 1983. Pope John Paul II left it in archdiocesan custody.

In 1988, the archdiocese authorized a series of scientific tests on pieces of the shroud, including independent carbon-14 dating by three laboratories. The archdiocese said the carbon-14 tests showed a 95 percent certainty that the cloth was made between the years 1260 and 1390. None of the 1988 tests shed light on how the image of the crucified man was made on the cloth. Many shroud experts have rejected the carbon-14 dating.

Signis (www.signis.net) Its secondary name is the World Catholic Association for Communication, founded in 2001 by the merger of Unda, the organization for Catholics in radio and television, and the International Catholic Organization for Cinema and Audiovisual. Capitalize only the first letter. Headquarters is in Brussels, Belgium. See **Catholic Academy for Communication Arts Professionals.**

sign of the cross Capitalize only in reference to the specific prayer: *The pope urged Catholics to learn the Sign of the Cross in Latin.* But *He made the sign of the cross as he entered the church.* See **prayers.**

Sinn Fein The legal political wing of the outlawed Irish Republican Army.

sister Capitalize when used as a title before the name of a woman religious or as part of the name of a religious order: *Sister Mary Agnes Jones, a Sister of Mercy, the School Sisters of Notre Dame.* Always identify a woman religious by the community to which she belongs. See **religious titles.**

Lowercase *sister* when it stands alone: *the sister, a group of sisters.* Except in direct quotes do not use it in the singular without an article, as if it were a substitute for a proper name: *Sister Julie said* or *the sister said* or *the nun said,* not: *Sister said.*

If it is not clear from the context whether *sister* refers to a woman religious or a female sibling, use more specific forms of reference such as *nun, woman religious, religious sister* and *blood sister.*

See **nuns, sisters; order, congregation, society; religious;** and **Appendix E: Religious Orders, Women.**

Slovak Catholic Sokol (www. slovakcatholicsokol.org) Headquarters is in Passaic, N.J.

small Christian communities Also called *small church communities, faith reflection groups, faith sharing groups* or various other names. In North America these are usually parish-based groups of about eight to 12 people seeking to make their faith more alive in their daily lives. While the emphasis differs from one group to another, generally their purposes include prayer, mutual support, reflection on Scripture and life, learning, mission and participation in the larger church. A 1999 study found that such small Christian communities are active in about half of U.S. Catholic parishes.

On other continents the characteristics of and names used for such small Christian communities may vary. In Latin America, where they first became a major force in church life, they often arose out of a need to address social or economic problems. There they are usually called *base communities* or *base ecclesial communities ("comunidades eclesiales de base").*

In North America such communities more often arise from a desire of members to know Scripture better or to find support for their spiritual life. Many such communities were sparked by participation in parish renewal programs such as Renew. Diocesan directors of such communities are linked by the *North American Forum for Small Christian Communities.* See that entry and **Renew.**

SNAP See **Survivors' Network of those Abused by Priests.**

SOAR See **Support Our Aging Religious.**

Societas Liturgica (www.so cietas-liturgica.org) Founded in the Netherlands in 1967, Societas Liturgica is an ecumenical, international society of liturgical scholars. It sponsors a biennial congress and publishes a newsletter in English, German and French.

societies of priests See **order, congregation, society.**

Society for the Propagation of the Faith (www.worldmissions-catholicchurch.org/spof) The largest Catholic organization for promoting missionary awareness and generating and distributing funds for the missions, it is one of four *pontifical missionary societies* under the jurisdiction of the Vatican Congregation for the Evangelization of Peoples. U.S. headquarters is in New York.

See **pontifical missionary societies.**

Society of Catholic Social Scientists (www.catholicsocialscientists.org) Founded in 1992 to further the study of Catholic social science, promulgate Catholic social teaching, influence society and aid the church. Open to Catholics involved in the social sciences or disciplines concerned with social questions such as theology or ethics, and who have earned a master's degree or doctorate. Headquarters is in Steubenville, Ohio.

Society of Friends See **Quakers.**

Society of St. James the Apostle (www.socstjames.com) A society of diocesan priests from the United States and other English-speaking countries on temporary leave from their dioceses for missionary work in Ecuador, Peru and Bolivia. Ordinarily the diocesan affiliation of such priests is more relevant to a story than their membership in the society. Headquarters is in Boston.

Society of St. Peter Apostle (www.worldmissions-catholicchurch.org/spa) The church's main fund for support of seminaries and seminarians in mission dioceses, it is one of four *pontifical missionary societies* under the jurisdiction of the Vatican Congregation for the Evangelization of Peoples. U.S. headquarters is in New York.

See **pontifical missionary societies.**

Society of St. Pius X (www.sspx.org) Do not use *Priestly Society of St. Pius X* or *Priestly Fraternity of St. Pius X* to refer to the international society founded in 1969 by traditionalist Archbishop Marcel Lefebvre, who was excommunicated in 1988 and died in 1991. The society does not accept the liturgical reforms of the Second Vatican Council and its concepts of religious freedom and ecumenism. Its priests celebrate the Tridentine Mass which was superseded by the revised order of the Mass after Vatican II.

See **Lefebvre, Archbishop Marcel** and **Tridentine Mass.**

Society of St. Sulpice (Sulpicians) (www.sulpicians.org) A community of diocesan priests whose ministry focuses on the training and education of priests and future priests. Its U.S. provincial house is in Baltimore.

See **order, congregation, society.**

Society of St. Vincent de Paul (www.svdp.org) Originally called the Conference of Charity, this association of lay men and women dedicated to personal service to the poor was founded in 1833 by Blessed Frederic Ozanam. In 2005, there were more than 120,000 U.S. members and 650,000 members worldwide in 135 countries. *Vincentians* is acceptable on second reference to members of the society.

U.S. headquarters (called the National Council) is in St. Louis. World headquarters is in Paris.

solemnity of In the general liturgical calendar of the Latin Church, 14 major feasts are classified as *solemnities.* Religious orders, dioceses or individual churches also may observe certain other feasts as solemnities. In news reporting, use the more widely understood *feast of* unless the technical liturgical ranking of the feast is relevant to the story.

See **feast of.**

Southern African Catholic Bishops' Conference It includes the bishops of Botswana, South Africa and Swaziland.

See **Inter-Regional Meeting of Bishops of Southern Africa.**

Southern Baptist Convention See **Baptist churches.**

Spanish and Portuguese names In the traditional rule, the family names of the father and the mother are both considered part of a person's full name. The normal sequence for men and unmarried women is given name or names, father's family name, mother's family name. If there is a *y* (Spanish for *and)* between the two family names, delete it: *Cardinal Jaime Ortega Alamino* (not *Ortega y Alamino), Cardinal Miguel Obando Bravo, Cardinal Eugenio de Araujo Sales.* Some people hyphenate the two to keep them together: *Joaquin Navarro-Valls.*

For married women, the sequence is given name or names, father's family name and husband's family name: *Ines Guadalupe Duarte Duran.* On second reference, use the husband's family name: *Duran.*

However, there is a growing tendency, especially in Brazil and Argentina, to drop the mother's family name in all references: *Cardinal Aloisio Lorscheider, Archbishop Carlos Galan.* Others in Portuguese-speaking countries use only their mother's family name on second reference: *Cardinal Sales.*

On first reference, use all names. On second reference, use the person's preference when this is known: *Cardinal Obando Bravo, Cardinal Lorscheider, Navarro-Valls.*

If preference is not known, for Spanish names use the father's family name on second reference: *Cardinal Ortega.* For Portuguese names, use the last name in the sequence: *Cardinal Sales, Cardinal Lorscheider.*

Spiritual Life Institute of America (www.spirituallifeinstitute. org) Founded in 1960 to promote the contemplative spirit in America, it has retreat centers in Crestone, Colo., and Skreen, Ireland.

spiritual works of mercy See **corporal, spiritual works of mercy.**

sports Sports writing is a specialized literary form with its own style. Sports coverage by Catholic News Service, however, ordinarily focuses on human interest or other aspects of a sports event rather than the event itself. Many clients use it outside sports pages. It should follow the norms of good general writing rather than a specialized sports style.

In any sports story, name the sport early. Not all readers of news pages immediately recognize the Chicago Bears as a football team or the Washington Nationals as a baseball team.

At the same time, a story about a sport would be stilted without elements of sports-writing style, particularly sports terms. Assume that in context the average reader recognizes the standard vocabulary of the nation's popular sports, but avoid more esoteric jargon such as hockey's *hat trick* or football's *nickel defense.*

square The ordinary translation in English for the large, open public areas, especially in front of major churches or public buildings, which are described by various terms in other languages, such as *"piazza"* in Italian or *"plaza"* in Spanish. Capitalize and do not abbreviate when part of a proper name: *St. Peter's Square.*

SS., Ss. Acceptable abbreviations for *Saints* only in formal names when the institution or organization so named uses one of these forms. In all other cases use the preferred abbreviation, *Sts.*

See **saint.**

state Catholic conferences Capitalize the formal name: *Texas Catholic Conference, New York State Catholic Conference, Catholic Conference of Illinois.* But: *the state Catholic conference, the conference.*

A state Catholic conference ordinarily consists of the Catholic bishops of the state as the only voting members. The size of staff varies, but usually the office is headed by an executive director and includes a general counsel who advises the bishops on legislative issues and other legal matters in the state.

A complete list of state Catholic conferences with addresses, phone numbers and chief staff officials is contained in the Kenedy directory and on the Web site of the National Association of State Catholic Conference Directors at www.nasccd.org. Not every state has a conference.

State Catholic conferences are independent of one another and of the U.S. Conference of Catholic Bishops, although they may cooperate in developing policies and strategies on common concerns. See **U.S. Conference of Catholic Bishops.**

A state Catholic conference should not be called a *conference of bishops* or *episcopal conference.* It is a civil entity, not a canonical one.

state councils of churches Capitalize the formal name: *Texas Council of Churches, Ohio Council of Churches.* But: *the state council of churches, the council of churches, the Ohio council,* etc.

Formed to encourage fellowship and cooperation among Christian churches at the state level, such councils vary from state to state in membership, structure and emphasis. Some have formal Catholic membership, others do not.

Stations of the Cross *Way of the Cross* is also acceptable for this traditional Catholic Lenten devotion.

See **liturgy, devotions.**

stem cell (n.), **stem-cell** (adj.) A master cell in any multicelled plant or animal that is capable of developing into several or all cell types of that plant or animal. Catholic moral teaching rejects harvesting of stem cells from human embryos for any purpose because it entails destruction of the embryo, which in Catholic teaching is already a human being. It does not reject research on or therapeutic use of human adult stem cells, since those may be obtained without killing a human being.

sterilization See **contraceptive sterilization.**

stewardship Theologically, the Christian understanding that all creation belongs to God and people are its stewards, not its owners; they are accountable to God for the use they make of his gifts. It is often invoked as a framework for offering one's time, talents and money to God through church support and action for others. It is applied also to issues such as care for the environment and responsible use, conservation and sharing of resources.

stigmata Bleeding wounds corresponding to those of the crucified Christ. The word is plural.

stipend Use *offering* or *Mass offering,* not *stipend.* Also avoid other terms that suggest a commercial exchange, such as *fee, payment* or *tax.*

The 1983 Code of Canon Law uses *offering,* not the word *stipend* used in the old code, in legislation governing the practice of contributing money to a priest for his or the church's support in return for his celebrating a Mass for the donor's intention. Although local law or custom may establish a recommended amount, the offering is voluntary, not mandatory, on the part of the person requesting a Mass for a particular intention.

Whenever a priest accepts such an offering, however, he undertakes an obligation: either to celebrate a separate Mass for the donor's intention himself or to give the offering to another priest who celebrates the Mass.

See **stole fee.**

stole The long, narrow strip of cloth, draped over the neck and falling to about the knees, worn by a priest or bishop when celebrating Mass or presiding at other liturgical ceremonies. A deacon wears a stole over his left shoulder, crossed and fastened at his right side.

See **liturgical dress.**

stole fee Use *offering,* not *stole fee,* for contributions given by Catholics in connection with administration of the sacraments or other religious services by a priest or other authorized minister. Under the 1983 Code of Canon Law any such contribution except a Mass offering is to go into parish funds unless it is clear that it was meant to be a personal gift to the minister. Local law or custom may establish recommended amounts of offerings, but they remain free-will offerings, not *fees* required as a condition for spiritual ministry.

See **stipend.**

subsidiarity The principle in Catholic social teaching that holds that decisions or actions should not be made on a higher level when a lower level of competence would suffice.

suburbicarian dioceses Not *suburban* or *suburbican* for the seven dioceses surrounding Rome which, together with Rome, form the ecclesiastical province of Rome.

The six Catholic cardinals with the rank of cardinal-bishop are their titular heads, but with the exception of Ostia each has its own residential bishop. Ostia, the ancient seaport of Rome, is governed by the head of the Vicariate of Rome. See **Rome, Diocese of.**

The cardinal who is made titular head of Ostia is the dean of the College of Cardinals. He is always titular head of another of the suburbicarian dioceses as well. That is why there are seven such dioceses but never more than six cardinal-bishops.

Capitalize *diocese* when it is used as part of the formal name of one of these dioceses, but lowercase *suburbicarian: the suburbicarian Diocese of Frascati.*

See **titular church.**

suffragan In Catholic usage, the archdiocese of an ecclesiastical province is the metropolitan see and dioceses under it are *suffragan sees.* The residential bishops of those dioceses are *suffragan bishops* of the province. The terms are not used except in contexts in which the relationship of the dioceses or their bishops to the metropolitan see or its archbishop is relevant.

In the Episcopal Church a bishop assigned to assist a residential bishop usually is called a *suffragan bishop.* This is the equivalent of an *auxiliary bishop* in Catholic practice. See **Episcopal Church.**

"sui iuris" The Latin phrase used in the Code of Canons of the Eastern Churches to characterize all patriarchal and major archiepiscopal Eastern Catholic churches and certain metropolitan and other Eastern churches, each of which stands as a church *in its own right.*

Patriarchal and major archiepiscopal churches (and, to a lesser degree, metropolitan churches "sui iuris") exercise a certain autonomy in internal governance and can establish their own laws on church practices and discipline, within the framework of their own traditions and the general laws of the code. The code spells out the authority exercised by each type of church "sui iuris."

Churches "sui iuris" of less than metropolitan status are immediately dependent on the Holy See. The pope establishes their particular laws and appoints their bishops.

The highest governing body of a patriarchal or major archiepiscopal church is its synod of bishops, convened by the patriarch or major archbishop. If the chief see is vacant, its administrator convenes a synod to elect a new patriarch or major archbishop. The highest governing body of a metropolitan church "sui iuris" is the council of hierarchs, convened by the metropolitan. The metropolitan and other bishops of a metropolitan church "sui iuris" are appointed by the pope. The synods of patriarchal and major archiepiscopal churches can elect bishops within their own territories, subject to the assent of the Holy See, but bishops serving outside the territorial boundaries of the patriarchal or major archiepiscopal church are appointed by the pope. This means, for example, that Ukrainian Catholic bishops in the United States, Canada and Australia are papally appointed, while those within the native territory of the Ukrainian Church are elected in synod.

Canons 55-176 of the code address the rights and responsibilities of Eastern Catholic churches "sui iuris." The English translation of the code repeats the Latin phrase without translation wherever it occurs. For news stories the phrase should be avoided unless the technical nature of the topic being treated requires it. If used, the Latin phrase should be placed in quotes and translated. It can be translated *of its own right* or *in its own right*, depending on context.

See **council of hierarchs; Eastern Catholic churches; mission; rite, -rite;** and **synod.**

Sukkot Preferred spelling for the Jewish Feast of Tabernacles. Observed in September or October, it celebrates the fall harvest and commemorates the desert wandering of the Jews during the Exodus.

Sullivan Principles A set of guidelines developed in 1978 by the Rev. Leon Sullivan, a Baptist minister from Philadelphia, for U.S. companies in South Africa during the apartheid era. Companies adhering to the Sullivan Principles pledged themselves to equal pay for equal work, fair employment practices, no segregation of the races in eating or workplaces, improved quality of life for employees, and training of black, mixed-race and Asian employees for management positions.

The Sullivan Principles served as a basis in 1984 for the MacBride

Principles in Northern Ireland, and they have been suggested as a model to combat workplace discrimination elsewhere as well.

See **MacBride Principles.**

Sulpicians See **Society of St. Sulpice.**

Sunday Capitalize such references to the liturgical year as *Fourth Sunday of Lent, 23rd Sunday of Ordinary Time,* etc.

See **liturgical time.**

Sunday, weekend Because many parishes schedule Saturday afternoon and evening Masses at which Catholics may fulfill their Sunday obligation, many news events connected with "Sunday" Mass actually take place over a two-day weekend period, not just on Sunday. Examples include parish, diocesan or national collections, announcements at weekend Masses, pastoral letters read at weekend Masses. When writing about such events, *Sunday* remains correct in some references, but *weekend* may often be the preferred or more accurate term. For example: *Oct. 24 was World Mission Sunday. Collections for the missions were taken up at all weekend Masses Oct. 23-24. The bishop met with parishioners after all weekend Masses July 16 and 17.*

Support Our Aging Religious (www.soar-usa.org) *SOAR* is acceptable on second reference. A lay-led campaign to raise funds for retired religious, it is distinct from the National Religious Retirement Office and its annual Retirement Fund for Religious campaign. Headquarters is in Silver Spring, Md.

See **National Religious Retirement Office.**

Survivors' Network of those Abused by Priests (www.snapnetwork.org) *SNAP* is acceptable on second reference. Headquarters is in Chicago.

suspended priests When a priest has been suspended, he is no longer permitted by the church to perform priestly functions such as celebrating Mass, preaching or administering the sacraments. However, he remains a priest.

If a priest has been laicized he should not be identified as *Father.* See **laicization.**

If he is *permanently* suspended, as has happened with a number of priests found credibly accused of sexual abuse of minors, he is no longer in active ministry and should not be identified as *Father.* If the suspension is *temporary,* as may happen because of a lesser crime or pending the outcome of the investigation of a major crime, he should be identified as *Father,* unless his bishop or religious superior has specified that while he is under suspension he may not be publicly identified as a priest. Mention in the story that he has been suspended: *Father John Jones, a suspended priest; Father Jones.* Or: *James Smith, a suspended priest who is forbidden to use the title "Father"; Smith.*

When possible, avoid the technical Latin phrase, *suspended "a divinis."* Instead, simply say what it means in English: He is suspended *from priestly ministry* or *from all priestly functions.*

In some cases a priest may not be suspended from all priestly ministry, but his authorization to perform specific acts such as preaching or hearing confessions may be withdrawn or suspended. See **defrock, defrocked** and **faculty.**

Swiss Guard(s) Papal body-guards. Use the singular for an individual or the entire corps, the plural only for references to two or more members. Uppercase *guard* when used alone as a shortened reference to the entire corps, but lowercase it when used alone to refer to corps members: *officers in the Swiss Guard, a Swiss Guard, three Swiss Guards, the Guard (the corps), a guard, three guards.* Give the military rank of a guard as a title before the full name on first reference. Use last name alone on second reference: *Col. Elmar Mader, commander of the Swiss Guard; Mader.*

synagogue A local congregation of Jews, an assembly of Jews for worship or religious study, or the building used for those purposes. In Reform and Conservative Judaism, some synagogues are called *temples.* See **temple.**

Capitalize only when used as part of a formal name. The adjective is *synagogal.*

See **Judaism.**

Synagogue Council of America Disbanded in 1998. See **Judaism.**

synod A gathering of designated officials and representatives of a church, usually with some degree of legislative and policymaking authority. In some churches it is the highest legal authority.

The structure and authority of a synod and its place in church life vary widely among denominations. See **Catholic Church; Eastern Catholic churches; Orthodox Churches;** and entries for individual denominations.

There are two correct adjectival forms in religious usage, *synodal* and *synodical.* Generally in Catholic references the preferred form is *synodal: a synodal decree, a postsynodal apos-*tolic exhortation. Follow the usage of the denomination in question.

In the Catholic Church:

— A *diocesan synod* is a gathering of priests, religious and laity called by the diocesan bishop to advise him on updating diocesan legislation and policies.

— An *Eastern Catholic synod of bishops* is a gathering of the bishops of a patriarchal or major archiepiscopal church to conduct business of the church such as updating laws and policies or electing new bishops. The rights and responsibilities of an Eastern church's synod of bishops are spelled out in the Code of Canons of the Eastern Churches.

— An *Eastern Catholic permanent synod* is a standing body of a patriarchal or major archiepiscopal church, composed of the patriarch or major archbishop and four other bishops designated for a five-year term.

— A *special synod* is a gathering of bishops of a particular country or region, called by the pope, to address special concerns of the church in that place.

— A *world Synod of Bishops* (note capitalization) meets every few years in Rome, generally for about a month, to discuss a major issue or issues in the life of the church. If it is an *ordinary session* the majority of members are elected by national bishops' conferences, with the number of representatives from each conference determined by a formula based on the number of bishops in the conference. If it is an *extraordinary session,* the majority of members are the presidents of national bishops' conferences.

In either type of session of a world synod, Eastern Catholic heads of churches "sui iuris" and top Vatican officials are automatic members, heads of men's religious orders elect a small number of members and the pope chooses a limited number of members at his own discretion. Papally selected laypeople may participate as auditors or experts, but only bishops and priests may be members.

For some terms often used in connection with world synods, see **auditor; "instrumentum laboris"; "lineamenta"; peritus; "placet"** and **"sui iuris."**

synod hall Lowercase in references to the hall at the Vatican where the world Synod of Bishops is held.

synoptic, Synoptics See **Bible.**

T

table Because of our international readership, this term must be explained when it is used in legislative references. In the United States, to *table a bill* means to *postpone its consideration indefinitely.* In Britain, Canada and other places, it means to *submit a bill for consideration.*

Taize community (www.taize. fr/en) An ecumenical society of more than 100 brothers who take the traditional monastic vows and commit themselves to the apostolate of reconciliation. It began in 1940 when Brother Roger Schutz, who came from a Swiss Reformed background, obtained a house in the French village of Taize. Many of its members prefer to use first names on second reference.

Talmud The collection of writings, pulling together a long history of rabbinic oral law, teaching, commentary and religious discussion, that constitutes the Jewish civil and religious law. The adjective, *Talmudic,* is also capitalized.

Do not confuse with the *Torah,* or law, which may refer to the whole body of Jewish law and tradition but more commonly refers to the Pentateuch, or first five books, of the Hebrew Scriptures.

See **Judaism** and **Torah.**

Tekakwitha Conference (www. tekconf.org) A U.S. gathering of American Indian Catholics and the organization that sponsors the annual conference. It is named for Blessed Kateri Tekakwitha, a Mohawk who is the first American Indian to be be-atified. Headquarters is in Great Falls, Mont.

televangelist, televangelism These are acceptable words for *television evangelist* and *television evangelism.* Do not use *televangelist* as a formal title before a name.

See **evangelist, Evangelist, evangelizer**.

temple A term used by some religious bodies to designate a place of worship. In Conservative and Reform Judaism it is sometimes used to designate a *synagogue.* See that entry.

Capitalize *Temple* when it stands alone only in references to the Temple of ancient Jerusalem — any of the three successive buildings considered the central place of worship of all Jews. Lowercase *temple* in all other uses unless it is part of a formal name.

Templeton Prize for Progress Toward Research or Discoveries About Spiritual Realities (www. templetonprize.org) Formerly the *Templeton Foundation Prize for Progress in Religion,* this annual religion award was founded by U.S. Presbyterian layman John Marks Templeton and first given in 1973. *Templeton Prize* is acceptable on all references, provided it is identified in the story as a religion award. The monetary value of the prize has changed from year to year but has always exceeded the value of any of the Nobel prizes. The prize is open to representatives of all religious faiths. Headquarters of the Templeton Foundation Inc. is in Nassau, Bahamas.

Ten Commandments Also *First Commandment, Tenth Commandment,* etc. Do not use figures.

Tenebrae A devotion of prayer in a darkened church on the evenings of Wednesday, Thursday or Friday of Holy Week. The name is taken from the Latin word meaning *shadows* or *darkness.* In the Catholic Church these services were formerly an optional form of liturgical prayer, commonly observed in religious communities, in which matins and lauds of the next morning's Liturgy of the Hours were recited in anticipation the evening before. With Vatican II reforms in the Liturgy of the Hours, the option of reciting morning prayer the evening before was ended, and such services now are considered strictly devotional, not liturgical. Elements of the former Tenebrae services remain in the liturgical morning prayer and the office of readings of Good Friday and Holy Saturday.

territorial abbeys First established around the 10th century, these church jurisdictions arose in some places where there was a monastery but no bishop in the area. The monks took over care of the Catholics in the area, and the abbot achieved a quasi-episcopal status. In 1976 Pope Paul VI said no more territorial abbeys would be erected except for "very special" reasons. In 2005 there were seven in Italy, two in Switzerland, and one each in Austria, Hungary and South Korea.

Because they are not under the jurisdiction of a diocese, territorial abbeys were formerly known as *abbeys "nullius."* The Latin modifier was short for "nullius dioceseos" — of no diocese.

See **abbey, abbess, abbot.**

territorial prelatures Church jurisdictions established by the Holy See, through the Congregation for Bishops, for "dioceses in formation." The prelates heading such jurisdictions are appointed by the pope and usually are ordained as bishops.

See **personal prelatures.**

tertiary See **third order.**

The Do not capitalize in the names of organizations or institutions: *Interfaith Alliance,* not *The Interfaith Alliance.* The only exception is *The Catholic University of America.*

thee, thy, thou Use only in direct quotations. Lowercase personal pronouns referring to God.

See **God, god(s).**

themes When the theme or major topic of a meeting — a convention, symposium, workshop, synod, assembly, etc. — is expressed by its organizers in the form of a title, use capitals and quotation marks: *the topic of the Synod of Bishops for Oceania, "Jesus Christ and the Peoples of Oceania: Walking His Way, Telling His Truth, Living His Life."*

Lowercase other topical descriptions of the meeting: *the 1998 Oceania synod on church life and witness in preparation for the new millennium.*

theologian Not a formal title. Do not capitalize before a name.

theophany Literally translated from the Greek, it means a manifestation of God to humans. In this sense, it would be lowercased. Eastern Catholics and Orthodox celebrate the feast of Epiphany, Jan. 6, as the feast of Theophany. Capitalize in this sense.

Theresian World Ministry, Theresians of the United States

(www.theresians.org) Headquarters (world and U.S.) is in Springfield, Ill.

third order The traditional name for lay associations whose members live in the world while sharing the spirit of a religious institute. These may also be called *secular third orders, third orders secular* or *secular orders*. Like religious, the members strive for Christian perfection, but they do not take public vows as religious and do not have a religious title. They sometimes are referred to as *tertiaries,* but *tertiary* should not be capitalized or used as a formal title before a name. Its meaning should be explained when it is used. Diocesan priests may also belong to such associations.

Do not confuse third orders secular with *third orders regular,* such as the Third Order Regular of St. Francis. A third order regular is a religious order, with religious vows and community life. See **order, congregation, society.**

Lowercase generic references to third orders but capitalize their formal names and certain variations: *Secular Franciscans, Third Order Franciscans, Third Order of Our Lady of Mount Carmel, Lay Carmelites.*

Thomism The school of thought that follows the philosophy and theology of St. Thomas Aquinas, a 13th-century Italian Dominican. Thinkers of that school are *Thomists.*

A 20th-century Catholic intellectual movement to revive Thomistic thought and integrate it with modern knowledge is often called *neo-Thomism,* especially in philosophy.

thurible, thurifer See **censer, censor, censure.**

tiara In religious usage, the three-tiered crown formerly worn by popes. The last pope to begin his pontificate with a coronation was Pope Paul VI in 1963. He then set the tiara aside and never wore it again. Popes John Paul I, John Paul II and Benedict XVI celebrated ceremonies of installation, not coronations, at the start of their pastoral ministry. Although the papal tiara is not worn in practice, no pope has formally renounced the right to wear it. In Pope Benedict XVI's papal coat of arms, the tiara was replaced by a pointed miter. It remains above the crossed keys in the Vatican flag.

See **reign (papal).**

time element Avoid time references that may be dated before the story is published. Instead, use precise dates or at least the name of the month.

WRONG: *yesterday, tomorrow, this morning, this week, last week, next week, last month,* etc.

RIGHT: Jan. 10, July 14-18, in mid-February, last August.

Phrases such as *two years ago, last year, earlier this year, next year* are acceptable in most contexts but become problematic near the end of every year. If in doubt, avoid them.

In general, avoid use of the present tense in news stories when there is a chance that events may change before the story is published.

WRONG: *Catholic health care leaders are praising the president's proposals to help the uninsured.*

RIGHT: *Catholic health care leaders were praising ...* (Opinions could change when more details come out.)

WRONG: *Police are investigating the bombing.*

RIGHT: *Police were investigating the bombing.* (The investigation might be completed in the next day or two.)

titular church When an individual is named a cardinal, he is given title to a parish church in Rome or to one of Rome's seven neighboring dioceses.

The six cardinals with the rank of cardinal-bishop hold honorary title to Rome's seven *suburbicarian dioceses.* The dean of the College of Cardinals always holds title to the Diocese of Ostia in addition to the titular diocese he was assigned when he was made a cardinal-bishop. See **suburbicarian dioceses.**

Eastern patriarchs who are named cardinals are not given a titular church or diocese, but are considered equal in rank to the other cardinal-bishops.

Cardinals with the rank of cardinal-priest — mainly cardinals who are residential bishops — are given title to *presbyteral churches* in Rome.

Cardinals with the rank of cardinal-deacon — mainly cardinals in the Roman Curia — are given title to *diaconal churches* in Rome. If a cardinal-deacon is promoted to cardinal-priest, his diaconal church becomes a presbyteral church for that instance but remains listed among the diaconal churches.

The titles are largely honorary and entail no jurisdiction. But many cardinals living in Rome are involved in the pastoral life of their titular churches, and those living outside Rome often visit their titular churches when they are in Rome.

Mention the titular church a cardinal has only when it is relevant to a story.

titular see A former diocese, now nonexistent, to which a bishop is given honorary title if he is not the residential bishop of a diocese or archdiocese. Auxiliary bishops and most bishops in Vatican service have titular sees. Titular bishops who have the rank of archbishop usually are named titular heads of former archdioceses.

Most titular sees are ancient cities of northern Africa, the Middle East or Spain that had to be abandoned as bishoprics because of schism or, especially in the Middle Ages, Islamic rule. Some titular sees, such as Walla Walla, Wash., and Allegheny, Pa., ceased to be active see cities simply because of a decision to merge dioceses or transfer diocesan headquarters to another city.

In the early 16th century Pope Leo X began giving cardinals of the Roman Curia title to such abandoned dioceses. From that practice grew the custom of naming auxiliary bishops as heads of abandoned dioceses. Titular sees were called sees "in partibus infidelium" ("in the lands of infidels") until 1882, when Pope Leo XIII changed the name to "titular sees" at the request of the Greek Orthodox Church.

Since a bishop's title to such a diocese is a legal fiction with no practical effects, it is rarely relevant to a story.

If the name of a titular see is used, there is no clear-cut rule for the best form. The Annuario gives the Italian name first. After that in parentheses it gives the modern name if known, but some modern names are listed with a question mark; some listings indicate two possible modern names; some listings say the ancient city consists of ruins of or near a modern city; and some listings provide no modern form. Few of the listings indicate the country in which the community is located. In general, use the Italian name of the see, which is listed first in the Annuario, unless you can determine another name by which the original community or the modern community can be more readily identified by English-speaking people. State the country if it can be determined.

To avoid any suggestion that titular bishops are not real bishops, never use *titular bishop* as a formal title before a name and never use the phrase apart from a reference to the titular diocese.

WRONG: *Titular Bishop Christie A. Macaluso, an auxiliary of Hartford, Conn.*

RIGHT: *Auxiliary Bishop Christie A. Macaluso of Hartford.*

WRONG: *Archbishop John P. Foley, a titular archbishop.*

RIGHT: *Archbishop John P. Foley, president of the Pontifical Council for Social Communications.*

RIGHT IF RELEVANT: *When Bishop Macaluso was made an auxiliary of Hartford, he was named titular bishop of Grass Valley, Calif., a former see city in what is now the Diocese of Sacramento.*

See **titular church.**

Torah Jewish name for the Book of Moses, the first five books of Scripture, which Christians generally call the *Pentateuch.* When used in a more general sense, it means the whole law and tradition governing Jewish religious life.

Do not confuse with the *Talmud.*

See **Bible; Judaism;** and **Talmud.**

Trent, Council of The 19th ecumenical council of the church, it was called to reform church practice and define Catholic teaching in the face of challenges of the Reformation. Considered the start of the Counter-Reformation, it consisted of 25 sessions held between 1545 and 1563, most of them in Trent, Italy. Its decrees were approved and published by Pope Pius IV in 1564. The adjective referring to the council is *Tridentine.*

See **Tridentine Mass.**

tribunal See **ecclesiastical courts.**

Tri-Conference Retirement Office Now called the National Religious Retirement Office.

See **National Religious Retirement Office** and **Support Our Aging Religious.**

Tridentine Mass Published in 1570 by Pope St. Pius V, this reformed rite of the Mass was used throughout the Latin rite of the Catholic Church, with some revisions from time to time, until it was replaced in 1969 with publication of the new Roman Missal. The last revised version of the Tridentine Mass was issued in 1962, and that is the version referred to when permission is given in the Catholic Church to celebrate the Tridentine Mass.

Tridentine comes from *Trent,* the site in northern Italy of the ecumenical council that mandated the 16th-century liturgical reform.

Both the Tridentine Mass and the revised order of the Mass are properly called the *Latin Mass* or the *Latin-rite Mass,* although the new rite also may be celebrated in an approved translation in any language. To avoid confusion use Latin Mass only to refer to a Mass celebrated in the Latin language. Do not use the term as if it refers only to the Tridentine rite and not to the revised one.

See **"Ecclesia Dei"; Lefebvre, Archbishop Marcel;** and **Trent, Council of.**

triduum A three-day period of prayerful preparation for a major religious feast. It is used especially for the *Easter triduum.* See that entry.

trinate See **binate, trinate.**

Trinity (n.), **Trinitarian** (n., adj.)
Capitalize these terms when used to
refer to the triune God of Christian
belief or one who holds that belief:
*the Trinity, Trinitarian theology, Uni-
tarians are not Trinitarians*. Note that
Trinitarian as a noun can refer to anyone who believes in three divine persons in God or to a priest or brother
of the *Order of the Most Holy Trinity*.
See **Holy Trinity.**

Lowercase *trinity* in reference to
any other group of three treated as
one.

triune (adj.) Lowercase. Like *all-
knowing, eternal* or *omnipotent*, it is
simply an adjective used to try to describe God, not part of a formal title or
name for God.

Twelve Apostles The disciples
of Jesus. An exception to the normal
practice of using figures for 10 and
above.
See **apostle, disciple.**

U

UCAN Acceptable in all references for *Union of Catholic Asian News,* an Asian church news agency based in Thailand.

UCIP Acceptable on second reference for *International Catholic Union of the Press,* but it must be explained that it stands for the initials of the organization's name in French.

See **International Catholic Union of the Press.**

Ukraine No *the* before the name, in datelines or text.

Use *Lviv,* not *Lwow* or *Lvov,* for the former see city of the chief archdiocese of Ukrainian Catholics.

Ukrainian Catholic Church See **Eastern Catholic churches.**

Unda See **Catholic Academy for Communications Arts Professionals** and **Signis.**

uniate churches A term that has been used with derogatory connotations, it is offensive to many Eastern Catholics and should be avoided in references to *Eastern Catholic churches* except in quotations. If it is used, it should be explained that it is a term used by some to describe those Eastern churches that are in union with Rome.

See **Eastern Catholic churches.**

Unification Church See **Family Federation for World Peace and Unification.**

Union of Brest See **Brest, Union of.**

Union of Utrecht See **Old Catholic churches.**

Unitarian Universalist Association (www.uua.org) An association of 1,000 autonomous Unitarian churches. Formed by a 1961 merger of the American Unitarian Association and the Universalist Church of America, in 2005 it claimed more than 220,000 members in the United States. Members or individual churches may be called either *Unitarian Universalist* or *Unitarian.*

Unitarianism is so named for its rejection of Trinitarian belief, which in turn entails rejection of the divinity of Christ. In the United States it developed in the early 19th century in New England Congregationalist churches, with William Ellery Channing as a leading proponent. *Universalism* is so named for its belief in universal salvation — a first-century doctrine revived in the United States in the late 18th century in reaction to the Calvinist teachings on the depravity of human nature. See **Congregational churches.**

Emphatically noncreedal, Unitarian Universalists reject all dogmatic tests of membership. They emphasize humanitarian social and ethical values, the goodness and dignity of the human person and freedom of religious belief.

Worship services vary from church to church but generally are simple and nonliturgical, usually consisting of hymns, prayers, readings and a sermon.

STRUCTURE: Strictly congregational, each church in the association is autonomous and governed democratically. Individual churches may have covenants or bonds of union, so long as such statements impose no creedal tests. Theists, agnostics and religious humanists are welcomed as members.

Ministers are ordained, but ordination is not considered a sacrament.

The association is governed by a president, a board of trustees and a general assembly.

It is not a member of the World Council of Churches or National Council of Churches, although it has observer status with the NCC. It is a member of the International Association for Liberal Christianity and Religious Freedom. Headquarters is in Boston.

United Church of Christ (www. ucc.org) Formed in 1957 when the Evangelical and Reformed Church and the Congregational Christian Churches held a uniting synod and merged. It has about 1.4 million members. Headquarters is in Cleveland.

The word *church* is properly applied only to each local church. Each church is responsible for the doctrine, ministry and ritual of its congregation.

The local churches also appoint delegates to *associations*. These recognize local churches, promote cooperation among them and oversee the licensing, ordination, installation and dismissal of ministers.

Conferences, generally organized along state lines, recognize associations and specialize in missionary and educational work.

A *general synod*, made up of delegates elected by associations and conferences, meets every two years. It is designed primarily to discuss questions of concern to all the churches and to handle communications with other denominations.

The separate National Association of Congregational Christian Churches (www.naccc.org), based in Oak Creek, Wis., was formed by a small group of churches that rejected the 1957 merger. Their combined membership is about 68,000.

BELIEFS: The United Church of Christ says it "claims as its own the faith of the historic church expressed in the ancient creeds and reclaimed in the basic insights of the Protestant Reformers." It regards Christ as Son of God, savior and sole head of the church. It does not require adherence to a particular creed as a condition for membership. It is a member of the *World Alliance of Reformed Churches*. See that entry.

It recognizes the two dominical sacraments, baptism and the Lord's Supper.

CLERGY: Members of the clergy are known as *ministers*. *Pastor* applies if a minister leads a congregation.

See **Congregational churches** and **religious titles.**

United Methodist Church See **Methodist churches.**

United Nations Stands alone in datelines. See **datelines.**

The Vatican has observer status at the United Nations. The delegation's headquarters is called the Permanent Observer Mission of the Holy See. In 2004, through a General Assembly resolution adopted by acclamation, the mission earned the right to participate in the general debate of the General Assembly; the right of reply; the right to have its communications issued and circulated directly as official documents of the assembly; and the right to co-sponsor draft resolutions and decisions that make reference to the Holy See. The head of the mission is referred to as the *Vatican nuncio*. See **papal nuncio**.

United States Conference of Catholic Bishops See **U.S. Conference of Catholic Bishops.**

United Synagogue of America See **United Synagogue of Conservative Judaism.**

United Synagogue of Conservative Judaism (www.uscj.org) Note that *synagogue* is singular. Until 1992, it was known as the *United Synagogue of America.*

See **Judaism.**

Unum Omnes See **International Council of Catholic Men-Unum Omnes.**

upper room, cenacle There are more than a dozen references to upper rooms in Scripture. Scripture scholars say the upper room or cenacle — which means *dining room* — used for the Last Supper could be the same place as the upper room in which Mary and the apostles gathered to pray between the Ascension and Pentecost, but this is not certain. In the scriptural references the terms are common nouns, not proper names. Capitalize only in reference to the officially designated Upper Room in Jerusalem or in organizations that use the terms in their name.

Urbanian University See **Pontifical Urbanian University.**

"urbi et orbi" Used to describe certain solemn papal blessings, and by extension the messages that accompany them, this Latin phrase means "to the city (Rome) and the world." A pope gives his blessing "urbi et orbi" at Christmas and Easter and at his first public appearance after he is elected pope.

Position the words in the sentence as the English phrase — after the noun or verb they modify, not before. Put the foreign phrase within quotes and follow it with a translation or an explanation of its meaning. For example: *Before giving his blessing "urbi et orbi" (to the city of Rome and the world), the pope offered Christmas greetings to people in 35 languages.*

See **apostolic blessing.**

U.S. Catholic Catechism for Adults Do not use quotation marks or spell out *United States* in the title.

U.S. Catholic Conference See **U.S. Conference of Catholic Bishops.**

U.S. Catholic Historical Society (www.uschs.com) Headquarters is in Yonkers, N.Y.

U.S. Catholic Mission Association (www.uscatholicmission.org) Headquarters is in Washington.

U.S. church, U.S. Catholic Church In stories about that portion of the Catholic Church that is found in the United States, *U.S. church* is acceptable in all contexts in which it is clear that reference is to the Catholic Church, not to another denomination or the U.S. Christian churches collectively.

Some Catholics object to phrases such as *U.S. Catholic Church, French Catholic Church,* etc., on grounds that the conjunction of capitalized words suggests that these are proper titles, implying the establishment of national churches within the Latin Church. Generally avoid the phrase *U.S. Catholic Church* outside quoted matter. But use it when needed — when *U.S. church* is not sufficiently clear but a longer form of expression such as *Catholic Church in the United States* would result in a stilted or awkward sentence.

See **American Catholic Church; American church, American Catholic Church;** and **Catholic Church.**

U.S. Conference of Catholic Bishops (www.usccb.org) Use this form, not *United States Conference of Catholic Bishops,* on first reference. USCCB is acceptable on second reference. Created in 2001 with the merger of the *National Conference of Catholic Bishops* and the *U.S. Catholic Conference.* The two conferences were established in 1967 after the Second Vatican Council called for such canonical national organizations of bishops. Although the U.S. bishops met annually before 1967 as the *National Catholic Welfare Conference,* that organization is more properly considered the predecessor of the *U.S. Catholic Conference,* not of the NCCB. See **Catholic Church** and **Appendix F: U.S. Conference of Catholic Bishops.**

State Catholic conferences are not branch or subsidiary offices of the USCCB. Nor are they canonical organizations, although in some cases their territorial boundaries coincide with those of ecclesiastical provinces. See **state Catholic conferences.**

U.S. Conference of Secular Institutes (www.secularinstitutes.org) Headquarters is in Washington.

usher Do not use *usherette* outside quoted matter, and never for female ushers in a church. *Usher* applies to both men and women.

See **minister, ministry.**

valid, licit The distinction between *validity* and *licitness* of an action is significant in Catholic church law, especially in the fields of decision-making and sacramental practice.

If an action is *valid,* it is effective. If it is *invalid,* it has no effect.

If an action is *licit,* it is legal or permitted. If it is *illicit,* it is a violation of a law, rule or norm. Generally in news reporting *legal* and *illegal* are preferable terms.

Among canon lawyers *liceity,* an Anglicized version of the Latin *"liceitas,"* often is used as the noun form of *licit.* Use the generally accepted English terms *licitness, lawfulness* or *legality* instead.

The distinction between validity and legality frequently is important in news concerning illegal administration of sacraments. For example, if a priest is barred from active ministry, a Mass or baptism at which he presides is valid even though it is illegal. But if he officiates at a marriage or hears a confession without the faculty to do so, the illegality affects validity: There is no sacrament.

Vatican agencies See **Catholic Church** and **Appendix G: Vatican Agencies.**

Vatican bank Founded in 1942, its formal name is the *Institute for the Works of Religion.* Do not capitalize *bank.*

It is sometimes referred to in Vatican documents as *IOR,* its initials in Italian. If *IOR* is used in quoted matter, explain its meaning. Do not use it outside quoted matter.

See **Appendix G: Vatican Agencies.**

Vatican City The proper dateline for stories originating either from civil entities of Vatican City State or from the Holy See or any of its central offices, including those housed on Vatican-owned extraterritorial properties elsewhere in Rome. The city name stands alone in datelines: *VATICAN CITY (CNS) —.*

See **Catholic Church; Holy See; Vatican City State;** and **Appendix G: Vatican Agencies.**

Vatican City State The official name of the independent state established by the treaty of the Lateran Pacts in 1929. It is the smallest in the world, at 108.7 acres. It is a sovereign nation, distinct from the Holy See but united with it in the person of the pope. Because the Holy See exercises sovereignty over Vatican City State, and not vice versa, the pope's diplomats are said to represent the Holy See, not the city state. In popular usage, however, it is acceptable to refer to the *Vatican Embassy, the Vatican representative in Nicaragua*, etc. See **Holy See** and **Lateran Pacts.**

The pope has full legislative, judicial and executive powers as head of Vatican City State, but in 1984 Pope John Paul II delegated the secretary of state as his representative in all matters relating to the civil state.

In civil matters the city state is administered by a governor under the supervision of the Pontifical Commission for Vatican City State. The commission and the civil government offices are not part of the Roman Curia.

Among the offices of the civil government are the agencies that handle Vatican stamps and coins, the post office and the Vatican monuments, museums and galleries.

In spiritual and pastoral matters the city state is part of the Diocese of Rome but, since 1929, has had its own religious administration, called the *Vicariate of Vatican City.* The head of the vicariate is a bishop, who is the pope's *vicar general of Vatican City.*

St. Peter's Basilica is part of Vatican City but is under a separate religious administration, headed by the archpriest of St. Peter's Basilica. The rest of the Diocese of Rome is administered by the Rome Vicariate. See **Rome, Diocese of.**

The official language of Vatican City State is Italian, but that of the Holy See is Latin.

Use *Vatican City State* when referring to the civil administration or its agencies, but *Vatican City* in datelines and *Vatican City* or *the Vatican* in other references to the place.

Vatican councils Of the 21 ecumenical councils in church history, only the last two have been held at the Vatican.

The *First Vatican Council* was held in 1869-70. *Vatican I* is acceptable on second reference. Abruptly suspended after the outbreak of the Franco-Prussian War and the Italian occupation of the Papal States, it is most noted for its definitions of papal primacy and papal infallibility.

The *Second Vatican Council* was held in 1962-65. *Vatican II* is acceptable on second reference. For a list and brief description of its documents, see **Appendix I: Vatican II Documents.**

Vatican Embassy The residence and offices of a papal ambassador, or nuncio, to another country. On second reference *the embassy* (lowercase) is acceptable. Such a building also may be called an *apostolic nunciature* or a *nunciature,* especially when a story concerns Vatican dealings with the church in a country, rather than diplomatic dealings with the country itself.

The technical diplomatic name of the nuncio's residence in Washington is *Embassy of the Holy See to the United States of America.* Its technical ecclesiastical name is *Apostolic Nunciature of the Holy See to the United States of America.*

Its popular name, however, is *Vatican Embassy.* Use *Embassy of the Holy See* or *Vatican Embassy* on first reference, and *Vatican Embassy* or *the embassy* on second reference.

The residence of an apostolic delegate is called an *apostolic delegation.*

See **apostolic delegate** and **papal nuncio.**

vespers Also called *evening prayer* or, especially among Anglicans, *evensong.*

See **Liturgy of the Hours.**

viaticum See **last rites.**

vicar Do not use *vicar* as a formal title before a name in any of its many ecclesiastical uses. See **religious titles.**

In Catholic teaching every bishop, including the pope, is a vicar of Christ. The main use of *vicar* in the Catholic Church, however, is to refer to someone deputized by a bishop or superior of a religious order to carry out certain functions on his behalf. Some examples:

— A *vicar general* assists the diocesan bishop in the governance of the entire diocese. If there is a coadjutor, he is vicar general. If there are auxiliary bishops (but no coadjutor), one is appointed vicar general. If there are no auxiliary bishops, a priest must be appointed to the post. The plural form is *vicars general*, but as a general rule there is only one in a diocese unless it is unusually large or populous.

— An *episcopal vicar* is a priest or bishop who assists the diocesan bishop, with the same ordinary power as the vicar general but only in a certain portion of the diocese, in certain types of business or with respect to certain groups of people. For example: *episcopal vicar for canonical affairs, episcopal vicar for the southern region.* Some dioceses may not use *episcopal* as part of the job description. For example: *urban vicar, western vicar, vicar for Region 4, vicar for the Spanish speaking.* If the person holding the post is an auxiliary bishop, he is an episcopal vicar because all auxiliaries hold that office. If he is a priest, he may or may not be an episcopal vicar. An unordained person cannot be an episcopal vicar. The number of episcopal vicars may range from none to many, depending on the size, population and diversity of the diocese and the governing style of the diocesan bishop.

— A *judicial vicar*, sometimes referred to as the *chief judge*, is the priest the bishop appoints to head a diocesan court. Assistant judges may be priests or laypeople, but only assistant judges who are priests may be called *adjutant judicial vicars.* A judicial vicar is not an episcopal vicar.

— A *vicar forane* is a priest assigned to oversee priests and promote and coordinate common pastoral activity among a group of parishes known as a *vicariate forane.* In the United States, *dean* and *deanery* are more commonly used to designate such a priest and the group of parishes for which he is responsible. He is also charged with other tasks, spelled out in church law.

— A *parochial vicar,* more commonly called an *associate pastor* or *assistant pastor* in the United States, is a priest assigned to help the pastor in a parish.

vicariate See **apostolic vicariate; military ordinariate; Rome, Diocese of; Vatican City State;** and **vicar.**

virgin birth Term used by Christians to signify belief that Mary remained a virgin during and after the conception and birth of Jesus.

The *Immaculate Conception* does not refer to the conception and birth of Jesus, but to the conception and birth of Mary. See **Immaculate Conception.**

Virtus (www.virtus.org) A safe environment program for those working as volunteers or paid employees in Catholic dioceses, developed by the National Catholic Risk Retention Group. The risk-retention group, owned by 61 dioceses, issues insurance and organizes programs to help church organizations reduce their risk liability. *Virtus* is a Latin word meaning "valor" or "moral strength." Do not use all caps, since it is not an acronym.

The Virtus program was started in 1998 and has special programs for adults and children. It also provides teachers with information on the recommendations of the American Academy of Pediatrics for age-appropriate education to prevent child abuse.

Voice of the Faithful (www.votf.org) Founded in 2002 in response to the clergy sex abuse crisis, this national organization describes itself as a "grass-roots Catholic lay movement committed to provide a prayerful voice, attentive to the Spirit, through which the faithful can actively participate in the governance and guidance of the Catholic Church." In late 2004, stated membership was more than 30,000 in more than 200 affiliates worldwide. Headquarters is in Newton, Mass.

vow, promise In ecclesiastical usage, a *vow* is a religious commitment made before God. Vows can be classified many ways, among them: private and public, simple and solemn, temporary and permanent, personal and real, conditional and absolute.

While all vows are promises, not all promises are vows. The *promises* made by believers at baptism and the *promises* of celibacy and obedience to his bishop made by a diocesan priest at ordination are not vows.

Among promises properly called *vows* are the marriage vows and the vows of poverty, chastity and obedience taken by men and women who enter religious orders.

See **celibacy, chastity** and **order, congregation, society.**

Vox Clara Committee A 12-member committee appointed by the Vatican in 2001 to advise the Congregation for Divine Worship and the Sacraments on matters related to the translation of Latin liturgical texts into English. "Vox clara" is Latin for "clear voice." Do not use quotes in the name of the committee.

vulgarities See **offensive language** in **Appendix A: Special Style Considerations.**

Way of the Cross *Stations of the Cross* also is correct.

See **church services.**

We Are Church (www.we-are-church.org) Founded in Austria in 1995, with chapters in 10 countries in 2005, this group seeks more lay participation in church decision-making and changes in doctrine or practice such as an end to priestly celibacy, the opening of the priesthood to women and an acceptance of homosexual activity.

Web site(s) See **World Wide Web.**

weekend Because of the wide popularity of Saturday evening Masses at which Catholics fulfill their Sunday obligation, it is usually more accurate to refer to *weekend Masses* and to use both the Saturday and Sunday dates when writing about events such as collections or announcements that occurred on both days.

See **Sunday, weekend.**

Western Catholic Union (www. wculife.com) Headquarters is in Quincy, Ill.

Western Hemisphere For certain purposes, including its annual statistical analysis of the church around the world, the Vatican divides the Western Hemisphere into two regions: Latin America (including all of the Caribbean region and Mexico) and North America (excluding Mexico and the Caribbean). In stories referring to these ecclesiastical groupings, it should be stated that the *North Amer-*

ica references do not include Mexico and the Caribbean.

Western Hemisphere Institute for Security Cooperation See **School of the Americas.**

White House Office for Faith-Based and Community Initiatives

White Mass See **Red Mass.**

Whitsunday Use *Pentecost.*

wholism, wholistic Use *holism, holistic.*

-woman, -women If reference is to an individual female or an exclusively female group, these endings usually can — and should — replace the endings *-man* or *-men*. For example: *layman, laywoman; chairman, chairwoman.* Sometimes the ending *-man* cannot be changed, as in the military designations *airman* and *seaman.*

See **inclusive language; layman, laywoman, layperson, laypeople;** and **-person, -people.**

women Women and men should receive the same treatment in news coverage. This means:

— Avoid demeaning stereotypes, condescending phrases and sexist language.

— Use the same standards for men and women in determining whether matters of marital or family relationships or personal appearance are relevant to a story.

— When both sexes are or may be involved, avoid male-only language unless an awkward construction would result.

See **inclusive language.**

Women for Faith and Family (www.wf-f.org) Founded in 1984 "to provide Catholic women with a means of expressing unity with the teachings of the Catholic Church." Headquarters is in St. Louis.

Women's Ordination Conference (www.womensordination.org) A predominantly Catholic organization founded in 1975 to promote the ordination of women as priests in the Catholic Church. National office is in Fairfax, Va.

Word of God institute See **National Institute for the Word of God.**

word, Word (of God) Lowercase *word* when it refers to the Bible or a part of it as God's revealed word: *This is the word of the Lord. You must obey God's word.*

When *word* is used to refer to the person of Jesus, Son of God, capitalize if it is the sole reference to Jesus in the sentence; lowercase it otherwise. See **Jesus.**

Capitalize *Liturgy of the Word* when it is used as the proper name of the first major segment of the Mass. Lowercase *liturgy of the word* when it is used as a generic reference to a religious service that involves readings or prayers from the Bible. See **Mass.**

World Alliance of Reformed Churches (www.warc.ch) Acceptable in all references to the *World Alliance of Reformed Churches (Presbyterian and Congregational)* formed in 1970 by the union of the former World Council of Reformed Churches and former International Congregational

Council. In 2005 it had 218 member churches in 107 countries, with an estimated combined membership of 75 million people.

It is governed by a General Council, also called the General Assembly, that ordinarily meets every seven or eight years. Between assemblies, an Executive Council, consisting of the president, five vice presidents, the heads of departments and 32 members, exercises general oversight over the work of the alliance. It meets annually. Alliance headquarters is in Geneva.

The alliance maintains close contacts with the World Council of Churches and executives of other world confessional organizations. It is the non-Catholic sponsoring partner of an international Presbyterian and Reformed dialogue with the Catholic Church.

See **Presbyterian churches; Reformed churches;** and **United Church of Christ.**

World Catholic Association for Communication A secondary name for *Signis.* See that entry.

World Council of Churches (www.wcc-coe.org) Established in 1948 as an international, interconfessional organization of Christian churches, its goal is to foster unity in fellowship, service and mission. In 2005 it counted as members some 347 churches of the Protestant, Anglican, Orthodox and Old Catholic traditions. On second reference *WCC* is acceptable, but generally *the council* is preferable.

The Roman Catholic Church is not a member but has an official dialogue with the council and cooperates with it in various programs.

Formation of the council marked the union of two parallel lines of ecumenical development in Protestant churches since the 1920s: the Life and Work movement, which sought Christian unity in service efforts despite doctrinal differences, and the Faith and Order movement, which sought to overcome doctrinal obstacles to Christian unity.

The highest authority in the council is the General Assembly, which ordinarily meets every seven years. Between assemblies it is governed by a 100-member Central Committee, which meets yearly, and a smaller Executive Committee, which meets twice a year.

Headquarters is in Geneva. There is a U.S. office in New York.

The national councils of churches that exist in many countries operate on a model of ecumenical cooperation similar to that of the world council, but they are not related structurally or organizationally to the world council. See **National Council of Churches.**

World Evangelical Alliance (www.worldevangelical.org) A global church-based organization of evangelicals that in 2005 had 120 country and regional members and 101 associate member organizations, with a constituency of 160 million. Its highest decision-making body is the International Council.

The World Evangelical Alliance theological commission co-sponsors the evangelical-Catholic consultation with the Vatican's Christian unity council.

The alliance's national office is in Seattle.

World Movement of Christian Workers (www.mmtc-wmcw-wbca. be) Headquarters is in Brussels, Belgium.

World Organization of Former Pupils of Catholic Education Headquarters is in Paris.

World Union of Catholic Teachers Headquarters is in Rome.

World Union of Catholic Women's Organizations (www.wucwo. org) Headquarters is in Paris.

World Wide Web The most commonly used system for finding and accessing Internet resources, including graphics. Do not abbreviate as *WWW* in news stories. Any area that can be accessed on the World Wide Web can be called a *Web site* or *Web page*. The main page set up on the World Wide Web by an organization, institution or individual to organize its information is a *home page*. All home pages are Web sites, but not all Web sites are home pages.

Note that some Internet addresses without the *www* are not Web sites. Refer to these sites as *Internet* sites. When giving an Internet address that is not a Web address, include the initial seven characters: *http://* to make it clear to readers that it is not a Web address. For example: *http://ace.nd.edu*, not: *ace.nd.edu*. See **Internet** and **on-line.**

When giving a Web address within a story or at the end, do not use the *http://,* which Web browsers will automatically insert. For example: *www. catholicnews.com*; not: *http: //www. catholicnews.com.*

XYZ

Xavier Society for the Blind A center for publications for the blind and partially sighted. It is located in New York.

Yom Hashoah The Day of the Holocaust, a modern holy day observed by many Jews in remembrance of the Holocaust before and during World War II. It occurs shortly after Passover, usually in April.

See **Holocaust** and **Shoah.**

Yom Kippur The Day of Atonement, a Jewish fast day observed in September or October. It and Rosh Hashana nine days earlier are the high holy days of Judaism.

you, your Lowercase personal pronouns referring to God.

See **God, god(s).**

Young Men's Christian Association (www.ymca.net) *YMCA* is acceptable in all references to this nondenominational Protestant lay group founded in 1844 to provide an opportunity for spiritual, physical and educational development in a wholesome atmosphere.

In the United States there are more than 2,400 local branches, units, camps and centers. Each local association is independent and self-governing, but they are grouped into area councils or state associations, which in turn form a national council. Headquarters is in Chicago.

The movement worldwide is represented by a service agency, the *World Alliance of YMCAs,* with headquarters in Geneva.

Young Women's Christian Association (www.ywca.org) *YWCA* is acceptable in all references to this nondenominational group founded in 1855. It is modeled after the YMCA but completely independent of it. It has a strong emphasis on ecumenical and interracial harmony.

In the United States there are more than 300 affiliates. Each local association is autonomous. A national board, elected by a triennial national convention of delegates from local associations, oversees general programs and provides assistance to local associations. Headquarters is in Washington.

The *World YWCA,* based in Geneva, holds world councils made up of delegates from about 85 national councils every four years.

yule Lowercase this loose synonym for Christmas derived from the name of a pagan festival for the winter solstice. Also: *yule log, yuletide.*

Zionism A Jewish nationalist movement to regain an autonomous Jewish homeland, begun in the 19th century and basically achieved with the establishment of modern Israel in 1948. It is primarily a political movement. Most Jews worldwide reject the religious view propagated by many Orthodox Jews in Israel that Jews outside Israel are in "exile" and can live a full life only in Israel.

Zionism takes its name from Mount Zion, one of the hills of ancient Jerusalem. *Zion* often is used in the Bible in figurative references to Jerusalem as the royal city and site of the Temple of Solomon, the place where God is especially present with his people. It also is used to refer to the land of Israel. See **Jerusalem.**

zucchetto The small, round skullcap worn by Catholic clergy. The plural is *zucchettos*, not the Italian *zucchetti.* Do not call them *beanies.*

The pope wears a white zucchetto, as do priests of certain religious orders whose habits are white. Cardinals wear red zucchettos. Patriarchs, archbishops and bishops wear zucchettos of a violet color known as amaranth red. Priests and deacons may wear black zucchettos, although the practice has fallen out of use.

Special Style Considerations

Certain style rules adapted especially to the religious press or to Catholic News Service in particular have been developed over the years by CNS editors. A sampling follows:

Book reviews: Each review should begin with a descriptive headline, book title (in quotes), author, publisher, place of publication, year of publication, number of pages, price and reviewer's byline. Example:

Three books on Harry Potter and Gospel messages

"Looking for God in Harry Potter," by John Granger. Tyndale (Carol Stream, Ill., 2004). 193 pp., $16.99.

"Imagining Faith With Kids: Unearthing Seeds of the Gospel in Children's Stories From Peter Rabbit to Harry Potter," by Mary Margaret Keaton. Pauline Books and Media (Boston, 2005). 282 pp., $19.

"Hour of the Witch: Harry Potter, Wicca Witchcraft and the Bible," by Steve Wohlberg. Destiny Image (Shippensburg, Pa., 2005). 216 pp., $13.99.

Reviewed by Jean Gonzalez
Catholic News Service

At the end of the review, there should be a brief identification of the reviewer, as in the following example:

- - -

Gonzalez is projects editor for The Florida Catholic newspaper in Orlando, Fla., and a parent.

Bylines: Religious titles such as *Bishop, Brother, Father* or *Sister* should be included in the bylines of writers who hold those titles. They should not be abbreviated. The title *Msgr.* should be abbreviated. For non-Catholic writers with religious titles, follow the guidelines for first reference in **religious titles.**

A byline should include reference to membership in a particular religious order only if the writer wishes it and always uses it in his or her byline. The byline should conform to normal style on religious orders: *By Dominican Father John Johnson, By Mercy Sister Maria Martin.* If a religious order is more than one or two words, it should not be used in a byline.

For guidance on when to use a byline, see **dateline selection** in the main section.

Composition titles: Do not use quotation marks around the names of the Bible and its individual books or the names of such resource and reference books as atlases, yearbooks, official prayer or liturgy books and similar publications. See **apostolic exhortation; Bible; court-case names; documents; encyclical; pastoral letter;** and **Appendix I: Vatican II Documents,** for the proper titles of those documents.

Datelines: For some specific datelines pertinent to Catholic news and for the lists of U.S. and foreign cities that stand alone in datelines without a state or country name, see **datelines** in the main section.

Editor's notes: Catholic News Service uses editor's notes in a variety of forms and for a variety of reasons. Among them are the following:

1) To alert readers about a special aspect of the story, such as first-per-

son accounts or stories from an area where coverage usually is not available. These editor's notes will appear between the byline and the text of the story (as the first item in the text field) and are intended for publication with the story.

Example:

RELIEF-KOSOVARS May-24-1999 (940 words) With photos.
Kosovars in Albania receive medical care from U.S. nurses
By Robert Pfohman
Catholic News Service

Editor's Note: Robert Pfohman, edior of the Catholic Sentinel, newspaper of the Archdiocese of Portland, Ore., accompanied a shipment of medical supplies and other goods donated by Oregon's Catholic community to Kosovo refugees in Albania.

SKODER, Albania (CNS) — When the exhausted grandmother ...

2) To alert and caution editors about an aspect of a story that may be offensive to some readers. See **offensive language**. These advisories will appear between the headline and the byline (in the alerts field) and are not intended for publication.

Example:

COPPS Jul-26-2004 (770 words)
FCC commissioner sees movement in Washington on broadcast indecency
Editors: Some readers may find description in 10th paragraph offensive.
By Mark Pattison
Catholic News Service

WASHINGTON (CNS) — Michael Copps, a Catholic who serves as one of five members of the Federal Communications Commission, ...

3) To give information on the author of a review or story. These appear at the end of the item, separated from the text by a line containing three dashes. They may be published.

Examples:

- - -

Forbes is director and DiCerto is on the staff of the Office for Film & Broadcasting of the U.S. Conference of Catholic Bishops.

- - -

Contributing to this story was Tracy Early in New York.

- - -

Mulhall works in the U.S. bishops' Department of Education as assistant secretary for catechesis and inculturation and serves on their Ad Hoc Committee on Native American Catholics.

4) To provide a source for further information about a story. These appear at the end of the story, separated from the text by a line containing three dashes. They may be published. The format differs according to whether or not they are intended for publication.

Example (intended for publication):

- - -

Editor's Note: Readers who want more information about getting English-language books by the new pope can visit a special Web site established by Ignatius Press at: www.benedictxvibooks.com.

Example (not intended for publication):

- - -

Editors: This story includes information from COLOMBIA-QUAKE of Jan. 26, COLOMBIA-HEROES of Feb. 1 and new material.

5) To alert editors to updates and corrections made since a previous version of a story. These appear immediately below the headline (in the alerts field) and are not intended for publication.

Example (for updated story):
BISHOPS-APPOINT (UPDATED) May-17-2005 (970 words)
Pope names bishop for Honolulu, co-adjutor bishop for Fort Worth
Editors: Updates with new information throughout.
UPDATED version of BISHOPS-APPOINT of May 17, 2005:
By Nancy Frazier O'Brien
Catholic News Service
WASHINGTON (CNS) —

Example (for corrected story):
BENEDICT-PROFILE (CORRECTED) *May-4-2005 (2,800 words)*
Pope Benedict likes verbal sparring, thinks God has sense of humor
Editors: Corrects date of baptism in 12th paragraph.
CORRECTED version of BENEDICT-PROFILE of April 21, 2005:
By Catholic News Service
VATICAN CITY (CNS) —

Foreign names: Ignore all diacritical marks. Do not add *e* after a vowel with an umlaut in Germanic words and names: *Father Hans Kung (not Kueng), Cardinal Christoph Schonborn (not Schoenborn).*

See **Asian names** and **Spanish and Portuguese names** for guidelines on last names in those areas.

Magazine and newspaper names: Consult the Catholic Press Directory published by the Catholic Press Association for the official names of U.S. and Canadian Catholic magazines and newspapers.

Offensive language: If CNS editors judge that a graphic description of sex or violence, a racial slur, or obscene, profane or vulgar word or phrase used in direct quotes is necessary to a story, the story will be flagged at the top. This advisory is not intended for publication.

Example:
Editors: The language in the third paragraph may be offensive to some readers.

An effort will be made to assure that editors wishing to drop the offensive paragraph will be able to do so without any need for extensive rewriting.

How to submit information to CNS

All news copy and press releases should be addressed to:

News Desk
Catholic News Service
3211 Fourth St. N.E.
Washington, DC 20017-1100

Phone: (202) 541-3250
Fax: (202) 541-3255
E-mail: cns@catholicnews.com

For faster, smoother handling of copy, do not address news items or send e-mail to individuals.

Photo Guidelines

Style rules that deal with spelling, capitalization, abbreviations, grammar, titles etc., are the same as for news stories.

A caption contains the following elements:

1. The headline consists of six to 10 words in all capital letters and gives a brief explanation of the photo.
2. The caption consists of two or three sentences.

The first sentence of the caption contains the who, what, when and where. The date and location the photo was taken should appear in the first sentence along with full names and titles of those appearing in the photo. Identify people from left to right. Those who are not identified by name should be labeled "unidentified."

The second sentence gives background on the news event or describes why the photo is significant.

For movie stills accompanying reviews, the last sentence includes the U.S. Conference of Catholic Bishops classification and the Motion Picture Association of America rating.

Indicate a file or archive photo within the caption and include the date the photo was taken. If the date is not known, call it "undated."

3. The credit line in parentheses follows the caption. The credit reads *CNS photo* followed by a backslash, the photographer's name and the publication or agency the photographer works for if other than CNS. If a photographer is not identified or is unknown, the credit will read *CNS photo* followed by a backslash and source of the photo.

Some credit line examples are:

CNS photo/Joe Jones
CNS photo/Jane Smith, Catholic Herald
CNS photo/Chris Cross, Reuters
CNS photo/courtesy of Pope John Paul II Cultural Center
CNS photo/Catholic Herald
CNS photo/Paramount Pictures

Illustrations or photo illustrations should be indicated as such in the credit line. Two examples are:

CNS photo illustration/Joe Jones
CNS illustration/Jane Smith

4. The date the image is posted to the CNS Web site follows the credit line in parentheses.
5. The refer line appears next and is included only in captions of images that relate directly to a CNS story. The refer line includes the slugline of the story in all caps followed by the date of the story.
6. Editor alerts or special instructions appear following the refer line.

Some caption examples are:

ARCHBISHOP LEVADA ADDRESSES MEDIA ABOUT HIS APPOINTMENT TO DOCTRINAL CONGREGATION
San Francisco Archbishop William J. Levada holds a press conference in San Francisco May 13 after the Vatican announced that Pope Benedict XVI had appointed him prefect of the Congregation for the Doctrine of the Faith. He will be the first U.S. prelate to head the Vatican office charged with protecting and promoting the church's teachings on faith and morals. (CNS photo/Greg Tarczynski) (May 13, 2005) See LEVADA-DOCTRINE and LEVADA-REACT May 13, 2005.

SWISS GUARD RECRUIT TAKES SOLEMN OATH DURING SWEARING-IN CEREMONY

A Swiss Guard recruit holds the flag of the Guard and raises three fingers — a symbol of the Trinity — as he takes a solemn oath at the Vatican May 6. Thirty-one new members joined the ranks of the elite corps during the swearing-in ceremony. Founded in 1506, the Swiss Guard consists of 110 young Catholic male volunteers who swear to protect the pope, even at the cost of their own lives. (CNS photo/Nancy Wiechec) (May 9, 2005) See POPE-GUARD May 9, 2005.

CHRISTIANS ENTER SYRIAN CHURCH IN BAGHDAD AT EASTER

Christians arrive at Al Najat Syrian-rite Catholic Church for Easter services in Baghdad, Iraq, in this file photo from March 27. A Catholic priest in the country recently told Catholic News Service that Iraqi bishops are concerned about monetary aid coming from the Kurdish regional government to Christian churches across Iraq. (CNS photo/Ali Jasim, Reuters) (July 8, 2005) See IRAQ-MONEY July 8, 2005.

EMMAUS ARTWORK BY CHINESE ARTIST HE QI

The risen Christ walks with two of his disciples in "The Road to Emmaus," a painting by contemporary Chinese Christian artist He Qi. His artwork blends Chinese folk customs and traditional Chinese painting techniques with Western painting methods. Easter, the feast of the Resurrection, is marked March 27 this year. It is the oldest and most important Christian celebration. (CNS photo/courtesy of He Qi) (Feb. 23, 2005) Editors: Image provided for one-time editorial use only. Credit to the artist is mandatory and must appear with the published image.

How to submit photos to CNS

Send digital files at least 1600 x 2000 pixels, or a size of 8 x 10 inches at 200 ppi. Send high-quality jpeg files in RGB color mode. Do not use sharpen or unsharp mask filters. CNS does not accept images where content has been manipulated or contrived unless such images are assigned as and labeled "photo illustrations." Fill out the IPTC or metadata categories within each individual jpeg file. The title and description of the primary categories are:

Document Title: Use the story slugline or a logical slugline if none exists.

Author: Name of person who took the photo.

Description: Full caption text, credit line and name of publication submitting photo.

Description Writer: Initials of people who wrote or edited the caption.

Date Created: Date the photo was taken.

Headline: Brief explanation of the photo.

City: Name of city where photo was taken.

State: Name of state (spelled out) where photo was taken.

Country: Name of country (spelled out) where photo was taken.

E-mail individual jpeg files as attachments to photos@catholicnews.com.

For information about sending groups of photos, contact the CNS photo desk.

<h1 style="text-align:center">Appendix C:</h1>

Endnotes

Endnotes in news stories

Part of the art of news writing is to incorporate any needed references to other materials into the news narrative itself. Because editors may crop a story or column, endnotes — or footnotes — should never be used in Catholic News Service news or feature articles. Within a story or column, avoid parenthetical citations whenever possible, using them only as a last resort when the reference cannot be incorporated into the narrative without creating an unduly long or awkward sentence.

WRONG: *He quoted from St. Paul, "These are shadows of things to come; the reality belongs to Christ" (Col 2:17).*

RIGHT: *He quoted from St. Paul, "These are shadows of things to come; the reality belongs to Christ."* (The parenthetical citation is simply dropped.)

OR, if there is a need to give the reader a fuller form of reference: *He quoted from St. Paul's Letter to the Colossians, "These are...."*

OR, if the precise reference is needed: *He quoted Chapter 2, Verse 17, of St. Paul's....*

For the handling of book information in book reviews and editor's notes on news or feature material, see **Appendix A: Special Style Considerations.**

Endnotes and citations in texts

Catholic News Service must deal with endnotes to a text and parenthetical citations within a text in documents from other sources. The section on Source Documentation in the "Editorial Style" chapter at the end of Webster's New World College Dictionary, Third Edition (but not contained in the Fourth Edition), provides guidance for both forms of source reference. Since the endnotes and citations are created by the source, not by CNS, and since different sources use different styles, the main goals of CNS are:

— To assure that a consistent style is used throughout the text.

— To assure that abbreviations and references to other resource documents are consistent from one text to another.

Parenthetical citations

The treatment of *citations within a text* differs from the treatment of endnotes in four key ways:

— The citation is placed in parentheses, with a space preceding the parentheses.

— If the citation follows a direct quotation, the quotation marks precede the citation, but any other punctuation comes at the end of the citation.

— The first word of a parenthetical citation is not treated as the beginning of a sentence. It is lowercase if it is not part of a title or proper name.

— The citation within the parentheses does not end with a period.

In other respects — internal capitalization and punctuation, the use of quotation marks, acceptable abbreviations — the rules for parenthetical citations within a text are the same as those for citations placed at the end of the text as endnotes. These rules are treated in more detail under *endnotes* below.

Some examples of *parenthetical citations:*

... peace of heart" ("Reconciliatio et Paenitentia," 32).

... that we "might be as gods" (Gn 3:5) in absolute autonomy ...

... which befits all the clergy (cf. 1 Tm 3:1-13). They are to be ...

Endnotes

Endnotes consist of sequential numbers within the text and correspondingly numbered citations at the end of the text.

The *endnote number within the text* is placed in parentheses. Treatment of the endnote number within the text differs from a parenthetical citation within the text in two ways:

— There is no space before the parentheses.

— There is no punctuation after the parentheses. Any punctuation in the sentence precedes the parentheses. For example:

... "kingdom of heaven," (12)

... as Pope Paul VI said in his encyclical,(13) or later in an address to the Synod of Bishops in 1977.(14)

Treatment of the note at the end of the text differs from a parenthetical citation in two ways:

— The first word is always capitalized, even if it is an abbreviation such as *Cf.* or *Ibid.*

— Every note ends with a period.

Each note is treated as a separate paragraph. It begins with the appropriate number and a period, then a space and the endnote information.

The rules that follow apply equally to *endnote citations* and *parenthetical citations.*

For use of quotation marks in place of italics or underlining in CNS copy, see **italics** in the main section.

Only biblical citations are abbreviated. Other titles of documents are capitalized and spelled out.

Use quotes around the Latin titles of documents *("Humanae Vitae," "Gaudium et Spes,"* etc.) and around English-language formal titles *("The Challenge of Peace: God's Promise and Our Response")* but not around English-language titles that are descriptive of a document or descriptions that are not formal titles *(Pastoral Constitution on the Church in the Modern World, Pope John Paul II's apostolic exhortation on religious life, the U.S. bishops' pastoral letter on war and peace).* Be consistent in the choice of language: In references to conciliar documents and to encyclicals and other major papal texts, generally use either all Latin or all English titles. For additional details on use or nonuse of quotation marks around titles or names of documents, see **composition titles** in **Appendix A: Special Style Considerations; court-case names; documents; encyclical; liturgical books; pastoral letter; reference works;** and **Appendix I: Vatican II Documents.**

For *biblical citations,* use the abbreviations listed under **Bible,** which are taken from the New American Bible. Do not use periods. When there are two books with the same name, use Arabic rather than Roman numerals: *1 Cor 5:11.* Cite Scripture passages this way: *name of book, space, number of chapter, no space, colon, no space, verses.*

If two or more biblical citations are given in the same endnote, separate successive references to verses within the same chapter by a comma and a space, but separate successive references to different chapters or to different books with a semicolon and a space: *Mt 3:10, 17; Jn 10:12; 14:3; 1 Pt 4:5.*

For references indicating inclusion of all material between the first and last point of the citation, use a hyphen with no space between the starting point and end point of the reference, whether within a chapter or going from one chapter into another: *Mt 3:10-12; Jn 10:12-11:2.*

When references to the Book of Psalms appear in texts from the Vatican, two numbers are usually given for the psalm: *Ps 79 (80).* This is because the Vulgate Bible combined Psalms 9 and 10 of the Hebrew Book of Psalms as Psalm 9, resulting in a difference of one in all subsequent numbering. Modern Catholic Bibles, including the New American Bible, have restored the Hebrew numbering. The first number in the Vatican's citation refers to the Vulgate numbering, the second to modern usage. Use only the higher number.

Almost all major church documents number paragraphs that introduce a new thought. Subsequent texts often cite those documents by reference to the numbered paragraphs — a system that permits consistent references to such documents regardless of which printed version is used. Whether in an endnote or parenthetical citation within a text, generally use this format: *"Populorum Progressio," 16.*

For Vatican II documents, use one of these formats: *"Lumen Gentium," 6; Dogmatic Constitution on the Church, 6.*

A list of abbreviations often used in Vatican documents is found in the books of Second Vatican Council documents edited by Dominican Father Austin Flannery.

In certain cases endnote abbreviations are used to make material more compact. The following are acceptable:

— *p.* for *page* and *pp.* for *pages.* Use a single *p.* only if the citation refers to a single page: *p. 27.* But *pp. 27-30; pp. 15 and 22; pp. 12f; pp. 12ff.* Note use of a period and space after the *p.* or *pp.*

— *f* for *following* (one additional page) and *ff* for *following* (two or more additional pages). The citation *pp. 14f* means the information is found on pages 14 and 15; *pp. 14ff* means it is found on page 14 and at least two following pages. Use the English abbreviations *f* and *ff,* not their Latin counterparts *(sq.* and *sqq.,* respectively), for all such references. Do not use a space between the number and the *f* or *ff.* Lowercase. Do not use a period unless it is the end of a sentence.

— *cf.* for *compare,* the accepted abbreviation in English for the Latin *"confer."* It invites the reader to compare the passage in the text with the passage cited in the footnote. The abbreviation *cfr.,* often used in Vatican documents, is not an accepted English abbreviation: Change it to *cf.*

— *ibid.* for *in the same place.* Used when two or more consecutive citations are from the same source. Uppercase only when it appears at the beginning of a sentence. The page or paragraph numbers may be different. For example:

26. "Mater et Magistra," 23.
27. Ibid., 14.

Religious Orders, Men

The *religious orders, congregations* and *societies* of men represented in the United States are listed here under the collective heading of *orders*. See **order, congregation, society.**

When identifying members of an order, the *shortened form* of the order's name is acceptable on all references. If the name of the order is longer than one or two words, do not use it before the name: *Jesuit Father John Jones,* but *Brother Sam Spade, a member of the Franciscan Friars of the Renewal.*

In stories about the order itself generally use the *formal name* on first reference, but the shortened form may be used on second reference. A shortened form acceptable on second reference may be used on first reference to avoid a cumbersome lead, but provide the formal name elsewhere in the story.

Do not use *initials* to identify a member of an order in news stories, book reviews or bylines. See **religious** and **Appendix A: Special Style Considerations.**

AA - Augustinians of the Assumption, Assumptionists

BCS - Brothers of Christian Service

BFCC - Brothers for Christian Community

BGS - Little Brothers of the Good Shepherd

BH - Brotherhood of Hope

BHS - Brother-Servants of the Holy Spirit

BSO - Basilian Salvatorian Fathers

CFA - Alexian Brothers

CFC - Congregation of Christian Brothers

CFMM - Brothers of Our Lady, Mother of Mercy

CFP - Brothers of the Poor of St. Francis

CFR - Franciscan Friars of the Renewal

CFX - Brothers of St. Francis Xavier, Xaverian Brothers

CICM - Missionhurst Congregation of the Immaculate Heart of Mary, Missionhursts

CJ - Josephite Fathers (Belgium)

CJM - Congregation of Jesus and Mary, Eudists

CM - Congregation of the Mission, Lazarists, Vincentians

CMC - Congregation of Mother Co-Redemptrix

CMF - Missionary Sons of the Immaculate Heart of Mary, Claretians

CMI - Carmelites of Mary Immaculate

CMLM - Congregation of Maronite Lebanese Missionaries

CMM - Congregation of the Missionaries of Mariannhill, Mariannhill Fathers and Brothers

CMVd - Mekhitarist Fathers

CO - Congregation of the Oratory of St. Philip Neri, Oratorians

CP - Congregation of the Passion, Passionists

CPM - Congregation of the Priests of Mercy

CPPS - Society of the Precious Blood

CR - Congregation of the Resurrection, Resurrectionists

CR - Congregation of Clerics Regular, Theatines

CRIC - Canons Regular of the Immaculate Conception

CRL - Canons Regular of the Lateran

CRM - Adorno Fathers

CRS - Somascan Fathers

CRSP - Clerics Regular of St. Paul, Barnabites

CS - Missionaries of St. Charles, Scalabrinians

CSB - Basilian Fathers

CSC - Brothers of the Congregation of Holy Cross *(no* the *before* Holy),* Holy Cross Brothers

CSC - Congregation of Holy Cross *(no* the *before* Holy),* Holy Cross Fathers

CSJ - Congregation of St. Joseph, Josephites

CSJB - Congregation of St. John the Baptist

CSP - Paulist Fathers, Missionary Society of St. Paul the Apostle

CSPX - Brothers of St. Pius X

CSS - Congregation of the Sacred Stigmata, Stigmatines

CSSp - Congregation of the Holy Spirit, Spiritans.

CSSR - Congregation of the Most Holy Redeemer, Redemptorists

CSV - Clerics of St. Viator, Viatorians

DLP - Diocesan Labor Priests

ErCam - Camaldolese Hermits of the Congregation of Monte Corona

FC - Brothers of Charity

FDP - Sons of Divine Providence

FFI - Franciscan Friars of the Immaculate

FFSC - Franciscan Brothers of the Holy Cross

FIC - Brothers of Christian Instruction, La Mennais Brothers

FJ - Brothers of St. John

FMM - Brothers of Mercy

FMM - Missionary Fraternity of Mary

FMS - Marist Brothers

FMSI - Sons of Mary Missionary Society, Sons of Mary Health of the Sick

FPM - Presentation Brothers

FSC - Brothers of the Christian Schools, La-Sallian Christian Brothers

FSE - Brothers of the Holy Eucharist

FSP - Brothers of St. Patrick, Patrician Brothers

FSR - Brothers of the Congregation of Our Lady of the Holy Rosary

FSSP - Priestly Fraternity of St. Peter

GHM - Glenmary Home Missioners

HJD - Los Hermanos de Juan Diego

HMC - Hermits of Mount Carmel

IC - Institute of Charity, Rosminians

IHM - Brothers of the Immaculate Heart of Mary

IMC - Consolata Missionaries

ISSS - Schonstatt Institute of Secular Priests

LBSF - Little Brothers of St. Francis

LC - Legionaries of Christ

MAfr - Missionaries of Africa *(formerly White Fathers)*

MCBS - Missionary Congregation of the Blessed Sacrament

MCCJ - Comboni Missionaries of the Heart of Jesus, Verona Fathers

MDes - Mercadarios Descalzos

MEP - Paris Foreign Mission Society

MFVA - Franciscan Missionaries of the Eternal Word

MG - Guadalupe Missioners

MHM - St. Joseph's Society for Foreign Missions, Mill Hill Missionaries

MIC - Congregation of Marians of the Immaculate Conception

MJ - Missionaries of St. Joseph

MM - Catholic Foreign Mission Society of America, Maryknoll Fathers

MS - Missionaries of Our Lady of La Salette, La Salette Fathers

MSA - Missionaries of the Holy Apostles

MSC - Missionaries of the Sacred Heart

MSC - Missionary Servants of Christ

MSF - Congregation of the Missionaries of the Holy Family

MSFS - Missionaries of St. Francis de Sales

MSP - Missionaries of St. Paul

MSpS - Missionaries of the Holy Spirit

MSSCC - Missionaries of the Sacred Hearts of Jesus and Mary

OAR - Augustinian Recollects

OCarm - Order of Our Lady of Mount Carmel, Carmelites

OCart - Order of Carthusians

OCD - Discalced Carmelites

OCist - Order of Cistercians

OCSO - Order of Cistercians of the Strict Observance, Trappists

OdeM - Order of Our Lady of Mercy, Mercedarians

OFM - Order of Friars Minor, Franciscans

OFM Cap - Order of Friars Minor Capuchin, Capuchin Franciscans, Capuchins

OFM Conv - Order of Friars Minor Conventual, Conventual Franciscans

OH - Hospitaller Brothers of St. John of God

OIC - Order of the Imitation of Christ

OLC - Brothers of Our Lady of Providence

OM - Minim Fathers

OMar - Congregation of Maronite Monks

OMI - Missionary Oblates of Mary Immaculate, Oblates

OMV - Oblates of the Virgin Mary

OP - Order of Preachers, Dominicans

OPC - Maronite Hermits of St. Francis

OPraem - Canons Regular of Premontre, Premonstratensians, Norbertines

ORC - Operarios del Reina de Cristo

OSA - Order of St. Augustine, Augustinians

OSB - Order of St. Benedict, Benedictines

OSBCam - Camaldolese Benedictines

OSBM - Order of St. Basil the Great, Basilians

OSC - Canons Regular of the Holy Cross, Crosiers

OSCam - Order of St. Camillus, Order of Servants of the Sick, Camillians

OSF - Religious Brothers of the Third Order Regular of St. Francis

OSF - Franciscan Brothers of Christ the King

OSF - Franciscan Brothers of the Third Order Regular

OSF - Franciscan Missionary Brothers of the Sacred Heart of Jesus

OSFS - Oblates of St. Francis de Sales

OSJ - Oblates of St. Joseph

OSM - Order of Friars Servants of Mary, Servite Fathers

OSPPE - Order of St. Paul the First Hermit, Paulines

OSsS - Order of the Most Holy Savior, Brigittine monks

OSST - Order of the Most Holy Trinity, Trinitarians

PIME - Pontifical Institute for Foreign Missions

RCJ - Rogationist Fathers

SA - Franciscan Friars of the Atonement, Atonement Fathers

SAC - Society of the Catholic Apostolate, Pallottines

SC - Brothers of the Sacred Heart

SC - Servants of Charity, Guanellians

SCh - Society of Christ

SchP - Order of the Poor Clerics Regular of the Mother of God of the Pious Schools, Piarist Fathers

SCJ - Congregation of the Sacred Heart of Jesus, Sacred Heart Fathers and Brothers.

SDB - Salesians of St. John Bosco

SDS - Society of the Divine Savior, Salvatorians

SDV - Society of the Divine Vocation, Vocationist Fathers

SF - Sons of the Holy Family

SFC - Society of the Brothers of Charity

SFM - Scarboro Foreign Missions

SJ - Society of Jesus, Jesuits

SLT - Servants of Our Lady of the Most Holy Trinity

SM - Society of Mary, Marianists

SM - Society of Mary, Marists

SMA - Society of African Missions

SMM - Montfort Missionaries

SMP - Society of Our Mother of Peace

SOCist - Cistercian Monks of the Strict Observance, Cistercians

SOLT - Society of Our Lady of the Most Holy Trinity

sP - Servants of the Paraclete

SPS - St. Patrick Missionary Society

SS - Society of St. Sulpice, Sulpician Fathers

SSC - Missionary Society of St. Columban, Columban Fathers

SSCC - Congregation of the Sacred Hearts of Jesus and Mary, Picpus Fathers

SSE - Society of St. Edmund, Edmundite Fathers

SSJ - St. Joseph's Society of the Sacred Heart, Josephites

SSP - Society of St. Paul for the Apostolate of Communications, Pauline Fathers and Brothers

SSS - Congregation of the Blessed Sacrament, Blessed Sacrament Fathers

SST - Missionary Society of St. Thomas the Apostle

ST - Missionary Servants of the Most Holy Trinity

SVD - Society of the Divine Word, Verbites

SX - Xaverian Missionary Fathers

TOR - Third Order Regular of St. Francis

VC - Vincentian Congregation

Religious Orders, Women

The *religious orders, congregations* and *societies* of women represented in the United States are listed here under the collective heading of *orders*. See **order, congregation, society.**

When identifying members of an order, the *shortened form* of an order's name is acceptable on all references.

In stories about the order itself generally use the *formal name* on first reference, but the shortened form may be used on second reference. A shortened form acceptable on second reference may be used on first reference to avoid a cumbersome lead, but provide the formal name elsewhere in the story.

Do not use *initials* to identify a member of an order in news stories, book reviews or bylines. See **religious** and **Appendix A: Special Style Considerations.**

AA - Sisters Auxiliaries of the Apostolate

AASC - Handmaids of the Blessed Sacrament and Charity

ABS - Auxiliaries of the Blessed Sacrament

ACJ - Handmaids of the Sacred Heart of Jesus

AD - Sisters of the Lamb of God

AIM - Association of Mary Immaculate

AMI - Handmaids of Mary Immaculate

ANG - Sisters of a New Genesis

AP - Nuns of Perpetual Adoration of the Blessed Sacrament

APB - Sisters Adorers of the Precious Blood

APG - Sisters of Perpetual Adoration of Guadalupe

AR - Congregation of the Handmaids of the Sacred Heart of Jesus for Reparation

AR - Augustinian Recollects

ASC - Adorers of the Blood of Christ

ASCJ - Apostles of the Sacred Heart of Jesus

ASSP - Angelic Sisters of St. Paul

Bethl - Bethlemita Sisters, Daughters of the Sacred Heart of Jesus

BPS - Sisters of Charity of Good and Perpetual Succor

BS - Sisters of the Good Savior

BVM - Sisters of Charity of the Blessed Virgin Mary

BVMC - Blessed Virgin Missionaries of Carmel

Cach - Carmelite Sisters of Charity

CBS - Congregation of Sisters of Bon Secours

CC - Carmel Community

CCVI - Congregation of the Sisters of Charity of the Incarnate Word

CCW - Carmelite Community of the Word

CDP - Sisters of Divine Providence

CDS - Congregation of the Divine Spirit

CFMM - Minim Daughters of Mary Immaculate

CFP - Feminine Congregation of the Passion, Mexican Passionist Sisters

CGS - Contemplatives of the Good Shepherd

CHF - Sisters of the Holy Faith

CHM - Congregation of the Humility of Mary

CHS - Community of the Holy Spirit

CIC - Sisters of the Immaculate Conception

CIJ - Congregation of the Infant Jesus, Nursing Sisters of the Sick Poor

CJC - Poor Sisters of Jesus Crucified and the Sorrowful Mother

CK - School Sisters of Christ the King

CLHC - Congregation of Our Lady, Help of the Clergy

CMC - Congregation of the Mother of Carmel

CMR - Congregation of Mary Queen

CMS - Comboni Missionary Sisters, Missionary Sisters of Verona

CMS - Cashel Mercy Sisters

CMST - Congregation of Missionary Carmelites of St. Theresa

CND - Sisters of the Congregation of Notre Dame

COC - Companions of Christ

CP - Religious of the Passion of Jesus Christ, Passionists

CP - Sisters of the Cross and Passion, Passionists

CPPS - Sisters of the Most Precious Blood

CPS - Missionary Sisters of the Precious Blood

CR - Sisters of the Resurrection

CS - Company of the Savior

CSA - Sisters of St. Agnes

CSA - Sisters of Charity of St. Augustine

CSA - Albertine Sisters

CSAC - Pallottine Sisters of the Catholic Apostolate

CSB - Congregation of St. Brigid

CSC - Sisters of the Holy Cross

CSC - Sisters of the Holy Cross and Seven Dolors

CSE - Carmelite Sisters of the Eucharist

CSFN - Sisters of the Holy Family of Nazareth

CSJ - Sisters of St. Joseph (of Carondelet, of Chambery, of Medaille)

CSJB - Sisters of St. John the Baptist

CSJP - Sisters of St. Joseph of Peace

CSM - Sisters of St. Martha of Antigonish, Nova Scotia

CSN - Congregation of Sisters of Nazareth

CSR - Sisters of the Holy Redeemer

CSSF - Congregation of the Sisters of St. Felix, Felician Sisters

CSSp - Sisters of the Holy Spirit

CST - Carmelite Sisters of St. Therese of the Infant Jesus

CVD - Sisters of Bethany

CVI - Congregation of the Incarnate Word and Blessed Sacrament

CVI - Religious of the Incarnate Word

DC - Daughters of Charity of St. Vincent de Paul

DC - Daughters of the Cross

DCJ - Carmelite Sisters of the Divine Heart of Jesus

DCPB - Daughters of Charity of the Most Precious Blood

DDL - Daughters of Divine Love

DHM - Daughters of the Heart of Mary

DHS - Daughters of the Holy Spirit

DLF - Daughters of Our Lady of Fatima

DLJC - Disciples of the Lord Jesus Christ

DM - Daughters of Our Lady of Mercy

DM - Daughters of Mary of the Immaculate Conception

DMJ - Daughters of Mary and Joseph

DSF - Daughters of St. Francis of Assisi

DSMP - Daughters of St. Mary of Providence

DW - Daughters of Wisdom

EFMS - Eucharistic Franciscan Missionary Sisters

FAS - Franciscan Apostolic Sisters

FC - Daughters of the Cross of Liege

FCJ - Society of the Sisters, Faithful Companions of Jesus

FCSCJ - Daughters of the Charity of the Sacred Heart of Jesus

FDC - Daughters of Divine Charity

FdCC - Canossian Daughters of Charity, Canossian Sisters

FDNSC - Daughters of Our Lady of the Sacred Heart

FDP - Daughters of Divine Providence

FDZ - Daughters of Divine Zeal

FHIC - Franciscan Hospitaller Sisters of the Immaculate Conception

FHM - Franciscan Handmaids of the Most Pure Heart of Mary

FHM - Franciscan Sisters Daughters of Mercy

FJ - Daughters of Jesus

FJ - Sisters of St. John

FLG - Franciscan Sisters of Our Lady of Grace

FMA - Daughters of Mary Help of Christians, Salesian Sisters of St. John Bosco

FMDC - Franciscan Missionary Sisters of the Divine Child

FMI - Franciscan Sisters of Mary Immaculate of the Third Order of St. Francis Assisi

FMI - Daughters of Mary Immaculate, Marianist Sisters

FMIJ - Franciscan Missionary Sisters of the Infant Jesus

FMM - Franciscan Missionaries of Mary

FMSA - Franciscan Missionary Sisters of Assisi

FMSA - Franciscan Missionary Sisters of Assisi for Africa

FMSC - Franciscan Missionary Sisters of the Sacred Heart

FMSJ - Franciscan Missionaries of St. Joseph, Mill Hill Sisters

FMSR - Daughters of Our Lady of the Most Holy Rosary

FPO - Franciscans of the Primitive Observance

FSE - Franciscan Sisters of the Eucharist

FSJ - Religious Daughters of St. Joseph

FSM - Franciscan Sisters of Mary

FSP - Franciscan Sisters of Peace

FSP - Daughters of St. Paul, Missionary Sisters of the Media of Communication

FSPA - Sisters of the Third Order of St. Francis of Perpetual Adoration

FSR - Franciscan Sisters of Ringwood

FSSE - Franciscan Sisters of St. Elizabeth

FSSJ - Franciscan Sisters of St. Joseph

FSSM - Franciscan Sisters of the Sorrowful Mother

FSSpJ - Franciscan Sisters of the Spirit of Jesus

GHMS - Home Mission Sisters of America, Glenmary Sisters

GNSH - Grey Nuns of the Sacred Heart

HCG - Hermanas Catequistas Guadalupanas

HFSJ - Franciscan Sisters of St. Joseph

HGS - Hermanas Guadalupanas de la Salle

HHCJ - Congregation of Handmaids of the Holy Child Jesus

HHS - Society of Helpers

HJ - Hermanas Josefinas

HM - Sisters of the Humility of Mary

HMSS - Mercedarian Sisters of the Blessed Sacrament

HOCarm - Hermits of Our Lady of Mount Carmel

HPB - Congregation of Handmaids of the Precious Blood

HRF - Sisters of the Holy Rosary of Fatima

HSH - Handmaids of the Sacred Heart

HSM - Hermit Sisters of Mary

HSpS - Daughters of the Holy Spirit

HT - Handmaids of the Most Holy Trinity

HVM - Sisters Home Visitors of Mary

IBVM - Institute of the Blessed Virgin Mary, Loretto Sisters

IC - Vietnamese Sisters of the Incarnational Consecration

ICM - Missionary Sisters of the Immaculate Heart of Mary

IHM - The California Institute of the Sisters of the Most Holy and Immaculate Heart of the Blessed Virgin Mary

IHM - Sisters of the Immaculate Heart of Mary

IHM - Sisters of the Immaculate Heart of Mary of Wichita

IHM - Sisters, Servants of the Immaculate Heart of Mary

IJ - Sisters of the Infant Jesus

IM - Sisters of Charity of the Infant Mary

ISSM - Secular Institute of Schonstatt, Sisters of Mary

IWBS - Sisters of the Congregation of the Incarnate Word and Blessed Sacrament

JC - Congregation of Benedictines of Jesus Crucified

JSOP - Dominican Oblates of Jesus

LB - Ladies of Bethany

LCM - Sisters of the Little Company of Mary

LHC - Lovers of the Holy Cross Sisters (Phat Diem)

LMSC - Little Missionary Sisters of Charity

LSA - Little Sisters of the Assumption

LSG - Little Sisters of the Gospel

LSIC - Little Servant Sisters of the Immaculate Conception

LSJ - Little Sisters of Jesus

LSJM - Little Sisters of Jesus and Mary

LSP - Little Sisters of the Poor

MC - Consolata Missionary Sisters

MC - Missionaries of Charity

MC - Poor Clare Missionary Sisters

MCDP - Missionary Catechists of Divine Providence

MCM - Cordi-Marian Missionary Sisters

MCS - Missionary Sisters of the Sacred Side

MCSH - Missionary Catechists of the Sacred Hearts of Jesus and Mary (Violetas)

MCSJM - Missionary Catechists of the Sacred Hearts of Jesus and Mary

MD - Mothers of the Helpless

MDPVM - Missionary Daughters of the Most Pure Virgin Mary

ME - Missionaries Ecumenical

MESST - Eucharistic Ministers of the Most Holy Trinity

MEST - Eucharistic Missionaries of St. Theresa

MFIC - Missionary Franciscan Sisters of the Immaculate Conception

MFP - Franciscan Missionaries of Our Lady of Peace

MGSpS - Guadalupan Missionaries of the Holy Spirit

MHS - Sisters of the Most Holy Sacrament

MHSH - Mission Helpers of the Sacred Heart

MIC - Sisters of the Immaculate Conception of the Blessed Virgin Mary (Lithuanian)

MJ - Missionary Sisters of Jesus

MJMJ - Missionary Sisters of Jesus, Mary and Joseph

MM - Maryknoll Sisters

MMB - Mercedarian Missionaries of Berriz

MMD - Servite Missionary Sisters of the Sorrowful Mother

MMM - Medical Missionaries of Mary

MMS - Society of Catholic Medical Missionaries, Medical Mission Sisters

MOM - Missionary Sisters of Our Lady of Mercy

MPF - Religious Teachers Filippini

MPH - Missionary Sisters of Our Lady of Perpetual Help

MPV - Religious Venerini Sisters

MR - Marianist Sisters

MS - Marian Sisters of Diocese of Lincoln

MSBT - Missionary Servants of the Most Blessed Trinity

MSC - Congregation of the Marianites of Holy Cross

MSC - Missionary Sisters of the Sacred Heart, Cabrini Sisters

MSC - Missionary Sisters of the Most Sacred Heart of Jesus

MSCG - Missionaries of the Sacred Heart of Jesus and Our Lady of Guadalupe

MSCK - Missionary Sisters of Christ the King

MSCS - Missionary Sisters of St. Charles Borromeo, Scalabrini Sisters

MSF - Missionary Sisters of the Holy Family

MSHF - Missionary Sisters of the Holy Family

MSHR - Missionary Sisters of the Holy Rosary

MSJ - Medical Sisters of St. Joseph

MSKCP - Missionary Sisters of Christ the King of Polonia

MSMG - Missionary Sisters of the Mother of God

MSOLA - Missionary Sisters of Our Lady of Africa, Sisters of Africa

MSSA - Missionary Servants of St. Anthony

MSSCB - Missionary Sisters of St. Charles Borromeo, Scalabrinis

MSSJ - Missionary Servants of St. Joseph

MSSp - Mission Sisters of the Holy Spirit

MSSS - Missionary Sisters of the Most Blessed Sacrament

MTG - Adorers of the Holy Cross

MXY - Yarumal Foreign Mission Institute

NAU-OLC - North American Union of Sisters of Our Lady of Charity, Eudist Sisters, Sisters of Our Lady of Charity in the Refuge

ND - Notre Dame Sisters

NDS - Congregation of Notre Dame de Sion

OAR - Augustinian Recollect Sisters

OBT - Sisters Oblates to the Blessed Trinity

OCA - Vietnamese Sisters of Our Lady of Mount Carmel

OCarm - Congregation of Our Lady of Mount Carmel

OCarm - Carmelite Nuns of the Ancient Observance, Calced Carmelites

OCarm - Carmelite Sisters (Corpus Christi)

OCarm - Carmelite Sisters for the Aged or Infirm

OCarm - Institute of Our Lady of Mount Carmel

OCist - Cistercian Nuns

OCD - Discalced Carmelite Nuns

OCD - Carmelite Sisters of the Most Sacred Heart of Los Angeles

OCSO - Cistercian Nuns of the Strict Observance

ODN - Company of Mary

OLC - Sisters of Our Lady of Charity

OLG - Sisters of Our Lady of the Garden

OLM - Sisters of Charity of Our Lady of Mercy

OLS - Sisters of Our Lady of Sorrows

OLVM - Our Lady of Victory Missionary Sisters

OMMI - Oblate Missionaries of Mary Immaculate

OMO - Oblates of the Mother of Orphans

OP - Dominican Nuns, Nuns of the Order of Preachers

OP - Dominican Sisters of Charity of the Presentation

OP - Dominican Sisters of Hope

OP - Dominican Sisters of Our Lady of the Rosary and St. Catherine of Siena

OP - Dominican Sisters of the Perpetual Rosary

OP - Dominican Sisters of the Roman Congregation

OP - Eucharistic Ministers of St. Dominic

OP - Religious Missionaries of St. Dominic

OP - Sisters of St. Dominic, Dominican Sisters

OSA - Augustinian Nuns of Contemplative Life

OSA - Congregation of Augustinian Sisters, Servants of Jesus and Mary

OSA - Sisters of St. Rita

OSA - Sisters of St. Augustine

OSA - Augustinian Sisters of Our Lady of Consolation

OSB - Benedictine Nuns of the Congregation of Solesmes

OSB - Benedictine Nuns of the Primitive Observance

OSB - Benedictine Sisters of Perpetual Adoration of Pontifical Jurisdiction

OSB - Benedictine Sisters of Pontifical Jurisdiction

OSB - Benedictine Sisters (Regina Pacis)

OSB - Missionary Benedictine Sisters

OSB - Olivetan Benedictine Sisters

OSB - Sisters of the Order of St. Benedict, Benedictine Sisters

OSBM - Sisters of the Order of St. Basil the Great

OSBS - Oblate Sisters of the Blessed Sacrament

OSC - Order of St. Clare, Franciscan Poor Clare Nuns, Poor Clares of St. Colette

OSCCap - Capuchin Poor Clares

OSCO - Cistercian Nuns of the Strict Observance

OSF - Bernardine Sisters of the Third Order of St. Francis

OSF - Congregation of the Servants of the Holy Child Jesus of the Third Order Regular of St. Francis

OSF - Congregation of the Third Order of St. Francis of Mary Immaculate (Joliet)

OSF - Franciscan Missionaries of Our Lady

OSF - Franciscan Missionary Sisters for Africa

OSF - Franciscan Missionary Sisters of Our Lady of Sorrows

OSF - Franciscan Sisters, Daughters of the Sacred Hearts of Jesus and Mary

OSF - Franciscan Sisters of Allegany, N.Y.

OSF - Franciscan Sisters of Baltimore

OSF - Franciscan Sisters of Chicago

OSF - Franciscan Sisters of Christian Charity

OSF - Franciscan Sisters of Little Falls, Minn.

OSF - Franciscan Sisters of Our Lady of Perpetual Help

OSF - Franciscan Sisters of St. Paul

OSF - Franciscan Sisters of the Immaculate Conception

OSF - Franciscan Sisters of the Immaculate Conception and St. Joseph for the Dying

OSF - Franciscan Sisters of the Sacred Heart

OSF - Hospital Sisters of the Third Order of St. Francis

OSF - St. Francis Mission Community

OSF - School Sisters of St. Francis

OSF - School Sisters of the Third Order of St. Francis

OSF - Sisters of St. Francis of Assisi of Christ the King

OSF - Sisters of St. Francis of Clinton, Iowa

OSF - Sisters of St. Francis of Millvale, Pa.

OSF - Sisters of St. Francis of Penance and Christian Charity

OSF - Sisters of St. Francis of the Perpetual Adoration

OSF - Sisters of St. Francis of Philadelphia

OSF - Sisters of St. Francis of the Congregation of Our Lady of Lourdes

OSF - Sisters of St. Francis of the Holy Cross

OSF - Sisters of St. Francis of the Holy Eucharist

OSF - Sisters of St. Francis of the Holy Family

OSF - Sisters of St. Francis of the Immaculate Conception

OSF - Sisters of St. Francis of the Immaculate Heart of Mary (Hankinson)

OSF - Sisters of St. Francis of the Martyr St. George

OSF - Sisters of St. Francis, Savannah, Mo.

OSF - Sisters of St. Joseph of the Third Order of St. Francis

OSF - Sisters of the Third Franciscan Order of Providence of God

OSF - Sisters of the Third Order of St. Francis of Penance and Charity

OSF - Sisters of the Third Order Regular of St. Francis of the Congregation of Our Lady of Lourdes

OSFS - Oblate Sisters of St. Francis de Sales

OSHJ - Oblate Sisters of the Sacred Heart of Jesus

OSM - Mantellate Sisters, Servants of Mary

OSM - Servite Sisters, Servants of Mary

OSM - Oblates of St. Martha

OSP - Oblate Sisters of Providence

OSS - Religious of the Order of the Blessed Sacrament and Our Lady, Sacramentine Nuns

OSSR - Oblates of the Most Holy Redeemer

OSSR - Order of the Most Holy Redeemer

OSSS - Brigittine Sisters, Order of the Most Holy Savior

OSST - Sisters of the Most Holy Trinity

OSU - Ursuline Nuns, Ursuline Sisters

PBVM - Sisters of the Presentation of the Blessed Virgin Mary

PC - Poor Clares

PCC - Order of St. Clare, Poor Clares of St. Colette

PCI - Pax Christi Institute

PCJ - Sisters of the Poor Child Jesus

PCPA - Poor Clares of Perpetual Adoration

PDDM - Sister Disciples of the Divine Master

PFM - Little Franciscans of Mary

PHJC - Poor Handmaids of Jesus Christ, Ancilla Domini Sisters

PM - Sisters of the Presentation of Mary

POSC - Little Workers of the Sacred Heart

PSN - Poor Sisters of Nazareth

PSSF - Little Sisters of the Holy Family

PSSJ - Poor Sisters of St. Joseph

PVMI - Parish Visitors of Mary Immaculate

QMHC - Quinhon Missionary Sisters of the Holy Cross

RA - Religious of the Apostolate of the Sacred Heart

RA - Religious of the Assumption

RA - Antonine Sisters

RAD - Sisters of the Love of God

RC - Congregation of Our Lady of the Retreat in the Cenacle

RCD - Sisters of Our Lady of Christian Doctrine

RCE - Religious of Christian Education

RCM - Sisters of the Immaculate Conception

RCSCJ - Sisters of the Cross and the Sacred Heart of Jesus

RDC - Sisters of Divine Compassion

RE - Religious of the Eucharist

RF - Sisters of St. Philip Neri

RFR - Sisters of Our Lady of Refuge

RGS - Sisters of Our Lady of Charity of the Good Shepherd

RHSJ - Religious Hospitallers of St. Joseph

RJM - Religious of Jesus and Mary

RMI - Religious of Mary Immaculate, Claretian Missionary Sisters

RODA - Sisters Oblates to Divine Love

ROIC - Religious of Our Lady of Charity of Refuge

RSC - Religious Sisters of Charity

RSCJ - Society of the Sacred Heart

RSHM - Religious of the Sacred Heart of Mary

RSJ - Religious of St. Joseph of Australia

RSM - Diocesan Sisters of Mercy

RSM - Religious Sisters of Mercy

RSM - Sisters of Mercy of the Americas

RSR - Congregation of Our Lady of the Holy Rosary

RT - Theatine Sisters of the Immaculate Conception

RU - Ursuline Nuns of the Congregation of Tildonk, Belgium

RVM - Religious of the Blessed Virgin Mary

SA - Franciscan Sisters of the Atonement, Atonement Sisters, Graymoor Sisters

SAA - Sisters Auxiliaries of the Apostolate

SAB - Sisters of St. Anne Bangalone

SAC - Missionary Sisters of the Catholic Apostolate, Pallottine Missionary Sisters

SND - Sisters of Notre Dame

SNDdeN - Sisters of Notre Dame de Namur

SNJM - Sisters of the Holy Names of Jesus and Mary

SOLM - Sisters of Our Lady of Mercy, Mercedarians

SOLPH - Sisters of Our Lady of Perpetual Help

SOLT - Society of Our Lady of the Most Holy Trinity

SP - Sisters of Providence

SPC - Sisters of St. Paul of Chartres

SR - Sisters of Reparation for the Sacred Wounds of Jesus

SRC - Congregation of Our Lady Queen of the Clergy

SRC - Servants of Our Lady Queen of the Clergy

SRCM - Sisters of Reparation of the Congregation of Mary

SSA - Sisters of St. Ann

SSA - Sisters of St. Anne

SSC - Missionary Sisters of St. Columban

SSC - Sisters of St. Casimir

SSC - Society of Sisters of the Church

SSCC - Sisters of the Sacred Hearts and of Perpetual Adoration

SSCh - Sisters of Ste. Chretienne

SSCJ - Servants of the Most Sacred Heart of Jesus

SSCJ - Sisters of the Sacred Heart of Jesus

SSCM - Servants of the Holy Heart of Mary

SSCM - Sisters of Sts. Cyril and Methodius

SSD - Institute of the Sisters of St. Dorothy

SSE - Sisters of St. Elizabeth

SSF - Congregation of the Sisters of the Holy Family

SSH - Sisters Servants of the Most Sacred Heart

SSHJP - Servants of the Sacred Heart of Jesus and of the Poor

SSJ - Servants of St. Joseph

SSJ - Sisters of St. Joseph

SSJ - Sisters of St. Joseph of Chestnut Hill

SSJ - Sisters of St. Joseph of St. Augustine

SSJ-TOSF - Sisters of St. Joseph - Third Order of St. Francis

SSJC - Sisters of St. Joseph Benedict Cottolengo

SSL - Congregation of the Sisters of St. Louis

SSLOG - Seton Sisters of Our Lady of Guadalupe

SSM - Sisters of the Sorrowful Mother (Third Order of St. Francis)

SSMI - Sisters Servants of Mary Immaculate

SSMN - Sisters of St. Mary of Namur

SSMO - Sisters of St. Mary of Oregon

SSND - School Sisters of Notre Dame

SSPC - Missionary Sisters of St. Peter Claver

SSpS - Missionary Sisters Servants of the Holy Spirit, Holy Spirit Missionary Sisters

SSpSdeAP - Sister Servants of the Holy Spirit of Perpetual Adoration

SSS - Servants of the Blessed Sacrament

SSS - Sisters of Social Service

SSTV - Congregation of Sisters of St. Thomas of Villanova

SSVM - Servants of the Lord and the Virgin of Matara

STJ - Society of St. Teresa of Jesus

SU - Society of the Sisters of St. Ursula of the Blessed Virgin

SUSC - Holy Union Sisters

SV - Sisters of Life

SVD - Sisters of the Divine Vocation, Vocationist Sisters

SVM - Sisters of the Visitation of the Congregation of the Immaculate Heart of Mary

VDC - Verbum Dei Community

VHM - Visitation Nuns

VS - Vestiarski Sisters

VSC - Vincentian Sisters of Charity

VZ - Sisters of Charity of St. Vincent de Paul

XMM - Xaverian Missionary Society of Mary

XS - Catholic Mission Sisters of St. Francis Xavier

U.S. Conference of Catholic Bishops

The U.S. Conference of Catholic Bishops, based in Washington, is both the membership organization to which all U.S. bishops belong and the public policy arm of the U.S. bishops. *USCCB* is acceptable on second reference.

The USCCB was created in 2001 with the merger of the *National Conference of Catholic Bishops* and the *U.S. Catholic Conference.* The two conferences were established in 1967 after the Second Vatican Council called for such canonical national organizations of bishops. Although the U.S. bishops met annually before 1967 as the *National Catholic Welfare Conference,* that organization is more properly considered the predecessor of the USCC, not of the NCCB.

Here are the formal titles of each of the committees, secretariats, departments or offices related to the USCCB. In general, it is not necessary to say that the committee or office is of the USCCB. Instead, use the *U.S. bishops' Committee on Vocations, the U.S. bishops' Committee on Pro-Life Activities, the U.S. bishops' Committee on Women in Society and in the Church, the U.S. bishops' Committee on Domestic Policy,* etc. All committees are listed in the *Membership Photo Directory* of the USCCB, which also is the primary source for the spelling of U.S. bishops' names.

Use the formal name of the committee or office on first reference. Shortened forms of the name and flip-flopped names *(doctrine committee, pro-life committee)* are acceptable on second reference and should be lowercased.

This list was up-to-date as of October 2005.

USCCB Offices
General Secretariat
Office of General Counsel
Office of Finance
    — Accounting
Office of General Services
Office of Government Liaison
Office of Human Resources
Office of Library Services
Office of Management Information Systems
Office of Publishing
Office of Child and Youth Protection
    — National Review Board

Executive-Level Committees
Administrative Committee
Executive Committee
Committee on Budget and Finance
    — Audit Subcommittee
Committee on Personnel
Committee on Priorities and Plans
    — Subcommittee on Planning

Standing Committees
Committee on African-American Catholics (Secretariat for African-American Catholics)
Committee on the American College of Louvain
Committee on Boundaries of Dioceses and Provinces
Committee on Canonical Affairs
Committee on Catechesis (Office for the Catechism)
Committee on Catholic Campaign for Human Development
Committee on Catholic Relief Services Collection
Committee on the Church in Latin America (Secretariat for the Church in Latin America)
Committee on Communications (Department of Communications)
    — Catholic Communication Campaign advisory board

— Subcommittee for Catholic News Service
— Subcommittee for Standards and Policy
Committee on Consecrated Life
Committee on the Diaconate (Secretariat for the Diaconate)
Committee on Doctrine (Secretariat for Doctrine and Pastoral Practices)
Committee on Domestic Policy (Office of Domestic Social Development, Department of Social Development and World Peace)
Committee on Ecumenical and Interreligious Affairs (Secretariat for Ecumenical and Interreligious Affairs)
— Subcommittee on Interreligious Dialogue
Committee on Education (Department of Education)
— Subcommittee on Bishops and Catholic College and University Presidents
— Subcommittee on Campus Ministry
— Subcommittee on Public Policy and Catholic Schools
— Subcommittee on "Sapientia Christiana"
Committee on Evangelization (Secretariat for Evangelization)
Committee on Hispanic Affairs (Secretariat for Hispanic Affairs)
Committee on the Home Missions (Secretariat for the Home Missions)
Committee on International Policy (Office of International Justice and Peace, Department of Social Development and World Peace)
Committee on the Laity (Secretariat for Family, Laity, Women and Youth)
— Subcommittee on Lay Ministry
— Subcommittee on Youth and Young Adults
Committee on the Liturgy (Secretariat for the Liturgy)
Committee on Marriage and Family Life (Secretariat for Family, Laity, Women and Youth)
Committee on Migration (Migration and Refugee Services)

Committee on North American College Rome
Committee on Pastoral Practices (Secretariat for Doctrine and Pastoral Practices)
Committee on Priestly Formation (Secretariat for Vocations and Priestly Formation)
Committee on Priestly Life and Ministry (Secretariat for Priestly Life and Ministry)
Committee on Pro-Life Activities (Secretariat for Pro-Life Activities)
Committee for the Protection of Children and Young People (Office of Child and Youth Protection)
Committee on the Relationship Between Eastern and Latin Catholic Churches
Committee on Science and Human Values (Secretariat for Doctrine and Pastoral Practices)
Committee on Selection of Bishops
Committee on Vocations (Secretariat for Vocations and Priestly Formation)
Committee on Women in Society and in the Church (Secretariat for Family, Laity, Women and Youth)
Committee on World Mission (Department of Education)

Ad Hoc Committees
Ad Hoc Committee on the Church in Africa
Ad Hoc Committee on Aid to the Church in Central and Eastern Europe (Office to Aid the Church in Central and Eastern Europe)
Ad Hoc Committee on Bishops' Life and Ministry
Ad Hoc Committee on Catholic Charismatic Renewal
Ad Hoc Committee on Catholic Health Care Issues and the Church
Ad Hoc Committee on Conciliation and Arbitration
Ad Hoc Committee on Diocesan Audits
Ad Hoc Committee on Economic Concerns of the Holy See
Ad Hoc Committee on Native American Catholics
Ad Hoc Committee on Nomination of Conference Offices
Ad Hoc Committee to Oversee the Use of the Catechism

Ad Hoc Committee on Review of Scripture
    Translations
Ad Hoc Committee on Shrines
Ad Hoc Committee on the Spanish-Language
    Bible
Ad Hoc Committee on Stewardship

Task forces
Task Force on Catholic Bishops and Politi-
    cians
Task Force on Catholic Use of the Bible
Task Force on Content and Flow of General
    Meetings

Separate Status
U.S. bishops' National Advisory Council
Catholic Legal Immigration Network board of
    directors
Catholic Relief Services board of directors
Confraternity of Christian Doctrine board of
    trustees

Appendix G:

Vatican Agencies

Use the following names for Vatican offices. Follow normal rules of capitalization, with the agency's full name capitalized as shown below. Any shortened or flip-flopped variations (such as *doctrinal congregation* for the Congregation for the Doctrine of the Faith and *Vatican press office* for the Press Office of the Holy See) should be lowercased. Do not use initials for any Vatican office.

Offices are listed according to their appearance in the Annuario. If an office under the jurisdiction of another agency has its main listing under that agency in the Annuario, that is how it is listed here. If its main listing is separate, however, it is also listed separately here. For example, the Pontifical Biblical Commission is subordinate to the doctrinal congregation but is listed separately under *Commissions and Committees.*

Consult the Annuario for names of officials and staff, addresses, telephone numbers, fax numbers, e-mail addresses and a complete list of all secondary sections or other organizational structures within each Vatican agency. All main offices and those subordinate offices which are frequently in the news are listed here.

The first group of entries in this listing is not part of the Roman Curia.

Noncurial Entities
Synod of Bishops
— Council of the General Secretariat
Council of Cardinals for the Study of the Organizational and Economic Problems of the Holy See

Secretariat of State
Secretariat of State

— Section for General Affairs
— Section for Relations With States
— Council of Cardinals and Bishops

Congregations
Congregation for the Doctrine of the Faith
Congregation for Eastern Churches
— Special Commission for the Liturgy
— Special Commission for Studies of the Christian East
— Special Commission for the Formation of Clergy and Religious
— Catholic Near East Welfare Association
— Pontifical Mission for Palestine
— Assembly of Societies for Aid to Eastern Churches
Congregation for Divine Worship and the Sacraments
— Vox Clara Committee
Congregation for Saints' Causes
Congregation for Bishops
— Central Office for Pastoral Coordination of Military Ordinariates
— Coordinating Office for "Ad Limina" Visits
— Pontifical Commission for Latin America
Congregation for the Evangelization of Peoples
— Supreme Committee of the Pontifical Missionary Societies of the Propagation of the Faith, of St. Peter the Apostle, of the Holy Childhood and of the Missionary Union
Congregation for Clergy
— International Council for Catechesis
Congregation for Institutes of Consecrated Life and Societies of Apostolic Life
Congregation for Catholic Education (of Seminaries and Institutes of Study)

Permanent Interdicasterial Commissions
Interdicasterial Commission for the Church in Eastern Europe
Interdicasterial Commission for the Formation of Candidates to Holy Orders
Interdicasterial Commission for a More Equal Distribution of Priests in the World

Courts
Apostolic Penitentiary
Supreme Court of the Apostolic Signature
Tribunal of the Roman Rota

Pontifical Councils
Pontifical Council for the Laity
Pontifical Council for Promoting Christian Unity
— Commission for Religious Relations With the Jews
Pontifical Council for the Family
Pontifical Council for Justice and Peace
Pontifical Council Cor Unum
— Caritas Internationalis
Pontifical Council for Migrants and Travelers
Pontifical Council for Health Care Ministry
Pontifical Council for Legislative Texts
Pontifical Council for Interreligious Dialogue
— Commission for Religious Relations With the Muslims
Pontifical Council for Culture
— Coordinating Council for Pontifical Academies
Pontifical Council for Social Communications
— Vatican Film Library

Offices
Apostolic Camera
Administration of the Patrimony of the Holy See
Prefecture for the Economic Affairs of the Holy See

Other Organisms of Roman Curia
Prefecture of the Pontifical Household
Office for the Liturgical Celebrations of the Supreme Pontiff
Press Office of the Holy See *(Vatican press office)*
— Vatican Information Service
Central Office of Church Statistics

Pontifical Commissions
Pontifical Commission for the Cultural Heritage of the Church (formerly *for Preserving the Patrimony of Art and History)*
Pontifical Commission for Sacred Archeology
Pontifical Biblical Commission

Pontifical Commission "Ecclesia Dei"

Other Commissions, Committees
International Theological Commission
Pontifical Committee for International Eucharistic Congresses
Pontifical Committee for Historical Sciences
Archives of the Second Vatican Council
Commission for Lawyers
Corps of Lawyers of the Holy See
Disciplinary Commission of the Roman Curia
Corps of the Pontifical Swiss Guards

Institutions Linked to the Holy See
Vatican Secret Archives
Vatican Library
Vatican Printing Office
L'Osservatore Romano (*Vatican newspaper*)
Vatican Publishing House
Vatican Radio
Vatican Television Center
Fabbrica di San Pietro *(paraphrase as the office in charge of construction matters relating to St. Peter's or the office of the Vatican's chief engineer)*
Central Labor Office of the Holy See

Vatican City State
Pontifical Commission for Vatican City State
Governor's Office for Vatican City State
— Vatican Philatelic and Numismatic Office
— Office for Pilgrims and Tourists
Vatican Museums
Vatican Gardens
Vatican Observatory
Permanent Commission for the Protection of the Historic and Artistic Monuments of the Holy See

Pontifical Academies
Pontifical Academy of Sciences
Pontifical Academy of Social Sciences
Pontifical Academy for Life
Pontifical Academy of Theology
Pontifical Ecclesiastical Academy

Institute for the Works of Religion (*Vatican bank*)

Use of the Annuario

The information in this appendix is based on the 2005 Annuario.

Structure

The first part of the Annuario deals with church jurisdictions worldwide and those who head those jurisdictions. It begins with a list of past popes and information on the current pope. Other listings follow in this order: *College of Cardinals, patriarchates, major archbishoprics, archdioceses and dioceses, titular sees, territorial prelatures, territorial abbeys, Eastern apostolic exarchates and ordinariates, military ordinariates, personal prelatures, apostolic vicariates, apostolic prefectures, apostolic administrations, personal apostolic administrations, missions "sui iuris."*

Also: *Synod of Bishops, the Council of Cardinals for the Study of Organizational and Economic Problems of the Holy See, episcopal conferences, synods of bishops of Eastern Catholic churches, international organizations of bishops' conferences, geographical distribution of sees* (both Latin and Eastern jurisdictions, organized by continent; within each continent by country; and within each country by metropolitan sees and their suffragans), *rites in the church* (a separate geographic listing of Eastern Catholic jurisdictions, organized by rite), *statistical data* and *deceased dignitaries* (a list of bishops who died the previous year).

For information on the different kinds of church jurisdictions, see individual entries in the main section of this stylebook.

The second part of the Annuario deals with the Roman Curia. It is divided as follows: *Secretariat of State, congregations, tribunals* (church courts), *pontifical councils, offices, other organisms of the Roman Curia, pontifical commissions, other commissions and committees, the Swiss Guard, pontifical equestrian orders, institutions connected with the Holy See* (archives, library, etc.), *pontifical administrations, pontifical delegations.* For English translations of the formal names of most of these offices, see **Appendix G: Vatican Agencies.**

The third part of the book deals with: *pontifical representatives* (diplomats representing the pope), *diplomatic corps to the Holy See, Vatican City State, the Vicariate of Rome, male religious orders, female religious orders, international and national federations of religious, cultural institutions* (primarily schools but also including institutions like the Pontifical Academy of Sciences and the Vatican bank) and *historical notes.*

The Annuario is not a very useful source for information on religious, because most of the orders' names are listed in Italian or another language. See **Appendix D: Religious Orders, Men** and **Appendix E: Religious Orders, Women.**

Finally, the Annuario has three indexes. The first is an alphabetical index of all persons named in the Annuario, with references to the page or pages on which their names appear. This index also includes names of monsignors, identifying them by diocese, but the list of monsignors is not complete. The second and third indexes are short lists of the contents of the Annuario, first alphabetically by key words of subjects and organization names, and then schematically — a table of contents. The inside covers, front and back, also contain lists of the main sections of the Annuario, with the page number on which each begins.

NOTE: In both its index of names and its listings of papal diplomats and of personnel in Vatican agencies, the Annuario almost always gives *last name first, with no punctuation between last name and first name.* When the full name given consists of more than two words, care is needed to determine what constitutes the last name, first name and middle name, if any. For example, *George Francis Eugene* is *Cardinal Francis E. George,* but in *Castillo Lara Rosalio Jose* the first name is *Rosalio,* not *Lara.* Cardinal Rosalio Jose Castillo Lara has a double last name.

In its listings in archdioceses, dioceses and titular sees, however, the Annuario gives first name first, followed by middle name if any, then the last name(s). In those listings the last name of the bishop of the diocese is given in bold type. Use the diocesan listings to assure that you have a bishop's name correct.

Abbreviations

The Annuario provides biographical information on each bishop and statistical data about each church jurisdiction. In its listings of personnel of various agencies it gives the religious or lay title of individuals. It uses standard Italian abbreviations in all these categories.

1. Statistical data

For each diocese or other church jurisdiction, the listing starts with the name and then gives certain historical information about it, as well as the address and telephone number. In the archdioceses and dioceses section, archdioceses are in larger type than dioceses.

The italicized entry under the jurisdiction's name gives statistics, using the following abbreviations:

su. — territory in square kilometers.

pp. — population.

ct. — number of Catholics.

pr. — parishes.

ch. — churches or mission stations.

sd. — diocesan priests resident in diocese.

dn. — diocesan priests ordained during the previous year.

sr. — religious priests resident in diocese.

rn. — religious priests ordained during the previous year.

dp. — permanent deacons.

sm. — seminarians in philosophy and theology courses.

rm. — men religious (brothers).

rf. — women religious.

ie. — educational institutions.

ib. — charitable institutions.

ba. — baptisms during previous year.

2. Clergy identification and bishops' biographical data:

In the index of names at the end of the book and in the diocese listings, the names of bishops are always preceded by a crosslike symbol. If *Prot. Ap. Sopr., Capp. di S.S.* or *Prel. d'On. di S.S.* follows a person's name in the index, he is a monsignor. The date that follows (in the European *date-month-year* format, not the American *month-date-year* format) is the date he was made a monsignor. *P.* in the index means a priest.

The biographical information on each *residential bishop or archbishop* follows his name in the *archdioceses and dioceses* section. Biographical information on each retired residential bishop is found under his former diocese. Cardinals' biographies are under *College of Cardinals* and those of patriarchs under *patriarchates.*

All other bishops — auxiliaries, papal diplomats, Vatican officials, etc. — have *titular sees.* The biographical information is given in the listing for his titular see.

The biographies use the following abbreviations:

n. — born.

ord. — ordained.

el. — elevated.

cons. — consecrated (ordained a bishop).

pr. — promoted.

rin. — resigned.

succ. per coad. — means he had been coadjutor before he became head of the diocese.

tr. — transferred.

q.s. — same see.

gia — former.

The biographical information also gives dates, with Italian abbreviations of months. Here are the translations:

genn. — January.

febb. — February.

mar. — March.

apr. — April.

magg. — May.

giu. — June.

lu. — July.

ag. — August.

sett. — September.

ott. — October.

nov. — November.

dic. — December.

Note that the date of the month precedes the name of the month: *16 genn. 1982* means *Jan. 16, 1982.*

3. Personal titles of personnel:

Especially in the listings of agency and embassy personnel, the Annuario uses abbreviations for each person's religious or courtesy titles.

See **religious titles** for proper use of formal titles before a name. Here are the main ones used in the Annuario:

Avv., Cav., Comm., Ing., Prof. and *Rag.* — ignore. They mean *lawyer, knight, commander, engineer, professor* and *accountant,* respectively.

Arciv. — an archbishop (name of see follows).

Card. — a cardinal.

Dott. — a *doctor,* but ignore it unless it refers to a medical doctor.

Mons. — a monsignor. Sometimes written *S.E. Mons.* But note:

S.E.R. Mons. — a bishop or archbishop, depending on the identification that follows the name.

Rev., Rev. P. or *P.* — a priest. But note:

Rev. Fr. — a brother.

Rev.da Sr. — a nun.

Sig. — a layman. No title in English.

Sig.na — an unmarried woman. No title in English.

Sig.ra — a married woman. No title in English.

Vesc. — a bishop.

The abbreviation *tit.* after *Arciv.* or *Vesc.* means a *titular* archbishop or bishop: The name of the see that follows, where his biographical information is given, is listed under the *titular sees.*

Job descriptions

The names of the departmental positions held by Vatican personnel are not abbreviated. Below the top posts in each agency, a description of what an official or aide actually does in his department will usually be more helpful to the reader than an English translation of his job classification. Often a literal translation is not merely unhelpful but positively misleading.

Here are the proper English renderings of some Vatican job descriptions:

prefetto — prefect.

presidente — president.

segretario — secretary.

segretario generale — general secretary.

sotto-segretario — undersecretary.

direttore — director.

assistente — assistant or aide.

aiutante, addetto — aide.

uditore — in the Rota, a judge; elsewhere, an aide.

consigliere — counselor.

consultore — consultor (not a full-time staff position).

Vatican II Documents

Here are the 16 documents approved by the Second Vatican Council and their dates of promulgation:

— **Constitution on the Sacred Liturgy** *("Sacrosanctum Concilium"),* Dec. 4, 1963. It ordered an extensive revision of worship so that people would have a clearer sense of their own involvement in the Mass and other rites.

— **Decree on the Instruments of Social Communication** *("Inter Mirifica"),* Dec. 4, 1963. It called on members of the church, especially the laity, to instill "a human and Christian spirit" into newspapers, magazines, books, films, radio and television.

— **Dogmatic Constitution on the Church** *("Lumen Gentium"),* Nov. 21, 1964. It presented the church as a mystery, as a communion of baptized believers, as the people of God, as the body of Christ and as a pilgrim moving toward fulfillment in heaven but marked on earth with "a sanctity that is real, although imperfect."

—**Decree on Ecumenism** *("Unitatis Redintegratio"),* Nov. 21, 1964. It said that ecumenism should be everyone's concern and that genuine ecumenism involves a continual personal and institutional renewal.

— **Decree on Eastern Catholic Churches** *("Orientalium Ecclesiarum"),* Nov. 21, 1964. It stated that variety within the church does not harm its unity and that Eastern Catholic churches should retain their own traditions.

— **Decree on the Bishops' Pastoral Office in the Church** *("Christus Dominus"),* Oct. 28, 1965. It said each bishop has full ordinary power in his own diocese and is expected to present Christian doctrine in ways adapted to the times. It urged conferences of bishops to exercise pastoral direction jointly.

— **Decree on Priestly Formation** *("Optatam Totius"),* Oct. 28, 1965. It recommended that seminaries pay attention to the spiritual, intellectual and disciplinary formation necessary to prepare priesthood students to become good pastors.

— **Decree on the Appropriate Renewal of the Religious Life** *("Perfectae Caritatis"),* Oct. 28, 1965. It provided guidelines for the personal and institutional renewal of the lives of nuns, brothers and priests belonging to religious orders.

— **Declaration on the Relationship of the Church to Non-Christian Religions** *("Nostra Aetate"),* Oct. 28, 1965. It said the Catholic Church rejects nothing that is true and holy in non-Christian religions, called for an end to anti-Semitism and said any discrimination based on race, color, religion or condition of life is foreign to the mind of Christ.

— **Declaration on Christian Education** *("Gravissimum Educationis"),* Oct. 28, 1965. It affirmed the right of parents to choose the type of education they want for their children, upheld the importance of Catholic schools and defended freedom of inquiry in Catholic colleges and universities.

— **Dogmatic Constitution on Divine Revelation** *("Dei Verbum"),* Nov. 18, 1965. It said the church depends on Scripture and tradition as the one deposit of God's word and commended the use of modern scientific scholarship in studying Scripture.

— **Decree on the Apostolate of the Laity** *("Apostolicam Actuositatem"),* Nov. 18, 1965. It said the laity should influence their surroundings with Christ's teachings.

— **Declaration on Religious Freedom** *("Dignitatis Humanae"),* Dec. 7, 1965. It said that religious liberty is a right found in the dignity of each person and that no one should be forced to act in a way contrary to his or her own beliefs.

— **Decree on the Ministry and Life of Priests** *("Presbyterorum Ordinis"),* Dec. 7, 1965. It said the primary duty of priests is to proclaim the Gospel to all, approved and encouraged celibacy as a gift and recommended fair salaries.

— **Decree on the Church's Missionary Activity** *("Ad Gentes"),* Dec. 7, 1965. It said missionary activity should help the social and economic welfare of people and not force anyone to accept the faith.

— **Pastoral Constitution on the Church in the Modern World** *("Gaudium et Spes"),* Dec. 7, 1965. It said the church must talk to atheists, a continual campaign must be waged for peace, nuclear war is unthinkable and aid to underdeveloped nations is urgent. It said marriage was not just for procreation and urged science to find an acceptable means of birth regulation.

Annual Church Observances

In addition to the fixed and variable observances of the Catholic liturgical calendar, here are other yearly worldwide or U.S. observances in the Catholic Church:

World Peace Day, Jan. 1.

National Migration Week (U.S.), first full week of January.

National Vocations Awareness Week, week in January beginning with the feast of the Baptism of the Lord.

Week of Prayer for Christian Unity, Jan. 18-25.

March for Life (U.S.), Jan. 22 or Monday after Jan. 22 when it falls on a weekend.

Catholic Schools Week (U.S.), week beginning last Monday in January.

Catholic Press Month (U.S.), February.

World Day of Consecrated Life, Feb. 2.

National Day of Prayer for the African-American Family, first Sunday in February.

World Day of the Sick, Feb. 11.

World Day of Prayer for Vocations, fourth Sunday of Easter.

National Day of Prayer (U.S.), first Thursday in May.

World Communications Day, Sunday before Pentecost.

World Youth Day, international celebration every two or three years around Aug. 15; national celebrations every other year on Palm Sunday; U.S. observance usually on third Sunday in October.

National Catechetical Sunday (U.S.), third Sunday in September.

Respect Life Month (U.S.), October.

Respect Life Sunday (U.S.), first Sunday in October.

World Mission Sunday, third Sunday in October.

World Migration Day, different dates in different countries.

Day of Prayer for Priestly Vocations (U.S.), different dates in different dioceses.

Copyright and Trademark Law

Copyright Basics

A copyrighted work is an original work of authorship fixed in any tangible medium of expression now known or later developed, from which the work can be perceived, reproduced or otherwise communicated either directly or with the aid of a machine. Copyrighted works include: literary works, musical works, including any accompanying words, dramatic works, choreographic or pantomime works, pictorial, graphic and sculptural works, motion picture and other audiovisual works, sound recordings and architectural works. Ideas, processes, systems and method of operations cannot be copyrighted works.

A copyright owner has the exclusive rights to:

— Reproduce the copyrighted work.

— Prepare derivative works, such as a translation, musical arrangement, dramatization, fictionalization, condensation or any other form in which a work may be recast, transformed or adapted.

— Distribute copies to the public by sale or other transfer of ownership, or by rental, lease or lending.

— Perform or display the copyrighted work publicly.

Computer functions that fall within these categories of exclusive rights include creating a Web site, downloading and uploading, linking and framing. Text, art works and computer software language are copyrightable works. Loading software into a computer constitutes creation of a copy under the Copyright Act.

Who holds the copyright in a work?

A copyrighted work is created when it is fixed in a tangible medium. The creator of the work is the copyright owner, unless the work is a work made for hire.

The Copyright Act defines a work made for hire as either: (1) a work prepared by an employee within the scope of his employment, or (2) a work specially ordered or commissioned for use as a contribution to (a) a collective work, (b) part of a motion picture or other audiovisual work, (c) a translation, (d) a supplementary work, (e) a compilation, (f) an instructional text, (g) a test, (h) an atlas, if the parties expressly agree in a written instrument signed by them that the work shall be considered a work made for hire.

An independent contractor owns his copyrighted work, even if he has been paid by the contracting entity, unless there is a written document, executed before the contractor creates the work, which states that the contracting entity will own the copyright.

Infringement and fair use

A direct infringement occurs when a person or entity (not the copyright owner), exercises one or more of the exclusive rights of the copyright owner without permission and when the exercise is not a fair use.

Vicarious liability for infringement: Vicarious liability for copyright infringement is imposed if defendant (1) has the right and the ability to supervise the infringing activity; and (2) has a direct financial interest in such activities. Vicarious liability is based on the tort concept of respondeat superior, which raises considerations of benefit and control.

Liability for contributory infringement is imposed when defendant, (1) with knowledge of the infringing activity, (2) induces, causes or materially contributes to the infringing conduct of another. Contributory liability is based on the concept of enterprise liability, which entails knowledge and participation.

Fair use of a copyrighted work is defined as reproduction of a copyrighted work for purposes such as criticism, comment, news reporting, teaching (including multiple copies of classroom use), scholarship, or research. A fair use is not an infringement of copyright. Four factors must be used to make an individual determination of whether copying a copyrighted work is a fair use: (1) the purpose and character of the use, including whether such use is of a commercial nature or is for nonprofit educational purposes; (2) the nature of the copyrighted work; (3) the amount and substantiality of the portion used in relation to the copyrighted work as a whole; and (4) the effect of the use upon the potential market for or value of the copyrighted work.

It is vital to recognize that fair use is not a blanket exception to the copyright laws for not-for-profit entities such as Catholic school and parishes.

Remedies a court may impose on an infringer include: permanent or temporary injunctions, impoundment of infringing copies during the pendency of an infringement suit, destruction of infringing copies following final judicial determination of copyright infringement, actual damages suffered as a result of the infringement and any profits acquired by the infringer as a result of the infringement, costs and attorney's fees, statutory damages (not less than $500 or more than $30,000, or, for willful infringement, $150,000 or less; to collect statutory damages or attorney fees, the copyright owner must first have filed a copyright registration for the work), or criminal penalties (if an infringer's acts were both willful and for commercial advantage or private financial gain). Civil actions have a three year statute of limitations; criminal actions have a 5 year statute of limitation.

Trademark basics

A trademark is "any word, name, symbol or device, or any combination thereof (used or intended to be used by a person) to identify and distinguish his or her goods, including a unique product, from those manufactured or sold by others and to indicate the source of the goods." A trademark is protected against confusingly similar use in connection with the sale of goods or services by others, and any false implied endorsement of another's goods or services by the trademark holder.

In determining whether a likelihood of confusion exists, courts may take into account (1) the degree of similarity between the owner's mark and the alleged infringing mark; (2) the strength of the owner's mark; (3) the price of the goods and other factors indicative of the care and attention expected of consumers when making a purchase; (4) the length of time the defendant has used the mark without evidence of actual confusion arising; (5) the intent of the defendant in adopting the mark; (6) the evidence of actual confusion; (7) whether the goods, though not competing, are marketed through the same channels of trade and advertised through the same media; (8) the extent to which the targets of the parties' sale efforts are the same; (9) the relationship of the goods in the minds of the public because of the similarity of function; (10) other facts suggesting that the consuming public might expect the prior owner to manufacture a product in the defendant's market.

Some considerations regarding computers

Linking: Hypertext linking and framing are two ways Web sites can connect the Internet user with other Web sites. Links are highlighted text, pictures or logos which the user can click on in order to access another Web site. A link can either take the user to the homepage of another Web site (linking), or to a site "below" the home page or several levels into the linked site ("deep linking"). Framing, on the other hand, allows the user to view the contents of another Web site within the borders of "framing" Web site. Thus, the contents of the framed website are surrounded by the pictures and advertising of the framing website.

Whether and to what extent links or deep links raise valid copyright, trademark and/or unfair competition claims is somewhat unsettled. In general, a simple hypertext link on one Web site to another by itself does not give rise to a claim of copyright, trademark or unfair competition violation. However, it is possible to create the link with language or use of trademarks which confuse the customer as to the source of goods or services provided by the Web site operator and the linked-to site. Further, state law defamation, false light or similar claims could be made depending on the language used on a Web site to describe a link to a Web site.

Domain names: The Federal Trademark Dilution Act makes actionable the use a famous trademark commercially to dilute the distinctive quality of the famous mark. Unlike the showing required to prove trademark infringement, proving dilution does not require proof that the wrongdoer competes with the mark owner, nor that there is a likelihood of consumer confusion. Dilution requires only a showing that the commercial use of a famous mark has lessened the mark's capacity to distinguish it from marks on dissimilar goods or goods of poor quality, or by associating the mark with an unwholesome or disparaging message. Fair use, noncommercial use and news reporting use of a mark that would otherwise dilute a famous mark are exempt.

Cybersquatting: The Anti-Cybersquatting Consumer Protection Act provides a statutory cause of action against persons who, in bad faith, register domain names incorporating the trademarks of others. It provides remedies against persons who, in bad faith, register, traffic in or use a domain name that is identical or confusingly similar to a distinctive or famous mark or which dilutes a famous mark or is a trademark owned by another. Remedies for cybersquatting are forfeiture or cancellation of the domain name or transfer of the domain name to the mark owner.

The Internet Corporation for Assigned Names and Numbers has established a dispute resolution process for domain name disputes. The policy's sole remedies are transfer of a domain name or cancellation of a domain name; no monetary damages are available. The arbitration process is usually completed within weeks and costs much less than trademark litigation. See www.icann.org.

— Katherine G. Grincewich,
Associate General Counsel,
U.S. Conference of
Catholic Bishops

Order Now!

Please accept my order for
_____ copies of the CNS Stylebook
on Religion.

CNS publishing clients — $14.95 per copy, plus shipping and handling.

All Others — $19.95 per copy, plus shipping and handling.

Shipping and handling — $4.00 for one to four copies; $6.00 for five to ten copies; more than 10 copies, call for shipping and handling charges.

Payment must accompany orders.

Name ____

Company ____

Address ____

City ___________________________ State __________ Zip __________

Phone ________________________________ Date ____________

Payment
❏ **Check or money order** (payable to Catholic News Service)
❏ **Credit Card** (Mastercard or Visa)

Card # _________________________ Exp. Date ____________

Name ____

Signature ____

Send your order to
Catholic News Service
Stylebook on Religion
3211 Fourth Street NE
Washington DC 20017

202.541.3250 t
202.541.3255 f
cns@catholicnews.com
www.catholicnews.com

Order Now!

Please accept my order for _______ copies of the CNS Stylebook on Religion.

CNS publishing clients — $14.95 per copy, plus shipping and handling.

All Others — $19.95 per copy, plus shipping and handling.

Shipping and handling — $4.00 for one to four copies; $6.00 for five to ten copies; more than 10 copies, call for shipping and handling charges.

Payment must accompany orders.

Name ____

Company ____

Address ____

City _________________________ State _______ Zip _____________

Phone _______________________ Date __________________

Payment
❏ **Check or money order** (payable to Catholic News Service)
❏ **Credit Card** (Mastercard or Visa)

Card # ______________________ Exp. Date _______________

Name ____

Signature ____

Send your order to
Catholic News Service
Stylebook on Religion
3211 Fourth Street NE
Washington DC 20017

202.541.3250 t
202.541.3255 f
cns@catholicnews.com
www.catholicnews.com